Domestic Tyranny

Domestic Tyranny

The Making of American Social Policy
against Family Violence from
Colonial Times to the Present

Elizabeth Pleck

University of Illinois Press
Urbana and Chicago

First Illinois edition, 2004
© 1987, 2004 by Elizabeth Pleck
Reprinted by arrangement with the author

This book is printed on acid-free paper.

Library of Congress Cataloging-in-Publication Data
Pleck, Elizabeth Hafkin.
Domestic tyranny : the making of american social policy
against family violence from colonial times to the present /
Elizabeth Pleck. — 1st Illinois ed.
p. cm.
Originally published: New York : Oxford University Press, 1987.
With new introd.
Includes bibliographical references and index.
ISBN 0-252-029127-7 (cloth : alk. paper)
ISBN 978-0-252-07175-1 (paper : alk. paper)
1. Family violence—United States–History.
2. Family violence—Law and legislation—United States—History.
I. Title.
HV6626.2.P58   2004
362.82'92'0947—dc22   2003015138

Contents

Acknowledgments

A faculty fellowship from the Ford Foundation on the Role of Women in Society enabled me to begin reading about contemporary family violence and search for historical documents about it. During a fellowship year at the Bunting Institute of Radcliffe, I began drafting this book. The Wellesley College Center for Research on Women has provided me with supportive colleagues and an excellent environment in which to write.

In the early stages of research Kathy Marquis and Michael Hanagan tracked down colonial court cases and American autobiographies. For his assistance during a summer reading case records at the Temple University Urban Archives, I thank Fred Miller. Mary Ritzenthaler provided similar help at the Archives of the University of Illinois-Chicago.

Philip Greven, June Namias, and Barbara Sicherman read chapters of the manuscript. For sharing her research with me, as well as reading my work, I am indebted to Linda Gordon. Ellen Fitzpatrick, Estelle Freedman, Judith Herman, and Louise Tilly gave extensive criticisms on the manuscript from which I have heartily benefited. Joseph Pleck has generously given of his time in commenting on successive drafts of this book. For his patience, diligence, and insights, I am deeply grateful.

Marie Cantlon helped me clarify and sharpen the themes of the book. Linda Grossman and Ruth Rose skillfully edited the manuscript and much improved its organization.

Many times I wish I had chosen a more lighthearted topic of inquiry. I have found the subject of family violence deeply depressing, confirming the most pessimistic assessments of human nature and family relations. But I have also been impressed with the ability of the victims of family violence I have known to remake their lives, and with friends and colleagues who are dedicated researchers, clinicians, and activists. In writing this book, I have tried to keep in mind their accomplishments and resourcefulness.

Introduction
to the Illinois Edition

In the early 1970s I was living in Ann Arbor, Michigan, when the local chapter of the National Organization for Women began organizing programs to encourage police to arrest wife batterers rather than mediate "domestic disputes." Inspired by these efforts, I became curious about the history of family violence. I was often asked why I wanted to write about this subject. My questioners assumed that I had a secret in my childhood or marriage that explained my interest in a topic seemingly so peripheral to historical scholarship. In my fields of women's history and family history, domestic violence was invisible and the impact of family violence on how the field understood the nature of family life was minimal. Danger and conflict in the family were regarded as peripheral, and family ideals and domestic realities were described in terms of harmony, partnership, and mutual interest.

After spending about a year reading through case records of the Pennsylvania Society to Protect Children from Cruelty and the Illinois Humane Society, I wrote "Challenges to Traditional Authority in Immigrant Families," which was published in 1983. I found that immigrant wives and children arrived in the United States with the belief that their husbands and fathers had a legitimate right to physically punish them. They soon discovered that they could complain to police and social agencies about being beaten. Until my article appeared it had been frequently argued that when outside agencies acted, they invaded the privacy of immigrant families and destroyed their autonomy. Instead, I found that immigrant families, composed of individuals with competing interests, were rife with internal conflict and that some family members actually invited and welcomed assistance from outsiders.[1]

After finishing research among these case records I wanted to learn more about the laws, policies, and institutions that set in motion formal social responses to family violence. This interest took me away from studying violent families and victims and toward the reformers concerned about family violence, their policies, and their ideas. Social responses to family violence varied enormously over more than three centuries of American history. I studied the well-known reforms, such as the establishment of societies to prevent cruelty to children, as well as more obscure efforts, which had much more limited impact and had never been written about.

In general, I was sympathetic to the difficulties reformers faced in overcoming public apathy. Nonetheless, some campaigns against family violence were of dubious merit. Among the latter was one in the late nineteenth century, led by judges and lawyers allied with feminists, to punish wife batterers with the whipping post. Three states enacted such laws and punished several hundred men accordingly. Demonizing all poor men as wife beaters, the judges and lawyers in favor of flogging abusive men affirmed that wife abuse was a crime deserving of punishment. Supporters of the whipping post for wife batterers employed Victorian rhetoric about the innocent wife and the brutish husband. The husband was portrayed as a dangerously violent, often drunken, brute who was typically either black or an immigrant, while his wife was presented as pure, sober, and nonviolent. This reform effort sent two messages. One was that punishing domestic violence had as much to do with class and race as with gender. The other was that the family unit could be breached when violence within it was perceived as a threat to public order.

Domestic Tyranny is the first book-length historical analysis of domestic violence; it begins with the first "reform" against family violence in American history—in colonial New England in the 1600s—and ends with the battered women's movement in the 1970s. Activists of the 1970s mainly thought of the past as "the bad old days" when children were maltreated, wives could be whipped with a stick no thicker than a man's thumb, and incest went unpunished. These kinds of overstatements and half-truths substituted for genuine understanding of how and why domestic violence emerged as a social issue in various cycles of reform. The politics of reform and the climate of the times shaped the understanding of family violence and the responses to it.

My book inspired considerable historical research but had its greatest impact on U.S. lawyers and social workers making contemporary policy. They wanted to know more about the successes and failures of previous reform efforts, with the hope of being able to avoid past mistakes.[2] Lawyers, especially feminist lawyers working on behalf of battered women, were interested in finding historical precedents for reform, the evolution of legal doctrines, and patterns of prosecution. Many of these activists assumed that they were the first to be concerned about domestic violence. My evidence of a long tradition of transforming a private harm into a public issue provoked mixed reactions. Some were pleased to discover that people who came before them shared their concerns, while others grappled with the discomfort of finding themselves in the company of reform campaigns they disliked.

From the beginning I decided against making large and difficult-to-prove claims about either the consequences or the causes of domestic violence. Philip J. Greven, for example, has insisted in *Spare the Child: The Religious Roots of Punishment and the Psychological Impact of Abuse* that much of American political conservatism was rooted in the corporal punishment of children.[3] That children who were routinely whipped or beaten grow up with distinct political stances has never been proven. I was also unwilling to offer any single explanation for the "causes" of domestic violence. If pressed now, I would refer to a variety of risk factors that can encourage family violence and a variety of protective factors that can subdue it or mute its negative effects on the individual. Such risk and protective factors would have to differ for each type of domestic violence—from incest to elder abuse. When I started my research, the term *patriarchy* might have served as sufficient explanation for domestic violence. The title of my book employed a phrase of John Stuart Mill, *domestic tyranny*, which seemed to come pretty close to an endorsement of that point of view. This explanation has merit but it is also difficult to prove. Some scholars saw patriarchy as both a cause of domestic violence and a limit on it. Even as a cause of domestic violence, patriarchal violence resulted from persons in authority exercising traditional rights of correction as well as from the exact opposite, subordinates resisting domination by those with power over them.

Contemporary research about violence in gay and lesbian couples has raised additional questions about the patriarchal explanation of domestic violence. Battering in gay male couples is a form of family violence that neither reflects nor reinforces the subordination of women or children. The existence of violence among gays and lesbians suggests that adult relationships, even ones devoid of some of the usual hierarchical structures and outside the bounds of legal marriage, are still fraught with tensions, stress, jealousies, and exercises in exerting power and control that lead to violence. This being so, one must conclude that struggles along the lines of gender and generation are not the sole determinants of domestic violence. Instead, couple violence among gays and lesbians is reinforced by the invisibility of homosexual relationships, denial about this kind of violence, and the nature of domestic privacy.[4]

Since *Domestic Tyranny* was published, twenty historical monographs on family violence, as well as one anthology and dozens of articles and dissertations, have appeared. Quite a few of these writings concern the representation of family violence in literature.[5] While my book and a few others dealt with several types of family violence at once most works have focused on either adult or child victims. Specialists in crime, family, and childhood have carved out distinct areas of study. The history of family violence among adults or sexually abused children has largely been written by scholars interested in criminology or those who study women, marriage, and the family. Feminist legal historians have been especially drawn to the history of marital rape and wife abuse. For the most part, those writing about child abuse and neglect have identified themselves as historians of childhood and located their works within the framework of developing notions of childhood and children's rights.

Scholars also sometimes defined their subject matter by the records they used. Some chose all violent crimes, infanticide, or the murder of older children. Others, sorting through criminal records to locate instances of wife beating, incest, and wife abuse, classified these crimes as "violence against women." Newspapers, police records of homicide arrests, and written trial records have made it relatively easy to write about family murder. Because family murder is the most visible form of family violence, it remains the most studied type. The subject of emotional abuse has been considered in relation to the history of marriage, especially as grounds for divorce. It also emerges in criminal records, since saying harsh words was considered assault in colonial New England and post-Revolution Philadelphia.[6] So as to reinforce the ideal of domestic stability, wives were arrested for beating their husbands back in the 1600s.[7] Some severe forms of sibling violence and elder abuse can be found in criminal records as well.

There are still many gaps in historical writing about domestic violence. Stalking, children witnessing family violence, abusing animals — all topics of recent origin in the social science literature about family violence — have yet to find their scholars. Historians of the nineteenth and early twentieth centuries have described out-of-home placements of abused and neglected children in institutions, as servants, or with farm or mining families, but there is no history of foster care in the twentieth century. The experiences of children in foster care and adoptive families is a crucial missing piece in the history of child maltreatment. Moreover, there are no reviews of recent historical work about family violence. Entries about child abuse or domestic violence in recently published encyclopedias on U.S. social or family history must suffice for now.[8]

Domestic Tyranny was intended to answer two main questions: What were the major barriers to recognizing family violence as a social issue? and How were these barriers overcome? The growth of public concern about family violence was relatively unrelated to the actual frequency of domestic violence (since, for example, family murder in colonial New England was low but concern about family violence was fairly high) but instead was much more attuned to the climate of reform at a particular time and public fears about dangerous criminals.

A key element of reform included naming the problem (crimes against women, battered child syndrome, and so forth), which provided insight into both what reformers thought caused family violence and the kinds of coalitions they assembled. Feminism was one key ingredient in reform in some epochs but not in others. It was not present in the colonial period, had little impact on the child protection movement in the late nineteenth century, and did not affect the discovery of the battered child syndrome in the 1960s. Public demand for law and order was as important as feminism, and the combination of the two was even more potent. Some victims and former victims were active in shaping reform, but for the most part, reformers were lawyers, judges, politicians, feminist activists, physicians—and now I would add journalists—who mainly came to know about family violence by coming into contact with victims.

I located barriers to reform in recurring arguments about the nature of the family, which I called the Family Ideal.[9] The Family Ideal consisted of beliefs in traditional rights of correction over dependents in the household, such as a wife, children, servants, slaves, and apprentices; an ideal of family and marital unity, harmony, and stability; and the ideal of family privacy.[10] The Family Ideal emerged from popular and religious attitudes and from legal decisions, statutes, and legislative debates. Many victims believed in it. Judges, the police, the general public, and opponents of reform offered elements of the Family Ideal as rationalizations for why they should not take action against family violence. They often combined rationales rather than offering only one. (In the colonial period legal rulings were sparse, and rationalizations for nonintervention consisted of brief statements rather than legal opinions).

Probably the major exponent of my argument about the Family Ideal as a barrier to intervention in family violence was the legal historian Reva Siegel. In "'The Rule of Love': Wife Beating as Prerogative and Privacy," she provided a detailed account of the shifting basis for the Family Ideal as found both in appellate court cases involving wife abuse and in tort cases, especially in the nineteenth century. She noted that by the 1870s, virtually no American judge accepted the argument that a husband had a right to administer moderate correction of his wife. She insisted that the absence of such defenses did not reflect enlightened thinking or even the impact of the nascent woman's rights movement but instead involved a substitution of one rationalization for another. She maintained that late-nineteenth-century judges retreated to rationales about privacy and domestic harmony (what I called family stability or marital unity) when the right of chastisement was challenged as ancient, barbaric, and hostile to women. In fact, most antebellum appellate court rulings, legal treatises, and a few colonial and nineteenth-century statutes rejected explicitly the idea that a husband had the right to chastise his wife. Rulings that affirmed the right were the exceptions. But Siegel was correct that the right of chastisement was wholly rejected after the Civil War. Siegel further argued that postbellum judges offered the family privacy rationale as an excuse for nonintervention. The influence of the new companionate ideal of marriage and laws giving married women greater property rights had dissolved the legal basis for the doctrine that husband and wife were one legal entity.[11]

Siegel's work was based on a close reading of appellate court rulings; she speculated in a footnote about how well such opinions matched local law enforcement. As it turns out, there was very little relationship between lofty judicial statements of the Family Ideal and the actual policing of families. The Family Ideal was not hegemonic and could be set aside by popular pressure from victims and neighbors. Indeed, it can be argued that appellate court judges acted conservatively because they regarded themselves as a brake on the justice provided to victims at the local level. At any rate, the records of urban police courts where such cases were routinely handled have not survived. Even historians trying to uncover how the law punished family violence can examine only the most serious cases of domestic violence that resulted in a jury trial or, even more rarely, in a conviction. Moreover, by the standards of today, there were few such cases.

Sean T. Moore, in "'Justifiable Provocation': Violence against Women in Essex County, New York, 1799–1860," argued that the temperance movement exerted pressure on local courts to redefine wife abuse as a public harm. He noted that in upstate antebellum New York local judges took wife beating more seriously than assault of single women because they perceived wife abuse as a threat to family stability. He studied cases that went to criminal trial in two counties and found that men who assaulted single women were fined, whereas husbands who beat their wives were more often sent to jail. Moore concluded that temperance agitation led judges to identify the drunken wife beater, usually seen as an immigrant—mainly German or Irish—as threatening not only to his family but also to the social order. Because the temperance movement was unconcerned about violence toward single women, Moore argued, the courts minimized the seriousness of such assaults, despite the public nature of the crime.[12]

In "The 'Ill-Use of a Wife': Patterns of Working-Class Violence in Domestic and Public New York City, 1860–1880," Pamela Haag contrasted male-on-male violence with wife abuse, although records did not permit examination of men who were violent in both arenas. As in the upstate counties, most of the batterers brought to trial in New York City after the Civil War were working-class immigrants. Men whose cases went to trial had usually committed serious assaults that caused injuries and sometimes led to death. Haag regarded a husband's violence against his wife as an expression of his belief in his patriarchal right to command her obedience but argued that men battled each other with knives or pistols in the street or in saloon brawls to prove their masculinity. The circumstances just prior to a husband's assault against his wife were quite similar to those today:

sexual jealousy, a wife's wish for housekeeping money, or complaints that a husband wasted money, and a husband's dissatisfaction with a wife's performance of her domestic duties. There were two major differences: wife assaults in postbellum New York City broke out not on weekends and holidays but on the day before pay day, when economic distress was the greatest. Moreover, unlike today, batterers in New York City did not offer excuses for their behavior, presumably because patriarchal ideas were much more strongly held then.[13]

Local law enforcement in the antebellum South conformed to national trends and reflected regional ones. As in the rest of the country, there were occasional arrests for domestic assault or incest, but not many. The usual argument from scholars was that the South was the last bastion of patriarchy. Several antebellum Southern appellate court rulings affirmed a husband's right to administer moderate chastisement of his wife because of respect for male dominance and authority and belief that the state should have limited power of family intervention.[14] Moreover, the South did lag behind the North in the prosecution of incest. Southern appellate court judges required corroboration by a third party for a conviction of incest; a conviction also required proof of physically forced sexual intercourse. Northern appellate courts did not impose such strict requirements for conviction.[15]

Southern girls raped or molested by their fathers, uncles, or stepfathers could expect very little justice from the courts, but Southern battered wives did seek protection from local sheriffs and justices and sometimes secured it. In "Keeping the Peace: Domestic Assault and Private Prosecution in Antebellum Baltimore," Stephanie Cole showed that in antebellum Baltimore battered women could initiate "peace warrants" against a batterer.[16] The peace warrant was the common means of handling family violence in some Northern jurisdictions as well.[17] If an abuser violated the warrant, he was fined. Like most remedies against family violence, the peace warrant was an unwieldy tool, since it relied on a woman's initiative to bring a complaint against a man upon whom she may have been economically dependent. But the peace warrant did give the battered woman, rather than the police or the local justice of the peace, the discretion to bring the complaint. Some Southern batterers were also prosecuted on grounds of vagrancy, which was the catch-all category used to punish disorderly conduct. Others were charged with assault. Thus, despite the conservatism of appellate courts toward family violence, victims in the antebellum South had access to some of the same legal remedies available in the North. There was, however, a strong racial bias to local justice. Free black women rarely swore out peace warrants against their husbands, apparently because they feared the punishment that might be meted out.

Although battered slave women had no access to legal remedies, some paternalistic planters did punish slave husbands who beat their wives. Until recently scholars overlooked domestic violence among slaves, largely because they sought to emphasize the horrors masters and overseers inflicted. This defensiveness was unwarranted, given the pervasiveness of domestic violence, then and now. It is difficult to distinguish between what slaves regarded as legitimate punishment and what they defined as abuse. Like everyone else, they had concepts of both and resented the master who interfered with the former. In meting out "legitimate" punishment, slave parents and husbands were demonstrating their belief in patriarchy. Northern abolitionists charged that white Southerners raped and viciously beat slave women. White Southerners, who defended slavery as a benevolent institution, claimed that paternalistic masters protected battered slave wives and children from their abusive husbands and fathers. Some masters did serve as justices of their own plantation courts and punished domestic violence and disputes between slaves; others handed over disciplinary power to their overseers.[18]

After emancipation former male slaves continued to assert their rights as family patriarchs, which were reinforced by their legal right to marry. At the same time, African American wives and their children brought complaints of household battery to local military courts and the Freedman's Bureau. Like many battered women, the former slaves seemed more concerned with securing their husbands' financial support than with complaining about abuse. Their husbands, like many batterers, insisted that they had the right to beat their wives as well as their children to discipline them. Courts responded variously, from counseling "forgive and forget" or claiming they had no jurisdiction to fining the man and threatening him with imprisonment.[19]

Patriarchy also shaped parental efforts to protect African American children. Emancipated fathers as well as mothers often insisted on the right of guardianship of children denied them under slavery. After the war the Freedman's Bureau allowed former masters to negotiate long-term apprenticeship contracts for former slave children, which amounted to a return to slavery. In some cases whites "adopted" slave children after claiming they had been orphaned. Emancipated parents brought complaints to the Freedman's Bureau and took whites to court seeking the return of their children, insisting both on their parental rights as well as on their right of domestic privacy.[20] These legal efforts prove that despite extensive patterns of communal and church oversight over African American life, emancipated parents did conceptualize the home in terms of the Family Ideal.

Southern appellate court judges, in deciding cases of wife or child abuse, tended to fall back on arguments about family privacy when middle- or upper-class white men were involved. It was assumed that violence in such families amounted to a "trifling matter" and that domestic privacy was more important than the public good that could be served by "lifting the curtain" separating domestic life from public view. Judges who issued these decisions tended to be former slaveholders who had not initially supported the Confederacy (and therefore could be appointed to the bench even during the era of Republican rule). Such men thought that the institution of marriage, even among whites, was threatened by the dissolution of slavery. If one critical relationship of authority, that of master to slave, could be overturned then perhaps another, that of husband to wife (or parent to child), was also threatened. Nonetheless, these judges wanted to underscore the state's power to intervene in cases of "gross abuse." Rationales about family privacy permitted them to make the distinction between trifling matters and "gross abuse," which was seen as characteristic of the lower class and of black men.

Arguments against invading the privacy of the family also flourished in judicial rulings in tort cases issued in Northern and Southern jurisdictions. The tort is a damage suit for injuries; under the doctrine of marital unity it was impossible for a wife to possess such a right because it would have amounted to the husband suing himself. After state legislatures passed married women's property acts in the mid-nineteenth century, it was more difficult to complain that a wife did not have a right to sue her husband for damages. Nonetheless, many judges did affirm an interspousal immunity from tort. Siegel argued that appellate court judges justified immunity based on two parts of the Family Ideal: privacy of the home and marital unity. In the Progressive Era the U.S. Supreme Court, seeking to slow a sexual and divorce revolution sweeping across the country, ruled that a battered wife could not sue her husband for damages arising from his assault of her.[21]

For the most part, research by lawyers and historians about family violence has not generated major controversies among scholars. Social scientists, in contrast, engage in many such debates since their studies evaluate how well reforms are working and produce results with direct implications for the policies of courts, the police, and child protection services. The major debate within the humanities has concerned how to interpret evidence about family violence produced not by victims but by social workers and other social agents. Linda Gordon in *Heroes of Their Own Lives: The Politics and History of Family Violence, Boston 1880–1960* studied patterns of child neglect, abuse, incest, and wife abuse using the case records of private social work agencies such as the Massachusetts Society for the Prevention of Cruelty to Children. She praised reformers for establishing new institutions but criticized the class assumptions and biases of social workers who carried out the work of these institutions. She tried to detect the motives within complainant families, even when those motives were not described directly in victims' and perpetrators' testimony but indirectly in case files.

The center of Gordon's book was the story of resistance to violence by "heroes of their own lives," victims of domestic abuse, single mothers, incest survivors, and the friends and relatives who assisted them. Gordon was reacting against the nineteenth-century view of the victim as passive, helpless, and dependent. This characterization had long proven necessary to gain sympathy, which could be easily diminished if proof of provocation, drunkenness, or physical resistance was found. In reaction against this stereotype advocates often spoke about "survivors" or about "empowered victims." Gordon acknowledged that some victims were also victimizers and that many victims did not survive but emphasized her "heroes." Gordon particularly applauded women who succeeded in gaining marital separations or mother's pensions through their "agency." Agency, it has been argued, flows "from the actor's control of resources."[22] Abused and neglected infants and young children had no agency, since they did not control resources and were totally dependent on neighbors or relatives to initiate a complaint on their behalf. Older children and adults could have agency; they sometimes brought their own complaints, relied on the aid of others, or fought back. The legal scholar Elizabeth Schneider acknowledged that victimization and agency were not opposites but two points along a continuum of responses to abuse. Moreover, the approval of resistance, with the implicit assumption that nonresistance was not heroic, applied unnecessary moral judgment to the difficult circumstances confronting victims of domestic violence.[23]

In her review of *Heroes of Their Own Lives* Joan Scott discussed the problems in reading case records to reveal the actions of clients and offered her view of the nature of agency among victims. In Scott's poststructuralist approach there is no such thing as truth, behavior cannot exist outside the mental categories people create for understanding it, and no standard exists for determining what is true. Scott never denied that family violence existed but was interested in the limitations on people's abilities to understand and respond to family violence based on the mental categories they used. She saw case records as mental maps of the way social workers understood domestic violence and argued that such records did not provide information about "the reality" of abuse. Scott also offered her own view of the victim/hero way of characterizing responses to family violence. Scott took the radical position that agency was entirely a linguistic construction. She wrote that agency is "a discursive effect, in this case the effect of social workers' constructions of families, gender, and family violence."[24]

For *Tramps, Unfit Mothers, and Neglected Children: Negotiating the Family in Late Nineteenth-Century Philadelphia* Sherri Broder read about ten thousand case records of two social agencies in late nineteenth-century Philadelphia. She was much more interested in the neighbors and neighborhoods where the societies intervened than in the consciousness and actions of the victims. There were no heroes in her book, although the villains tended to be those in the middle class who accepted and endorsed various stereotypes about the poor.

Broder focused particularly on class distinctions within working-class neighborhoods. She portrayed working-class neighborhoods in Philadelphia as deeply divided and saw the societies to prevent cruelty to children as resources in ongoing struggles within these neighborhoods. Broder distinguished between the respectable working class, which regarded family violence as a moral failing among individual families, and those she termed the rough working class, which resented social agencies and refused to cooperate with their investigations. She suggested that in cases of child neglect, neighbors were willing to feed and care for hungry children but called an agency for assistance when their patience reached a breaking point. She noted the number of false accusations (still common) and speculated that neighbors who feuded with each other used intervention by a social agency as a new way to threaten each other. She also saw division among ethnic and racial groups about filing formal complaints. While it was common to see complaining as an act of racial or ethnic betrayal (airing one's dirty laundry in public), she also recognized that it could affirm standards of respectability within a group.

Just as the working class was split in attitudes toward family intervention, the social agencies did not speak with one voice either. Gordon claimed that instead of encouraging battered mothers and mothers of incest survivors to find employment, which would have provided financial stability to allow an escape from a violent household, agencies acted on the basis of prevailing attitudes, such as opposition to maternal employment. She argued that most agencies encouraged mothers to remain at home, even if their children were eventually sent to orphanages or foster care. Subsequent research has shown that a bureau that counseled deserted or widowed white mothers to remain at home nonetheless urged black mothers in similar circumstances to take paying jobs because black children were not seen as deserving of maternal care as white ones were. Moreover, while societies to prevent cruelty to children may have discouraged maternal employment, social workers at charity societies and courts of domestic relations encouraged it.[25]

Of the twenty books published about domestic violence since 1987, nine were on British history. British historians have long been interested in Victorian marriage and childhood and possess a rich record of campaigns against wife beating in the nineteenth century. Studies soon followed in the Commonwealth countries of Canada and Australia, where reform against child abuse and wife abuse could also be traced to the late nineteenth century. Scholars studying other parts of the world began to write about family violence by the 1990s, seemingly keeping pace with growing global interest in domestic violence. This research is still in its early stages, however, and has been published only in articles rather than in book-length studies. On the whole, such studies have been concerned with family violence within a single nation or a local area. Nonetheless, sociologists around the globe are beginning to compare reforms against domestic violence across countries.[26]

Political changes on the national scene as well as the rise of cultural history shaped U.S. scholarship about domestic violence. Most historians writing about family violence favored an expanded welfare state and greater spending on social services. For them President Clinton's welfare reform act (the Personal Responsibility and Work Opportunity Act of 1996) was a retreat from governmental responsibility for the poor and an attack on the safety net for disadvantaged children. Broder saw the present repeating the past in the social attitudes that encouraged the act's passage. In the late nineteenth century and in the contemporary era, she argued that a "charged term" (like *waif* or *tramp* in the Gilded Age and *welfare queen* or *deadbeat dad* in the 1980s) limited "Americans' abilities to formulate compassionate and constructive solutions to the problems the nation faced."[27] In addition, sensational murder trials, such as O. J. Simpson's, led to numerous articles about family murder trials, crimes of passion, and analysis of fictional representation of family murder.[28]

The general shift from social to cultural history apparent in historical writing by the 1980s led to more interest in the representation of domestic violence in murder trials as well as in women's fiction and temperance writings. My own work and that of Jerome J. Nadelhaft showed how antebellum temperance literature could attack the prevailing view of the home as a place of refuge. Advocates of temperance insisted that drunkenness could destroy the home and contribute to the victimization of women and children.[29] Karen Sanchez-Eppler, a literary scholar, examined temperance literature as a study in denial of incest as well as an acknowledgment that alcoholism (and maternal absence) could raise the prospects of it. For "Temperance in the Bed of a Child: Incest and Social Order in Nineteenth-Century America" she read more than seventy-five nineteenth-century temperance stories written for an audience of children. They had one theme: a drunken father climbing into bed with his young daughter. The father did not rape his daughter but instead was saved from his alcohol addiction by his daughter's love. Temperance newspapers and stories written for adults were filled with wife and child abuse. Those intended for a young audience sought to portray children as redeemers of errant drunkards. Nonetheless, these circumspect children's stories also revealed that of the various types of abuse, incest was the most taboo.[30]

In employing a literary and cultural approach to family violence some historians were seeking to illuminate cultural values of a distinct historical period. They used family violence as evidence of the trauma of not being able to live up to the manly ideal of independence in the new republic or about class-conscious debates about family values in the late nineteenth century. They also discussed family violence as evidence of the disempowering nature of Victorian marriage for women, the degree to which poor whites and former slaves in the South challenged elite political control during Reconstruction, and (in the case of Sanchez-Eppler) about the cultural belief in the redemptive power of the innocent child.[31] Family violence was thus providing evidence about the values that shaped marriage, family, childhood, class, and gender relations. Ironically, family violence had once been so invisible that it had no past but its "discovery" was seen not as revealing deviance but as shedding light on fundamental beliefs.

At the same time that cultural historians were shifting questions about family violence from social policy to representation and values, historians of crime were seeking a more detailed account of the incidence of family violence. Scholars in this field hold two somewhat contradictory views about whether there is more family violence now than in the past. The first is that the post-1960 increase in reports of child abuse and adult domestic violence is largely the result of increased public awareness rather than increased incidence; it may be impossible to determine the level of domestic violence for any period since its definition is constantly changing. The second is that family murder, as the most serious and most well-reported form of domestic violence, serves as the most reliable indicator of the level of severe domestic violence. (Yet the definitions of murder and manslaughter are changing and the matter of what charges to bring against mothers murdering their infants is open for debate.) In an appendix in *Domestic Tyranny*, I present findings from my research in colonial crime records as well as summaries of other studies about family murder. In medieval England I found a high incidence of family murder but this fell gradually for several centuries in England and in North America as part of "the civilizing process" and then rose again in the twentieth century in the United States. Subsequent research has confirmed this overall trend.

Two studies by Randolph A. Roth, "Spousal Murder" and "Child Murder in New England," have provided a much more detailed portrait of family murder and violent crime immediately after the American Revolution. Roth, in careful, detailed reconstructions using criminal records, concluded that the safest locales for families in American history was eighteenth- and early-nineteenth-century New Hampshire and Vermont, safer even than colonial New England. He offered many explanations for the low rate of family murder there. The first was that the population of these New England states was relatively homogeneous, so little tension arose because of religious or cultural differences. Physical chastisement of wives was disapproved of and neighbors, servants, and relatives frequently intervened in violent marriages. Roth further argued that in farm families each partner was needed to make the enterprise profitable. Most child murder was committed by seduced and abandoned unmarried servants who could not face the shame of bearing an illegitimate child and consequently killed their infants within twenty-four hours of giving birth.[32]

According to G. S. Rowe and Jack D. Marietta, although family murder was also uncommon in Philadelphia soon after the American Revolution, the overall murder rate in Philadelphia was quite high. One possible reason for this disparity is that while Philadelphia was not peaceable it was neighborly, and interventions in violent families may have limited the number of abusive incidents that led to murder. According to their essay "Personal Violence in a 'Peaceable Kingdom': Pennsylvania, 1682–1801," Benjamin Rush's Revolution-era Philadelphia was almost as violent as 1990s Philadelphia. Law enforcement in Philadelphia after the founding of the new nation may have been quite weak because of the religious and ethnic pluralism of the city. Poverty and alcoholism also produced considerable child neglect among poor families living in the back alleys of the city and was occasionally punished in the courts.[33]

As is evident already, a considerable amount of U.S. research concerns the history of the South, which has long been thought of as the most violent region in the country. Historians are interested in linking patterns of violence and justice administered by southern courts to race and to slavery. The South was clearly different from the North not just in the antebellum decades but also as far back as the colonial period prior to the widespread adoption of slave labor. In this book I emphasize the "reform" against family violence in colonial New England, where explicit laws against wife and servant abuse were enforced, but I did not study domestic violence in other colonial regions. In general, I assumed that southern colonies that modeled their laws on English rather than biblical precedents did not usually prosecute family violence. There are still few domestic violence studies using criminal records from the mid-Atlantic colonies, the French ones, or the areas of the Southwest governed by Mexico. After 1700, as colonial New England lost some of its religious mission and become more English in its legal rulings, enforcement efforts dwindled. This was true not only in Plymouth Colony, which I studied, but also in nearby New Haven Colony.[34]

Colonial New England had a more interventionist bent and a more humanitarian inclination than the South, at least up through about 1700. In the colonial South, the Family Ideal was held in high esteem. There were a handful of prosecutions for wife or servant abuse in colonial Virginia and Maryland, but fewer than in colonial New England. In the South the church and courts played a limited role in family intervention. Moreover, in the sparsely settled South, fewer kin were nearby to provide aid. Most cases of servant abuse in the colonial South were brought by victims, as opposed to the situation in New England, where kin often intervened.[35]

In all the colonies it was difficult to secure a divorce on grounds of cruelty; in Southern colonies a separation, not a full divorce complete with the right to remarry, was granted. The ability to secure a divorce rather than simply a separation in colonial New England was not a defining regional characteristic, however, since in no colony was a battered woman able to obtain a divorce or a separation solely on grounds of cruelty. Instead, she had to attach evidence of cruelty to what was then regarded as a more compelling claim of desertion or adultery. Nonetheless, women in colonial Virginia fared especially poorly. Servants in colonial Virginia might have been too afraid of being abused themselves to come to the aid of their mistresses. A battered wife who received alimony in a successful separation could find that the order was not enforceable and might end up dependent on public charity.[36]

David Peterson del Mar, in examining the incidence and response to wife abuse in Oregon in *What Trouble I Have Seen: A History of Violence against Wives*, concluded that domestic violence also flourished on the western frontier. He studied wife abuse from the settlement of Oregon in the 1840s until the present day using as his evidence divorce and court records.[37] Like many other western states, Oregon offered relatively easy access to divorce, since divorce solely on grounds of cruelty was permitted. His is the only study of the history of domestic violence among Native Americans, mainly Klamath Indians. Before the pioneers arrived, jealousy was the primary cause for a Native American husband to beat his wife. But the hunger confronting Native Americans after white settlement added stress to their marriages. Native American villagers did step in to stop familial abuse, but Indian women married to white trappers and traders lived isolated from their kin and seem to have gone unaided when they were battered. Wife beating was punished less severely in frontier Oregon than in the East, Peterson del Mar concluded, because the law did not take the matter seriously and because divorce court judges tended to believe that a husband had the right to chastise a wife who nagged or provoked him. In part because of the lack of law enforcement, in part because women had necessarily gained physical strength through tough pioneer life, western wives often fought back, verbally or physically.

Peterson del Mar argued that the decline of the frontier ethic and the rise of a Victorian emphasis on manly self-restraint made wife beating less acceptable and less common in the West as the decades passed. He concluded that wife abuse in twentieth-century Oregon mirrored national trends. The consumer ethic of self-indulgence and individualism, he argued, unleashed both good and violent impulses. Abusers began to offer less patriarchal explanations for their actions and instead tended to pity themselves, doubt themselves, and see themselves as powerless rather than powerful. Peterson del Mar's condemnation of consumer culture as a cause for increased wife abuse in Oregon is difficult to prove and ultimately reveals more about the hostility of intellectuals toward consumer culture than about domestic violence.

Both Peterson del Mar and Gordon concluded that the years between the world wars were a turning point for battered women. Peterson del Mar concurred with Gordon, who claimed that greater availability of divorce and increased employment options led women to turn to social agencies for escape from violent marriages rather than for assistance in securing child support from abusive husbands.[38] It has been argued that before the 1930s a battered woman brought a complaint only when she had been beaten and her husband had failed to provide financial support. One cannot but wonder, however, whether the decline in claims for child support by the 1930s was related to jurisdictional changes, as more battered women may have taken their claims of nonsupport to courts of domestic relations rather than to private social agencies.

On the whole, most studies of nineteenth-century cities such as Portland and rural areas, including rural Oregon, have found that neighbors often intervened in violent families. (To some extent this may be an artifact of the sources used, since Gordon and Broder examined investigations in which some neighbors refused to cooperate with an agency, whereas Peterson del Mar relied on divorce records, which included testimony from witnesses who did provide help). At any rate, using divorce records Peterson del Mar concluded that the importance of family privacy in the social sphere was rising in the twentieth century. Increasingly, battered women tended to turn to the police rather than to neighbors for aid. They did so presumably not because the police were especially helpful but because neighbors were unknown or unwilling to get involved.

At least since the 1960s the courts have both contracted and expanded the Family Ideal, in tune with changing public pressure and growing awareness of domestic violence. The courts limited the concept of marital unity by overturning the marital rape exemption, which protected husbands from being prosecuted for raping their wives. But court rulings about family privacy were contradictory. Especially since the 1960s family privacy has become a key component of social liberalism, synonymous with freedom of personal and sexual expression. Social movements from abortion rights to gay liberation pressed the courts to move some matters of sex, marriage, and childrearing into the realm of the private (meaning confidential or secret). A right to privacy has been used to argue in favor of abortion, the sale of contraceptives, interracial marriage (overturning state laws barring it), gay rights, gay marriage, and the rights of parents in child custody cases. The feminist lawyer Elizabeth Schneider, even though suspicious of the argument about privacy when it came to family violence, nonetheless insisted that family privacy "provides an opportunity for individual self-development, for individual decision making, and for protection against endless caretaking."[39] The black feminist lawyer Kimberle Crenshaw defended family privacy for blacks as necessary to creating a domestic sanctuary from racial discrimination.[40] The historian Nancy Cott sought to explain why so many contemporaries saw married life as a refuge of privacy. She wrote, "Traditionally a 'yoke,' marriage more recently and paradoxically signifies freedom in a chosen space—a zone marked from the rest of the world. While it promises to defend against the sense of estrangement haunting our cosmopolitan world, marriage can now also symbolize freedom."[41]

As conservatives gained political power, especially with the election of Ronald Reagan to the presidency in 1980, concern about most types of family violence (except for the newly discovered phenomenon of prenatal abuse by drug-addicted mothers) was largely in retreat, associated with diminished enthusiasm for liberalism and feminism. Commitment to the Family Ideal resurfaced, with greater support for the right of parental correction of children and for measures to bring about marital stability. New Right organizations, especially Christian evangelical ones, defended the parental right to use corporal punishment and decried child protection services that enforced child abuse and neglect laws, which they saw as an infringement on parental rights. Significant reforms, such as mandatory reporting of child abuse, mandatory arrest of wife abusers, and no-drop policies related to the prosecution of batterers, were said to be unworkable.[42]

Meanwhile, the public was also alerted to the prevalence of child sexual abuse, as feminists joined with child advocates who wanted to bring to light this form of child maltreatment. To Lela Costin, Howard Karger, and David Stoesz in *The Politics of Child Abuse* and Philip Jenkins in *Moral Panic: Changing Concepts of the Child Molester in Modern America*, this movement did not necessarily achieve its desired results. They claimed that the media, lawyers, and child advocates exploited public fears to create unnecessary panic about child abduction and molestation, satanic ritual abuse, incest, and Internet sex rings. They further argued that the public was too much absorbed with these topics to give attention to the more mundane but far more numerous instances of child neglect, which occurred mainly in poor families. Probably the most controversial area of reform has been civil damage suits brought against parents by incest survivors after recalling repressed memories. Costin, Karger, and Stoesz as well as Jenkins argued that because so many of the victims were white and middle or upper class, the media gave such stories undue attention.[43]

The phrase *moral panic* implies that the allegations of child sexual abuse were not real but instead were products of public hysteria whipped up by the media. Charges of satanic abuse, that is, incest, sexual torture, cannibalism, and child murder occurring as part of satanic worship, had no basis in fact. Sexual abuse alleged at day-care centers was generally not proven in a court of law. But other instances of abuse were corroborated, and still others, though hard to substantiate, may have been real. Moreover, some family violence researchers seem to want to have it both ways. Some claim that talking about family violence as a problem of the poor is a form of class and race bias yet insist that coverage of abuse among the middle and upper classes drains attention from the needs of poor families.

The sensationalism, doubt about reform, and suspicion of government agencies that characterized the 1980s gave way to the passage of major domestic violence legislation in 1992, the Year of the Woman. The rekindling of feminist public activism along with the election of a Democratic president during this period helped create the climate for reform. The Violence against Women Act, concerned with domestic violence and rape, was enacted in 1994. It represented the first federal effort to define domestic violence as a violation of a victim's civil rights. The Senate Judiciary Committee in 1991 held hearings on the appointment of Clarence Thomas to the U.S. Supreme Court. Thomas, an African American judge who had served as head of the Equal Employment Opportunity Commission, effectively employed rhetoric about his "high-tech lynching" by the committee to defend himself against charges that he had sexually harassed his employee, the lawyer Anita Hill. Outrage at Hill's treatment by the skeptical all-male, all-white Senate Judiciary Committee spurred the election of five female senators in 1992.

Women in both houses of Congress became major sponsors of legislation concerned with rape and battered women. A feminist lawyer who drafted the Violence against Women Act explained, "Congress was looking for ways to make amends to women."[44] Feminist lawyers, women legislators, male Democratic Senators eager to prove their feminist credentials, and an occasional law-and-order Republican found common ground. Joseph Biden, a liberal Democratic Senator, gained the support of the conservative Republican Orrin Hatch on the Senate Judiciary Committee in securing passage for the act. As had been the case before, domestic violence succeeded when it was framed as a law-and-order issue. The legislation provided funding for battered women's shelters, more prosecutors, and training hospital personnel, special police units, and judges. In its most controversial provision victims were given the right to sue their assailants for damages in federal court. The U.S. Supreme Court in *U.S. v. Morrison* struck down this provision in 2000 on grounds that the Fourteenth Amendment was not designed to provide remedies to private citizens. Nonetheless, the rest of the law remained on the books. The Columbine massacre of high school students in Colorado by fellow students in 1999 made it easier to pass the reauthorization bill two years later as yet another necessary crime control measure.

Despite the success of the act, the hysteria of the 1980s cast doubts about the merits of public intervention against domestic violence. Witch hunts, bizarre charges, and therapists who promised to restore to victims their repressed memories of incest gave reform efforts a bad name. Nonetheless, taken as a whole, there had been huge successes in the institutional and legal responses to family violence since the official recognition of the battered child syndrome in 1962. In 1974 the United States had only a couple of shelters for battered women; twenty-five years later there were about two thousand.[45] The federal government has now assumed responsibility for helping to fund these shelters. All states had criminalized marital rape by the 1990s.[46] Never before in American history have so many victims participated in providing comfort and services to others facing similar situations.

However, the public was still largely focused on child murder and did not comprehend the general nature of child protection work. The passage of legislation against child abuse in 1974 and the requirement that various professionals report suspected abuse to child protection services led to a huge increase in allegations of child abuse and neglect. The number of reports of abuse rose from 10,000 in 1962 to 3 million in 1999. Even while a large minority of these reports were screened out as unsubstantiated, child protection services were still overwhelmed by a huge volume of substantiated cases. Because more children were being removed from their homes, the number of children in foster care more than doubled between 1962 and 1999. Most of these children were racial minorities, and black children were overrepresented in foster care by a factor close to three.[47]

As these facts became known, the first legislative response was to reverse the trend toward out-of-home placement of abused and neglected children. Liberals concerned about the removal of so many minority children from their homes and conservatives eager to protect parental rights helped achieve passage of the Adoption Assistance and Child Welfare Act of 1980. Keeping abused and neglected children in the home was also cheaper than placing them in foster care. This law put the weight of the government behind "family preservation programs," including short-term efforts by social service professionals who moved into the home where the neglect or abuse was occurring to provide assistance. Such efforts proved largely ineffective. Initially the adoption act did have the effect of discouraging child removal. However, by the mid-1980s, the crack epidemic, high levels of unemployment, AIDS, and homelessness were taking their toll on poor families. Once again, child removals were increasing, as were placements in foster care. By 1997 federal policy affirmed the trend underway. The Adoption and Safe Families Act of 1997 placed the emphasis on putting the safety of the child ahead of family preservation. In *Domestic Tyranny* I wrote that "concern about abused children can be measured by the amount and quality of foster care available and the likelihood that a child can be placed permanently with adoptive parents" (203). By that measure, efforts to protect vulnerable children still fall appallingly short.

Some critics favor an end to mandatory child abuse reporting so as to decrease the number of complaints and avoid overwhelming the system. But the point is not to return to the days when child abuse and neglect were underreported and the only discussion of incest was on *Peyton Place*. Adequate funding is needed so that child protective services can function effectively. Family violence, as my work showed, is an elastic, malleable category. The more aware we become, the more family violence will be uncovered. Awareness also leads to naming and comprehending more types of abuse. The public recognition of family violence outstripped the public services necessary to undergird increased reporting. Undoing the reforms of the 1960s and 1970s seems an unwise overreaction. Although the third cycle of reform against family violence ended more than twenty years ago, it is imperative to hold onto the gains that have been made and recognize that caring for the needy and vulnerable is part of what makes for a decent world.

Notes

1. Elizabeth H. Pleck, "Challenges to Traditional Authority in Immigrant Families," in *The American Family in Socio-Historical Perspective*, 3d ed., ed. Michael Gordon (New York: St. Martin's Press, 1983), 504–17.

2. Reva B. Siegel, "'The Rule of Love': Wife Beating as Prerogative and Privacy," *Yale Law Journal* 105.8 (June 1996): 2117–207.

3. Philip J. Greven, *Spare the Child: The Religious Roots of Punishment and the Psychological Impact of Abuse* (New York: Knopf, 1991).

4. Claire M. Renzetti, *Violent Betrayal: Partner Abuse in Lesbian Relationships* (Thousand Oaks, Calif.: Sage, 1992); Claire M. Renzetti and Charles Harvey Miley, *Violence in Gay and Lesbian Domestic Partnerships* (New York: Harrington Park Press, 1996).

5. LeRoy Ashby, *Endangered Children: Dependence, Neglect, and Abuse in American History* (New York: Twayne, 1997); Louise Barnett, *Ungentlemanly Acts: The Army's Notorious Incest Trial* (New York: Hill and Wang, 2001); George K. Behlmer, *Friends of the Family: The English Home and Its Guardians, 1850–1940* (Stanford: Stanford University Press, 1998); Sherri Broder, *Tramps, Unfit Mothers, and Neglected Children: Negotiating the Family in Late Nineteenth-Century Philadelphia* (Philadelphia: University of Pennsylvania Press, 2002); Irene Quenzler Brown and Richard D. Brown, *The Hanging of Ephraim Wheeler: A Story of Rape, Incest, and Justice in Early America* (Cambridge, Mass.: Harvard University Press, 2003); Shani D'Cruze, *Crimes of Outrage: Sex, Violence, and Victorian Working Women* (DeKalb: Northern Illinois University Press, 1998); Maeve E. Doggett, *Marriage, Wife-Beating, and the Law in Victorian England* (Columbia: University of South Carolina Press, 1993); Frances E. Dolan, *Dangerous Familiars: Representations of Domestic Crime in England, 1550–1700* (Ithaca, N.Y.: Cornell University Press, 1994); Linda Gordon, *Heroes of Their Own Lives: The Politics and History of Family Violence, Boston 1880–1960* (New York: Viking, 1989); Greven, *Spare the Child*; E. James Hammerton, *Cruelty and Companionship: Conflict in Nineteenth Century Married Life* (New York: Routledge, 1992); Joseph M. Hawes, *The Children's Rights Movement: A History of Advocacy and Protection* (Boston: Twayne, 1991); Louise A. Jackson, *Child Sexual Abuse in Victorian England* (London: Routledge, 1999); Mark Jackson, *New-Born Child Murder: Women, Illegitimacy, and the Courts in Eighteenth-Century England* (Manchester: Manchester University Press, 1996); Philip Jenkins, *Moral Panic: Changing Concepts of the Child Molester in Modern America* (New York: Yale University Press, 1998); David Peterson del Mar, *What Trouble I Have Seen: A History of Violence against Wives* (Cambridge, Mass.: Harvard University Press, 1996); Saenz Eugenia Rodriguez, *Hijas, Novias, y Espoas: Familia, Martimonio, y Violencia Domestic en el Valle Central de Costa Rica (1750–1850)* (San Jose: University of Costa Rica Press, 2000); Lionel Rose, *The Erosion of Child-*

hood: *Child Oppression in Britain, 1860–1918* (London: Routledge, 1991); Eric A. Shelman and Stephen Lazoritz, *Out of the Darkness: The Story of Mary Ellen Wilson* (Lake Forest, Calif.: Dolphin Moon Publishing, 1999); Marlene Tromp, *The Private Rod: Marital Violence, Sensation, and the Law in Victorian Britain* (Charlottesville: University Press of Virginia, 2000). The anthology is *Over the Threshold: Intimate Violence in Early America*, ed. Christine Daniels and Michael V. Kennedy (New York: Routledge, 1999).

6. Robert L. Griswold, "Law, Sex, Cruelty, and Divorce in Victorian America, 1840–1900," *American Quarterly* 38.5 (Winter 1986): 721–45; Robert Griswold, "The Evolution of the Doctrine of Mental Cruelty in Victorian American Divorce, 1750–1900," *Journal of Social History* 20.1 (Fall 1986): 127–48; Michael Grossberg, *A Judgment for Solomon: The d'Hauteville Case and Legal Experience in Antebellum America* (Cambridge: Cambridge University Press, 1996); G. S. Rowe and Jack D. Marietta, "Personal Violence in a 'Peaceable Kingdom': Pennsylvania, 1682–1801," in *Over the Threshold*, 22–44.

7. Ann M. Little, "'Shee Would Bump His Mouldy Britch': Authority, Masculinity, and the Harried Husbands of New Haven Colony, 1638–1670," in *Lethal Imagination: Violence and Brutality in American History*, ed. Michael Bellesiles (New York: New York University Press, 1999), 43–66.

8. Jerome J. Nadelhaft, "Domestic Violence," in *Encyclopedia of American Social History*, vol. 3, ed. Mary Kupiec Cayton, Elliott J. Gorn, and Peter W. Williams (New York: Charles Scribner's Sons, 1993), 2115–24; Barbara Finkelstein, "Child Abuse," in *The Family in America: An Encyclopedia*, ed. Joseph M. Hawes and Elizabeth F. Shores (Santa Barbara: ABC Clio, 2001), 133–41; Elizabeth Blair Clark, "Domestic Violence," in *The Family in America*, 279–85.

9. Barbara Finkelstein offered her own formulation of how the Family Ideal operated with respect to child abuse. She added another element to the Family Ideal, the individualism of American society, which "prevented the development of universally available health and education benefits." Barbara Finkelstein, "A Crucible of Contradictions: Historical Roots of Violence against Children in the United States," *History of Education Quarterly* 40.1 (2000): 1–22.

10. The legal historian Hendrik Hartog argued that the notion of marital unity was the primary justification for a husband's exemption from being charged with raping his wife. Yet he also claimed that the concept of marital unity was primarily formulated in relation to cases of separated spouses. He further insisted that the argument about marital unity was not altogether used to keep women in their place, since it was also employed to enforce a husband's economic support for a wife who had separated from her husband. Hendrik Hartog, *Man and Wife in America: A History* (Cambridge, Mass.: Harvard University Press, 2000).

11. Siegel, "'The Rule of Love,'" 2142–50.

12. Sean T. Moore, "'Justifiable Provocation': Violence against Women in Essex County, New York, 1799–1860," *Journal of Social History* 35.4 (Summer 2002): 889–918.

13. Pamela Haag, "The 'Ill-Use of a Wife': Patterns of Working-Class Violence in Domestic and Public New York City, 1860–1880," *Journal of Social History* 25.3 (Spring 1992): 447–78.

14. Peter W. Bardaglio, *Reconstructing the Household: Families, Sex, and the Law in the Nineteenth-Century South* (Chapel Hill: University of North Carolina Press, 1995), 39–48.

15. Peter W. Bardaglio, "'An Outrage upon Nature': Incest and the Law in the Nineteenth-Century South," in *In Joy and Sorrow: Women, Family, and Marriage in the Victorian South, 1830–1900*, ed. Carol Bleser (New York: Oxford University Press, 1991), 32–51. For national, rather than regional, denial of incest, see Lynn Sacco, "Sanitized for Your Protection: Medical Discourse and the Denial of Incest in the United States, 1890–1940," *Journal of Women's History* 1403 (Fall 2002): 80–104.

16. Stephanie Cole, "Keeping the Peace: Domestic Assault and Private Prosecution in

Antebellum Baltimore," in *Over the Threshold*, 148–72; Laura F. Edwards, "Law, Domestic Violence, and the Limits of Patriarchal Authority in the Antebellum South," *Journal of Southern History* 56.4 (Nov. 1999): 733–70.

17. Randolph A. Roth, "Spousal Murder," in *Over the Threshold*, 65–93.

18. Christopher Morris, "Within the Slave Cabin: Violence in Mississippi Slave Families," in *Over the Threshold*, 268–85.

19. Leslie A. Schwalm, *A Hard Fight for We: Women's Transition from Slavery to Freedom in South Carolina* (Urbana: University of Illinois Press, 1997), 260–66. On abuse during the Civil War, see Darla Brock, "'Domestic Recreation' and Household Amusements: Spousal Abuse in Memphis, 1861–1865," *West Tennessee Historical Society Papers* 48 (1994): 81–90.

20. Laura F. Edwards, *Gendered Strife and Confusion: The Political Culture of Reconstruction* (Urbana: University of Illinois Press, 1997), 43–44, 47–53.

21. Siegel, "'The Rule of Love,'" 2162–70; Nancy F. Cott, *Public Vows: A History of Marriage and the Nation* (Cambridge, Mass.: Harvard University Press, 2000), 161–63.

22. William H. Sewell, "A Theory of Structure: Duality, Agency, and Transformation," *American Journal of Sociology* 98.1 (July 1992): 19.

23. Elizabeth Schneider, *Battered Women and Feminist Lawmaking* (New Haven: Yale University Press, 2000), 74–86.

24. Joan Scott, "Review of *Heroes of Their Own Lives: The Politics and History of Family Violence*," *Signs: Journal of Women in Culture and Society* 15.4 (Summer 1990): 851.

25. Gordon, *Heroes of Their Own Lives*; Emily K. Abel, "Valuing Care: Turn-of-the-Century Conflicts between Charity Workers and Women Clients," *Journal of Women's History* 10.3 (Autumn 1998): 32–52; Joanne L. Goodwin, *Gender and the Politics of Welfare Reform: Mothers' Pensions in Chicago, 1911–1929* (Chicago: University of Chicago Press, 1997).

26. Diane Mitsch Bush, "Women's Movements and State Policy Reform Aimed at Domestic Violence against Women: A Comparison of the Consequences of Movement Mobilization in the U.S. and India," *Gender and Society* 6.4 (Dec. 1992): 587–608.

27. Broder, *Tramps, Unfit Mothers, and Neglected Children*, 202.

28. Jeffrey S. Adler, "'My Mother-in-Law Is to Blame, but I'll Walk on Her Neck Yet': Homicide in Late Nineteenth-Century Chicago," *Journal of Social History* 31.2 (Winter 1997): 253–76. See also Hartog, *Man and Wife in America*, 218–41; and James D. Rice, "Laying Claim to Elizabeth Shoemaker: Family Violence on Baltimore's Waterfront, 1808–1812," in *Over the Threshold*, 185–201.

29. Jerome Nadelhaft, "Wife Torture: A Known Phenomenon in Nineteenth-Century America," *Journal of American Culture* 10.3 (Sept. 1987): 39–59; Jerome Nadelhaft, "Alcohol and Wife Abuse in Antebellum Male Temperance Literature," *Canadian Review of American Studies: Revue Canadienne d'Études Américaines* 25.1 (Winter 1995): 15–43.

30. Karen Sanchez-Eppler, "Temperance in the Bed of a Child: Incest and Social Order in Nineteenth-Century America," *American Quarterly* 47.1 (Mar. 1995): 1–33.

31. Edwards, *Gendered Strife and Confusion*, 178–82; Dawn Keetley, "Victim and Victimizer: Female Fiends and Unease over Marriage in Antebellum Sensational Fiction," *American Quarterly* 51.2 (June 1999): 344–84.

32. Roth, "Spousal Murder"; Randolph A. Roth, "Child Murder in New England," *Social Science History* 25.1 (Spring 2000): 101–47.

33. Rowe and Marietta, "Personal Violence."

34. Little argued that there was a crisis of authority in the colony during the period of the restoration of King Charles II. The colony of New Haven was joining with the neighboring colony of Connecticut. The efforts at prosecution, she pointed out, were attempts to shore up the authority of the colony and shame both husband and wife into acting in a more orderly manner. Little, "'Shee Would Bump His Mouldy Britch'"; Cornelia Hughes Dayton,

Women before the Bar: Gender, Law, and Society in Connecticut, 1639–1789 (Chapel Hill: University of North Carolina Press, 1995).

35. Terri L. Snyder found that courts in Virginia paid more attention to servant abuse as the race line became more firmly drawn in the law. The assumption is that as whites rose in status and became more clearly defined as the superior race, they received better treatment from the courts, even when white servants were abused by white masters. She concluded that after that, justifiable brutality was largely reserved for judgment on abuse of slaves. The number of cases she examined seems too few to make these generalizations. There were sixteen cases of servant abuse in York County, Virginia, between 1646 and 1720. In fact, the courts sided strongly with servants as early as 1661. Moreover, the number of cases between 1700 and 1720 that showed concern about servants was three. Terri L. Snyder, "'As If There Was Not Master of Woman in the Land': Gender, Dependency, and Household Violence in Virginia, 1646–1720," in *Over the Threshold*, 219–36; Irminga Wawrzyczek, "The Women of Accomack versus Henry Smith: Gender, Legal Recourse, and the Social Order in Seventeenth-Century Virginia," *Virginia Magazine of History and Biography* 105.1 (Winter 1997): 5–26; Mary Beth Norton, *Founding Mothers and Fathers: Gendered Power and the Forming of American Society* (New York: Alfred A. Knopf, 1996), 114–15.

36. Wawrzyczek, "The Women of Accomack."

37. Peterson del Mar's arguments about the incidence of domestic violence were based on cases in which the complainant had an incentive to falsify a report of abuse to secure a divorce on grounds of cruelty. He also reported absolute numbers of divorce without taking into account changes in population. Peterson del Mar, *What Trouble I Have Seen*, 175–77.

38. Ibid., 131–32; Gordon, *Heroes of Their Own Lives*, 257–64.

39. Schneider, *Battered Women and Feminist Lawmaking*, 89; Martha Albertson Fineman, "What Place for Family Privacy?" *George Washington Law Review* 67.5–6 (June–Aug. 1999): 1207–24.

40. Kimberle Crenshaw, "Mapping the Margins: Intersectionality, Identity Politics, and Violence against Women of Color," in *Applications of Feminist Legal Theory to Women's Lives*, ed. D. Kelly Weisberg (Philadelphia: Temple University Press, 1996), 363–77.

41. Cott, *Public Vows*, 226.

42. Richard J. Gelles, *The Book of David: How Preserving Family Can Cost Children's Lives* (New York: Basic Books, 1996).

43. Lela Costin, Howard Karger, and David Stoesz, *The Politics of Child Abuse* (New York: Oxford University Press, 1997); Philip Jenkins, *Moral Panic: Changing Concepts of the Child Molester in Modern America* (New Haven: Yale University Press, 1998). See also Dorothy Rabinowitz, *No Crueler Tyrannies: Accusation, False Witness, and Other Terrors of Our Times* (New York: Free Press, 2003).

44. Sally Goldfarb, "Symposium: The Violence against Women Act of 1994: A Promise Waiting to Be Fulfilled," *Journal of Law and Policy* 4.2 (1996): 397–98.

45. E-mail message from Melissa Wakeman, National Coalition against Domestic Violence, July 1, 2002.

46. For a history of marital rape in the nineteenth century, see Jill Elaine Hasday, "Contest and Consent: A Legal History of Marital Rape," *California Law Review* 88 (Oct. 2000): 1375–1505.

47. Kathy Barbell and Madelyn Freundlich, *Foster Care Today* (Washington, D.C.: Case Family Programs, 2001).

Domestic Tyranny

The domestic life of domestic tyrants is one of the things which
it is the most imperative on the law to interfere with.

JOHN STUART MILL
Principles of Political Economy

Introduction

MANY PEOPLE READ about horrible instances of family violence in the newspaper, but do not want to know much more about it, let alone to ask the fundamental question: What can be done? The first reason for grappling with this unpleasant, unnerving subject is its prevalence. Every police station, hospital emergency room, and shelter for the homeless can testify to this fact. Current statistics on the incidence of family violence show that the number of reports have risen dramatically, but it is difficult to know if this is the result of heightened social awareness or an actual increase in domestic abuse. Historical data are even less reliable. Still, the rate of family murder—the one form of domestic abuse most likely to be reported in any period—was higher in the late 1960s and the 1970s than at any previous time in American history.[1] The second reason for dealing with domestic violence is concern for its devastating effects—the physically and sexually abused swell the ranks of the homeless; they also make up a large share of runaways, violent criminals, prostitutes, and even assassins. Some victims of abuse suffer depression, social isolation, and are prone to suicide; others lash out at their friends, relatives, and even strangers on the street.[2]

Even if the incidence of domestic violence declined, it would still require public attention for a third reason. Family violence violates the conditions necessary for human well-being. The individual has a fundamental right to personal safety, and one of the prime responsibilities of government is to secure that right.

Many people think that family violence was discovered in the 1960s. It is true that the scale of effort on behalf of victims has been greater since that period than ever before. Yet there were two earlier periods of reform against family violence in American history. From 1640 to 1680, the Puritans of colonial Massachusetts enacted the first laws anywhere in the world against wife beating and "unnatural severity" to children. A second reform epoch lasted from 1874 to about 1890, when societies for the prevention of cruelty to children (SPCCs) were founded and smaller efforts on behalf of battered women and victims of incest were initiated. The third era of interest began in 1962, when five physicians published an article about "the battered child syndrome" in the *Journal of the American Medical Association*.[3] In the early 1970s, the women's liberation movement rediscovered wife beating and, somewhat later, marital rape. Since then many other types of family violence, from abuse of the elderly to sibling violence, have come to light.[4]

Family violence is a recent term referring to different types of abuse between relatives. (It was coined in the 1970s and is used here, even though other words—if the topic was at all openly discussed—were employed before then.) I define family violence as consisting of sexual coercion or threats or the use of intentional physical force with the aim of causing injury. Various types of family violence, from infanticide and murder to marital rape, spousal abuse, sibling violence, incest, and sexual molestation of children fall under this definition. Spanking, slapping, and emotional neglect do not. Child neglect has also been excluded because it comprises acts of omission rather than commission, such as failure to provide food, clothing, medical care, or adequate supervision of children. Social policies on behalf of neglected children will be mentioned only insofar as they have overlapped with programs for physically or sexually abused children.

Why did family violence become a matter of public policy in these three periods of American history? One explanation is that the incidence of it was rising, thus contributing to public alarm. But not all historical statistics support this. The Puritans of Massachusetts Bay Colony were the first to pass laws against family violence, although the domestic murder rate in their settlement was the lowest ever reported in American history. On the other hand, during the 1870s a violent crime wave made the public fearful. The family homicide rate was rising then, too, so an increase in the incidence of family violence may have been one reason for noticing "child cruelty." But the rediscovery of battered children in the early 1960s was not prompted by an epidemic of family murder. In 1962 the rate of domestic murder, by twentieth-century standards, was quite low. (However, unprecedented levels of it were soon reached, a decade or more *after* the battered child syndrome had already become public knowledge.)

Reform against family violence has mainly occurred as a response to social and political conditions, or social movements, rather than to worsening conditions in the home. The Puritans of Massachusetts Bay drafted a criminal code that reflected their religious principles and humanitarian ideas about the treatment of women and children rather than any assessment of current domestic disarray. The SPCCs, as we have noted, were in part a response to public outcries for sterner measures against a rising crime wave. In the late 1950s and early 1960s, new programs against family violence developed out of the general atmosphere of social reform and the belief that government should protect minority rights. The civil rights movement, along with the growth in women's employment and education, eventually led to the rebirth of the women's movement in the 1960s. In turn, the burgeoning of the radical wing of feminism contributed to the rediscovery of wife beating a decade later.

In all the reform periods, small organizations and dedicated individuals— ministers, millionaires, physicians, temperance activists, and women's liberationists—have made family violence a social issue that demanded public attention. Some have tried to pass legislation against domestic violence; others have also founded institutions—from SPCCs in the 1870s to shelters for battered women in the 1970s—on behalf of the victims of abuse. All of these activists were concerned about alleviating human suffering. Some were directly involved with victims of abuse, while for others domestic violence was an abstract, even philosophical issue.

Reformers against family violence challenged the general apathy and derision with which the problem is so often greeted. Yet the history of their efforts is not simply one of humanitarianism triumphing over prejudice and indifference. Altruism was rarely unalloyed, and many of the reformers had motives other than helping the victims. The Puritans, for example, wanted to stamp out family violence because they felt it, along with other forms of wicked behavior, threatened to disrupt their divinely sanctioned settlement. In the 1870s reformers sought to control dangerous and violent lower-class men. Even in contemporary times, the desire to deter and prevent crime has been one reason for creating social policies against family violence—a stronger motive in the battered women's movement than in programs on behalf of abused children. Leaders of the battered women's movement in the 1970s also wanted to demonstrate the importance of feminist ideas as well as aid the victims. Along with helping to alleviate human suffering, the pediatricians and radiologists who rediscovered child abuse helped enhance the reputation of their professional specialties and strengthen medical control of social problems.

Mixed motives have been characteristic of reformers in periods of interest in family violence; nonetheless, lack of concern about the issue has been the normal state of affairs. Inattention to the problem of domestic abuse lasted from about 1680 to 1874 and from 1890 to 1960. The first signs of declining attention are easy to detect: ministers, writers, or judges would urge a return to a more private family life or argue that the state should refrain from interfering in the family.[5] Greater suspicion of government intrusion or increased respect for family privacy would diminish support for social policies against family violence.

During the two long periods of inattention, laws from the previous reform epoch remained but were unlikely to be enforced. Victims still appealed to outside agencies for help; the police and the courts continued to receive complaints. But the level of social resources and general notice of the problem declined. Some institutions or policies begun during the reform era remained, but the priorities of courts or other social organizations responsible for enforcing laws against family violence changed. Domestic abuse came to be thought of as a problem of the past; the methods once appropriate in dealing with it were viewed as outmoded. New, more "modern" ways of thinking made family violence seem a less serious matter. At the lowest point of interest, there was a denial it existed at all, except in a few highly unusual instances.

This book traces the ebbs and flows in attention to the social issue of family violence through different periods of American history. Chapter 1 examines the first American reform against family violence—unique laws enacted in the New England colonies beginning in 1641. After the decline of the Puritan experiment, no significant public reform against family violence emerged until the formation of the first SPCC in 1874. Yet the American family was undergoing a reordering of its power relations. By the 1830s writers for women's magazines and authors of family advice books declared the private sphere of the family a female zone of influence. As Chapter 2 demonstrates, greater maternal authority in the home led to a decline in whipping as an acceptable form of corporal punishment among the educated middle class. (It remained the legitimate form of child discipline among most Americans, however.) Mothers were assumed to be able to govern their children without resorting to the rod. Later on, ideas about proper mothering and child nurture helped to define the standards of parental care that social welfare institutions sought to enforce. But in the early nineteenth century the curtain was drawn on family life, closing off private troubles from public view. The feminist movement of the 1850s, chronicled in Chapter 3, exposed the abuses that occurred at the domestic fireside and sought women's entrance into the public world. In the 1850s Elizabeth Cady Stanton and Susan B. Anthony, leaders of the woman's rights movement, sponsored but failed to pass legislation to add physical cruelty as grounds for divorce in New York state.

The punitive approach toward family violence reached its apex in the last third of the nineteenth century. The three reform efforts against domestic violence of that era defined it as a crime requiring stern punishments. The largest and most successful of these resulted in the formation of the SPCCs; the reasons for their founding and the results of their policies are discussed in Chapter 4. Chapter 5 examines the smaller-scale feminist and temperance programs to protect battered women and victims of incest. The efforts of male lawyers, district attorneys, and other law enforcement officials are detailed in Chapter 6. These professionals wanted to protect battered women by punishing abusers. They believed that fines and imprisonment had failed to reduce wife beating, and called for corporal punishment of batterers. Chapter 7 describes the specialized tribunals for children or families founded in the early twentieth century. These courts introduced a new, noncriminal approach to family violence and furthered the decline of interest in it already under way. Psychoanalytic thought influenced American clinical practice beginning in the 1920s. These ideas, as Chapter 8 indicates, relegated abuse to the world of childish fantasy. When the reality could not be denied, clinicians were trained to inquire into the victim's complicity. In the 1960s, after more than seventy years of neglect, private family troubles again became an important social issue. Chapter 9 examines the largest single reform against family violence, the programs begun in this era to prevent child abuse. Chapter 10 chronicles the feminist battered women's movement, and their significant innovation, shelters for abused women and their children.

The history of reform against family violence is not unlike that of other social movements in the United States. Campaigns against poverty, alcoholism, drug addiction, and mental illness have all gone through periods of sustained attention followed by periods of apathy. Highly educated people have frequently offered solutions for social problems that did not directly affect them. Proposed changes often combined the desire to control the lower classes with humanitarian compassion.[6] The underfunding of programs made it difficult for reformers to achieve their objectives. But the campaign against family violence, although similar in some respects to many other efforts, has had one aspect that necessarily limited it and made it more controversial.

The single most consistent barrier to reform against domestic violence has been the Family Ideal—that is, unrelated but nonetheless distinct ideas about family privacy, conjugal and parental rights, and family stability.[7] In this ideal, with origins possibly extending into antiquity, the "family" consists of a two-parent household with minor children. Other constellations, such as a mother and her children, were seen not as a family but as a deviation from it. One crucial element of the Family Ideal was belief in domestic privacy.

The family, it was held, should be separate from the public world. To Aristotle, the private sphere of women, children, and slaves was inferior to the *polis*, where men pursued the common good. Since the ancients, other philosophers, theologians, psychiatrists, and lawyers have offered a number of different rationales for family privacy. Little is certain about the concept of family between classical times and the sixteenth century; the kinship group rather than the husband-headed household may have been the dominant family ideal, and the home may have been more of a public than a private institution. But in the sixteenth century, Luther and Calvin's emphasis on the individual's direct relationship to God, unmediated by church ritual, affected the view of the family. The home became a more important center of worship and began to appear as a more distinct and separate institution from the rest of society. The husband, as the minister of the home, guided his wife, children, and servants, and led them in prayer.[8] A seventeenth-century Englishman, Sir Edward Coke, coined the phrase "a man's home is his castle." Because the privacy of the family was believed to be valuable yet fragile, government was to refrain from interfering in it. Notions of family privacy did not appeal to the English Puritans who migrated to the New World, however. They believed that neighbors and the church had a duty to regulate family life.[9] Nonetheless, although the Puritans did not have a modern notion of family privacy, they believed divorce or removal of children from abusive parents was justified only in unusual circumstances.

By the 1830s the private sphere came to acquire a deeply emotional texture; it became a refuge from the hard, calculating dealings of the business world. Relations between family members were seen as qualitatively different—more affectionate, lasting, and binding than those between strangers. Nothing was more sacred and socially useful than mother love—it made children righteous and responsible. Even more than before, intervention in the family was viewed as problematic, a violation of family intimacy. Although there have been many periods of American history since the 1830s when family privacy declined in importance, belief in it has persisted to the present day. Modern defenders are likely to argue that the family has a constitutional right to privacy or insist that the home is the only setting where intimacy can flourish, providing meaning, coherence, and stability in personal life.[10]

A second element of the Family Ideal is a belief in conjugal and parental rights. In ancient times, the head of the household had the power to compel obedience from his wife, children, and servants and maintain domestic harmony. A husband also had the "right" to demand sexual intercourse with his wife at his pleasure. Traditionally, the husband and father possessed the "right of correction" (physical discipline) over his wife, servants, apprentices, and children. He was permitted, even expected, to use the rod or the whip in a moderate fashion. A mother, whose power to punish was delegated by her husband, could also use force in disciplining her children. Although abuse has always been separate from correction, the right of discipline has served as a justification for virtually all forms of assault by parents and husbands short of those that cause permanent injury.

The Romans had the most extensive legal definition of these traditional rights. A Roman wife remained under the guardianship of her husband, who possessed *patria potestas*, including the power to sell his wife and children into slavery or put them to death.[11] Since Roman times, the husband's power has been gradually restricted, and the rights of women and children have correspondingly increased.[12] Yet in many areas of law a stranger is entitled to more legal protection than a family member. In most states, a wife does not have the right to charge her husband with rape, nor in many can a family member sue a relative for damages arising from assault. Although courts have overturned the common law custom of "moderate correction" of wives, parents still have the right to physically discipline their youngsters; indeed, most Americans spank their children and approve of it as a general method of punishment.[13]

A third element of the Family Ideal is belief in the preservation of the family. Marriage was supposed to be life long, for religious reasons and for the responsibility of raising children. Conservatives in the nineteenth century argued that women were dependent on the family for their happiness. They were tethered to it because of their children and in order to make the home a place of affection.

Thus—for the sake of their children, or the redemption of their husbands—wives have traditionally been urged to renounce their personal liberty. Many women have been bound to marriage and the family by this sense of duty and obligation. It follows, then, that the desire for personal autonomy, especially among women, would threaten family stability. Since the nineteenth century, but especially in modern times, feminism and the more generalized quest for self-realization have encouraged women to question the sacrifices they made automatically in the past.

In sum, reform against family violence is an implicit critique of each element of the Family Ideal. It inevitably asserts that family violence is a public matter, not a private issue. Public policy against domestic violence offers state intervention in the family as a major remedy for abuse, challenges the view that marriage and family should be preserved at all costs, and asserts that children and women are individuals whose liberties must be protected.

The fate of proposed legislation against family violence has depended to a

large extent on how reformers regarded the Family Ideal. Those who criticized it most directly and vehemently were defeated. Nineteenth-century
advocates of women's rights, for example, attacked the Family Ideal as a
hypocritical belief that denied the seriousness of abuse. They posed the issue
of divorce for battered women as a choice between the Family Ideal and
women's rights to freedom and autonomy. By thus making divorce reform a
referendum on the politics of the Family, they ensured legislative failure. In
the 1970s as well, feminist espousal of divorce for battered women and a
conservative backlash against the women's movement led to initial Congressional defeats of domestic violence legislation.

The more successful reformers have been politically circumspect. Conservative feminists and female advocates of temperance after the Civil War
avoided criticizing power relations in the family and presented their remedies
as a means of preserving the home. Because women and children were
economic dependents, they argued, there was no viable alternative other than
ensuring that the home was a place of safety and happiness. In the 1970s
modern feminists, after their first defeat, were far more successful than their
nineteenth-century counterparts. Their early encounters with the political
process taught them to mute their rhetoric; some feminists claimed they were
helping to restore the family, and others tried to conceal or sidestep the
controversy. Federal legislation funding shelters for battered women finally
passed because the feminist movement and its Congressional supporters
formed a coalition with conservative legislators.

Other than avoiding a broad philosophical critique of power in the family,
the use of personal influence, intriguing new definitions of family violence,
and unusual reform coalitions have contributed to legislative success. The
Puritans buried provisions against wife beating and child abuse in a highly
popular criminal code. Although some of its provisions provided for the
liberties of women and children, others safeguarded parental authority.
Founders of the SPCCs succeeded partly because they were wealthy and
politically well-connected. While deliberately reassuring the public that they
supported "good wholesome flogging of children," they also capitalized on
public concern about the plight of helpless, innocent children. Moreover,
they made clear that "child cruelty" applied to public exploitation of children, not just to domestic assault. In the 1960s the physicians who discovered
"the battered child syndrome" successfully defined child abuse as a public
health problem and quickly focused public attention on it, with the aid of
television and the press. But continuing federal support for child abuse prevention programs required dedicated Congressional leadership. The women's
movement of the 1970s succeeded in passing new state laws because it relied

on a coalition with representatives who favored other women's rights issues. It employed the same strategy in Congress, but found success, after incurring several defeats, through compromise with conservatives.

Before the founding of the SPCCs, no formal institutions other than secular or church courts aided the victims of family violence. Beginning in the 1870s, concerned groups established new organizations. Thereafter reform against family violence became part of the history of social welfare. The SPCCs of the late nineteenth century were private institutions staffed by semiprofessionals and volunteers. The juvenile and family courts founded in the early twentieth century received public funds and employed probation officers, social workers, and psychiatrists. They regarded domestic violence as a family problem, not a violation of the criminal law. In the 1920s, another layer of institutions was added. Mental health and child guidance clinics and family service associations provided individual or marital therapy. Like the family courts, these services were not designed to meet the needs of victims of family violence, although some of their clients were families where abuse was occurring. In the 1960s pediatricians and social workers helped to establish hospital treatment teams for battered children and new social services for abusive and neglectful parents. Women's groups a decade later founded shelters for battered women and their children.

Evaluating programs against family violence is considerably more complicated than charting legislative failure or success. In the provision of services, the complicated dynamics of family abuse that reformers had rarely grasped came fully into view. Women and children suffered the most severe consequences from family violence. Although mothers often committed child abuse, they rarely sexually assaulted children. Still, the family situation did not often fit the moralistic categories of innocent victim and guilty victimizer. The wife who suffered at the hands of her husband, for example, could also abuse her children. Moreover, battered children or incest victims often refused to complain. Many did not want to be removed from home, despite the physical pain or emotional anguish they had suffered. Abused women, who brought complaints of abuse to SPCCs, family courts, or legal aid societies, often refused to press charges and decided to reconcile with their husbands.

But the institutions and services provided since the 1870s have changed in response to the demands of clients. The victims of family violence had rarely formulated legislation or founded institutions to aid others like themselves. But abused adolescent children, neglectful mothers, battered wives, even abusive husbands pressed social agencies for action and thus helped to affect actual policies and their goals.[14]

Many influential historians, lawyers, and social theorists argue that public programs against family violence have done more harm than good. Noting that reform has never been simply an act of disinterested benevolence, they have uncovered the class bias of specific agencies—SPCCs in the late nineteenth century, the juvenile courts of the early twentieth century, diverse child and family clinics begun in the 1920s, the programs aimed at preventing and treating child abuse beginning in the 1960s. The clients of these institutions were mainly poor or working class; the founders were the more privileged. The critics claim that such programs have attempted—and succeeded—in imposing their own standards on their clients, while strengthening the political power and cultural dominance of the reforming elite. The bureaucratic "invasion" of the home, they have argued, trampled on the domestic life of the poor.[15] Too often, so the argument goes, children have been removed from home on grounds of parental poverty alone, rather than because of parental abuse or malfeasance.[16]

These critics make two crucial assumptions about the family. First, they believe that it was better off in some "golden age" before the state intervened. Second, they view the family as a single unit with shared interests and a common stand against state intrusion.[17] My sampling of several thousand case records of the Pennsylvania Society to Protect Children from Cruelty for the late nineteenth century and the Illinois Humane Society from 1880 until 1940 indicates that the critics have confused the Family Ideal with the reality of domestic life. The Pennsylvania and Illinois records show that family conflict was a persistent fact of life—family unity the myth. The household was comprised of individuals who had divergent goals and points of view. The interests of the husband were not the same as those of his wife. A daughter's perspective differed from that of her mother. Moreover, neighbors and relatives often "meddled" in abusive families and believed they had the right to do so. Far from accepting the ideal of family privacy, victims and their kin or their neighbors invited outside agencies to intervene. But those closest to the family were often unsympathetic or more supportive of the abuser than the victim. A decision in favor of traditional authority was less certain in complaining to an anticruelty society or a juvenile or family court instead of depending on help from relatives, neighbors, or the parish priest.[18]

Families in which abuse occurs need the protection offered by the police or outside agencies. Yet assistance has also been accompanied by efforts at social control and class domination. Still, some policies and programs have worked better than others. Those that blamed the victim for having caused abuse added psychic damage to the original injury; those that attempted family reconciliation at any price left victims in danger. The most successful efforts were those that made protection of victims their highest priority and offered them concrete resources—emergency housing, relief or welfare, legal aid for divorce, child support agreements, foster care leading to permanent adoption. By these criteria, the policies against family violence established since the 1960s receive the highest marks.

The policies before the 1960s deserve more criticism. Yet historical study provides more than a scorecard for evaluating past programs, and more than a repository of past cruelties and barbarities. It also reveals inherited domestic ideals, and their impact in shaping and distorting social policy regarding family violence.

I

Reform of the Moral Code

1

Wicked Carriage

"WE ARE A COMPANY professing ourselves fellow members of Christ," wrote John Winthrop, a Cambridge-educated lawyer describing English passengers on a ship bound for America in 1630. Puritans such as Winthrop believed that the Church of England, although nominally Protestant, had not been purged of the "detestable enormities" of Roman Catholicism.[1] Persecuted for their beliefs, and desirous of bettering themselves in a New World where land was plentiful, many English Puritans saw no choice other than to leave England. Winthrop made Boston the colony's capital, although many settlers quickly dispersed inland and elsewhere along the coast. Within a decade, sixteen thousand English immigrants were living in the colony of Massachusetts Bay.

The Puritans hoped that their "city upon a hill" would set an example of religious devotion for the rest of the world. The family was vital to their endeavor; it conveyed religious values and prepared the young for a pious life. It was also the foundation upon which a religious commonwealth was built. An institution so necessary to the Puritan mission could not become a sanctuary for cruelty and violence; family violence was "wicked carriage"— assaultive and sinful behavior—that threatened the individual's and the community's standing before God. Only if the Puritans maintained their vigilance in punishing sin would God extend to them his protection from fire, plague, disease, earthquakes, and Indian attacks. Moreover, family violence threatened the social and political stability of the Puritan's godly settlement. As a sacred institution, the family stood as a model for all other social relations. Harmonious family life helped to create a peaceful community, but a quarrelsome household endangered the social order. Any disturbance within the family, from verbal to physical abuse, was considered a failure to achieve domestic peace. With this view of the family, combined with advanced humanitarian ideas on the rights of women and children brought with them from England, the Puritans developed the concept of family violence as a public concern.

The Puritans attacked family violence with the combined forces of community, church, and state. In Puritan society meddling was a positive virtue. Neighbors informally but vigilantly watched each other for signs of aberration; church courts extracted confessions of sin from their errant members, and civil and criminal courts upheld the laws and punished wrongdoers.

They acted against family violence in ways without parallel in Western history. But they intervened in quarrelsome families only to correct the most severe abuses rather than to protect the rights of individuals. Despite their lack of a modern notion of family privacy, the Puritans regarded outside intervention as disruptive, justifiable only to the extent that it restored family order. Faced with the choice between preserving the family unit and permitting a victim of family violence to be removed from an abusive household, they invariably chose to preserve the male-dominated family.

The major form of protection for victims of domestic violence was the watchfulness over family life that Puritan communities provided. Neighbors were expected to watch each other so that the sins of a few would not jeopardize the standing of the entire community in God's eyes. Disorderly families defiled the institution of the family; a husband who beat his wife, for example, disgraced himself in the eyes of his neighbors. In one of his sermons, the Puritan religious leader Cotton Mather preached that for "a man to Beat his Wife was as bad as any Sacriledge. Any such a Rascal were better buried alive, than show his Head among his Neighbours any more."[2] Another Puritan minister castigated the wife-beating husband as a man who "shames his profession of Christianity, he breaks the Divine law, he dishonours God and himself, too." The husband-beating wife was "a shame to her profession of Christianity, she dishonours God and provokes the glorious God, tramples his Authority under her feet; she not only affronts her Husband, but also God her Maker, Lawgiver and Judge."[3]

One suspects that in the majority of Puritan households, family life was harmonious, although by no means free of conflict or physical violence. In the model household, the husband and father was looked upon as a benevolent guide and leader, wives accepted their place as subordinates in the family enterprise, and children were regarded as obedient servants. Everyone had a well-defined position in the family hierarchy; it was a stable system of domestic government. Yet in the midst of their devout settlement, the Puritans found "bad" and jealous husbands who drank heavily, frequented prostitutes, and took sexual advantage of servant girls; bad wives who cursed their husbands, flogged their servants, and stole their neighbors' pigs; and disobedient children and servants who lied, stole, and ran away from home.

Puritan neighbors regarded malcontents and deviants as disturbers of the peace, who needed to be put right. Thus they visited families suspected of moral lapses, praying with them for divine guidance. This neighborly surveillance encouraged at least the appearance of domestic tranquillity, carrying as it did the threat of public shame. It also had a darker side. A wife who refused to bend to her husband's will, abused her children, or raged against her neighbors could be accused of witchcraft. In the Puritan mind, only a thin line separated the nag from the woman who convenanted with the devil. Some accused witches had been abused by their husbands or sons; others, although not victims of family violence, were part of a household where it occurred. One wife, tried for witchcraft, was also accused of "railing" at her husband and calling him a "gurley-gutted Devil." A mother abused by her son was later charged with witchcraft. Another suspected witch had never committed any violence, although her son had been brought to court and convicted of "high misdemeanors" in "abusing of his father, and throwing him down, and taking away his clothes." An abusive husband testified in Connecticut that the bruises on his wife's thighs came not from the beatings he gave her, but from his wife's secret practice of witchcraft.[4]

The fear of being suspected of witchcraft exerted a powerful pressure to conform, particularly to maintain a harmonious family. This Puritan domestic order is attested to by the low rate of family murder in Massachusetts Bay Colony or nearby Plymouth. Murder is the one form of disharmony in the home that least escapes the notice of authorities—the one instance of physical violence almost never considered reasonable or justifiable. There were only six indictments for family murder in the seventeenth-century Massachusetts Bay and Plymouth colonies among a population of about 6,000 inhabitants. On a per capita basis, the family murder rate was only 0.3 per 100,000 in Massachusetts Bay Colony between 1630 and 1692 and 0.1 per 100,000 if only husband-wife murders are included. The family murder rate was approximately the same in Plymouth Colony during the same years.[5] By contrast, in Houston and Philadelphia about 1970, the family murder rate was 3.6 and 3.7 per 100,000, respectively, or about twelve times greater than in Puritan Massachusetts. It is possible that modern methods for detecting murder can uncover more murders, which could help explain the disparity in murder rates. But it is likely that the modern American home is a far more dangerous place to live than its Puritan counterpart.

In the small, dense Puritan villages, a neighbor or relative quickly alerted the local minister to any serious verbal or physical assaults occurring in families. The minister could then visit with the errant couple and warn them to correct their behavior. During this visit, he might also have led them in prayer for God's counsel and forgiveness. With so much informal pressure to conform, only the truly recalcitrant had to be brought before a church court. These courts served to reinforce more informal methods of community pressure. Still, the influence of the courts was somewhat limited, since they could punish only their own members. Even in these religious communities, many people did not belong to a church and thus were not subject to its jurisdiction.

Church courts tried cases of spouse abuse, cruelty to children and servants, assaults, threats against parents, and child neglect; they also punished drunkenness, murder, adultery, fornication, and even lying. The procedure of a church court was designed to shame and disgrace the sinner. The ruling church elders investigated complaints and sought out two witnesses who would testify at a hearing convened before the entire congregation. The accused were given an opportunity to respond to the accusations of the witnesses. The goal of the hearing was not to determine innocence or guilt but to wring from the person on trial a confession of sin in the hope of securing for the wayward soul the promise of salvation.

The congregation of the church decided whether to accept a sinner's confession. Sometimes the minister called for a show of hands, other times, he asked his congregation to raise their voices to indicate acceptance of a confession. If they remained silent, as they did in a particular case after hearing the confession of a man who drank and beat his wife, it signaled rejection. The minister pronounced sentence on those whose repentence had been rejected as trifling. Before doing so, he delivered a blistering sermon chastising the evildoer and urging continued vigilance against immorality.

The total number of persons disciplined in various church courts never numbered more than a few dozen per year, in contrast to the several hundred cases of various kinds that appeared every year in the secular courts of Plymouth and Massachusetts Bay colonies. Accusations of family violence, incest, or rape were infrequent in church courts, as were complaints against masters for cruelty to servants or slaves. The most frequent cause of complaint was "fornication," premarital sexual activity usually discovered because a woman gave birth to her first child less than nine months after marrying.

Even when the rare instance of family violence was brought before the church court, the kind of justice meted out indicated a desire to preserve the family rather than to punish wrongdoing. The wife who was beaten was considered to be almost as much at fault as her husband. In the trial of Lemuel Phelps, an accused wife beater, his wife was called upon to confess that she had "transgressed the Rules and Duties of a Wife towards her husband in some of my past conduct in assuming too much authority over him and controlling him in civil and religious matters." She promised to reform. Then Phelps acknowledged that he had beaten his wife and had accused her of bearing a child not his own. He promised to behave "for the future as a kind and tender husband." Following the standard procedure in being restored to full church membership, Phelps stood before the entire congregation on Sunday, pleaded for their forgiveness, and read his confession:

> I acknowledge to this Church that I have broken a Christian rule and thereby dishonoured God and brought a scandal upon the holy Religion which I profess by my unchristian treatment of my wife in beating her and in speaking to others of her as having committed the unpardonable sin, in speaking unadvisedly concerning her death and the Birth of her last child, and in not having that love and affection towards her I engaged by my Marriage Covenant, for which I am heartily sorry and ask the Foregiveness and restoration to your church and ask your Prayers for me.[6]

Three years later Phelps was brought before the church court on the same charge; he again accused his wife of adultery. Presumably he underwent the same process of examination and confession as before.

In addition to church courts, the magistrates of the New England colonies—especially the colonies of Massachusetts Bay and Plymouth—enforced a criminal code that punished many types of family violence. Massachusetts Bay and Plymouth were the only two American colonies to pass laws against the beating of spouses; indeed, theirs were the first laws against spousal abuse enacted anywhere in the Western world. It is often thought that wife beating was not made illegal until the late nineteenth century. Indeed, one eighteenth-century English judge suggested that the size of the beating instrument a husband could legally use should be no thicker than a man's thumb. In 1824 a Mississippi appellate court held that a husband had the right of "moderate chastisement" over his wife, and some decades later other Southern judges concurred with this ruling.[7] Yet, almost two centuries earlier, the Massachusetts *Body of Liberties* of 1641 provided that "Everie marryed woeman shall be free from bodilie correction or stripes by her husband,

unlesse it be in his owne defence upon her assault." A few years later the law
was amended to prohibit husband beating as well. The Pilgrims were probably
following Massachusetts Bay in enacting a law against spouse abuse in 1672.
This law punished wife beating with a five-pound fine or a whipping and
husband beating with a sentence to be determined by the court.[8]

The Massachusetts *Body of Liberties* also protected the "liberties of children." A provision that prohibited parents from choosing their child's mate
included a clause that forbade parents from exercising "any unnatural sever-
itie" toward children. If unnatural severity occurred, children were granted
"free libertie to complaine to Authorities for redresse." The *Body of Liberties*
also forbade cruelty toward any creature "usuallie kept for man's use" and
permitted servants to flee from abusive masters without penalty.

The impetus for the formation of this code came in the 1630s when resident
stockholders in the investment company backing the colony demanded a
written constitution and a civil and criminal code to protect their liberties.
Acting upon their request, and with the experience of several decades of
governing themselves with minimal interference from the crown, the colony's
General Court appointed a committee to devise a written legal code. A draft
by Puritan minister John Cotton was rejected because it contained too many
provisions for capital punishment, including one specifying hanging for
incest. The Court turned to Reverend Nathaniel Ward, a Puritan minister
with English legal training. He pruned some of Cotton's provisions for the
death penalty and added sections protecting the liberties of women, children,
servants, and foreigners.[9] It is not known whether there was any public
discussion of the sections on the liberties of women and children. But Ward's
draft was debated and voted upon by the freemen of the colony and the
General Court.

The passage of the Massachusetts *Body of Liberties* was the first American
reform against family violence. And, like many reforms that came later in
history, legislative success depended on unusual social and political circumstances that had nothing to do with the prevalence of domestic violence.
Parliament had granted the colony permission to govern itself as long as it was
in accord with English law, but when civil war broke out in England in 1640,
the colonies were left on their own. Taking advantage of their freedom from
imperial rule, the Puritans drafted laws that reflected their religious principles.

Although most of the criminal laws in the Massachusetts *Body of Liberties*
were adapted from biblical law or English custom, the one against wife beating
was not. The precise origins of this law are unclear, although advanced opinion
in seventeenth-century England held that moderate correction of a wife was
an outmoded custom. At an Oxford debate held about 1630, a Dr. G sup-

ported the view that a husband possessed the right of moderate correction over his wife. His opponent, William Heale, an Anglican clergyman, later published a pamphlet in which he argued that striking a wife was not only unlawful, but unnatural, since humans were the only species where the male used violence against his mate. The English Puritans seem to have concluded that wife beating should not be permitted even before this debate, however. In 1599 one Puritan minister argued—somewhat cynically—that a wife beater should be whipped because "he is worthy to be beaten for choosing no better." In 1622 Puritan theologian William Gouge insisted in his popular *Domesticall Duties* that it was immoral for a husband to beat his wife. The great Puritan preacher William Perkins also opposed wife beating, as did Richard Baxter, another Elizabethan Puritan writer.[10]

Although the *Body of Liberties* made wife beating illegal, Puritan courts placed family preservation ahead of physical protection of victims. They were reluctant to separate wives from husbands, and infrequently granted divorce, attempting instead to reconcile unhappy and quarrelsome couples. When Puritan magistrates encountered couples who were living apart, they urged them to move back together. Courts sometimes forced runaway wives to return to their husbands. In one instance of repeated physical abuse, a wife in Plymouth Colony was permitted to live separately from her husband, and her husband was ordered to pay her maintenance.[11] She was only allowed to do so, however, until her husband reformed.

Divorce was not unknown in Massachusetts Bay Colony, where the laws regulating it were less stringent than in England.[12] Marriage, the Puritans believed, was not a sacrament but a civil contract based on the mutual consent of both parties. Nevertheless, divorce was still a rarity. Fewer than forty full divorces were granted in Massachusetts Bay Colony from 1639 to 1692. In no instance was a divorce granted solely on account of cruelty. Cruelty was grounds for divorce, but only in combination with other grounds, such as adultery and neglect of family, a condition that remained in effect well into the eighteenth century.

All divorce petitioners in eighteenth-century Massachusetts who cited cruelty as one of the grounds for divorce were women, and most of them were unsuccessful. Out of twenty-three such petitions brought to the Governor's Council from 1692 to 1789, only nine led to divorce from bed and board (a legal separation without the right to remarry).[13] Three suits resulted in separations based on mutual consent, six were dismissed because of insufficient evidence, and five went unresolved. Several women applicants had been abused for many years before suing for divorce; many of them had been living separately from their husbands, but sought divorce to protect their property or inheritance from being seized by their husbands.

Physical cruelty, then, although disapproved of, was not regarded as sufficient reason to sunder the bonds of matrimony. Nagging wives, the courts appeared to believe, provoked their husbands into beating them. A violent husband who could show that his wife had committed adultery stood a good chance of securing a divorce. But a petitioning wife was expected to prove that she had "acted dutifully" and had not given her husband "provocation" for hitting her; in fact, "[he] beats her without provocation" was a recurring phrase in women's divorce petitions. Yet even women who could furnish sworn witnesses to testify of beatings and murder threats still lost their suits on grounds of insufficient evidence. Divorce on the grounds of extreme cruelty or abusive treatment, with the right to remarry, was not permitted in Massachusetts until 1870.

The Puritans did regard incest as grounds for divorce, however. In Massachusetts Bay Colony one divorce was granted on grounds of incest and desertion; and in Plymouth Colony, one husband, Thomas Hewitt, secured a divorce on grounds of incest alone. When his wife, Martha, bore a child less than nine months after his marriage, Thomas realized that he was not the child's father. Martha Hewitt had been made pregnant by her father, Christopher Winter, and, with his active encouragement, married Hewitt. (There is no evidence as to whether Winter forced his daughter to have sex with him, although there is always some element of coercion when a father takes sexual advantage of his daughter's love—or fear—of him.) When Martha Hewitt was in labor, she was interrogated by a midwife who demanded to know the name of the father of her child, a method often used to extract confessions from unwed mothers. Martha still refused to name the child's father. Soon after the child was born, Thomas Hewitt instituted divorce proceedings, and Martha Hewitt was punished with a public whipping. Her father was suspected because he did not interrogate his future son-in-law when he learned his daughter was pregnant, nor did he "reprove or bear witness against her [his daughter's] wickedness, as would have become a father that was innosent."[14] There is not enough information in the Hewitt divorce case to know why Martha Hewitt chose to remain silent when interrogated or why her husband sued for divorce. The motives of Puritan judges were clear, however; they punished a woman sinner and freed her husband from marriage to her; Christopher Winter fled and thus escaped punishment.

Incest was viewed as a crime as well as a ground for divorce. The Bible called for capital punishment of those who committed incest, but English law at that time did not. The colony of New Haven followed the Bible and made incest a capital offense; the colony of Massachusetts Bay copied English law. In all the New England colonies, the definition of incest was more extensive than current views; besides a father's sexual relations with his daughter, it included consensual sex or even marriages between near relatives. A man who married his brother's widow, for example, was tried in church court for incest. In any case, one survey of seventeenth-century New England court records found only six cases of incest in the criminal courts in addition to the church court case mentioned above.[15]

The Puritans sided with the weak, the dependent, and the helpless only if they were seen as blameless; they punished the sinful, stubborn, and disobedient. Although there were humanitarian and biblical dimensions to the Puritan legal code, the major purpose of their laws was to reinforce hierarchical relationships, either in the family or in society. As people who respected authority, the Puritans accepted and even justified the use of "legitimate" physical force by parents, masters, and husbands. Thus a clause in the *Body of Liberties* punishing wife beating stated that if a husband had "any just cause of correction complaint shall be made to Authoritie assembled in some Court, from which onely she [a wife] shall receive it." Occasionally, the state allowed a husband to punish an abusive wife or a disobedient child at home (presumably with a whipping).[16] The courts never granted permission for a child to punish a parent, or a wife a husband. The obvious reason for this difference is that the husband and father was the highest ranking figure in the household. Only he could act on the basis of authority delegated by the state.

Many of the Puritan laws designed to uphold proper authority invoked capital punishment. The *Body of Liberties*, for example, punished by death a child over the age of sixteen who cursed or struck a father or mother. Several colonies had other laws for the punishment of "rebellious sons." In the Massachusetts Bay and New Haven colonies, a stubborn and rebellious son could be put to death. In Connecticut and Rhode Island, the rebellious son faced confinement to the house of correction.[17] Rebellious daughters, sons under sixteen, and servants were subject to other laws that provided for whipping or a short term in the house of correction.

The Puritans were following the Bible in punishing crimes such as rebellion in sons, witchcraft, and blasphemy with death.[18] In fact, each capital crime listed in the *Body of Liberties* was followed by a biblical annotation, a kind of footnote to the word of God. Not every biblical injunction was taken literally, however. For example, the Bible called upon the elders of a town to stone to death a stubborn or rebellious son. The Puritans did not call for stoning and limited the death penalty to a son over sixteen years of age. In addition, although the Book of Exodus held that "he that curseth his father or mother shall surely be put to death," Puritan law exempted children who had been provoked by extreme and cruel correction to the point of facing permanent injury or death, and those whose Christian education had been neglected and so could not be expected to know better.

The Puritan law punishing a child who cursed his or her parents was intended mostly as a moral example. Only one offender was ever prosecuted under it. A Suffolk County Court in 1654 pronounced an adult son guilty of cursing his father (calling him a drunken sot and a liar), kicking his sister in the belly, and threatening to burn down his father's house. Still, the court was unwilling to sentence him to death. Instead, it ordered him to be whipped and to stand in the pillory for about an hour with a sign pinned on him that read: "This is for reviling and unnatural reproaching for his naturall father and most desperate Cursing of himself."[19] (Pinning such signs upon an offender was a not uncommon form of punishment.)

No stubborn or rebellious son was ever hanged at the gallows in an American colony, and only one rebellious son was ever tried under the Puritan law. Joseph Porter, a thirty-year-old bachelor living with his parents in Salem, was brought before the Essex County Quarterly Court in 1655. He had called his father a "liar and simple Ape, shittabed" and had told his mother she was a "Rambeggur, Gamar Shithouse, Gamar Pisshouse." He had also unsuccessfully attempted to burn down his father's house and kill his father's cattle. Having beaten his father's servants, even threatening the life of one of them, Porter then attempted to stab one of his brothers. In order to convict Porter, the court required the sworn testimony of two witnesses. When Porter's mother refused to testify against her son and instead pleaded for leniency, he could not be hanged. Instead, he was sentenced to stand upon a ladder at the gallows with a rope around his neck for an hour, a severe whipping, and a jail term. Porter appears to have escaped before enduring any of these punishments.[20] Massachusetts Bay Colony repealed its rebellious son law in 1681, although the state of Massachusetts continued to have on its books—and to enforce—a "stubborn child law" up through 1973.[21]

While the Puritans passed laws to hang rebellious sons and blasphemers of their parents, many other types of family violence received only mild punishment. For most assaults between family members, the most common sentence was a fine, a whipping, or both; then the wrongdoer was quickly restored to his or her family. The disgrace of punishment and the "holy watching" by neighbors, magistrates believed, would deter further violence.

Repeat offenders were sometimes asked to post a bond of surety. If they failed to do so, they were sent to jail. If they did post a bond and committed another act of violence, the bond was forfeited.

In all their laws and punishments, the Puritans demonstrated their belief in the state's responsibility to enforce morality and instill respect for legitimate authority. Thus, Puritan laws against family violence conformed to their views about the importance of proper, but not excessive, authority in all relationships, including those in the family. Nonetheless, many Puritan laws against family violence were rarely enforced. Capital punishment was not invoked against rebellious sons or parental blasphemers because the punishment was considered too severe to fit the crime. However, since the punishments for wife beating, child abuse, and assault of servants were relatively mild, one might have expected to find a number of such cases. But the court records of Plymouth Colony from 1633 to 1802 contradict that supposition. In more than a hundred and fifty years there were only twenty-three cases of wife beating, husband beating, assault between masters or servants, or incest in the Plymouth courts.

Does this evidence suggest that family violence rarely occurred in Plymouth, or that it was under-reported? The family murder rate in seventeenth-century Plymouth, as we have already noted, was exceedingly low, and in the twenty-three complaints of abuse in the Plymouth courts, not one concerned child abuse. If there were occasional cases of assault between spouses, or servants and masters, one might have expected at least a few reports of parental assault on children.

The absence of complaints about child abuse extended beyond the boundaries of colonial Plymouth. Despite the *Body of Liberties* provision permitting children to complain of unnatural severity, none ever did so. Only one natural father was brought before any New England colonial court on charges of abusing his child. Michael Emerson of Haverhill, Massachusetts, was tried for "cruel and excessive beating of his daughter with a flail swingle and for kicking her." (A flail swingle was a large wooden handle attached to a free-swinging stick, which was used in threshing grain.) Emerson's daughter was eleven at the time, and she later said of herself, "I was always of an Haughty and Stubborn spirit."[22] Six months later the court abated Michael Emerson's fine and released him on a bond of good behavior. Emerson was found guilty of "excessive beating." Was nonexcessive beating then acceptable? Elizabeth Emerson, the abused daughter, grew up into a rebellious teenager who kept "bad company." She eventually gave birth to a child out of wedlock and murdered it.

It should be noted that stepfathers were sometimes accused of cruel treatment of a child, but probably because the natural father's kin sought custody of the child. Still, contemporary studies find that physical and sexual abuse is more common among stepfathers than among natural fathers. Thus these complaints may have reflected both the family's desire to gain custody of a child as well as the stress and conflict inherent in families with stepchildren.

In "Child Abuse in Context: An Historian's Perspective," John Demos used the dearth of complaints of parental assault on their children to argue that child abuse rarely occurred among the Puritans.[23] Demos readily acknowledged that corporal punishment was accepted and widely practiced, but insisted that the Puritans had a genuine concern for the well-being of children that confined parentally administered beatings within carefully circumscribed limits. Demos maintained that deliberately causing bruises, marks, or injuries to the child fell outside the bounds of acceptable punishment. But it is hard to prove this simply from the absence of criminal prosecutions for child abuse.

The few cases there were suggest that the Puritan definition of child abuse would be different from our own. Acceptable punishment appears to have included most beatings and bruising that fell short of maiming or *permanently* injuring the child. The numerous complaints by servants assaulted by their masters offer some insight into Puritan attitudes toward child abuse. Because Puritan mothers and fathers were expected to treat a servant as they would a son or daughter, it seems likely that the same kind of punishment meted out to servants was also inflicted on children. One mistress excused the whipping her husband had given a servant by explaining that "it broke no bones and brought no blood, there were no permanent bruises or contusions." A master and mistress proved in court that the beating they had administered "hath never hurt her body nor limes [limbs]." Cotton Mather argued that the punishment of a disobedient servant should be so "moderate with Humanity, that he may not be thereby *Killed* or *Maimed*." Masters were not permitted to hang their servants by their heels, a punishment that still persists in India today. When Philip Fowler did so, the Essex County court held that he was "justified . . . in giving meet correction to his servant, which the body deserved," yet it did not approve of "hanging him up by the heels as butchers do beasts for the slaughter," and cautioned Fowler against using this form of punishment."[24] Although a servant, the servant's relatives, and neighbors might complain against a cruel master, hardly anyone did more than issue threats and warnings to a brutal father or mother.

The hesitancy to charge a natural father or mother with child assault or to remove abused children from their parents can be attributed to the Puritans' reverence for the two-parent, father-dominated household and the belief in the bond between a child and his or her natural parents. The courts removed or "put out" a few children to live with relatives or neighbors because of parental neglect of the child's Christian education or parental criminality, but not on grounds of abuse.

Wife beating was the single most common case of family violence in the Plymouth courts. Between 1663 and 1682, there were four complaints of wife assault, but thereafter the number of accusations dwindled to only one complaint per decade from 1683 to 1702. In the first half of the eighteenth century, virtually no complaints of wife assault came before Plymouth magistrates, and in the second half of the century, there were at most two complaints per decade. By 1690 accusations of other types of family violence—husband beating, violence between servants and masters, a child beating a parent, or incest—disappeared from the Plymouth courts.[25]

Colonial courts were under pressure to bring their practice of law enforcement in line with English jurisprudence. In the 1680s, the crown, no longer preoccupied with domestic and international warfare, sought to exert more control over the political affairs of the king's American subjects. Colonial governors and royal commissioners established a court of appeal to review sentences handed down in the courts of Massachusetts Bay. Several New England colonies passed infanticide laws to conform to English law.

In addition to these imperial influences on colonial law, domestic social changes were also threatening religious orthodoxy. The Puritan ideal of a community of saints engaged in "holy watching" began to dissolve by the 1670s. Waves of immigration from England, Scotland, and Ireland, and an increase in non-churchgoers diminished some of the doctrinal uniformity of Puritan settlements. Further, the younger generation of Puritans underwent a spiritual crisis of sorts. Many of them failed to experience a religious conversion, which had been the criterion for full church membership. As the settlement became more heterogeneous, the public began to doubt the state's responsibility to enforce morality. One Puritan minister, wondering about the merits of mutual surveillance, argued that wise men would "very hardly be drawn to make or intermeddle in Fray, lest they get a broken head for their pains."[26]

Community life grounded in a common faith had become less important than maintaining good fences between neighbors. The Massachusetts legislature in 1677 made one last attempt to impose communalism when it revived the ancient post of tithingman. The tithingman was to visit ten families in a neighborhood and report stubborn and disorderly children and servants, prostitutes, drunkards, and sabbath breakers to a magistrate for punishment. The job proved so unpopular, however, that it was impossible to find anyone to fill it.[27]

The growing reluctance of Puritans to become involved in fights between husbands and wives, unless the quarrel threatened to disrupt the entire neighborhood, is evident in the lack of assistance rendered to Elizabeth Ela by her Haverhill neighbors in 1681. Elizabeth Ela was a widow who had married a quarrelsome, and probably heavy-drinking, farmer and former tanner, Daniel Ela. Ela fumed whenever his wife questioned his authority. In the midst of a snowstorm, Elizabeth Ela fled her home one night, and failing to find the county magistrate, pounded on William White's door. She told White that her husband had beaten her on the head and threatened to stab her to death. White refused to let her into his house. Elizabeth Ela screamed at White, "Sorry . . . if you will not entertaine mee and lett me abide in your house I will lie in the street in the snow & if I perish, my blood be upon your head."[28] White then permitted Elizabeth Ela to enter and sought out the local magistrate, who urged him and his neighbor, Andrew Greely, to take Ela home. White and Greely left Elizabeth Ela in the yard of her house (again in the snowstorm) while they went inside to talk with her husband. Daniel Ela lashed out at them as "meddling knaves" who should go home and order their own wives around and threatened to get even with them. After the two men left, Daniel Ela again threatened to kill his wife. Greely ran into Elizabeth Ela as she was fleeing in fear and escorted her to another neighbor's home, where she probably spent the night.

Two months later Elizabeth Ela appeared in court and dropped her complaint against her husband. Her "unadvised speeches," she said, had led to their quarrel. She denied that her husband had thrown her out of the house that night; she claimed in court she had left of her own will in order to avoid further conflict. Ela's neighbors pressed charges against him, and he was fined forty shillings. Presumably he paid the fine and he and Elizabeth Ela went home together. In subsequent years, the Elas did not again appear in court, nor were they brought before a church court.

The circumstances that wintry night in 1681 suggest that Puritan neighbors acted reluctantly and suspected women who complained of abuse almost as much as they disapproved of men who committed it. After all, in the middle of a snowstorm, William White refused to allow a woman neighbor whom he had probably known for years, who claimed that her husband had tried to kill her, to enter his house. Perhaps it showed concern that he and one of his neighbors visited Daniel Ela. Even so, why did they force Elizabeth Ela to accompany them rather than permitting her to remain at White's home?

We can only surmise why Elizabeth Ela's neighbors were so reluctant to help her. They do not appear to have agreed with Daniel Ela's blustery assertion that he was "Lord paramount in his own house" since they considered him someone who spoke in a manner "unbeseeming a man." They may have been afraid of him. Yet William White was unwilling to allow Elizabeth Ela into his home, even before Daniel Ela threatened him. Townswomen also observed Daniel Ela attacking his wife with a cudgel. They were probably afraid to interfere, but they do not appear to have offered Elizabeth Ela assistance even after Daniel Ela retreated. Most residents of the small settlement of Haverhill wanted to avoid meddling in the family life of their more troublesome neighbors. In short, there were severe limits to the extent of Puritan communal vigilance.

In the last two decades of the seventeenth century, the tapestry of Christian morality that had woven together the interest of family, the state, and the church began to unravel, one thread at a time. The church courts no longer took an active role in punishing morals offenses. Indeed, by the end of the eighteenth century many churches had abolished their courts. Another sign of the declining enforcement of morals laws was that single individuals were permitted to live alone, rather than being forced to reside with a family. Similarly, the conviction rate for attempted rape fell in Massachusetts from 93 percent between 1690 and 1779 to 62 percent between 1780 and 1799.[29] (Rape was not a capital crime, but a felony generally punishable by a whipping and a jail term.) Moral laxity was also discernible in a small item of gossip entered in a clergyman's diary. He noted that several ministers were upset to learn that one of their own was repeatedly beating his wife. They discussed the matter several times but did not bring a legal complaint against the man or try him before a church court.[30] Would Cotton Mather have allowed such wickedness to go unexposed? Public criticism of corporal punishment was beginning to have some effect. Boxing the ears was eliminated as a punishment at Harvard in the 1750s; the provision permitting it disappeared from the college's laws by 1767. The pillory was removed from the Boston Common in 1803, and the whipping post and stocks were taken down a decade later.[31]

The most telling evidence of the decreased enforcement of Puritan morality can be found in the changing prosecution rate of infanticide. Even before the passage of colonial laws against infanticide in the 1680s, infanticide was prosecuted as murder, although the accused was actually tried for concealing the body of a dead infant. If a body was found, the presumption was that a mother had killed her infant, unless a midwife or another witness testified otherwise. The Puritans assumed that a mother who concealed her pregnancy and her child's birth was immoral, and that a sinful woman was capable of committing murder. Concealing a sin among the Puritans—whether the sin was fornication or murder—showed bad character and lack of proper contrition for wrongdoing. In the known dispositions of infanticide cases in the New England colonies, fourteen mothers were hanged, ten were acquitted, three were whipped, and one was flogged and sent to prison. Most of those brought to court were single mothers, often Irish, Indian, or black, who took the lives of their infants soon after birth. A few married women were also tried for having burned or severely bruised their infants and thus caused their deaths.[32]

Although the number of infanticide cases increased threefold in colonial Massachusetts from 1630 to 1780, the rate of prosecution was cut in half. Even in prosecuted cases, the rate of acquittals in infanticide trials grew and outstripped the acquittal rate in other murder trials.[33] Jurors increasingly accepted pleas of extenuating circumstances from an accused mother. If an accused mother was able to show that she made preparations for the birth of the child or that she showed "maternal love" towards her infant, a jury was likely to consider her child's death an accident. In 1784, the state legislature of Massachusetts revised the infanticide law. Concealment of the death of a bastard child was made punishable by a fine of not more than one hundred dollars or imprisonment of not more than one year. Although it was possible to bring charges of murder instead of concealment of death, most prosecutors chose not to.

Another indication of changing morality was the decrease in prosecutions of fornicators. The Puritans had punished men and women who engaged in "fornication before marriage." They brought charges against not only mothers of illegitimate children but also husbands and wives who had produced a child less than nine months after marriage. In Middlesex County, Massachusetts, by 1740 men were no longer prosecuted for the crime of fornication, although they could still be sued for support of a bastard child. Taking to court a married woman who gave birth early also declined.[34] About the same time, Benjamin Franklin's satiric essay about a Miss Polly Baker appeared. The heroine of his story was an unwed mother hauled before a judge for bearing a fifth bastard child. Franklin, a man of cosmopolitan sexual habits himself, greatly enjoyed poking fun at Puritan morality and making his case for a criminal code that distinguished sin from crime.[35]

Franklin believed that sex between unmarried people and adultery were not the concern of the state. Commercial expansion and the influx of diverse peoples into a homogeneous community contributed to the development of secular attitudes. As the prosecution for morals crimes declined, the prosecutions for crimes of violence outside the family and crimes of property rose.[36] The state sought to protect the citizenry from public violence—robberies and mob disorders—rather than physical and sexual assault that occurred in the privacy of the home. Private morals crimes receded into the background, and morals crimes affecting the public welfare, such as drunkenness, vagrancy, and prostitution, rose in importance.

In *Commentaries on the Laws of England*, first published in the late 1760s, William Blackstone stated that a crime was an act that produced mischief in civil society, whereas private vices lay outside the legitimate domain of law. Even the vice of drunkenness, he argued, if committed in the privacy of one's home, fell beyond the reach of the law, but the public drunkard set an evil example for others and deserved to be prosecuted. Disharmony in the home was no longer perceived as a threat to the stability of the community. The family became a more private institution, clearly separate from public life. The belief that the state was responsible for the enforcement of morality stimulated the punishment of family violence; doubts about the state's imperative to intervene in the family or private matters contributed to the waning of interest in family violence. The Puritans defined violence both as a sin and a crime. But enforcement meant intervening in the family, and there lay the crux of the problem. The Puritans intervened in the family only to restore and preserve the home. And they intervened reluctantly, realizing how shameful and humiliating it was to reveal family troubles in public.

The vigilance of neighbors and church courts against wife beating did not entirely disappear, however. In Boston in 1707, seven or eight white men and a black youth tore the clothes off a neighbor and flogged him for having beaten his wife. In the 1750s the Regulators of Elizabethtown, New Jersey, painting their faces and dressing up as women, whipped reputed wife beaters. Among religious Presbyterians or black Baptists in nineteenth-century America, an occasional husband who assaulted his wife was brought to trial. But these isolated incidents of community regulation were remnants of a much more extensive form of social policing that ended with the demise of the Puritan experiment.[37]

What, then, was the significance of Puritan laws against family violence, if they were rarely enforced? Laws not only prescribe punishment for crimes; they also function as a guide to the community's moral principles. The purpose of the Puritan laws against family violence was less to punish abusers than to define the boundary between the saint and the sinner, demonstrate to each other and to God a vigilance against sin, and shore up proper authority in the household and in society. As a religious community gave way to a more pluralistic one, the state gradually relinquished its commitment to enforcing morality. Thus the campaign to eradicate wicked behavior yielded to tolerance and indifference.

2

Parental Tyranny

THE BELIEFS ABOUT PHYSICAL PUNISHMENT of children—its necessity, methods, and effectiveness—can be traced by a perusal of childrearing literature. Such published advice to parents on how to raise children dates from as early as the 1500s. Only one out of the four advice pamphlets in sixteenth-century France and England did not approve wholeheartedly of corporal punishment; in the next century, only two out of seven counseled moderation in physical discipline. By the eighteenth century, all four major childrearing books printed in England advocated limiting the use of corporal punishment. Childrearing manuals published during the first half of the nineteenth century in the United States and England showed six supporters and three opponents of the physical chastisement of children. By the last half of the nineteenth century, however, six out of the seven English or American books and pamphlets of parental advice favored only limited use of corporal punishment.[1] And, during this period, the first childrearing book to oppose corporal punishment under any circumstances appeared. The author was an English physician, Pye Henry Chavasse. The American edition of his *Advice to a Mother on the Management of Her Children* was published in 1862. Using a question-and-answer format, Chavasse gave his opinion that mothers, rather than fathers, would be able to govern children without hitting them. This gradually shifting stance toward childrearing practices constituted a kind of private reform movement against family violence.

Probably the single most influential childrearing advisor was the Scottish philosopher John Locke. In 1693 Locke published a treatise entitled "Some Thoughts Concerning the Education of Children." In it he gave corporal punishment a secure but nonetheless circumscribed place. He advocated an entire system of childrearing rules based on the concept of reward and punishment. Locke differed from previous writers of advice to parents in the detailed attention he devoted to corporal punishment and the circumstances that justified its use. He believed that children should be treated as "rational creatures" and rewarded with esteem and praise; parents were to withhold approval until the child obeyed completely. Caress and commend children when they do well, he urged, but show a cold and neglectful countenance when they disobey. In his view of the child as a rational creature, Locke had moved one step away from the Calvinist belief in the innate sinfulness of the infant—the child as bearer of Adam's sin. He did not endorse the idea that the child was an innocent being, however. Children, in his view, were guilty of disobedience and stubbornness unless proven otherwise.

Corporal punishment, Locke believed, was needed most to discipline young children, who were incapable of being governed by reason; the parent could then put aside the rod when the child matured. Whipping was to be used "only on great occasions, and in cases of extremity." Even with the older child, a whipping might be necessary if other punishments failed: "*stubbornness*, and *obstant* [sic] *disobedience*, must be master'd with force and blows, for there is no other remedy."[2] Unlike later writers of childrearing advice, Locke was not distressed that a whipping caused the child pain. Instead, he worried that the parent who wielded the whip had secured only superficial obedience; once the threat of punishment receded, he feared that the child would become just as obstinate as ever.

Samuel Richardson's *Pamela*, about a sexually exploited servant girl who marries well and rears her children according to the principles of reason, popularized Locke's ideas.[3] Locke's emphasis on a deliberate use of rational authority seemed to harmonize with the sense of moderation and balance Enlightenment philosophers called for. Although Locke wanted to consolidate rather than challenge parental dominance, he gained adherents among colonial rebels who opposed tyranny in the home or the state, and his ideas on childrearing greatly influenced American attitudes during the Revolutionary period. Jay Fliegelman, in *Prodigals and Pilgrims*, has argued that the American Revolution was part of a larger revolution against established patterns of authority. American patriots often lapsed into familial metaphors in criticizing British imperial rule; they thought of themselves as sons or daughters in rebelling against a brutal and tyrannical parent. John Adams wrote, "But admitting we are children, have not children a right to complain when their parents are attempting to break their limbs, to administer poison, or to sell them to their enemies for slaves."[4] The Americans described themselves as sometimes seeking independence from the mother country, England, other times from their brutal father, the king. Discontented colonists likened themselves to neglected, or sometimes disobedient children who were no longer obligated to love or revere a brutal parent, and so had retreated to the wilderness of a new world to found a more perfect society.

The colonists also referred to ancient history—in particular, the downfall of ancient Rome—to prove that political authoritarianism caused the demise of civilization. The rule of tyrants such as Nero, they argued, brought the Roman republic to its ruin. In their own time, George III and his ministers were seen as conspiring to establish "an absolute Tyranny over" the colonies; only the overthrow of a despotic king could thwart their aims.

The colonists not only applied a familial analogy to their struggle against the British Empire; they also analyzed domestic relations in political terms. Prominent women in the colonies, for example, selected as their target tyrannical marriages. If a husband was similar to a king, then a wife had the right to rise up against him. Just after the Revolution broke out, Abigail Adams wrote to her husband to "remember the ladies" in the code of laws the Continental Congress was about to draft. She told him "not [to] put such unlimited power in the hands of the Husbands. Remember all Men would be tyrants if they could." Because men were by nature tyrannical, she cautioned, laws were needed "to put it out of the power of the vicious and lawless to use us with cruelty and indignity."[5] The term "cruelty" referred to a variety of ill-uses, not necessarily physical in nature. One has no way of knowing whether Abigail Adams had in mind physical or sexual abuse of wives, the squandering of a wife's fortune, or other grievances. Her ideas, playfully dismissed by her husband, never appeared in national legislation, but they reverberated in *Lady's Magazine, American Museum,* and other Revolutionary era literary magazines that upheld a new ideal of romantic love, companionate marriage, mutual understanding between spouses, and power for mothers in childrearing.

The political concepts of self-government and independence were reflected in the ideals regarding childrearing as well as marriage. If the new nation was to prosper, values of thrift, industry, and morality had to be taught to the generation that was too young to have fought the Revolution; habits of responsibility and patriotism needed to be encouraged. Since mothers cared for the young, they were given the task of educating sons in Christian morality and civic-mindedness. In the republic, a child was seen as a figure to be molded into a good citizen and as possessing the right to develop his or her capacity for reason and independence. By raising sons who obeyed not out of fear or duty, but out of reason, an American mother made an important patriotic contribution.[6] However, although mothers educated their sons for citizenship, fathers still provided the necessary discipline. Mothers were believed to be too kindhearted and inconsistent in their disciplinary methods to be in charge of such an important matter.

Family violence never appeared among the instances of tyranny singled out in the literary journals published soon after the republic was founded. Writers deplored arranged marriages, neglect of a child's education, irrational preference of parents for the eldest sons, or unjust denial of a child's inheritance. But the family crisis closest to the heart of the Revolutionary generation was the conflict between parents and children.

By the late 1790s a conservative reaction in politics set in. Congress passed the Sedition Act in 1798 that made writing, printing, or pronouncing defamatory statements against the government a punishable offense. As the U.S. government sought to censor its critics, literary journals became less willing to publish articles denouncing parental excesses. The American government had not reverted to despotism, but the purity of political motivation was questioned. As the sole remaining repository of republican virtue, the family had to cut itself off from the corrupt public world. Only in the privacy of the home could patriotic values be realized.[7]

The one group that seems to have maintained most closely the republican ideas on childrearing was the Society of Friends, commonly called Quakers, among whom Locke appears to have enjoyed his greatest influence. Locke's views of childrearing did not reach the educated American public until the American Revolution, although they influenced the Quakers as early as 1700. William Penn, the founder of the Quaker colony named after him, had been an intimate acquaintance of Locke, and Penn's disciplinary philosophy resembled his friend's. Penn recommended shaming as an appropriate punishment and opposed disciplining the child in anger. He also believed that parents should make disobedient offspring feel guilty, by showing "a grieved" countenance when they misbehaved.

Locke's ideas found a receptive audience among the Quakers because social, economic, and political changes in the eighteenth century had transformed their attitudes toward children. For one thing, a steep decline in fertility occurred among Quaker women in the decades from 1780 to 1800.[8] The most likely explanation for this decline is the practice of some form of birth control, spurred in part by the women's desire for smaller families. Forming a child's character, Quaker women believed, required maternal attention; having fewer children permitted a mother to spend more time with each child. The new view was evident in the London edition of the Friends' catechism, published in 1807. It no longer contained biblical injunctions; the interrogator of a child, instead of being a third party or a stern master, became a soft-voiced mother, strolling in a field of wildflowers with her two small children.[9]

A second force influencing Quaker family size and thus attitudes toward children was land scarcity. As the population increased, the size of farm plots available for children to inherit diminished. Limiting family size became a means of enabling Friends to establish their adult children nearby. Another development that influenced Quaker attitudes toward the family was that many Friends of Pennsylvania became less involved in political affairs. During the French and Indian War, Quakers in Pennsylvania were torn between their allegiance to England and their feelings of sympathy for the Indians. Those who adhered to neutrality and pacifism turned their backs on public life and took as their task the strengthening of church and family life.

The Quakers' increased time for children was reflected in their childrearing practices. Their methods were calculated, consistent, and effective—designed for the improvement of the child rather than for the convenience of the adult. Mothers and fathers were urged to remain calm in administering discipline so as not to arouse the child's anger. Parents taught their children to inhibit aggressive sexual impulses and indeed practiced self-control themselves. Strict Friends did not drink, smoke, or gamble, and some even refused to play the piano. It was felt that making a child feel guilty for wrongdoing was the most effective form of punishment, and to stir pangs of conscience, parents sometimes delayed punishment for hours or even days. The Quaker son or daughter chastised according to these methods was believed capable of self-control rather than mere outward obedience.[10]

Although the Friends were not the first or the only parents to employ the Lockean technique of withdrawal of love to punish children, they appeared to have used it more frequently and with better effect precisely because the child's relationship with the mother was a warm, affectionate one. New methods of discipline required intense and constant maternal surveillance of children. Quaker mothers were noted for watching their youngsters and keeping them "out of the way of corrupting company." Quaker epistles mentioned the parent's "constant watchful eye." In autobiographies of Quaker children fathers "looked reproachfully" and mothers expressed disapproval of errant behavior with "a mean look." One Quaker son recalled that his mother conquered his stubborn nature not by whipping or scolding him "but by looking at me in *her way*. I could stand anything but *that*."[11]

In their schools as well as their homes, Quakers managed to discipline without much resort to the rod. In the late seventeenth century, teachers at the William Penn School in Philadelphia were told that if they governed children through love rather than fear, the rod could be put aside. Graduates of a Quaker school in the early eighteenth century wrote to praise their master for not hitting them, even though they thought that he should have.[12]

Not all Quakers were such paragons of self-control. Some schoolmasters in the colonies whipped their pupils badly enough to draw blood. A Quaker mother living in Rhode Island during Revolutionary times used a horsewhip on each of her fourteen children, including her adult sons. In the middle of the nineteenth century, a Quaker mother in Maryland beat her five-month-old infant son black-and-blue because he would not stop crying. She later achieved fame for her book of childrearing advice! Other nineteenth-century Quaker parents used the rod but not the whip. Ann Branson of Belmont County, Ohio, recalled that her mother, who was an elder of the Society of Friends, "seldom resorted to the rod, yet she did not wholly discard it." The Thomases of Baltimore put away the slipper or rod they used on their first-born in disciplining their other children.[13]

These Quaker parents and teachers broke or at least stretched the unwritten code governing discipline of children. A few parents protested when teachers whipped their children but others encouraged instructors to do so. Even among Quakers, then, there were significant differences in attitudes toward corporal punishment. The distinctive feature of the Quakers was not uniform opposition to corporal punishment, but the development of general principles of childrearing. Quakers viewed a child's misbehavior as an infraction of a set of well-defined rules. They connected the adoption of rather time-consuming practices of discipline with beneficial changes in the personality of the child.

In the first stage of childrearing reform, Locke's ideas were reflected in a concern for the proper exercise of authority by enlightened parents, under the guidance of the father. In the second stage, beginning in educated middle-class America in the 1830s, there were two major trends. The mother, rather than the father, was seen as the most powerful agent in developing a child's character (an idea that had gained momentum since the Revolution), and less emphasis was placed on physical punishment, while correspondingly more importance was given to psychological methods of discipline. Various types of childrearing literature advocated these changes. Most pamphlets on childrearing were written by male ministers and physicians—the first by an American mother was published in Boston in 1811. "Mother's magazines" dispensing childrearing advice first appeared in the 1830s and their popularity and circulation grew rapidly. Finally, children's books and stories depicted model behavior in parents and children and showed the consequences of children's bad behavior.[14]

A survey of American magazines from 1741 to 1825 noted that most articles advocated "mutual cooperation" between husband and wife in childrearing. Between 1825 and 1850, however, an increasing number not only favored putting mothers in charge of childrearing, but asserted that they already were.[15] Women, in the opinion of many writers of childrearing literature, were uniquely suited to discipline because they possessed "a mother's heart." Mothers were believed capable of expressing their love naturally, but also of withholding it when necessary. Fathers were occasionally advised to punish the reprobate child, but the dominant authority became the mother. The origins of these changes could be traced to the new domestic circumstances of the urban middle class. Commercial life became more risky. Men, who carried the heavy burden of providing for the family, wanted the home to serve as a refuge from cut-throat competition. Thus the "empire of the mother" served not only as a response to the political vagaries of the post-Revolutionary period, but to economic instability as well.[16]

As "angels of the house," mothers modified Locke's techniques and ideas to accommodate "nurture," or taking advantage of a child's affection for its mother. This was a decided shift from Locke's selective reinforcement methods. Louisa Hare, an English writer widely read in early nineteenth-century America, cautioned that "if we desire to perform our duties to children, it is not their outward conduct, but to the heart, that we must direct our attention."[17] Manipulating the child's feeling of affection for the mother was the surest way to achieve the desired goal of obedience and self-control.[18] Antebellum writers made parental love contingent on a child's good behavior. In T. S. Arthur's *The Iron Rule, or, Tyranny in the Household*, published in 1853, a mother tells her son, "You must be an obedient, good little boy, and then your father will love you." Arthur repeated the same advice in *The Mother's Rule, or, the Right Way and the Wrong Way*, published three years later. In this novel, Arthur referred to a being whose withdrawal of love was even more devastating to the child than that of the parent. A father, schooled in the maternal principles of domestic government, tells his daughter, who has just deliberately bloodied her brother's head, "How sorry He must be that any little girl can have so bad a heart as you have. God never can love the bad girl in this world or the next."[19]

It was believed that one of the greatest dangers of corporal punishment was that it "hardened the heart" of the child, who would no longer be able to "reverence or love the parent."[20] The child so treated would become bitter, angry, and resentful. Techniques of withdrawing love were similar to Locke's in relying on selective reinforcement, but the goal was different. Whereas Locke sought to develop the child's capacity for reason, antebellum advisors wanted to create in the child a conscience. Their methods were designed to produce children who felt responsible for their actions, confessed their misdeeds to parents, becoming restrained and orderly rather than spontaneous and impulsive. The dictum of Theodore Dwight, author of a childrearing book addressed to fathers, was that "the child must be made his own disciplinarian."[21] One historian has described maternal methods of discipline as "a set of strategies for the reproduction of a middle-class personality."[22] The kind of adult traits the childrearing advisors hoped to inculcate were the bourgeois virtues of thrift, temperance, industry, honesty, frugality, and self-control.

Children's books of the antebellum period also aided parents in the psychological reform of their offspring and counseled children against hitting each other. Henry Clarke Wright's *A Kiss for a Blow* (1842), for example, appealed "to the hearts of children" in advising them not to strike each other with fists and clubs or pelt each other with stones. Wright cautioned children not to strike back when they were hit and instead to "show a kind and loving spirit" toward an assailant. The protagonist in one of Wright's stories threw a stone at his brother, damaging the joint in his brother's leg, and the leg had to be amputated. Another of Wright's characters was a boy who lost his eye because of an accident caused by his brother.[23]

Antebellum childrearing writers believed that a mother's kindly manner, rather than an extensive set of Lockean rules, led to good behavior in a child. The more liberal ones favored using the mildest methods possible to achieve the desired result. Yet by our standards, these techniques could be quite harsh. Indeed, the phrase "gentle measures," which appeared often in childrearing literature, included not only spanking but also depriving a child of food or locking him or her in a closet, even for an entire day. Corporal punishment was still an alternative, of course. Six out of nine childrearing books published in the early nineteenth century advocated it (the three opposed were written by women). Some Presbyterian ministers advised parents to pick up "old hickory" and perform their painful duty.

Most childrearing writers of the antebellum period accepted Locke's argument that corporal punishment should be resorted to only if other means had been exhausted. Lydia Maria Child, probably the most permissive childrearing advisor of this period, favored corporal punishment "when the same wrong thing has been done over and over again, and when gentler punishments have failed. A few smart slaps do good when nothing else will; but particular care should be taken not to correct in anger."[24] (She also sometimes referred to a mother administering a whipping, although she made clear that it should not be done frequently.)

The type of corporal punishment most favored by these writers was spanking rather than whipping. The word "spanking" appears to have been used as early as the 1780s, although it came into common use in the 1830s. Spanking was defined as a legitimate discipline that involved hitting the child's bare or clothed buttocks or palms with an open hand. It referred to planned, deliberate actions by a steadfast but emotionally controlled parent. In the nineteenth century, spanking could include light strokes with an instrument, such as the "maternal slipper" or hairbrush. Spanking was distinguished from whipping, which involved hitting a child with a branch of a tree or a whip. The child about to be whipped was usually standing up, perhaps with one or both of the child's hands tied so as not to protest. Thus the parent could deliver telling blows without resistance from the child.

Despite these distinctions, many Americans confused spanking and whipping; they were often equally as severe. One woman recalled a good "spanking" from her childhood that consisted of being hit with a buggy whip; a boy hit on the hand with a ruler referred to the "spanking" he received.[25] Mothers were also permitted to whip disobedient sons. Still, it was assumed that a mother would use a switch—a small twig cut from a tree—rather than a whip. A mother was also expected to intercede to protect her children against a father's excessively severe whippings.

Fictional mothers who governed according to the principles of the affectionate heart populated childrearing advice books and children's fiction throughout the nineteenth century. In the confines of comfortable American homes, real mothers tried strenuously to live up to the standards of childrearing advice.

One such mother was Lucy Buffum Lovell, born of a prominent and wealthy Rhode Island family, and living with her Baptist-minister husband in Amherst, Massachusetts. Much of Lucy Lovell's diary was devoted to the training of her first child, Caroline, who was born in 1837. Many of the passages in the diary concerned disciplining four-year-old Caroline. (A sickly child, Caroline died the following year.) As an educated mother interested in applying modern ideas of domestic government, Lucy Lovell devoured the childrearing advice of her day. In one passage from her diary she referred to "the famous story of Dr. Weyland's [sic] child"—a harsh struggle between a Baptist father and his son, in which the boy was kept isolated and deprived of food for thirty-six hours. She hoped to be able to exert her authority over her daughter without having to engage in such a long contest of wills.

Caroline Lovell was often stubborn, willful, and disobedient, however. One morning she refused to say good morning to a visitor, even when her mother requested several times that she do so. Caroline continued to resist; finally her mother led her into a bedroom and left her there. Lucy Lovell soon returned, but Caroline still would not obey. Mrs. Lovell then decided that she must "chastise" Caroline, which, according to her diary, she "did, but without any good effect; repeatedly." It appears that the chastisement referred to here was spanking, not a whipping. Mrs. Lovell began to waver, and her husband called to her from his study that she "must not yield." Mr. Lovell appeared in the bedroom and prayed with his daughter, who remained obstinate. He went outdoors to procure a stick for a whipping, but Caroline, now realizing her fate, decided to give in. Her mother led her downstairs. In tears Caroline said good morning to the visitor and soon thereafter appeared, according to her mother's diary, "unusually mild and lovely, a sweet submissive spirit seemed to influence all her conduct."[26]

It is remarkable how many Lovells one encounters in diaries and magazine articles: educated, highly religious parents who engaged in bitter struggle for power with a young child. Countless "sweet submissive smiles" overcame children who submitted eventually to insistent parents. A single dramatic incident aroused in the child deep fear of parental rejection. As a result, the child hoped to placate the parent through smiles and elaborate displays of affection. Modern psychologists characterize such behavior in children as "overly dependent"; antebellum parents valued such excessive compliance, which they interpreted as evidence of obedience and self-restraint.

Conscientious mothers such as Lucy Lovell tried isolation of the child and other punishments before resorting to a spanking. If threats failed, a father was called upon to deliver a whipping. Antebellum parents, who judged themselves "gentle" because they rarely used the rod, were experimenting with punishments that operated on the child's mind, rather than the body. Extreme withdrawal of love represented rejection of the child and could cause excessive anxiety. Nonetheless, these early experiments seemed to work quite well; parents who tried them were satisfied with the results they achieved. Considering themselves enlightened, "affectionate" parents did not much ponder the lasting negative effects of these kinds of punishments on the child's personality. One cannot unreservedly praise a mode of discipline that created insecurity in the child. Yet it seems too harsh to say that the educated middle-class mother substituted "emotional cruelty" for physical abuse of the child. One does not have to approve of these forms of discipline to notice how innovative they were. Social change never progresses in a straight line; in this instance, as in many others, new, milder measures would be necessary to undo some of the worst effects of these changes.

Lucy Buffum Lovell was putting into practice exactly the kind of mothering childrearing advisors favored. How many others like her were there? Indeed, what can be discovered about the actual, as opposed to the recommended, disciplinary measures used by parents in the early nineteenth century? Since parents often ignore childrearing advice, writers of such literature may have influenced each other more than they managed to modify parental behavior. Oblivious to expert opinion, many parents learn from observing the way friends and relatives handle children, and they remember—or react against— how they were raised. A few hours spent with a young child is enough to convince most adults that parents do not entirely control their offspring— crying babies, demanding young children, and youngsters who light matches or step out into the street without looking often compel parents to respond.[27] Even those mothers and fathers who wanted to institute milder methods of childrearing may still have found themselves unable to govern according to the advice offered in books and magazines. A Vermont schoolteacher, when questioned about her methods of discipline, summed up the all-too-common dilemma with her frank admission that "moral suasion's my belief but lickin's my practice."

In order to ascertain the extent of corporal punishment among American parents in the past, I conducted a comprehensive survey based on documentary sources. Hundreds of autobiographies, biographies, diaries, letters, and published interviews were scanned to assemble a collection of 110 reminiscences concerning children raised in the American colonies and the United States between 1650 and 1900. These accounts, where sometimes only a sentence or a paragraph mentioned punishment in passing, were mainly reflections in later life on childhood discipline; most came from the child, a few from parents. Very few diaries kept by parents alluded to how they punished their children. No diaries of children described the discipline they received, perhaps because punishment stands out only in retrospect. The absence of information in parent's or children's diaries does not prove that parents were unduly severe or extremely kind; it suggests instead that most parents did not give much thought to the punishment of their children.[28] The authors of autobiographies generally recalled one incident from childhood—usually, the most severe punishment they ever received—and perhaps commented on how they were treated in childhood. Because use of the rod was so accepted in colonial America, only the unusual, self-conscious mother or father considered the matter worthy of mention. After mother's magazines directed attention to the procedures of childhood discipline, physical punishment of children became a matter deserving observation and commentary; thus nineteenth-century accounts contained more references to childrearing practices than earlier ones.

Far more of these recollections came from children of the wealthy and the middle class than of the poor. The largest group were the sons and daughters of farmers, artisans, store owners, and traders, followed by the educated middle class—the children of librarians, writers, schoolteachers, and ministers. Only a few mothers earned wages, although many, as wives of farmers and small businessmen, participated in the family enterprise. Accounts of families from the South and West, as well as Catholics, Jews, and other ethnic minorities were under-represented, although by no means entirely absent. Because of these gaps in resources, it is much more difficult to reach conclusions about the childrearing methods of later European immigrants, blacks, Indians, or white Southerners. Thus the first-person accounts reflect only the typical childrearing practices of a specific group at a particular time. Further, the extent of the child's injuries was not a matter for note and cannot therefore be adequately researched; only five accounts out of 110 mentioned the bruises or marks the children suffered when their parents hit or whipped them.

For the century before 1750, there are written accounts describing the punishment of only six children in the American colonies. These were the sons and daughters, nephews and nieces of merchants, plantation owners, and clergymen. The stern Presbyterian father of Sarah Homes boxed her ears when she stayed out late at night. It is not known how often the Virginia planter William Byrd whipped his niece and nephew; he seems to have left most of their discipline to their tutor. "Better whip't than damn'ed," urged New England's most prominent Puritan minister, Cotton Mather. But his diary indicates that he did not follow his advice in punishing his children or grandchildren. When young Sammy Mather pummeled his sister, his father merely refused to give him a piece of candy. The diary of another devout New Englander, Judge Samuel Sewall, only twice referred to whipping his children.[29]

In the half century after 1750, physical punishment appears to have become more severe. Few boys and girls were raised according to the methods Locke advocated. Every single child in this group was hit at least once with an instrument, ranging from a hickory stick to a horsewhip. Fathers were the major disciplinarians, and mothers were no more reluctant than fathers to use the whip. The children from this period, which encompassed the American Revolution, were raised according to the principle of not sparing the rod; some boys ran away from their brutal fathers and uncles, and one daughter was raped and horsewhipped by her father. An unusual case was that of Arthur Tappan. His father, the major disciplinarian in the household, never whipped a child on the Sabbath. Tappan's mother punished him with whippings or cold water baths, but she did not pull his hair, scold, or box his ears—these latter punishments, she believed, belonged to a more barbaric age.[30] Nonetheless, the Tappans appear to have been exceptional among parents of the Revolutionary generation regarding the rules and prohibitions they employed.

It is possible to argue that the Revolutionary generation was harsher in its childrearing discipline than its predecessors, although the Enlightenment is usually thought to have produced a significant critique of parental tyranny that had been absent before then. The available sources dated between 1650 and 1750 were written by unusual, highly educated parents and probably are not representative. If more evidence was available for this period, it would likely demonstrate frequent use of the rod.

A statistical analysis of the childhood recollections leads to the conclusion that whipping gave way to spanking in the first half of the nineteenth century. Corporal punishment had not disappeared, but it became milder in form.[31] All the children in my sample born between 1750 and 1799 were hit with an object. Among children born between 1800 and 1849, about 80 percent were hit with an instrument at least once in their childhood; among children born between 1850 and 1899, the figure was 73 percent (statistics for both groups based on forty-six cases). Thus, a substantial decline in the prevalence of whipping occurred in the first half of the nineteenth century.

The twentieth century has been one of increasingly mild forms of parental discipline. Contemporary sociologists who have assembled a representative sample of childhood punishment from interviews with American families in the 1970s find that about 20 percent of American children have at some time in their childhood been hit by their parents with an instrument.[32] The changes of the antebellum period pale in comparison with this dramatic downturn in the frequency of whipping.

But while the diffusion of less severe forms of corporal punishment took place in very recent times, credit must go to the Childs and Lovells for inventing new methods of child nurture. My survey of childrearing recollections up to 1900 indicates that mothers, the major disciplinarians in educated middle-class families, introduced spanking as a common childhood punishment. Children born in the nineteenth century often described "gentle" mothers and "stern" fathers. Mothers did use corporal punishment, but the number and force of their blows was less than those of the father. Furthermore, mothers employed corporal punishment as a last resort, whereas fathers did not hesitate to take a son or daughter to the woodshed. And mothers often interceded to save their children from a father's blows.

For the most part, daughters were spared the beatings inflicted on their brothers; girls were to be treated more gently than boys. Contemporary psychologists note that boys are more likely than girls to engage in rough-and-tumble play and to act aggressively at early ages; therefore, boys may have deserved more discipline of some sort than girls. Until the early nineteenth century, however, these gender distinctions appear to have gone unnoticed, and daughters as well as sons suffered cuffings and whippings.

Reform of childrearing, appealing mainly to the educated middle class, did not greatly permeate American society as a whole. In the recollections studied, the vast majority of American parents wielded the rod "on old Adam's account" without much reflection. Most fathers and mothers used an instrument in hitting their children, ranging from a belt to a horsewhip. Whippings did not occur daily but were not overly rare, either. Davy Crockett ran away from home because his father continually whipped him with a hickory stick. Robert E. Lee was raised by his aunt whose principle of childrearing was "whip and pray and pray and whip." John D. Rockefeller's mother tied him to a tree in the back of their home on several occasions to administer sharp whippings. Abraham Lincoln's father was often drunk and beat his son unjustifiably with his fists or a horsewhip.[33] These four boys, each of whom became a national leader, hero, and cultural icon, did not think of themselves as abused children, yet the treatment they received, while not preventing great accomplishment, may have harmed them. And their experiences with discipline were certainly not atypical of nineteenth-century America.

It is important to note that in some of the printed recollections, girls were subjected to sexual assaults by their fathers or uncles. There were no boys in the recollections who were sexually abused. Sexual assault falls outside the domain of legitimate corporal punishment, but it deserves mention here as part of the complete story of mistreatment of children—especially daughters—by their fathers. The girls raped by their fathers felt deep shame; they left their families as soon as they could. Fathers of these girls were brutal and authoritarian; the mothers were dead or relatively powerless.

Modern methods of childrearing had been influenced by diverse intellectual and social changes extending as far back as the Enlightenment, when philosophers hoped for progress through furthering people's capacity for reason. To give in to the passions of sexuality, rage, cruelty, and aggression was to become a "domestic tyrant."

The lesson of the Revolution was that a self-governing child served the best interests of the nation. Also, the decline of strict Calvinist doctrine diminished belief in original sin and allowed a more tolerant view of children. Although children had a capacity for reason and conscience, they required moral instruction from someone predictable, kind, and gentle. Mothers, who benefited from hired help or servants, could give more attention to the needs and instruction of each child. They exercised more power in deciding how many children to have, and thus had fewer children to raise.

Whereas a modern family might employ humane and moderate methods of child discipline, most nineteenth-century American families were decidedly traditional. All of the influences that created modern childrearing—the decline of Calvinism, the rise of the Enlightenment, the impact of American nationalism, the growth of maternal control over childrearing—were confined to a small but highly influential segment of the American people in the Northeast, the Mid-Atlantic, and the northern California coast.

The private reform of domestic discipline contributed to public prohibitions against corporal punishment in the early nineteenth century. As early as 1810 many Sunday schools eliminated corporal punishment. The managers of orphan asylums and houses of refuge, seeking to institute principles of self-government, hoped to resort to the rod only as the punishment of last resort. School reformers in the North led the way in abolishing or at least limiting corporal punishment. Massachusetts educator Horace Mann succeeded in restricting the use of the rod in the common schools of his state; several city school systems in other states outlawed corporal punishments in the schools as well.

The campaign against corporal punishment reflected a general trend against physical cruelty to subordinates or the helpless. In 1850, Congress passed a law prohibiting flogging in the Navy. Anglo-American reformers campaigned to abolish slavery, capital punishment, dueling, and cruelty to animals.[34] Often these movements were buttressed by the religious and moral fervor of liberal Protestantism, which found expression in secular reform dedicated to the principles of human rights.

Enlightened antebellum educators and writers of advice literature were concerned about corporal punishment rather than child abuse. There were no organized efforts to punish parents who were deliberately cruel. Causing permanent injury to a child was always considered wrong, but before the Civil War there was no palpable interest in defining what cruelty to children was. A parent, it was believed, possessed a natural right to chastise a child, which the state should not interfere with.

Even anticruelty societies, established in the 1870s, held to the principle of a parent's right to administer "a licking when necessary." The societies had no consistent definition of child battering; it varied from case to case and from one SPCC to another. But these agencies did charge mothers with neglect, thus incorporating new childraising standards of the middle class. Permitting youngsters to play on the street and leaving young children at home unattended were considered neglectful. Alcoholic wives and mothers were branded as unfit; equally neglectful were mothers who lived in sin. The belief in mother-dominated childrearing also affected attitudes toward child placement. If every child required a mother's love, then foster homes, rather than institutions, were the best environments for abused and neglected children.

The model of the affectionate family, with the mother as the major child-raiser, reshaped the Family Ideal. Women were to exert their reforming impulse within the confines of the homes, where they were granted greater authority in childrearing. But they were also to make the home a refuge from the public world, thus further sealing off domestic activities from community surveillance. This revitalized belief in family privacy made state intervention appear even more problematic, disruptive, and unnatural. The family restructuring of the antebellum years was thus an ambiguous legacy for reform against domestic violence, creating new standards for childrearing but erecting higher barriers between the family and the outside world.

3

The Drunkard's Wife

THE TEMPERANCE MOVEMENT became the first American reform campaign to depict for the public the cruelty of domestic violence. Temperance reformers regarded family violence not as a distinct social problem, but as an evil consequence of alcohol. Although they believed that prohibiting the sale of liquor would help to end male violence, they did not advocate policies to aid its victims directly. By the 1840s, however, the temperance crusade attracted large numbers of women activists, who recognized in male drunkenness a grave threat to family life. These women organized their own societies, raised funds, and urged men to take a pledge to abstain from drinking. Many women, unhappy with their shabby treatment from male-dominated temperance societies, abandoned the temperance cause in favor of the campaign for what they called "woman's rights." As activists in this crusade, they fought for legislation to grant divorce on grounds of drunkenness and secure for drunkards' wives the right to their own earnings. They subsumed the issue of domestic violence under the rubric of the ills caused by intemperance.

This was the first public effort against family violence led by women on behalf of women, and it gradually became more radical. Until the 1850s male and female temperance reformers urged wives and mothers to appeal to the drunkard's sense of family responsibility. Woman's rights leaders eventually rebelled against this idea. Believing that wives had a moral duty to divorce their drunkard husbands, antebellum feminists placed the emancipation of women ahead of the preservation of the family. In their minds it was preferable for a mother and her children to live alone rather than to remain bound to the inebriate husband. They reformulated the issue of the drunkard's wife so that it became one of wrongs done to women by men. The very survival of a drunkard's wife, they argued, depended on a woman's rights—her right to custody of her children, her right to her own earnings, and her right to secure a divorce.

Divorce for the drunkard's wife was a radical proposal, which some woman's rights leaders regarded as fundamental. They set forth the issue of divorce for the drunkard's wife as a conflict between the claims of the traditional male-dominated family and a woman's right to autonomy and personal safety. The vehemence of their rhetoric may have helped defeat divorce reform legislation. Indeed, their crusade confirms the observation stated in the Introduction: the more radical the critique of the family underlying proposed legislation, the lower the chance that legislation has of passing. In spite of their legislative defeats, the woman's rights crusade earned for antebellum feminists a place in history as women who dared to challenge the traditional domestic hierarchy and struggled for the emancipation of their sex.

Early nineteenth-century lecturers against temperance described with characteristic hyperbole the husband who, under the influence of cider alone, savaged with an axe his loving wife and the baby nursing at her breast.[1] No one can say for sure if alcohol causes wife beating. In many cultures, heavy drinking is not associated with aggressiveness. In fact, some have argued that wife beaters use alcohol as a rationalization for assault. Nevertheless, there are many ways that drinking indirectly contributes to family violence. Male drinking companions at saloons often encourage each other to put women in their place; when these men stumble home, they take out their aggression on their wives. A husband's spending of his wages on alcohol also leads to quarrels at home, which can escalate into violence.

Temperance advocates in the nineteenth century assumed there was a simple relationship between alcoholism and wife beating. Most naively believed that excessive drink was *the* cause of domestic violence, rather than a precipitating factor or convenient excuse for violent behavior. Family murder and physical assaults between family members, they argued, were among the many consequences of intemperance.

Drunkenness was common in antebellum America. Women as well as men drank a great deal of homemade whiskey, hard cider, beer, and West Indian rum. In 1770, per capita annual consumption of alcoholic beverages was 3.7 gallons; in 1830, 5.2 gallons. (National per capita consumption of hard liquor in 1982 was a little less than half that of 1830.) Scholars have offered several reasons for the increase in alcohol consumption from the colonial period to the 1830s. For one thing, the success ethic of the early nineteenth century led to increased stress. Some of the men who failed in business or farming in that competitive era turned to drink. Moreover, the decline in the enforcement of religious morality and the migration of men to new frontier areas far from friends and relatives removed the heavy drinker from social pressures to control his intake of alcohol. Finally, an overabundance of corn on the Western frontier encouraged the production of cheap domestic whiskey.[2] The increase in alcohol consumption appears to have occurred even before the large-scale immigration of the Germans and Irish, who came from heavy-drinking cultures.

Drunkenness was prevalent among men, especially men of the working classes. In antebellum shops and factories, employers customarily furnished their workers with a daily ration of rum or gin. Craftsmen and laborers often drank several glasses of rum at work breaks, and they celebrated the end of a project, a holiday, or the arrival of the weekend with an alcoholic binge that included homemade whiskey, hard cider, and beer. In drink-related divorce suits filed in Santa Clara County, California, between 1850 and 1890, 8 percent of the husbands sued for divorce were in middle-class occupations, as compared to 40 percent employed as common laborers.[3] One might expect to find the same class distinctions in the first half of the nineteenth century as well.

Temperance reformers correctly noted that alcoholism contributed to dissension, conflict, and violence in marriage. Still, they were primarily concerned with drunkenness rather than family violence and initially ignored the effect of male drunkenness on the family. Temperance speakers instead reminded their audiences that taxpayers had to foot the bill for the custodial care of drunkards in state asylums, prisons, and poorhouses. Intemperance, they insisted, contributed to murder and caused property damage, fires, and shipwrecks.

The drunkard's family was occasionally depicted in speeches and in the temperance literature of the time, however. The "trembling family" first emerged as a metaphor in a temperance speech delivered in 1813, and the image of the suffering wife "doomed to mourn without hope and to suffer without alleviation" began to appear by the 1830s.[4] In 1835, *The Pennsylvania–New Jersey Almanac* printed the first drawings of family violence in America: drunken husbands lifting a chair or tongs to bludgeon a wife and children.

Thirty years passed between the founding of the first formal American temperance society in 1808 and the appearance of temperance rhetoric about family violence. What needs to be explained is not why the movement was so late in raising the issue but why it was raised at all. As a social problem, domestic violence inevitably exposes the worst features of family life. Reformers must demonstrate that family violence is not a private concern, but a public matter, and that domestic abuse violates deeply held cultural values. To achieve success, many reformers against family violence have deliberately avoided challenging the Family Ideal. In the eighteenth century, a wall had been built dividing the family from community surveillance. At the same time, the public lost interest in punishing crimes of morality. By the first half of the nineteenth century, the family was effectively isolated from the community; it had become a more private unit, exempt from public scrutiny.[5]

Antebellum women magazine writers, educators, and novelists defined the home not only as private but as a woman's special domain. *Godey's Lady's Book, Ladies Magazine,* and dozens of other publications celebrated women's increased domestic authority. Men, the journals proclaimed, no longer ruled the household; commerce and politics made up their world. The home stood as a bastion against the crass material values of the outside world. As guardians of the domestic fireside, women presented to their husbands and children the female values of modesty, self-sacrifice, and piety. This division of the world into two spheres and the assignment of each sex to its separate sphere has been referred to as the ideology of domesticity.

This ideology promoted the view that women had the power to reform the morals of fathers, sons, and brothers. As noted in Chapter 2, belief in the purity of women and the power of mothers encouraged more maternal control over child discipline. Women were urged to rear their children gently and to exert their influence over all other domestic matters. Women's power over men, however, was to remain within the private confines of the family cottage. Women were to use their influence only in their own homes, rather than acting collectively. The impulse toward moral reform, however, carried women into public charitable activities and organizations. Some who joined women's moral reform associations tried to publish the names of men known to visit prostitutes, while women in temperance societies urged men to take the pledge before they brought ruin to themselves and their families. Out of their sense of religious and family responsibility, thousands of women entered temperance reform in the 1830s and 1840s. They even claimed special abilities as speakers because while "men can deal in statistics and logical deductions . . . women can describe the horrors of intemperance—can draw aside the curtain and show us the wreck it makes of domestic love and home enjoyment—can paint the anguish of the drunkard's wife and the miseries of his children."[6] The temperance cause gave women a platform to speak out against the economic dependency of mothers and children on the male provider.

Temperance reformers also spoke out against physical abuse, which they saw as violating domestic ideals and destroying female virtue. If women were the purer sex, as antebellum domestic ideology insisted, then they deserved a life free from terror and cruelty. The public had not grasped the extent of women's suffering, the reformers argued, because family privacy concealed it from public view. One woman advocate of temperance insisted that "intemperance assaults the wife at her domestic hearth, and there she must bear her sorrows until her heart breaks, shut up without the world's observation, and the world's sympathy."[7]

However, male and female temperance reformers avoided speaking on rape, incest, and to some extent, prostitution. Discussion of these, as well as many other sexual issues, was rare in the Victorian Age, and the morals of those who openly discussed them were called into question. Antiliquor speakers were cautious in discussing certain topics. Even so, the airing of domestic travail, however circumspectly presented, offered an implicit critique of prevailing family mores.

Victorian sexual attitudes sharply differentiated between the sexual natures of men and women. The ideal woman of the early nineteenth century was expected to be sexually pure and lacking in passion and governed more by the rational faculties. However, male sexuality was considered essentially brutish. Although man required his "animal passions," he also needed to keep them under control. Indeed, the ability to keep sexual impulses in check was seen as the ultimate moral act. Lustful indulgence in sex and alcohol were thought to neutralize the small amount of self-control men possessed. The concept of male brutishness, referring to both sexuality and violence, was divided along class lines. The middle and upper classes were theoretically self-policing; the lower classes were not. In America brutishness was a term often applied to the frontiersmen or the newly arrived immigrants (at that time predominantly Irish Catholics). Although there were references to brutish women, the term was generally reserved for men. Most of those who expressed an opinion held that men were not by nature brutish, but that drink caused them to degenerate. The idea of the brute in man did not lead to any specific program of action, but throughout the nineteenth century, it fueled public discourse and provided a satisfying attribution for male behavior.

Beliefs in male brutishness and female purity were necessary to gain a sympathetic public hearing for the plight of the drunkard's wife. The miserable children and anguishing wife of the temperance tale were presented as victims of male drunkenness; the drunkard was invariably portrayed as a "brute." These were the terms in which family violence was understood throughout the nineteenth and well into the twentieth century. The image of the brutish wife beater seems to have appeared first in the 1830s. Samuel Chapman, a Quaker temperance reformer, concluded in 1834 that only a small proportion of the "brutes in human shape" who abused their families had been punished. William Alcott, in his marital advice book published in 1838, described as "brutes in the shape of men" those husbands "who will inflict bodily pain on those whom it should be their highest interest to treat with tenderness."[8]

Because the effects of male brutishness were felt so gravely by women, and as it was believed that drink "embruted" men, there could be no reform other than temperance in which women could more appropriately take part. In joining the temperance crusade, women were taking steps to defend the family. But in the early period of reform, their activities were limited to fund-raising and listening with rapt attention to male temperance lecturers. As women became more involved, however, they became convinced that legislative action against alcoholism was required; moral appeal alone had proven ineffective. They took on political activities, lobbying state legislatures through petition campaigns for the passage of laws prohibiting the sale of liquor, establishing dry districts, and imposing saloon closings on Sunday.[9]

In the 1850s the growth of political activism in the temperance movement coincided with new ideas on the rights of women. Feminism in America originated in the egalitarian ideals of the Revolution and the moral fervor of abolitionism. The Revolution contributed the belief that women, like men, possessed inalienable natural rights. Abolitionism served as a training ground for women in political action and taught women that to secure the rights of others, they had to emancipate themselves.

A tiny village in upstate New York, Seneca Falls, proved to be the meeting ground for abolitionism, temperance, and woman's rights agitation. The town had been the center of a Protestant revival belt as early as the 1820s. The spirit of the revivals continued to attract men and women to reform activities for decades; Methodists protested against slavery, and Quakers, relatively untouched by evangelical enthusiasm, became active in the abolitionist and temperance movements. Some women from the Seneca Falls region secured the passage of married women's property legislation in New York in 1848.

Emboldened by success, the women called a convention on women's rights to meet in Seneca Falls later that year. The men and women who attended it identified a series of women's grievances against male tyranny. They drafted a Declaration of Human Sentiments containing a bill of particulars modeled after the list of grievances of the colonists outlined in the Declaration of Independence. Among women's complaints was the fact that man "has so framed the laws of divorce, as to what shall be the proper causes, and in case of separation, to whom the guardianship of the children shall be given, as to be wholly regardless of the happiness of women—the law, in all cases, going upon the false supposition of the supremacy of man, and giving all power into his hands."[10] The Declaration did not call for legislation expanding the grounds of divorce, although it implied that new laws were welcome and necessary.

Seneca Falls was the home of a leading advocate of temperance and woman's rights, Amelia Bloomer. She helped organize and served as an officer of the local female temperance society in 1848. Bloomer had been the co-editor of her husband's newspaper, *the Seneca County Courier,* and decided to publish a temperance newspaper for her own society. Although there had been many men's temperance journals, *Lily,* established in 1849, was the first one edited by a woman in the United States. Under Bloomer's editorship, *Lily* carried stories about woman's rights as well as temperance. (Bloomer is most known for having lent her name to a costume of Turkish pantaloons worn under a belted knee-length dress. The Bloomer outfit was intended to provide women with a loose and comfortable attire. Designed by another woman's rights activist, the costume carried Bloomer's name because she printed a sketch and patterns of it in *Lily.*)

Letters demanding divorce for the drunkard's wife had been appearing in *Lily* almost since its inception. Some correspondents even claimed that the law should compel a wife to leave her drunken husband. Jane Swisshelm, an advocate of woman's rights from Pennsylvania and an aggrieved wife herself, suggested in a letter to *Lily* that drunkards should be horsewhipped. Any wife willing to remain married to a drunkard, she argued, should be committed to a lunatic asylum. Such a woman was free to chose her own fate, but she had no "right to entail misery and degradation upon a helpless offspring."[11] She regarded it as a criminal act for a woman to become the mother of a drunkard's child.

Few favored solutions as radical as these. At this time, it was easier to secure a divorce on grounds of drunkenness than on the ill-defined grounds of cruelty. Most of the nineteen states that granted divorce for cruelty by 1850 were in the South or the Midwest. Legislators in these states felt freer to depart from English precedent and respond to the demands of a mobile, frontier society. At first, divorces were granted on a more or less ad hoc basis. When the number of divorce bills mounted, lawmakers began to reform the divorce codes as a means of relieving the burden on their legislative calendar. State statutes granting divorce on grounds of cruelty varied widely. Some permitted full divorce with the right to remarry; others sanctioned only a legal separation. Some statutes applied to husbands and wives, others only to wives. There was a wide range in the definition of cruelty in these laws. The more restrictive the definition of cruelty, the greater the difficulty in securing a divorce. Even in states that defined cruelty more liberally, many judges granted divorce only to wives who appeared submissive, chaste, and protective of their children. In the late nineteenth century, however, judges began to accept "mental cruelty" as a reason for divorce.

Nonetheless, the typical divorce of the time was granted for desertion, not cruelty. Between 1867 and 1871, a national commission on divorce gathered statistics from each state and territory and found that only 13 percent of divorces in the United States in those years were secured on grounds of cruelty. Divorce for this reason was nearly always requested by women. Women made up 67 percent of all divorce applicants and 87 percent of those seeking divorce for cruelty.[12] But almost twice as many states granted divorce for drunkenness as for cruelty. By 1871 thirty-four states permitted divorce on grounds of habitual drunkenness; two-thirds of these states were in the South and West.

The divorce law of New York state was far behind that of other states. It modeled its domestic relations law after English law, which permitted absolute divorce only for those who could prove a spouse's adultery. The New York state legislature had considered various divorce reform bills for more than thirty years. By 1852, state law permitted a legal separation, but not a divorce, for cruel and inhuman treatment, abandonment, refusal to provide economic support, and husbandly conduct that made it "unsafe and improper for the wife to cohabit with him." State legislators often received requests from wealthy constituents for passage of a "private divorce bill" granting legislative divorce. A steady stream of these requests, along with a general revision of state laws, spurred the effort for divorce reform. The legislature appeared willing to act in 1852. A judiciary committee, reviewing the entire legislative history of New York's divorce law, recommended abolishing legal separation and instead broadening the grounds for absolute divorce to include cruel and inhuman treatment, willful desertion, and "other cases of extreme hardship and peculiar inconvenience." The recommendations did not add drunkenness as a grounds for divorce.[13]

As men in the temperance movement still felt that women should not become directly involved in politics, the break between men and women in this movement was imminent, and the women's groups would focus on issues much larger in scope than the plight of the drunkard's wife. In January 1852, Susan B. Anthony attended a state temperance meeting as a delegate from the Rochester, New York, Daughters of Temperance. Trained as a schoolteacher, Anthony had given up her profession to manage the family farm in western New York. Her mother and sister had attended the Seneca Falls convention. Woman's rights ideas interested Anthony, but she had given her primary allegiance to the temperance and abolitionist causes. At the age of twenty-eight, she joined a local chapter of the Daughters of Temperance and distinguished herself as an articulate speaker and tireless fund-raiser. At this

1852 temperance meeting, she spoke out against the exclusion of women from political life, but her speech was drowned out by boos and catcalls. That evening Anthony and several other women speakers met separately and called a convention to establish a new women's temperance society, unaffiliated with any men's temperance organization. Five months later, Elizabeth Cady Stanton, introduced to Anthony by Amelia Bloomer in 1851, was elected the first president of the New York State Woman's Temperance Society.

By this time Stanton, in her late thirties and the mother of three small children, was already a veteran activist on behalf of abolition, woman's rights, and temperance. She had come into frequent contact with women victims of male cruelty, having opened her home to abused women neighbors, most of whom were poor or working class and Irish. Under the pseudonym of "Sun Flower," Stanton had contributed articles on temperance and woman's rights to *Lily*, published by her friend in Seneca Falls, Amelia Bloomer.

In addressing the first convention of the New York State Woman's Temperance Society in 1852, Stanton hoped to gather support for a divorce bill that had just passed the New York House of Representatives and was before the state Senate. Speaking to an audience of more than a thousand men and women, Stanton, four months pregnant, dressed in a Bloomer costume and sporting a short haircut, pictured for her audience the "moral monster" of the drunkard and his wife, who was "helpless, outraged, hungry, cold and in rags."[14] Women were the greatest victims of intemperance, she argued, yet they did not possess the power to end their suffering by the ballot. They were forced to use more personal methods at their command. Stanton resolved:

> 1. Let no woman remain in the relation of wife with the confirmed drunkard. Let no drunkard be the father of her children. Let no woman form an alliance with any man who has been suspected even of the vice of intemperance; for the taste once acquired can never, never be eradicated. Be not misled by any pledges, resolves, promises, prayers, or tears. You cannot rely on the word of a man who is, or has been, the victim of such an overpowering appetite.

> 2. Let us petition our State governments so as to modify the laws affecting marriage, and the custody of children, that the drunkard shall have no claims on either wife or child.[15]

She added that the wife of a drunkard who insisted upon remaining married should not have sexual intercourse with him, so as to "bring no children to that blighted, dreary, desolate hearth."[16] Her advice was based on the belief, quite common at the time, that the drunkard's children inherited a propensity toward insanity, lunacy, pauperism, and criminality. In endorsing Stanton's resolution, a former wife of a drunkard insisted that it was foolish to expect that a drunkard could reform. Amelia Bloomer spoke next. No wife, she argued, should submit to a drunken husband's "blows and curses, and submit to his brutish passions and lusts."[17] Any woman who remained married to a drunkard and anyone who forced her to do so was helping to perpetuate drunkenness. Bloomer demanded that the law compel the drunkard's wife to secure a divorce, especially if she had children. A separation or divorce would punish the drunkard and perhaps encourage him to stop drinking because he would fear the loss of his wife, property, and children. The victimization of the drunkard's children was mentioned merely as an adjunct to the suffering of women. For Stanton, the condition of women and children were one and the same.[18]

Had Stanton and Bloomer deliberately offered radical proposals to stir their audience to action? Or had they simply been carried away by the emotional tenor of the meeting? Stanton and Bloomer recognized that women's enthusiasm for temperance often brought to the surface suppressed rage against their vulnerability and dependence on irresponsible and abusive men. They believed that latent female anger could be channeled into feminist activism. Their strong moral antipathy toward the evil of alcohol stirred them to discuss features of married life others had feared to recount. The drunkard's wife symbolized for them the abject status of women in marriage. This convention marked the first time that women had publicly denounced the rape of a wife in marriage and questioned a husband's right to demand sexual intercourse from his wife. Stanton and Bloomer tried to show that in bearing the drunkard's child, the sacred calling of motherhood was perverted into reproducing another generation of drunkards. They attacked the view that a wife was to sacrifice herself in the hopes of reclaiming her husband, and that duty compelled a wife to submit to her husband. A woman deserved nothing less than a right to life and happiness equal to that of any man.

The plight of the drunkard's wife demonstrated forcefully that women were a distinct "sexual class" whose interests were separate from those of men. Stanton had argued that the drunken husband could not be trusted to exercise his power wisely or use the ballot to represent fairly his family's interests. Male judges and state legislators collaborated with the drunkard, she argued, in that they regulated marriage on his behalf. In so doing, they helped to perpetuate drunkenness and women's suffering. Women required the suffrage, Stanton claimed, so they could use the ballot to prohibit the sale of liquor.

In the summer of 1852, women temperance activists crisscrossed New York state, securing 28,000 women's signatures on a petition requesting the legislature to ban the sale of alcoholic beverages. State lawmakers, upon receipt of these petitions, told temperance women they had acted unwomanly by involving themselves in petition campaigns. When the Woman's State Temperance Society met the following winter, some of the men in the organization (men were allowed to join, but not to hold elected office) wanted the society to rename itself the "People's Temperance Organization" and eliminate women's issues entirely. Stanton's radical views on divorce had shocked them and other members. She responded by pointing to the hypocrisy of those who recited the sufferings of drunkards' wives with no interest in securing such women their rights.

> [I]n discussing the question of temperance, all lecturers, from the beginning, have made mention of the drunkards' wives and children, of widows' groans and orphans' tears; shall these classes of sufferers be introduced but as themes for rhetorical flourish, as pathetic touches of the speaker's eloquence; shall we passively shed tears over their condition, or by giving them their rights, bravely open to them the doors of escape from a wretched and degraded life? . . . If in pointing out her social degradation, we show you how the present laws outrage the sacredness of the marriage institution; if in proving to you that justice and mercy demand a legal separation from drunkards, we grasp the higher idea that a unity of soul alone constitutes and sanctifies true marriage, and that any law or public sentiment that forces two immortal high-born souls to live together as husband and wife, unless held there by love, is false to God and humanity; who shall say that the discussion of this question does not lead us legitimately into the consideration of the important subject of divorce. [19]

Stanton insisted that women in the temperance movement were obliged to discuss women's rights because men had challenged their right to speak and petition. The majority of the membership did not wish to be associated with Stanton's radicalism. Having lost her bid for reelection to the presidency of the society, she and Anthony resigned. Neither of them ever again belonged to a temperance organization. Stanton took her defeat in stride and wrote to her friend soon after the meeting, "Now, Susan, I do beg of you to let the past be past, and to waste no powder on the Woman's State Temperance Society. We have other and bigger fish to fry."[20]

Stanton and Anthony, ending their association with the temperance cause, decided that only the woman's rights movement represented the interests of drunkards' wives. After this, divorce reform surfaced periodically as one of several women's demands. Although women in the temperance movement had a special interest in the plight of the drunkard's wife, for woman's rights activists divorce for the drunkard's wife was just one of several legislative priorities. Stanton was attracted to the divorce question precisely because it made apparent the need for a separate women's organization to raise issues of special concern to her sex. However, once involved in the woman's rights movement, she was forced to recognize that other matters were more appealing to her constituency.

In spite of the fact that the New York state legislature continued to consider divorce legislation to include habitual drunkenness as grounds for divorce, Stanton and Anthony did not discuss the issue of divorce until 1860. They apparently felt that they were pressing too many women's demands at the same time. Divorce was the most controversial part of their agenda, and they seem to have decided to shelve discussion of it, at least temporarily. Passage of married women's property legislation became their highest priority. Stanton and Anthony tried to show that married women's property rights would benefit drunkards' wives. Such women were forced to support themselves and their children, they argued, yet a husband could seize his wife's earnings and sell off her property. Moreover, a husband separated from his wife and who had forfeited custody of his children still retained his right to appoint a guardian other than his wife in his will.[21] Stanton and Anthony agitated for legislation to grant to the drunkard's wife (and deserted wives) the right to their own earnings and to control over their property.

Even without the active efforts of Stanton and Anthony, the issue of divorce for the drunkard's wife would not die. A few New York state legislators in 1855 and again in 1856 introduced new divorce bills, responding to pressure from wealthy constituents. Several cases of aggravated cruelty to daughters of the wealthy Dutch landholding aristocracy had stirred the state senator from their district. He introduced a divorce bill to grant absolute divorce on grounds of desertion, cruelty, and drunkenness. In their lectures Stanton and Anthony never mentioned the pending legislation, but influential editors of the state's major newspapers were adamantly opposed. *The Albany Evening Journal* referred to such bills as legislation "to promote adultery."[22] The editor of the *New York Tribune*, Horace Greeley, published a stinging editorial in opposition to the proposed legislation. Although an opponent of divorce, Greeley was by no means an enemy of woman's rights. He was even a personal friend of Stanton and Anthony.

Greeley's attitude toward divorce reflected the popular view of the time. He opposed divorce, in part, because it was un-Christian; he pointed out that Jesus had advocated divorce only on grounds of adultery. Greeley further believed marriage was the best institution for raising children. Liberal divorce, he feared, endangered civilization, opening the way to selfishness, egotism, and immorality. Still, for "a virtuous and worthy girl" who was married to a "miserable loafer and sot," he would permit a legal separation with the right to guardianship of her children and property legislation securing for a wife the right to her earnings.

Greeley was opposed to giving any woman the right to remarry while her husband was alive. He seemed to believe, as most of the public did, that a man or woman who sued for divorce was adulterous. No applicant for divorce could be entirely virtuous and blameless, he wrote. In Greeley's way of thinking, a woman should suffer for having made a rash decision, and her children should not have to endure the awkward situation of having both a living father and a stepfather. On these issues, he upheld the domestic ideals of the age. Divorce not only challenged the institution of marriage but also permitted women to remarry; it appeared to offer divorced women too much opportunity for a normal sexual life. By contrast, married women's property legislation seemed merely to aid deserving women who wanted to support themselves and their children without giving them the freedom to begin life anew.

For her part, Stanton refused to believe that Greeley's views represented public attitudes. She had been encouraged by the fact that the last divorce reform bill in the New York state legislature, in spite of Greeley's opposition, had lost by only four votes. Her feminist beliefs had grown stronger, and she seemed oblivious to the caution of her friends. In 1860 Stanton and Anthony engaged in direct action for the first time. Anthony found safe and secret lodgings for a "fugitive wife," the sister of a U.S. Senator, who had kidnapped her daughter and fled from her abusive husband, a Massachusetts legislator.[23] The desperation of this woman convinced Anthony and Stanton that many wives were nothing more than slaves, who had to flee the institution of marriage because the law did not treat them justly.

Woman's rights conventions had met yearly during the 1850s to consider resolutions on women's issues, but no convention had ever endorsed liberal divorce. In fact, most woman's rights activists believed that the "marriage question" was too controversial for their movement. Divorce was only one of the issues that discussion of marriage encompassed; it also included a woman's right to decide when and how often she became pregnant and her right to refuse her husband's demands for sexual intercourse. Prior to the 1860 convention, most of these matters had only been addressed in the private correspondence of Stanton and her friends. At the 1860 convention, Stanton introduced ten resolutions designed to gain support for yet another version of the divorce bill to be reintroduced in the New York state legislature the following term. In an hour-long speech, she argued that the institution of the family could not survive amidst the "violence, debauchery, and excess" often manifest in marriage. She insisted that the married woman was as much in bondage as the slave. The dignity of womanhood, far from being protected by the institution of marriage, was actually sullied by it. Religious custom and government had conspired to make women the property of their husbands. Stanton argued that divorce ought to be a private matter, unregulated by church or state. If government was to interfere, its proper role in her view was to make divorce easier and marriage more difficult to secure. Stanton was no longer content to argue in favor of divorce for the drunkard's wife. She now insisted that marriage should be a simple contract to be dissolved in cases of drunkenness, insanity, desertion, cruel or brutal treatment, or mere incompatibility.

Stanton's views were echoed by Ernestine Rose, an important advocate of married women's property legislation, who went on to suggest "that personal cruelty to a wife, who he swore to love, cherish, and protest, may be made a heinous crime—a perjury and a State's prison offense, for which divorce shall be granted."[24] Her speech was applauded, but her proposal was not pursued. Indeed, the majority of woman's rights supporters at the convention strongly opposed Stanton's ideas. Congregationalist minister Antoinette Blackwell conceded that legal divorce was sometimes necessary "for personal and family protection" but she argued that even an ex-wife was still morally responsible for the regeneration of her drunken and abusive husband. Wendell Phillips, a noted abolitionist also active in the woman's rights cause, argued that Stanton's resolutions should be ruled out of order. To Phillips, divorce affected men and women equally and was therefore not a woman's rights issue. Phillips also added more pragmatically that "the marriage question" associated the woman's rights movement with radical free-love theories. Having heard all these arguments, the convention allowed Stanton's resolutions to stand, but did not adopt them. Although not completely rebuffed by her colleagues, Stanton was roasted in the press and inundated with letters denouncing her as a reviler of Christian marriage.[25]

Although dozens of states permitted divorce on grounds of habitual drunkenness and most Americans were quite sympathetic to the deserving and virtuous wife of a drunkard, Stanton's stance was too radical for many people. Her views aroused antipathy from ministers who opposed woman's rights, conservatives who were frightened by social instability, and some woman's rights advocates who did not want to damage their movement. The arguments against divorce reform were a virtual restatement of the domestic ideology of the time: belief in female sexual purity, Christian morality, and female self-abnegation. Divorce for the drunkard's wife, as posed by Stanton, was a threat to the institution of the family.

Despite lack of support for her position, Stanton persisted in advocating divorce reform. In 1861 she testified before the judiciary committee of the New York state Senate. She appeared to sway the committee, which reported in favor of a divorce reform bill. When the bill reached the floor of the Senate, however, it was easily defeated. A few months later, guns were fired at Fort Sumter and interest in the divorce issue quickly subsided. New York's divorce law remained substantially unchanged until the 1950s. Stanton and Anthony had succeeded in creating greater awareness about the suffering of drunkards' wives, without being able to translate their perception into the passage of legislation.

Some of Stanton and Anthony's colleagues sought to aid drunkards' wives and other abused women by calling for more strictly enforced criminal laws on behalf of battered women. Amelia Bloomer, for example, believed that abused women should be persuaded to press criminal charges against their husbands. In fact, two American states had passed laws punishing wife beating as a misdemeanor—Tennessee in 1850 and Georgia in 1857.[26] There is no information about the sponsors of this legislation. During these years Stanton and Anthony appear to have been unaware of these laws and generally uninterested in the criminal punishment of wife beaters.[27]

English reformers were more interested in the issue of wife beating and more successful in passing legislation and establishing new programs on behalf of victims than the Americans. Indeed, the term "wife beating" was first devised in England in 1856 during a campaign for divorce reform. English legislation to punish wife beating stemmed from the fear that violent crime was getting out of hand. In 1852 Thomas Phinn, a London magistrate, published statistics on the number of assaults by men on women and children in London. His data showed that about one in six assaults occurred within the family. Alarmed by these figures, Phinn advocated punishing wife beaters at the whipping post. His suggestion was taken seriously—flogging was an accepted form of punishment for a variety of crimes—but not acted upon. Instead, Henry Fitzroy, a member of Parliament who wanted to prevent dastardly blows "constantly perpetrated upon defenceless women by brutes who . . . [call] themselves men," devised an alternative. Fitzroy worried that the "evil" of assault was growing rapidly, and "constituted . . . a blot upon our national character."[28] In 1853, Parliament passed Fitzroy's legislation, the Act for the Better Prevention of Aggravated Assaults Upon Women and Children, popularly known as the "Good Wives' Rod." It punished aggravated assault on women or children under the age of fourteen with up to six months in prison, a fine, and an order to keep the peace for six months. Fitzroy succeeded for two reasons. First, Parliament had previously enacted into law a number of statutes against cruelty to horses, cattle, dogs, and against cock baiting. Animal anticruelty legislation demonstrated that the government had a legitimate interest in outlawing various forms of human cruelty hitherto regarded as legitimate popular custom. In doing so, Parliament had accepted responsibility for expressing a new and more expansive humane sentiment. Supporters of legislation to punish the assault of women and children could effectively insist that Parliament should extent "the same protection to defenseless women as they already extended to poodle dogs and donkeys."[29]

Most historians conclude that the English preceded the Americans in their concern about cruelty to animals because industrialization occurred there earlier and because a large proportion of the English population lived in cities.[30] The goods and services of the industrial order were produced by workers and machines; animals played only a small part in the manufacturing process. The beneficiaries of industrialization, the urban upper classes, were the first to express humane sentiment about animals. Their compassion for animals was part of a nostalgia for the rural life they longed to enjoy on country weekends.

Also, English judges and the public worried about the presence of dangerous and violent criminals. Members of Parliament believed that punishing wife beating would help reduce other forms of violent crime. The growth of the factory system and its abuses spawned not only criminals but a large movement demanding greater economic and political participation of the masses. The swarms of robbers and petty criminals who could not be absorbed into the new economic order made the control of crime an urgent matter for Parliamentary legislation. Thus, fear of the lower classes was a much more powerful impetus behind reform in industrialized England than in America because English authorities equated criminality with social and political unrest.

Although this English legislation on behalf of women and children was passed without any feminist agitation, woman's rights activists took advantage of it to found a Society for the Protection of Women and Children in 1857. The society provided legal advice to women and child victims of battering by advertising for information about assaults and guaranteeing informants confidentiality. It stationed observers in courtrooms to monitor cases involving women and child victims. The society also established a lodging place for victims of assault, the first shelter of its kind in Western Europe or North America.

In reshaping their criminal law and founding an institution to aid victims of assault, the English had taken the first step toward a more extensive reform against family violence. During the 1850s the issue of wife beating continued to be discussed in Parliament; some reformers proposed to expand the grounds for divorce and others favored punishing wife beating with the whip. English newspapers and magazine articles throughout the decade carried dozens of stories of family murders and extremely cruel assaults by husbands on their wives. In 1850 and 1851 John Stuart Mill and Harriet Taylor published a series of newspaper articles expressing shock at the prevalence of wife beating and pointing out the similarities between men who beat their wives and owners who cruelly treated their animals. In 1853 and 1856 Parliament considered legislation to punish wife assault with flogging.

American reformers were not as concerned about wife beating as their English counterparts, and the American public was unprepared to support English-style measures. The vital ingredients in making English reform— animal anticruelty laws, legislators and a public fearful of criminals—were missing in America. There is no reason to suspect that wife beating was more prevalent in England than in the United States; instead, the English were simply more interested in the issue. British politicians and advocates of temperance and women's rights focussed public attention on wife beating, as their colleagues were unable to do in America. It took about twenty-five years before American law-enforcement officials began to fear the labor unrest and social disruption that violent, brutal family assault might cause.

Just after the end of the Civil War, Victorian silence about the double standard gave way to public discussion of sexuality, prostitution, and abuse in marriage. The popular press fed its audience a steady diet of sensational divorces, scandalous courtroom trials, and crimes of passion. Stanton sought to expose the secrecy upon which traditional marriage rested. Between 1868 and 1870, Stanton and Anthony actively wrote, spoke, and demonstrated on behalf of women who were victims of violence or sexual exploitation. In these years they championed the cause of Hester Vaughn, a servant accused of infanticide, demanded the conviction of Albert McFarland, a wife beater who murdered his ex-wife's fiancé, and called for the death penalty for rape.[31] If anything, they appeared more willing to engage in controversial causes than they had been before the Civil War. They may have been encouraged by the more liberal atmosphere of this period; they may also have felt that it was time to make up for the absence of women's agitation during the War.

By the early 1870s, the climate of the country turned more conservative. The Comstock law, passed in 1873, banned dissemination through the mail of birth control information and pornography and helped to end the brief period of free discussion of such topics as rape and incest. Many liberal divorce laws dating from the antebellum period were removed from the statute books. In a sensational divorce scandal, the Beecher-Tilton affair, Stanton and Anthony were tarnished by their association with presumed adulterers and known advocates of free love. The scandal not only damaged their reputation, but also closed the door on revealing the darker side of marriage. Those who insisted on doing so were branded as obscene and as advocates of free love. In 1870, Stanton had delivered her standard lecture on "Marriage and Divorce," arguing that abuse of children and wives arose out of a man's ownership of a woman as his property. Five years later, Stanton still favored liberalized divorce and even denounced male domination in the family, but she did not mention the abuse of wives and children.

Although temperance women and conservative feminists in the late nineteenth century avoided advocating divorce for the drunkard's wife, they turned their attention to the use of the criminal law as a means of punishing the violent man. As might have been anticipated, a more conservative women's rights movement was able to achieve greater success than the more radical antebellum feminists in establishing programs of behalf of female victims of physical and sexual assault.

II

Reform of the
Criminal Law

4

Protecting
the Innocents

IN 1874 A SINGLE CASE of abuse and neglect of a little girl named Mary Ellen led to the founding of the first society in the world dedicated to protecting children from cruelty. Forty years later, there were 494 such anticruelty societies in the United States. Child protection became a national movement that swept aside the fear of outside intervention in the family. Publicity about Mary Ellen's plight stirred reformers to action, increased public awareness of child abuse, and helped alter the balance between the rights of parents and those of the state. Anticruelty societies were the largest and most successful reform against family violence yet undertaken.

The societies, which helped pass and enforce legislation concerning child cruelty, were special institutions devoted to the protection of children. Their founding initiated a new phase of reform against family violence. Writers on childrearing and temperance reformers had hoped appeals to conscience would end domestic violence; even some antebellum feminists concerned themselves only with freeing women from the constraints of civil law. The establishment of anticruelty societies represented an attempt to use the criminal as well as the civil law to punish abusers and remove abused and neglected children from parental custody.

After the failure of antebellum feminists to pass divorce legislation on grounds of cruelty, and the rather sporadic interest of temperance advocates in family violence, the sudden explosion of social concern about child cruelty appears to have been spontaneous in origin. The case of Mary Ellen ignited the public's interest, but fundamental social and political changes had prepared the way. Why did these societies finally emerge? Why did reformers against child cruelty succeed when antebellum feminists had failed? The humanitarian desire to protect children from cruelty was the main reason behind the founding of a society for the prevention of cruelty to children (SPCC). But a wealthy, urban elite was also fearful of social disorder and dismayed by the poverty, disease, and lawlessness of urban life. They blamed the immigrant, largely Catholic, poor and hoped to rescue their children from a life of pauperism, drink, and petty thievery. The Civil War had increased public consciousness about pain and suffering and ushered in more public acceptance of state intervention to protect minority rights and shore up domestic life.

The law enforcement rhetoric of the SPCCs was considerably stronger than their actions. They rarely prosecuted parents for child cruelty. There is thus a considerable confusion between the stated goal of the societies—the prevention of cruelty to children—and their actual work, which was primarily threatening and cajoling neglectful, often drunken parents and sometimes removing their children from them. Physical abuse of children served as the emotional subject that generated funds and popular support for a much larger range of child welfare activity. Measured against all previous attempts at family violence reform, the work of the anticruelty societies was distinctive in placing protection of children ahead of the goal of preserving the family. Still, in hoping to maintain proper parental authority in the family, the agents of these societies often sided with cruel parents at the expense of the child's safety.

Mary Ellen was born in New York City around 1864. Her parents hired a woman to look after her, but when the monthly payments ceased, her caretaker took her to the office of the Superintendent of Outdoor Poor. This New York City charity indentured Mary Ellen to a couple who were required to report once a year as to her welfare. The charity lost contact with Mary Ellen after its records were burned in a fire. Unbeknownst to them, they had placed the little girl with her natural father, Thomas McCormack, a butcher, and his wife, Mary. Mary McCormack consented to taking the girl, even though she knew Mary Ellen was her husband's illegitimate daughter. After Thomas McCormack died, Mary McCormack remarried a man named Connolly, and the three of them moved to a New York City tenement.

The Connolly's neighbors complained to Etta Wheeler, a charity worker and the wife of a journalist, about a little girl whose screams constantly pierced the thin walls of their apartment building. Few of them had actually seen the girl because she was locked in the apartment all day and not allowed to go outside except at night. Etta Wheeler persuaded Mrs. Connolly to permit her to enter the apartment. She found a malnourished, barefooted girl about nine or ten years old clad in a tattered calico dress and skirt clearly not warm enough for the bitter cold of the New York winter. On a table was a large whip with long leather strands. Mary Ellen's arms and legs bore many marks. Mrs. Wheeler did not want to intercede unless she could be assured of success. Fearful of making Mrs. Connolly suspicious, she took no action. But the abuse Mary Ellen suffered grew worse in the next several months.

After being told by several asylums in the city that they would care for Mary Ellen only if she could be removed from her parents, Wheeler applied to Henry Bergh of the American Society for the Prevention of Cruelty to Animals (ASPCA), an organization founded in New York City in 1868 to rescue helpless and abused animals from their cruel owners. Mrs. Wheeler appears to have believed that an agency charged with animal protection was capable of child rescue. Bergh, although interested in the case, was also concerned about whether his society had the legal right to take a child from the custody of her guardians. Nonetheless, he sent a detective to the family's apartment the next day, and within twenty-four hours, little Mary Ellen was removed from her home. She was brought into the courtroom weeping, her ragged clothes covered by a carriage blanket. Bergh explained that he was acting as a private citizen rather than as a representative of the ASPCA. He told the court that although this case did not fall under the rubric of animal protection, "the general laws of humanity" had been violated, and he feared that Mary Ellen would be beaten to death if she was returned to Mrs. Connolly. It has often been claimed that Mary Ellen was removed temporarily from Mrs. Connolly's apartment on the grounds she was a member of the animal kingdom, entitled to protection under animal anticruelty statutes. In fact, she was brought into court under an old English writ, *de homine replegando*, that allowed a magistrate to remove one person from the custody of another.[1]

Sobbing and tearful, Mary Ellen recounted the details of her life to a packed courtroom filled mainly with women. She had been beaten almost daily with a rawhide whip and less often with a long cane, although she never knew why she had been whipped. "Mamma," as she called Mrs. Connolly, had struck her with a pair of scissors, causing a deep and still unhealed gash from her left eyebrow down to her cheek. She was not allowed to play outside with any children; in fact, she was only permitted to leave the apartment after dark. At night she slept on a rug stretched on the floor underneath the window, her covering only a thin quilt. After about twenty minutes of deliberation, the jury found Mary Connolly guilty of felonious assault and sentenced her to the maximum penalty, one year at hard labor in the penitentiary. Little Mary Ellen was committed to an orphanage, the Sheltering Arms Children's

Home. Later she was placed with a farmer's family outside New York City, where she grew up. She married a farmer who lived near her adopted family.[2]

When Etta Wheeler was leaving the courthouse, she thanked Henry Bergh for the rescue of Mary Ellen. Could there not be a society for the prevention of cruelty to children, she asked, which would do for the abused child what anticruelty societies had done for mistreated animals? Bergh, taking Wheeler's hand, replied, "There shall be one."[3] The trial of Mrs. Connolly for assault and battery occurred in April 1874; in December of that year, the New York Society for the Prevention of Cruelty to Children (NYSPCC) was founded.

Elbridge Gerry, rather than Henry Bergh, seized the opportunity presented by this case to found a society to prevent cruelty to children. A grandson of one of the signers of the Declaration of Independence, Gerry was born into a wealthy New York City family. After graduating from Columbia College at twenty, he studied law, becoming financially successful from his private practice and from investments in New York City real estate and Rhode Island banks. But he had tired of legal work on behalf of corporations and wealthy individuals, and at age thirty-three he became Bergh's counsel for the ASPCA. He helped achieve passage of several laws for the prevention of cruelty to animals transported by rail. He served as counsel of the NYSPCC from its founding until 1879 and then became its president, a position he held for twenty-two years until he retired. Reflecting his importance to the agency, the NYSPCC was popularly known as the Gerry Society.

After Mrs. Connolly was convicted of assault, Gerry recognized that, while there were several children's asylums and refuges, no organization existed to rescue children from an abusive home. He could not find anyone interested in founding such a society until he met John Wright, who was a living embodiment of the Quaker virtues of business success and humanitarianism. Born into a family whose wealth had come from shipping, he had enlarged his fortune as a leather importer and dealer. After retiring from business when he was fifty-nine, Wright devoted himself to the Society of Friends, of which he was an active member. Fond of children and concerned about the poor, he liked to pass out candy and tell stories to the orphans at the Home for Friendless Children in New York City. At seventy-five, he announced to his children that he considered it his "religious duty to found a society for the prevention of cruelty to the little ones." John Wright became the first president of the NYSPCC and held the post up to his death. Almost daily he appeared at the office of the NYSPCC.[4]

Together Wright and Gerry recruited the board of directors and the nine vice presidents of the Society. Wright's son was appointed, and, in addition to Henry Bergh, three other directors of the NYSPCC had also served on the board of the ASPCA. The board was a reflection of the privileged, upper strata of society—its members were white, male, Protestant, and well-to-do. A few of the younger men on the board had known Gerry from undergraduate days at Columbia. Among the vice presidents of the Society was Peter Cooper, who had amassed a fortune in the manufacture of glue and iron and made an even larger one through his acquisition of the Baltimore and Ohio Railroad. A major New York City philanthropist, he founded an institute for adult education, Cooper Union, which bore his name. The only non-Protestant on the board was August Belmont, a German-Jewish banker who handled the U.S. operations of the Rothschilds and was active in the Democratic Party. Besides Belmont, another vice president of the NYSPCC was Robert Stuart, who after selling his sugar refinery, devoted himself to serving on the boards of such institutions as Princeton University and the Presbyterian Hospital. John Wright recruited Cornelius Vanderbilt as another vice president of the Society. One of the wealthiest men of the Gilded Age, Vanderbilt had parlayed a small fortune in steamboats into a gigantic one in railroads, and he created the New York Central system that dominated railroad transportation between New York and Chicago. When asked by Wright to become involved in the Society, Vanderbilt replied, "John, I haven't got the time to go into this thing myself, but I'll give you all the money you want."[5] Vanderbilt gave liberally to the Society before his death two years after its founding. It is possible that Vanderbilt's attitude was typical of some other directors, who not only had their industrial empires to oversee but served on boards of numerous organizations.

The presence on the NYSPCCs board of directors of some of the richest men in the nation reassured the public and state officials about the conservative nature of anticruelty work. The vast fortunes of these men helped the NYSPCC establish an endowment that provided a steady annual income and financial security. Not only wealthy men could establish new institutions; in cities such as Boston, women helped found child protection societies and held fairs to raise funds for their operation. But it was probably crucial that the first anticruelty society recruited for its board of directors titans of industry and finance.

Why did these millionaires establish a society to prevent cruelty to children? How did child cruelty become a social issue when there had been little public clamor about it? A number of interpretations have been advanced to explain the origins of children's anticruelty societies. Some trace the growth of the societies to the increasing prominence of philanthropic work after the Civil War. Others consider the organizations a social response by the middle class to the problems of industrialization, urban growth, poverty, and crime. In this view, the middle class reacted to dramatic social changes by trying to refashion the family life of the poor.[6] But it was actually the upper rather than the middle class that founded the NYSPCC.

Other scholars believe anticruelty societies grew out of a steady increase in humanitarianism, especially a recognition of childhood as a separate and protected stage of life. Yet the view of children as angelic, innocent creatures had appeared as early as the eighteenth century. Some detect a new interest in children's rights during Reconstruction, a period when freedmen were granted their constitutional rights of citizenship and suffrage.[7] However, the anticruelty societies contributed to the growing recognition of children's rights, rather than vice versa. Although the idea of child protection gradually developed in the first half of the nineteenth century, the earliest appearance of the phrase "the rights of children" in anticruelty literature did not appear until eight years after the founding of the NYSPCC. In 1882 the first annual report of the Massachusetts Society for the Prevention of Cruelty to Children (MSPCC) stated that it hoped to further "just ideas of the rights of children and duties of guardians."[8] A few English reformers in the 1880s began to formulate a children's charter, in which they held out for children a right to decent food, clothing, and affection—the right to "an endurable life."[9] Aided in part by the formation of anticruelty societies, the literature on children's rights expanded greatly from the 1890s to the 1920s. Oddly enough, however, as the rhetoric about children's rights intensified, the attention devoted to child cruelty faded.

If child rescue was not a movement for children's rights, what was it? Scholars seem divided between those who emphasize the humanitarianism of reformers and those who point to the desire for social control over the lower classes. Both motives could be detected in the rhetoric of the SPCC founders and the actual operation of their societies. Yet even this combination of motives does not completely explain all the factors that led to the establishment of the world's first SPCC in 1874. Ministers, judges, and other public officials had been concerned about child cruelty as early as the Puritans; fears of illiterate, unruly immigrants had stirred reformers since at least the middle of the nineteenth century; the new maternal style of childrearing was prominent from the 1830s. Thus many of the social changes that prepared the way for the anticruelty societies had been present for decades.

The necessary institutional developments upon which SPCC work depended were established by the 1830s. For there to be child rescue, there had to be a children's home to which the rescued child could be committed. New York City's house of refuge became the first of its kind in the nation when it opened in 1825. Boston and Philadelphia soon followed. Houses of refuge, places of incarceration for youthful petty criminals, often took in neglected children. New York state alone had twenty-seven public and private child-care institutions by 1850.[10] In other cities, homeless minors were committed to almshouses. Many children's institutions, even those that were publicly supported, had a Protestant religious character. Catholics often feared that children of their faith committed to these institutions would be converted. As a result, Catholics constructed their own orphanages and asylums. Thus, Catholic as well as Protestant children's institutions were in operation before the Civil War.

Local authorities had the power to remove abused children from parental guardianship. In fact, the state had long possessed the legal right to act against parents on behalf of minor children. This right derived from the medieval English doctrine of *parens patriae* ("parent of the nation"), which permitted the crown, through Chancery court proceedings, to intervene on behalf of a child whose welfare was threatened. After the consolidation of the king's power in the thirteenth century, the English monarch was declared the guardian of the person and property of idiots and lunatics, according to the principle that the king was bound to protect the interest of those subjects who were incapable of caring for themselves. The doctrine was generally applied to preserve the estates or further the education of wealthy children, or protect adolescents from improper marriages.[11]

In nineteenth-century America *parens patriae* was broadened to sanction removal of children from homes of drunken or neglectful parents. The state possessed not only common-law justification for intervention in the family, but also statutory grounds for doing so. Many of the colonies had enacted legislation providing apprenticeship for neglected or poverty-stricken children. In the first decades of the nineteenth century, a few states passed laws to bind out or commit to an almshouse children of beggars or youths found begging on the streets. Several state statutes called for the apprenticeship of a girl or boy whose parents were unwilling to provide support, or for the child who was not being educated or was "living in idleness." Other antebellum laws added abandonment of the child or immorality of the mother as justification for terminating parental guardianship. In theory, instances of abuse could be prosecuted as neglect, but in practice, they were not. Intervention against parents on behalf of an abused child was more controversial than removing a neglected child from home. Depriving a child of food or a place to live was unconscionable; abuse could always be justified as necessary punishment for disobedience. Even though abusive parents could be charged with assault and battery, few of them were.

The general concern about the suffering of children in the antebellum era was simply outweighed by the belief in the privacy of the family. Unlike parental criminality and drunkenness, which were regarded as reasonable grounds for removal of a child, physical cruelty to a child was not considered a special category of maltreatment requiring state action. The image of policemen dragging children from their homes inspired fear. In 1875, critics voiced fears that the newly formed NYSPCC would "take children away from their parents." The New York *Sun* opposed legislation that would give the NYSPCC the power to remove children from their parents and commit them to institutions. After all, they knew of "more babies in New York who are about to be spanked too hard than there are animals that are cruelly treated. . . . Would Mr. Bergh confiscate all these babies. . . . Where would he take them?"[12]

Like antebellum feminists, the NYSPCC was perceived to be trampling on the privacy of the family. Yet the anticruelty societies were able to overcome these anxieties, while antebellum feminists had not. Instead of attacking the institution of the family, Bergh and Gerry reassured the public about their commitment to traditional values and sincerely believed in the efficacy of corporal punishment. At the founding meeting of the NYSPCC, Henry Bergh made clear that he advocated "a good wholesome flogging for disobedient children," although he favored the protection of children from "undue parental severity."[13] Bergh argued that parents (and the authorized representatives of the state) possessed the right to beat a child, so long as it was done for the proper reasons and in a moderate manner. He and other directors of the NYSPCC rarely spoke about the nature of the family, but instead dwelled on the importance of rescuing children from a future life of crime, a strategy that English reformers in the 1850s had found successful. Moreover, the leaders of SPCCs did not regard child cruelty as a family problem, but as an instance of exploitation and faulty moral character that occurred in public as well as in the home.

The perennial difficulty for reformers against child abuse lies in drawing the line between legitimate corporal punishment and child cruelty. Although most people favor the former but abhor the latter, few agree as to the difference between the two. The NYSPCC succeeded because of the elite social standing of its founders, their desire to avoid controversy, and the public's willingness to embrace a more humanitarian definition of child cruelty.

Greater judicial interest in child cruelty began to appear about the time of the Civil War. Before then, only two state appellate courts had ruled in child cruelty cases, one advancing a liberal, the other a conservative, legal definition of child cruelty. In *Johnson* v. *State* (1840) a Tennessee appellate court held that any punishment that exceeded the bounds of moderation was cruel. In *Pendergrass* v. *the State of North Carolina* (1838) the North Carolina appellate court decided that child cruelty was limited to those acts that endangered life, limbs, health, or caused disfigurement or permanent injury. Between 1862 and 1874, nine state appellate courts ruled in cases of child cruelty.[14] In several different decisions, North Carolina appellate courts reaffirmed the standard that child cruelty constituted only those acts that threatened a child's life or limbs.[15] Other state appellate courts, however, defined child cruelty as those actions that exceeded moderate standards of correction, irrespective of whether the parent had caused bruises, marks, or burns, or had threatened the child's life. The Illinois Supreme Court in 1868, in an opinion that mirrored most judicial sentiments of the time, held that parental authority must be exercised "within the bounds of reason and humanity," in the case of a stepfather and stepmother who had kept their blind son in an unheated and damp cellar for several days during the middle of winter. To rid his stepson's body of the vermin covering it, the father had poured kerosene over the boy and lit a match to the boy's clothes. The boy fled. Town officials took him in and indicted his parents for unjust imprisonment. Although this youth must have sustained severe burns, the degree of his injuries was never mentioned in the indictment. In rejecting the view that only life-threatening actions constituted child cruelty, the Illinois Supreme Court stated that it was "monstrous to hold that under the pretense of sustaining parental authority, children must be left, without the protection of the law, at the mercy of depraved men or women, with liberty to inflict any species of barbarity short of the actual taking of life."[16] Still, state appellate courts differed as to what acts, injuries, or evil intentions went beyond moderation. In a Pennsylvania case in 1867, cruelty depended on "the mode and severity of punishment," "the nature of the offence [and], the age, size and apparent powers of endurance of the child." A Texas court, however, ruled that judges had to take into account the "age, sex, condition and disposition of the child and attending circumstances."[17]

Historian James Turner has shown that the moral revulsion against physical suffering was one of the central ideas of the animal protection movement in the latter half of the nineteenth century. Turner points out that in earlier times, individuals endured pain as a personal misfortune, an act of God, and a punishment for sin. Because the next life would bring everlasting joy, agony in this one was seen as a temporary annoyance to be stoically endured. Scientific advances brought the ability to control pain; no longer was pain viewed as part of divine retribution.[18] John Locke had argued that the sensation of pain was necessary in the discipline of young children because they were incapable of reason. Most antebellum childrearing writers agreed with him and worried not about children who endured bodily anguish, but about parents who were reluctant to inflict whippings when they proved necessary.

But by the 1870s child protection advocates had come to insist that children possessed "a far greater capacity for suffering" than animals.[19] Advice to parents in that decade warned of the dangers of corporal punishment. The new attitude was evident by the change of heart in the writings of Congregationalist minister, educator, and writer, Jacob Abbott. He was the author of 180 books, most of them stories for children, including his famous "Rollo" series. Abbott was by far the most widely read author of childrearing literature of his day. In his article on "Punishments" written in 1841, Abbott justified whipping, if administered in a mild manner, as an acceptable, even a preferable form of child discipline. However, his *Gentle Measures in the Training of the Young*, published in 1871, represented an abrupt departure from his previous view. If the mother applied proper discipline, he now believed that the rod could be laid aside. In rejecting corporal punishment, he announced to his readers that whipping was an act of violence, exciting pain and terror in the child. Whipping, he noted, caused "bodily suffering" shocked the child's nervous system, and if done often enough, could cause brain damage. Abbott even suggested that the biblical admonition not to "spare the rod" was intended only as a statement about the importance of some form of discipline, not necessarily physical. Abbott's *Gentle Measures* may not have had any bearing on public outrage at the case of Mary Ellen three years later. But he had circumscribed the definition of acceptable corporal punishment, and thus helped to widen the distance between discipline and abuse.

There was some similarity between the 1870s, a period of reform against family violence, and the 1640s. In both decades, government passed laws to guarantee the freedom of dependent groups—women and children in the *Body of Liberties* of 1641, and ex-slaves through the passage of constitutional amendments in 1865, 1868, and 1870. However, unlike the colonial period, Reconstruction era reform grew out of rising social dependency and disorder.

The industries in major American cities attracted some of those left destitute by the Civil War. New York City was inundated by crippled veterans, widows, and orphans. European immigration resumed in large numbers after the war ended, and the immigrants found jobs in sweatshops or as menial laborers. Many, however, were forced to beg or steal. It is significant that the first anticruelty society in the world originated in the nation's largest metropolis, where the highest concentration of wealth and philanthropic zeal was combined with the greatest visibility of poverty and crime.

The incidence of violent crimes increases after all major wars, and the Civil War was no exception. Almost as soon as the Union and the Confederacy signed a treaty of peace, violent urban crime began to get out of hand. Arrests for assault and rape in major cities skyrocketed. The American home was not isolated from the violence swirling outside it, at least according to the limited statistics available. The family homicide rate in Philadelphia between 1867 and 1874 was 2.5 per 100,000, almost double that for the previous seven years, and higher still than in the antebellum period. After 1874, the domestic murder rate continued to rise, reaching a peak of 4.1 per 100,000 from 1874 to 1880 before declining. (The general trend in family homicide is presented more fully in Appendix B.) Newspapers and crime gazettes that carried lurid stories of crimes of passion and ax murders sensationalized a national crime wave of major proportions. Some of the public called for drastic measures, and many wanted to prevent children of immigrants from becoming violent criminals. [20]

More favorable attitudes toward government intervention were coupled with a belief that the family was facing a major crisis. Some women were demanding the right to vote, others were openly securing abortions, and children were becoming unruly and criminally inclined. As in colonial times, the state was expected to strengthen the American family and preserve morality. In many domains of sexuality and family life, once considered private and sealed off from public view, outside agencies now claimed the right, the duty, even the sacred obligation to intercede. [21]

As in Puritan Massachusetts, the common law of domestic relations gave way to new legislation. Parents were seen as exercising authority delegated by the state. Only so long as parents fulfilled their responsibilities were they permitted to govern their children. If they failed to do so, the state had the duty to safeguard the child's interests. Some antebellum judges had made a case for limited intervention, arguing only for the state's right to commit neglected children to reform schools. After the Civil War the state broadened its powers of intervention to include child cruelty.

In England and America, animal protection preceded child protection not because the public was more concerned about animals than children, but because child rescue involved interference in the fundamental unit of the family. Yet SPCCs borrowed the quasi-police style that animal anticruelty societies had developed. Several of the founders of the NYSPCC had belonged to the ASPCA, but they chose to establish a new organization rather than broaden the functions of the ASPCA. For example, Bergh remained as vice president of the NYSPCC until his death in 1888. He also permitted the Society to establish its offices in the ASPCA building. Yet Bergh does not appear to have suggested or even favored the idea of combining the two. He may have felt that an organization had to have a single priority.

Societies devoted exclusively to child protection were established in the urban centers of Boston and Philadelphia and in small towns such as Keene, New Hampshire, and Bangor, Maine. The early SPCCs were founded in a large band of cities across New York state. The movement spread to the Mid-Atlantic region and the Midwest. There were few societies established in the Pacific Northwest, the Rocky Mountain states, or the South. Child rescue in these regions remained a haphazard and largely informal matter, mostly handled by the police. The regional concentration of the anticruelty societies was quite typical of the geography of American social reform at this time.

Child protective work was separate from animal protection in most Eastern cities, where interest in both causes was strong. Elsewhere the two were often combined so as to conserve scarce resources. A "humane society" handled animal and child protection; the first one was founded in Cleveland in 1876. In the 1880s, as the reform impulse began to wane, most of the new organizations formed—many in Midwestern cities—were humane societies. By 1906, there were 240 of them but only sixty-one devoted exclusively to child rescue.

As the newer and less well-endowed branch of the movement, child anti-cruelty reformers sought to preserve their affiliation with animal protection. They initially met with indifference, as in their efforts to join the American Humane Association, a national organization of animal rescue leagues established in 1877. Two years later, a representative of the San Francisco SPCA proposed a resolution to add child protection to the activities of the AHA. His motion was defeated. It took eight more years of lobbying and the concerted efforts of Elbridge Gerry to include child protective work under the rubric of humane activity.[22] Even then protection of animals still remained the main priority of the association. Articles to promote kindness to animals filled the pages of the association's *Humane Review*, alongside only an occasional and very brief report about efforts on behalf of children.

Despite the problems in allying child with animal protection, Gerry copied directly the model of protective work he had developed at the ASPCA. The basic idea was to establish a privately chartered corporation to enforce specially enacted state laws. The society would arrest and prosecute abusive parents or guardians and take legal action if necessary to remove children from their custody. The agents would also work closely with the police. Although Gerry recognized the need for preventing cruelty to children, his organization was only equipped to punish child cruelty after it occurred. Modern ideas of prevention or rehabilitation were noticeably absent. Gerry and the other founders made a deliberate decision that the NYSPCC should remain a law enforcement agency, rather than a child welfare organization. As a practicing lawyer, Gerry emphasized the criminal work of his agency. "Our societies for the prevention of cruelty to children," he liked to insist, "were instituted for the express purpose, and for none other, of applying the arm of the law to the protection of the helpless."[23] The aim of the NYSPCC, he stated, was "to aid suffering childhood, through the law, by the law, and under the law. It is the hand of the law, the fingers of which trace charges of injury to children and fasten the grasp of the law upon the offender."[24] Several Eastern state legislatures granted societies in their state the power to arrest anyone found violating statutes regarding children, or obstructing or interfering with the work of the society's agents. The police were required to aid agents in bringing offenders to court for a hearing. Magistrates were granted the power to issue a warrant so that agents of the society could enter the homes of suspected abusers. By 1880 police court judges in New York called upon the NYSPCC to investigate cases and report to them. The society was also made the collector of child-support payments. In addition, it conducted criminal investigations for state boards of charities to determine if a child was completely destitute and therefore qualified to enter a state institution.

The agents of anticruelty societies were men of working-class or lower-class backgrounds, with no special training in child welfare work. Most of them had previously been employed as policemen, salesmen, or firemen. The vast bulk of the cases handled by the early anticruelty societies involved working-class or poverty-stricken immigrant families.[25] In Philadelphia most complaints concerned Irish and German families; in Chicago, the Irish and Poles; in Boston, Irish and Italians.

Many of the generalizations about the work of the anticruelty societies are based on reading the annual reports of the agencies and the speeches of men such as Gerry; the case records of the agencies describe the actual manner of handling complaints and the problems brought to the SPCCs. I examined the cases that concerned child and wife abuse and incest in the records of two major urban societies: the Pennsylvania Society to Protect Children from Cruelty (PSPCC) of Philadelphia from 1878 to 1893, and the Illinois Humane Society of Chicago every tenth year from 1880 up to 1940. These came to 1292 cases of the PSPCC and more than 1200 for the Illinois Humane Society. Those who committed physical abuse of children described in these case records were parents, grown siblings, aunts and uncles, adoptive parents, stepparents, and grandparents. Nearly as many women as men were abusers. In the Philadelphia society's case records for the late nineteenth century, 46 percent of the assailants of children were men acting alone, 35 percent were women acting alone, and the rest were men and women acting in concert. The percentages in the Illinois Humane Society case records were similar. Girls were as often the victims of physical abuse as boys. About a third of those who committed physical abuse used some kind of instrument, such as a strap, rope, horsewhip, rattan, or sometimes even a hot poker. Women were no more reluctant than men to inflict cruelty with one of these instruments. In almost all cases, the victims of sexual abuse were girls, and their assailants were mainly their fathers and stepfathers, and upon occasion, an uncle, older brother, or male boarder. As compared with the circumstances described in these records, the case of Mary Ellen was an extreme instance of abuse and neglect, not the typical kind of complaint these agencies received.

An agent of the society had the power to investigate cases and take action. He could choose to do nothing, issue a warning, arrest the adults, and/or remove abused and neglected children from their parents. The agency did not provide supervision of families where no legal proceeding was justified, nor did they make available any social services for families. They seemed willing to overlook deliberate cruelty in parents who were otherwise temperate and industrious. Agents urged fathers to be good providers, and mothers to be homemakers, not income-earners. The poor were divided into the worthy and the depraved, and "intemperate and abusive" language was almost as serious an offense as physical cruelty.[26]

The day-to-day work of the agents was quite mundane. Neighbors, relatives, and sometimes the victimized child appeared at the office of the society, described the nature of the abuse, and furnished a list of witnesses. Incest victims often complained on their own behalf.[27] In Boston, where the records of the MSPCC were quite detailed, 60 percent of the complaints of known origin from 1880 to 1930 were brought by family members, mainly women and children. Victims and mothers distressed that they were unable to feed and care for their children requested assistance.[28] Some complaints came from letters sent anonymously. Upon receiving a complaint, an officer, identified by the badge of the society adorning his jacket lapel, was dispatched. He generally turned to neighbors first before visiting the family to interview the alleged assailant and victim. He also visited the employer of the abuser, especially in cases in which the man was known to be an alcoholic. The agent sometimes made several visits before deciding if any action was required. Occasionally he may have found that there was no such address as the one provided in a postcard or learned that the family against whom a complaint had been made had moved to a unknown destination. He had to determine if accusations were "spite work," acts of revenge perpetrated by quarrelsome neighbors, or efforts to ensnare the agency in a family feud.

At the society's office, the agent filed his report. In the late nineteenth century this document was rarely more than a paragraph in length, consisting of a description of the family, the child's condition, and statements by the neighbors. Only a few case records were more substantial. The other noticeable feature of these records was the frequent reappearance of a few of the same families. One year a drunken father was failing to provide for his wife and children, the next the oldest daughter had run away from home and was believed to have entered a house of prostitution, and the year after that, the younger son was truant from school, caught stealing, and his parents sought assistance in committing him to the house of refuge.

Although the majority of the public assumed that child protection work meant shielding children from extreme physical cruelty, the societies had in mind a much broader view of their function. They used the word "cruelty" in a specific sense to refer to physical abuse and more generally to include many forms of neglect, mistreatment, and exploitation. The annual report of the Brooklyn Society for the Prevention of Cruelty to Children, published in 1884, defined cruelty as:

(a) All treatment or conduct by which physical pain is wrongfully, need-lessly, or excessively inflicted, or

(b) by which life or limb or health is wrongfully endangered or sacrificed or

(c) neglect to provide such reasonable food, clothing, shelter, protection, and care as the life and well-being of the child require;

(d) the exposure of children during unreasonable hours of inclement weather, as peddlers or hawkers, or otherwise;

(e) their employment in unwholesome. degrading, unlawful, or immoral callings;

(f) or any employment by which the powers of children are overtaxed or their hours of labor unreasonably prolonged; and

(g) the employment of children as mendicants, or the failure to restrain them from vagrancy or begging. [29]

The Brooklyn society's definition of cruelty could be found in cruelty statutes in many states and in England. The exact language in these statutes varied, but always included physical abuse as only one form of child cruelty. The societies were aware that of the variety of concerns they held, the one that most deeply shocked the public was extreme physical cruelty toward children. The annual report of the Massachusetts Society to Protect Children from Cruelty in 1885 admitted that "the prominence of the word cruelty in our title carries the impression that protection from blows and other forms of torture is the main purpose of our work." They acknowledged that the greater part of their work was "to relieve children from various forms of suffering, by neglect of food and clothing and exposure to examples of intemperance, dishonesty, falsehood, and vice." The societies used the issue of child cruelty as a means of gaining public acceptance for their entire range of activities. Recognizing that the public was more willing to contribute to their organization because of a shocking case of physical torture than because of hundreds of reports of neglect and malnutrition, the MSPCC looked forward to the day when "it would be easier to excite and maintain a public interest and a more generous support for cases other than physical cruelty."[30]

In fact, cases of physical cruelty constituted only a small part of the case load of the societies. Because of the consistently high quality of its annual reports, one can determine the exact percentage of physical abuse cases handled by the Pennsylvania Society to Protect Children from Cruelty. During the first decade of its work, reports of cruelty fluctuated between 6 and 13 percent of the total cases. From 1878 until 1935, when this information was no longer collected, 12 percent of the PSPCCs cases concerned child cruelty.[31] The agents of the PSPCC and other societies were limited by the willingness of those involved to come forward. Complainants were generally women neighbors and relatives of the victims, who preferred to alert the agencies rather than act directly or persuade their male relatives to intercede. They were less willing to notify agencies about physical cruelty than about parental drunkenness. To be sure, the inebriated father or mother was often a child beater. The majority of drunkenness cases the societies handled, however, noted no physical violence in the family.

Agents had some discretion in deciding what actions to take. They, like most parents, believed in the necessity of corporal punishment. Thus, when an anticruelty society received a complaint, its agents often reassured parents of their duty to correct children, so long as the punishment was administered in "a proper manner" and intended "for the good of the child." Among infractions thought to deserve corporal punishment, even if a whip or strap was used, were running away from home or school, stealing, telling lies, acting insolent, beating up a sibling or a friend, or going swimming on Sundays and staying away from home all day.

The annual reports of the NYSPCC from 1887 to 1913 describe the number of cases they prosecuted.[32] The NYSPCC was the one large urban agency to record these figures each year. Under Gerry's firm command about a third of all children's cases in the last decades of the nineteenth century resulted in criminal trials of abusive or neglectful parents and guardians. Even after he retired, the rate of prosecution increased. Between 1900 and 1913, three out of seven cases were taken before a criminal court judge. After 1913, however, the rate of prosecution began to fall off.

When the anticruelty society with the greatest reputation for prosecution was taking only a third of "cruellists" to criminal court, what did most of its work consist of? No action was taken in cases of "spite work." Nothing was done when the parties were perceived as equally guilty, an incident was believed to be insignificant, or the victim was regarded as having deserved to be beaten. Agents were called to investigate wife beating as well as child abuse. They were convinced that drunken, slothful, or adulterous wives provoked beatings. In some cases of wife beating, agents tried to reconcile the couple, and in others, they referred the wife to the police, a divorce lawyer, or a women's protective agency that handled legal cases for the poor. [33] In some cases, agents formally warned a father that "on account of no marks, we could not prosecute him for cruelty to his son."[34] But in other similar cases, they did not prosecute or even issue a warning. Abused children sometimes told the agents they deserved to be whipped. Agents tried to uphold parental authority when confronted with unruly, disobedient children. They sided with husbands against provocative or drunken wives, and relied on threats and warnings to keep the peace.

The societies did sometimes remove children from their parents and place them in the custody of others. The PSPCC was the one agency to publish a yearly record of such removals. In the late nineteenth century, three out of every ten children's cases led to the placement of the child outside the home. Few of these children were abused. Most were neglected; some were "stubborn children." Parents often asked the society to place an "incorrigible" child in an institution. When children were removed from home, they were generally placed in children's institutions, such as orphanages or reform schools. Sometimes these placements were only temporary; many children were later returned home. Others were sent to foster care or hired out to work as a servant, laborer, or an apprentice with a family. [35]

In sum, most of the work of anticruelty societies consisted not in the rescue of physically abused children but in the investigation of complaints against drunken and neglectful parents. In enforcing a variety of laws concerning children, the child cruelty societies operated in a manner similar to the police—they carried a big stick, but rarely used it. Sometimes, children were the innocent parties, other times, the guilty ones. Like the police, the societies tried to maintain order by prodding and cajoling potentially dangerous, drunken, or disreputable characters. Most that were arrested paid their fines and went home. Only a few offenders were sent to prison to serve a long sentence. The anticruelty societies intervened primarily in immigrant poor and working-class homes. The occasional investigation of a middle-class family was handled more gently, because such households were better able to maintain a facade of respectability.

Had the founders of the anticruelty societies accomplished their objectives? The purpose of the societies was to deter others from treating children cruelly, to rescue abused and neglected children, and prevent children from growing up to become criminals. At a more pragmatic level, the societies sought to induce fear of "the Cruelty" among the lower orders and the immigrant poor. They were not equipped to handle the kind of extensive policing that would have been required had they tried to arrest even a fraction of parental "cruellists." With those considerations in mind, their strategy was to appear at opportune moments in a threatening manner and on occasion, take highly punitive actions as a means of deterring others. The SPCCs decided upon a realistic strategy; still, it is doubtful that much abuse was actually prevented in this manner.

Different types of reform campaigns against family violence continued through the 1890s, and their achievements, failures, and reasons for being will be chronicled in the next two chapters. The record of the anticruelty societies ends here at the high point of their concern about child cruelty. The story of their declining interest in family violence deserves brief mention, if only as another example of the retreat from reform that inevitably follows a period of advance. The founders of the anticruelty societies created a new awareness about physical cruelty to children, which they translated into action. The aggressive fund-raising and expansive aims of many anticruelty societies in the 1920s contributed to a major growth in personnel and programs. During the Great Depression the budgets of the agencies were drastically cut, however, and never recovered after that. Since the problem of child abuse was considered the preserve of the anticruelty societies, it is difficult to separate the fate of the societies from the fate of the issue. The public assumed the purpose of the societies was to protect children from physical abuse. Although the budgets and the staffs of these societies mushroomed, the societies were no longer interested in child abuse after about 1890.

Around that time many of the societies came under the influence of modern methods of social casework and hired professionally trained staff. Social workers hoped to prevent the recurrence of conditions that made intervention in families necessary. Some of the most influential leaders of the anticruelty societies in the twentieth century, believing that curing social ills would eliminate abuse, lobbied for the juvenile court, mothers' pensions, laws protecting illegitimate children and child laborers, and segregating the feeble-minded. With the plight of the poor alleviated, child cruelty would become an issue of the past.

The forward-thinking directors of the anticruelty societies wanted to separate child cruelty work from its association with animal protection. The prosecutorial methods of the late nineteenth-century societies conflicted with the interest of the modern agencies in rehabilitation and treatment. The staff of the modern anticruelty societies wanted to think of themselves not as police but as social workers. The head of the Boston SPCC stated "there are limits to the work of prosecuting, there is a point where no improvement can be made except in the number of children reached," whereas they believed that in child welfare work, "the opportunities of development are as infinite as nature itself."[36] An expanded domain of child welfare work also carried with it the practical benefits of being able to hire more agents, open new local bureaus, and develop new programs.

The heads of the societies believed they could expand their original mission because they had already succeeded in eliminating child cruelty. The first statements of this kind appeared as early as the 1880s, but began to recur with more frequency in the twentieth century. As early as 1883 the Massachusetts Society to Prevent Cruelty to Children was "led to report a lessening of the number of cases of extreme cruelty by blows and other methods of physical torture." They attributed the decline to the "wholesome fear of the knowledge of the law and knowledge of its probable enforcement."[37] In 1907 the MSPCC reported that they were gratified "to see . . . a considerable decrease in brutality in its various forms."[38] In 1927 the agency's annual report noted that physical cruelty had decreased even more. The reason "is undoubtedly due in good measure to the lessons taught parents and others by this and other child protection agencies everywhere."[39] The White House Conference on Children, which met each decade since 1909 to recommend changes in national child welfare policy, in 1933 endorsed the view that "the grosser forms of physical cruelty are not so prevalent as they were a few decades ago."[40] The SPCCs' statements implied they were responsible for the decline in child abuse. A few of the societies with substantial endowments simply shifted their interest from child abuse to neglect. Among most anticruelty societies the lack of interest in child cruelty contributed to the demise of the organizations. An incomplete understanding of family violence gave rise to a false sense of optimism that the problem had been solved.

5

The Pure Woman and
the Brutish Man

BEFORE THE NYSPCC WAS FOUNDED in 1874, there was as much or even more social concern about wife abuse as there was about child cruelty. To antebellum feminists, the drunkard's wife, rather than his child, was considered the major victim of family violence. By 1860, two states had passed laws to prohibit wife beating, but no state had enacted laws making child cruelty a crime. After the formation of the child protection societies, however, the efforts to protect wives from cruelty paled in comparison to those on behalf of children. There was only one society in the United States, established in 1885, to prevent cruelty to wives.

Why was there no movement to protect wives from cruelty? Certainly women reformers faced greater obstacles than advocates of child protection. Women's organizations, funded by women, could never expect to match the endowments of the anticruelty societies, some of which had the backing of the America's wealthiest men. Of course, child protection reformers also had to counter the charge that they were invading the privacy of the family. But taking children away from their parents was never as controversial as encouraging abused women to secure divorces. Because the child was viewed as helpless, innocent, and defenseless, terminating parental rights was looked upon as more justifiable than encouraging women to secure a divorce. A woman was expected to sacrifice her personal happiness for the sake of her children.

Even though in the post-Civil War period there was less interest in cruelty to wives than children, the two decades after 1870 represented a high point of feminist interest in "crimes against women" not again attained until the

1970s. In contrast with the antebellum women's campaign that failed in its single effort on behalf of drunkards' wives, women reformers after the Civil War enjoyed far greater success in passing legislation and founding new institutions to aid women victims. In the 1840s and 1850s, the temperance cause attacked the subordinate status of women only indirectly. After the Civil War, the woman's movement forthrightly challenged male dominance. Female organizations grew larger, more powerful, and enjoyed some success promoting a more equitable standard of sexual morality.

Why was there so much more interest in crimes against women in the 1870s? The Civil War had led to more public acceptance of state intervention in the family. Both government and private organizations broadened their concept of social affairs that fell under their legitimate control. In the post-Civil War era public fear of the violent and dangerous classes increased. Thus, the social milieu that promoted the formation of the anticruelty societies was also conducive to women's reform regarding cruelty. The campaign to protect abused women focused as much on appeals to morality as on efforts to pass laws and develop new institutions.

Women activists concerned about family violence were often involved in other movements—temperance, women's suffrage, and most of all, the campaign to promote and maintain "social purity." As much a moral crusade as an effort to pass legislation, social purity attracted suffragists, such as Elizabeth Cady Stanton and Susan B. Anthony, and temperance advocates, such as Frances Willard of the Woman's Christian Temperance Union (WCTU). The campaign for social purity was unusually strong in both the United States and England and was associated with efforts to outlaw prostitution, and secondarily, with legislative initiatives to raise the age of consent, so that men who engaged in intercourse with girls under a certain minimum age could be charged with statutory rape. Advocates of social purity favored a number of other measures, ranging from sex education in the schools to prison reform. They estabished a network of municipal "vigilance" societies to stamp out prostitution and pornography and founded homes for "wayward girls."[1]

A large number of social purity reformers were Quakers or Unitarians; many were former abolitionists. Several leaders of the anticruelty movement were members of social purity organizations: Elbridge Gerry, for example, belonged to the largest social purity organization, the National Purity Alliance.

American social purity reform began when small groups of moral reformers sought to rescue prostitutes and reshape the sexual conduct of men. A handful of mostly female members of Protestant churches in New York City in the 1830s pledged themselves to exposing and uprooting male vice, going so far as to publish the names of men who frequented New York's most fashionable brothels. Female moral reform societies—fearless in their disregard for public disapproval—carried their message to local groups of women in many Eastern and Midwestern cities and villages. The emergence of female moral reform in the 1830s was one result of the dislocations of a burgeoning commercial economy and rapidly changing society.[2] The prostitute, bereft of family and friends, became a symbol of the powerlessness of women in new industrial order. Whereas male reformers had focused their condemnation on the cruel temptresses who corrupted innocent young men, female moral reformers placed the blame for prostitution on male sexual greed and tried to help the so-called fallen women. Although female reformers were primarily concerned with the rescue of prostitutes, they also tried to protect servant girls harassed by their employers and paid Bible-carrying visits to the homes of the poor.

The impetus for a second wave of moral reform, which began in the 1870s, came from opposition to governmental regulation of prostitution. By this time, several European cities permitted commercial sex in carefully circumscribed red-light districts. In the 1860s the English Parliament passed the Contagious Diseases Acts, providing for government registration of prostitutes in seaport towns frequented by the Royal Navy. Prostitutes were forced to submit to medical exams and confinement to a hospital if they were found to be carriers of venereal disease. A few American doctors and civil officials suggested trying this policy in the United States, provoking public outrage. Regulating prostitution, American opponents insisted, was a European invention designed to corrupt American morals; government involvement in prostitution was represented as the capitulation of the republic to the morality of Sodom and Gomorrah. In 1871 Elizabeth Cady Stanton and Susan B. Anthony helped defeat a bill in the New York state legislature to regulate prostitution.[3] Similar legislation in other cities and states also failed resoundingly.

Social purity reform always combined personal appeals with efforts to create pressure groups and pass new legislation. The reformers sought to abolish prostitution entirely. They also believed in converting males to the female sexual standard, theoretically higher and purer, so that prostitution and other forms of male vice would be completely eliminated. Most woman's rights advocates before the Civil War discussed female sexual subservience only in their private correspondence; now they spoke about it in public. Elizabeth Cady Stanton, in her speeches in favor of divorce, proclaimed that "false marriage" was nothing less than legalized prostitution. A few courageous free-love advocates, writers, and lecturers insisted that a loveless marriage and a union in which the husband forced his wife to submit to sex was an unsavory commercial transaction. Divorce was the sole remedy for such a marriage, they argued, freeing each partner to search for a compatible mate. Victoria Woodhull, an outspoken defender of free love, liked to claim that "the marriage law is the most damnable Social Evil Bill—the most consummate outrage on women—that was ever conceived. Those who are called prostitutes . . . are free women sexually, when compared to the poor wife. They are at liberty, at least to refuse; but she knows no such escape."[4]

Feminist thinkers and social purity reformers attacked the belief that a wife must submit to intercourse with her husband because it was her duty. Physical and sexual cruelty toward wives, they argued, arose from a husband's ownership of his wife's body. In referring to sexual abuses in marriage, women social purity writers had in mind not simply physical and sexual attack but also excessive sex, oral sex, disregard for a woman's pleasure, and intercourse when the husband was intoxicated or infected with venereal disease. (Anal sex appears to have been so taboo that it went unmentioned.) Revulsion against forced sex was partly a reflection of the antisexual attitude of the Victorian period, as well as a legitimate response to the physical vulnerability of women. In an age without reliable contraception, when frequent pregnancy endangered a woman's health, nothing was more crucial for a woman than the freedom to determine when and how often she wanted to conceive. Childbearing had always been dangerous for women. But the combination of the rhetoric of women's rights and Victorian outrage at male brutishness furnished middle-class women with their first opportunity to demand a sexual code that served their own needs. When a bride failed to restrain her husband's animal impulses, then the wedding night became "a night of rape and torture." Marital advice writers recounted tales of sexual assault among primitive tribes that bore an uncanny resemblance to the Victorian honeymoon. (Women missionaries pointed to the prevalence of wife beating and wife murder among Muslims as instances of the degradation of marriage in non-Christian countries.[5]) One groom married a week compelled his wife at knife point "to perform the office of 'sucker.'"[6]

Eliza Bisbee Duffey, the author of *The Relations Between the Sexes*, one of the most widely read marital advice books of its day, believed that a woman's right "to say no" was absolutely essential to female happiness in marriage. Although Duffey never used the term "marital rape," she described and decried the practice of a husband forcing his wife in sexual intercourse. She argued against the prevalent wedding-night custom that made the deflowering of a virgin bride into a traumatic event, during which the young husband firmly pinned down his bride and quickly completed his thrusts, ignoring his wife's cries of pain. Instead, she urged the groom to awaken the sexual interest in his bride, even if he had to wait the whole night or even a week. Any other mode of conduct constituted an abuse of marriage. Duffey counseled the young man to "practice in lawful wedlock the arts of the seducer, rather than the violence of the man who commits rape; and you will find the reward for your patience very sweet and lasting." She also recommended the frequency for marital intercourse as once a month.

Nineteenth-century women probably enjoyed sex much more than the marital advice writers thought they did. Peeping through the keyhole of the Victorian bedroom would also reveal husbands who were more clumsy than brutal, for whom the wedding night was less an evening of conquest than an unwelcome trial of their manhood. Even social purity writers were willing to admit that not every Victorian bridegroom was a lusty animal waiting to pounce, but they were less concerned about the the reality of male behavior than about the denial of women's sexual rights. [7]

Social purity reformers shared with temperance advocates the belief that males were not inherently brutish but possessed the capacity to control their sexual aggression. However, since men were seen as the initiators of sex, and women as the passive objects, they defined women's freedom mainly in terms of the right to refuse intercourse. Catharine Beecher, the leading proponent of the view that women had a moral mission to uplift the home, suggested that women's organizations establish "mothergartens" for pregnant wives who sought to protect themselves from the threat of sexual attack by their husbands. [8]

No survey was undertaken of Victorian sexual practices to determine the success of social purity advice. But judges of divorce courts listened to the cries of anguish from those wives who had not succeeded in restraining the sexual brutality or demands of their husbands. It is often thought that Anglo-American common law permitted a husband to rape his wife. The appearance of complaints of sexual violence in Victorian divorce applications, however, indicates that judges regarded marital rape as legitimate grounds for divorce. Elaine May examined divorce suits that appeared in Los Angeles courts in the 1880s. Many applicants for divorce, she found, complained of "sexual brutality," sexual abuses, and of their husbands' "unbridled passions."[9] Although some of the complaints about male sexual appetites sound rather puritanical by today's standards, it is very likely that women had real, rather than imaginary, reasons for describing sexual intercourse as painful. Frequent childbirth can often tear muscles and cause permanent injury to the organs of the pelvic region. Also, the female diseases and sicknesses these women suffered from were never spelled out, but one suspects venereal diseases, or gynecological and urinary tract disorders.

In the divorce applications May examined, wives complained about having sexual intercourse with their husbands as often as two or three times a night, not just during the early months of marriage, but on a regular basis. Frequently, the husband would awaken his wife out of her sleep and compel her to submit to him. Wives seeking divorces charged that their husbands' sexual demands caused them to become frail and sickly. Grace Thomas, a plaintiff for divorce in Santa Clara County, California, in 1890, swore in her affidavit that her husband "would not . . . obey the instructions of the Doctor but would force me to submit to him . . . many times so that often I could not get out of bed . . . I would beg him not to do it as I was so very sick. The only answer he gave me was 'you damned bitch, you have no business to be a woman.'" The judge granted her a divorce.[10] Melvina Harris complained specifically about her husband's "brutal violence and indecency," which "he used to satiate his lust."

> That during the whole of said five months he had sexual intercourse with her every day not less than twice, and as often as six times each day—and during all of her periods of menstrual discharges during said time, he did with force and violence and with indecent frequency have sexual connection with her against her protests . . . with beastly indifference to her feelings and cries of pain did hurt and injure her and seriously impair her health.[11]

Wives who were victimized by excessive sexual demands felt they had a right to a divorce. No husbands in the Los Angeles petitions that May looked at accused their wives of making excessive demands for sex, which is not surprising given the Victorian sexual norm of male initiative and female acquiescence. Although most husbands in these divorce applications denied making unwarranted demands on their wives, a few insisted on their conjugal rights. One California husband told a divorce court judge that "he would not give two cents and a half for a wife like her who did not give a man all he wanted . . . It did not seem to hurt whores to be treated in that way, and he did not see why it should hurt his wife."[12]

Social purity reformers viewed education of the young in a sexual standard that applied equally to men and women as their best hope for lasting change. During the 1870s small groups of mothers and women doctors in major Eastern cities founded moral education societies. At meetings of these societies, the members discussed a woman's right to her own body and proper rearing of children. Mothers were advised to warn their sons against frequenting prostitutes and to instruct them to view sex as a moral activity for the purpose of procreation. Mothers were urged to dress their daughters modestly, so as to keep in check the sexual passions of men, and to educate their daughters about menstruation and female anatomy. Moral education societies also campaigned in favor of sexual education in the schools.[13]

Most nineteenth-century rape laws did not specify whether a husband could be charged with raping his wife. It was not until the twentieth century that statutes exempted husbands from prosecution for marital rape. Nonetheless, no husband in nineteenth-century America was ever prosecuted on this charge. Wives in many states had the option of bringing suit for divorce on grounds of sexual brutality. It was assumed that a wife who complained of sexual assault by her husband could sue for divorce. Reformers did not discuss the legality of marital rape, with the exception of the moral education society of Washington, D.C. This organization, founded by a Quaker reformer, Lucinda Chandler, attempted in 1873 to repeal the law of coverture in the District of Columbia, under which the wife's separate legal identity was submerged under her husband's. Chandler wanted to give every woman "the legal custody and control of her person in wifehood to govern according to her wisdom and instinct the maternal office and protect her children as well as she may from the dangers of selfish passion, alcoholism, and vice."[14] It is not known whether she succeeded.

Moral education societies believed that maternal duty compelled women to secure legislation that would protect the virtue of their daughters. Likewise, social purity reformers realized that appeals alone would not promote changes in male sexuality. Women reformers met the challenge of ensuring that the law was enforced fairly on behalf of victimized women and girls. Because sexual purity was such a delicate subject, adult women of upstanding moral character were deemed the most appropriate agents to rescue prostitutes and aid women victims. Their efforts differed from those of antebellum women's rights advocates in two respects: they gave equal attention to the punishment of the perpetrator as to the rights of women, and they sought to establish permanent institutions to protect women victims. Thus, social purity reform actively embraced outside intervention in the family and did not simply rely on moral appeals for self-control. The difficulty lay in aiding the victims of violence without appearing to attack the institution of marriage. Anticruelty societies had successfully reassured the public that they intervened only in the most extreme circumstances. Women reformers had a harder time refuting the charge that they were helping to destroy the traditional family.

In spite of Victorian reticence to discuss sex, in the middle of the 1880s newspapers became willing, even eager to publish the details of sex crimes. In England, a sensational exposé on child prostitution rings touched off a torrent of public demands to end "the white slave traffic." American newspapers followed the progress of English reform and carried their own revelations of young girls enticed into prostitution. These stories aided women's reform groups. In the United States, legislative campaigns to raise the age of consent were achieving success. Nowhere were women reformers better mobilized for action than in Chicago, where the local WCTU, the Chicago Woman's Club, and the Protective Agency for Women and Children enjoyed unparalleled community respect and legislative influence.

The Protective Agency for Women and Children was founded in 1885 by women from Chicago's Moral Education Society, who called a meeting to address the problem of sex crime in Chicago, to which they invited representatives from the Illinois Humane Society, the WCTU, and the Chicago Woman's Club. Some of the members of the society had been reading in a Chicago newspaper about sex crimes committed against women and children in the city over the last several months. The article contended that judges tended to ignore rape or punish rapists leniently. Speakers also denounced the "debauching" of women clerical workers by their male employers and the extremely low age of sexual consent under Illinois law (at that time, only ten years). Edith Harbart of the Cook County Suffrage Association suggested that the Chicago Woman's Club establish a separate department devoted to the protection of women and children. She believed that the club, which included so many wives of Chicago's lakefront millionaires, would lend respectability to a protective agency. The society would hire its own agents. Membership was to be restricted entirely to women, and services were to be available free of charge.

Half of the officers of the agency were required to be members of the Woman's Club and the other half were recruited from diverse city and suburban women's organizations. Most of the officers were wealthy, with the possible exception of the representatives from the Swedish and Bohemian women's clubs. The governing board of the agency consisted of delegates from fifteen associations of women in Chicago, including the WCTU, the Chicago Woman's Club, the Cook County Woman's Suffrage Association, and the Moral Education Association. Originally, most of the funds for the agency came from the small gifts of individual women. As the agency grew, Chicago area women's clubs provided a larger share of its revenue. Some club members donated office space. The agents of the society listened to women's complaints of sexual molestation, incest, rape, sexual harassment, wife beating, and consumer fraud.

The Protective Agency was the most significant organizational effort to aid female victims of violence in nineteenth-century America. It provided diverse forms of legal aid and personal assistance to female and child victims of assault and monitored courtrooms to see that women victims were treated fairly. In these respects, it resembled the Society for the Protection of Women and Children from Aggravated Assaults founded in England some thirty years earlier. The agency sometimes sent homeless girls or abused women to a shelter operated by the Woman's Club of Chicago, where women victims could stay for a maximum of four weeks. Through their efforts, a battered woman could secure property held in her husband's name. The agency also provided legal counsel for women victims. In a typical situation of this kind, the agency's lawyer represented a Russian immigrant girl who had been raped by her father. The lawyer cooperated with a representative from the Illinois Humane Society in terminating the father's right to custody; the girl was placed in an orphan asylum.[15]

The Chicago Protective Agency also sought out women believed to be rape victims, based on the reports of friends or witnesses. Women of the agency located the victims, visited them at home, and inquired as to the circumstances of the assault. If a victim had enough money, they advised her to hire her own lawyer and take the case to court. If she did not, they engaged one on her behalf, and upon occasion, provided her with a place to live and a new job. These activities drew criticism from detractors who told the agency "that to go out in the highways and byways of life, and lift up those who are downtrodden, under the feet of wicked men, [was] very dirty business."[16]

Agency members hoped that the presence of respectable women would create an atmosphere of moral support for the rape victim in the courtroom. They encouraged victims to bring their cases to court. These victims, they believed, felt ashamed to testify and did not want to subject themselves to cross-examination, especially about their sexual history. Since no lawsuit could restore a woman's virginity, the public believed it was better for a victim to remain silent and accept her misfortune as best she could rather than tell her story in court. But the annual report of the agency countered that "the shame and scandal of these crimes lies in the fact, not the telling of it." It attacked the double standard, whereby a rape victim had to demonstrate to a jury "an unblemished reputation."[17] The agency took credit for the fact that rape charges were no longer dismissed or reduced to a lesser charge of disorderly conduct.

Social purity ideas provided the justification for the work of the Chicago agency. Women, they insisted, were the natural protectors of other women and children. Only women were capable of understanding another woman's predicament. Single females and working women needed special protection because they were removed from their families and forced to fend for themselves in a world of unsympathetic, even predatory men; young girls were especially vulnerable because they were sexually innocent. Although social purity reformers hoped to strengthen the purity of the home, the Protective

Agency had to act when moral redemption proved impossible. In cases of wife beating and incest, the initial policy was to discourage divorce. The case of a man who had raped his two stepdaughters, however, forced the agency to conclude that the mother of these girls should be given legal assistance in securing a divorce. Still, the Protective Agency defended itself against the charge that it was helping to break up the family. The marriages it helped to terminate were not "true marriages" but instead "a falsity and a sham" because of the violence, cruelty, or immorality that occurred within them.[18] By the third year of their work, the women of the agency began to question the nature of marriage: "We come to ponder much more on these great questions—the sexual and financial relations of men and women, and often wonder what is wrong."[19]

Efforts on behalf of assaulted wives led Protective Agency members to consider "the most embarrassing of all questions which come before us"—the issue of divorce.[20] The agency began cautiously by securing legal separations for women, and later began to help women obtain divorces, but only on the grounds of extreme cruelty or drunkenness. Thus the agency became involved in the controversial issue of outside intervention in marriages. However, opponents of divorce went on the offensive, in part because the number of complaints—most of them from women—began to rise. Magazine writers worried about the future of the American family. Even societies for the prevention of cruelty to children were pressed to defend themselves against the accusation that they were breaking up the family. Generally, when the public becomes frightened by the rapidity of social change, it looks to the traditional family (or an idealized image of the home) to provide security and continuity with the past. At a time when many men and women alike believed that woman's suffrage endangered the domestic unit, directly aiding women in securing separations or divorces was perceived as a frontal assault on family life. In responding to the conservative tide, women reformers were led to support laws that forced men to assume child support and made desertion a crime, rather than actions that would dissolve marital ties. The Protective Agency was even criticized for its involvement in the heretofore all-male domain of the police court. Despite the fact that the Protective Agency was perceived as immodest and antifamily, its members continued their work decade after decade. But few other women reformers followed their lead. Where there were so many other areas of public reform for a modest woman to undertake, why enter protective work only to invite derision and scorn?

The agency proposed the idea of a national organization to assist in establishing other protective agencies across the country. In 1891 one of the agency's founders reported on the society's work before the National Council of Women, a coordinating body comprised of representatives from every major national women's group. No action resulted from her speech. A women's group in Peoria, Illinois, appears to have established an agency, but after the 1890s, no new institutions were founded.

Eleven years after its founding, the Protective Agency merged with a larger, better funded, and predominantly male organization, the Bureau of Justice, which furnished legal aid to indigent clients of both sexes. Usually, when women's organizations join with men's, female concerns often disappear and women's power to make important decisions declines. As part of the Bureau of Justice, however, the Protective Agency continued to enjoy autonomy and influence for many years. The Protective Agency received from the Bureau sole jurisdiction over the cases affecting women and children, since they believed it "a self-evident truth that women can do better work for the wronged of their own sex than men can do." As a result of the merger, the caseload of the agency grew rapidly. The agency began to provide assaulted wives who had children with legal assistance in securing a divorce, rather than just a legal separation.[21]

In 1905 the agency and the Bureau of Justice joined with the Legal Aid Society of Chicago. The Protective Agency retained its separate identity and was represented on the board of directors of Chicago Legal Aid. In the agreement of consolidation, the president of the Protective Agency became the vice president of Legal Aid, and half of the directors of the Legal Aid were to be women. By 1912, however, information about the agency's work disappeared from the annual report of Chicago Legal Aid. Rape cases were being handled by other agencies. Among other signs of change was the replacement of the old motto, "woman's work for women," with another, "men's and women's work for the wronged and helpless." By the 1920s, the official policy of Chicago Legal Aid was to discourage divorce and seek marital reconciliation whenever possible.

In contrast to the charges against the Protective Agency, women active in the temperance cause maintained that their work helped preserve the institution of the family and made sons into virtuous men. In many ways, the temperance campaign of the Gilded Age continued the aims of the pre-Civil War movement. Alcohol, not family violence, remained the major concern. Temperance reformers, as always, bemoaned the fact that alcohol and lust had turned gentle men into vicious brutes. In comparison with the antebellum temperance crusade, the late nineteenth-century effort was larger, more influential, and more accessible to women's participation. Temperance literature continued to be filled with wife murderers, brutal gin fiends, and even the occasional drunkard who assaulted the corpse of his dead wife![22] But this later temperance movement tended to downplay a wife's duty and obligation to reform her drunken husband in favor of emphasizing a mother's influence over her sons. The most damnable drunkard became the drunken son who abused his mother. An aristocratic but troubled mother queried a temperance lecturer as to whether such a son was responsible for his actions.

> "You have had experience, but have you ever known or heard of a son striking his mother?" "More than once," I said, "but never unless that son was influenced by drink; indeed, I cannot believe that any young man, in his sober senses, would strike his mother." She seemed relieved to know that hers was not a solitary case, and she informed me that she had a son who had been dissipated for years. [23]

Temperance speakers portrayed drunkards' mothers as ferocious protectors of their cubs, but depicted drunkards' wives as passive, submissive, and weak. What remedy was available for the drunkard's wife? Stanton and Anthony had counseled such women to flee from their homes with their children and sue for divorce and child custody. Women reformers after the Civil War encouraged the drunkard's wife to attack the wicked rum seller, or persuade her husband (or son) to take the pledge. Because there was so little that could be done for a woman who married a drunkard, the only true protection was to select wisely at the outset. Antebellum reformers had implied that no woman knowingly married a drunkard; most men, they seemed to think, succumbed to drink only after marriage. Gilded Age temperance advocates counseled young women against choosing a prospective husband who might be inclined to imbibe. The lyrics of the "Drunkard's Wife" painted a grim picture of what happened to women who did not choose well. The drunkard's wife who narrates the song hears her husband stumble home, insanely drunk. She rushes to the room of her "two little girls at rest," where she finds them, "mangled, cold and dead." Having bludgeoned to death his daughters, the drunkard "then with a thrust . . . took his life." But widowhood did not put an end to this woman's suffering, as her lyrical lament made clear.

> Then I fell to the floor and was born from the room,
> A wreck since that night I've been,
> And the boy that was left had a passion for drink,
> The sad mark of his father's sin.
> It claimed him, though young a hopeless slave,
> And early he filled a drunkard's grave.
>
> I beg of you girls, as you value your lives
> From the drunker to turn aside,
> And give heed to no plea, whatever it be
> Of a drinker to be the bride.
> To save from such sorrow as wrecked my life,
> Oh never become a drunkard's wife. [24]

Women were not only writing temperance lyrics to convey their point of view but also developing an entire program of social action. The Woman's Christian Temperance Union, founded in 1874, was the largest national woman's organization of its day. Although temperance was their main concern, the WCTU established its own social purity organization (the White Cross) and led state campaigns to raise the age of consent. They even invited Anthony Comstock, Victorian America's most famous crusader against pornography, to censor impure literature for them.

Women's temperance organizations hoped to strengthen the traditional family by forcing men to realize their responsibilities.[25] Rather than criticizing female dependency, as feminists did, women temperance reformers called upon decent men to protect helpless females. Women of the WCTU seemed more concerned with uplifting men than with raising the status of women. They believed in a marriage not of equals but of respectables, headed by a worthy husband, with his wife, an acquiescent subordinate, at his side. Nonetheless, even the WCTU was forced to take a stand on the matter of divorce on grounds of drunkenness. An 1886 editorial in the *Union Signal*, the newspaper of the WCTU, maintained that so long as saloons remained open, drunkenness should remain grounds for divorce. They later insisted they favored only legal separation.[26]

Janet Zollinger Giele compared the rhetoric and image of men and women in a suffragist newspaper, the *Woman's Journal*, with that in the *Union Signal*. The women of the WCTU perceived themselves as mothers acting in defense of home and family. They favored woman's suffrage—"the home protection ballot"—as a means of defending the family. The followers of Frances Willard were rarely castigated for being unwomanly or immodest. "The temperance women," Giele wrote, "were oriented primarily to the warm affectional world in which they stood. In humanitarian endeavor, they turned to helping the weak rather than to interceding with the powerful. They were satisfied with the image of the traditional woman and rather than change her, they wanted only to pull up imperfect man to her level. Their explicit reform objective was much more strongly directed at consolidating woman's status within the home, rather than trying to find a place for her outside of it." The WCTU believed that anything that "breaks down the home, hurts the woman most" because a woman was dependent on the family for her happiness. No friend of the advancement of women would ever encourage a woman to leave her husband.[27]

Because the enemy of temperance women was not the husband, but the saloonkeeper, the WCTU was able to devise innovative means of aiding drunkards' wives. No nineteenth-century court granted a battered woman the right to sue her husband for damages arising from his assault upon her. Suffragists and women's temperance advocates never even considered this legal approach. But if the major enemy of the home was the saloonkeeper, then a wife ought to be able to bring suit against the man who served her husband. In 1873 New York and Arkansas became the first states to pass laws giving the injured party the right to sue the saloonkeeper or owner for damages caused from an assault committed by an intoxicated person. Eventually, twenty states enacted such laws. In some states, only the wife could sue for damages, although in others, several injured parties, including a husband, child, parent, or employer, were permitted to do so. In order to be awarded damages, the law generally required the wife to notify the saloonkeeper in advance not to serve her husband alcohol.[28]

Only a few drunkards' wives could afford to hire a lawyer to take their complaint to court. In those few cases that reached a judge, women plaintiffs generally won their suits and were awarded damages. Ann J. Wilson of Genessee, Michigan, was one of the successful claimants. She had informed the town saloonkeeper not to serve her husband. When her husband finally came home from the saloon, he attacked her in front of their children, striking her on the head with a chair. She won her suit, although the amount of the award of damages was not stated. Courts also upheld other cases that favored the assaulted wife. One Illinois husband who pleaded with his wife not to separate from him signed a note promising to pay her $600 if he became drunk or abused her. He did, and she sued him for divorce. The Illinois Supreme Court in 1877 upheld the validity of the husband's promissory note.[29]

Although the WCTU acted on behalf of women, it did more for dependent, neglected, and abused children. When there was no other society for the prevention of cruelty to children, the WCTU founded one. In 1887, the San Diego Union, a local chapter of the WCTU, established a refuge for homeless women, generally mothers and women who had been deserted by their husbands; some of these women probably had been abused. Soon the Union founded a day-care center for the children of homeless women. A few years later, they decided to expand the children's center but close their shelter. They gave the reason that women's emergency housing was no longer needed since the town's land boom had ended, but the day-care center was forced to turn children away. This decision, while sensible enough, reflected the general priorities of the WCTU.[30] In part, women did not establish societies to prevent cruelty to wives because they put most of their efforts into providing social services for children.

Although Stanton and Anthony had ceased to mention family violence in their speeches by the middle of the 1870s, the interest of Lucy Stone, a relatively conservative suffragist, was just beginning. A white lace cap perched on top of her silver-gray hair, Stone resembled an elderly matron more than a crusader on behalf of woman's rights. Her interest in "crimes against women" coincided with the founding of the first society for the prevention of cruelty to children. She noted in the *Woman's Journal* of 1879 that beaten horses and dogs received more protection than bruised and battered wives. She called for a society to prevent cruelty to wives, although she herself never organized one.[31] Stone is best known for having kept her maiden name, even after her marriage to Cincinnati merchant and abolitionist Henry Blackwell. She was perceived to be the conservative of the woman's rights movement, more proper and respectable—more willing to cooperate with male reformers— than Stanton and Anthony. She sided with such antebellum feminists as Wendell Phillips, who believed the marriage question was not a woman's rights issue. Stone opposed divorce reform and insisted that motherhood was a woman's highest calling. She and Blackwell helped pass a resolution at a national suffrage convention "that the ballot for woman means stability for the marriage relation, stability for the home, and stability for our republican government."[32] The issue of "crimes against women" had found its most respectable advocate, a suffragist who could not be tarred by association with advocates of free love or other radicals.

Soon after the Civil War, Lucy Stone and Henry Blackwell took over the editorship of a Boston woman's rights newspaper, the *Woman's Journal*. Before Stone and Blackwell assumed control, the *Woman's Journal* featured articles that called divorce for women "an escape out of tyranny into freedom." Under their editorship, such articles quickly disappeared. They avoided controversial issues in promoting woman's rights. In 1876, however, Stone announced her intention of publishing a weekly catalog of "crimes against women" culled from brief stories in New England newspapers. She believed the law was too lenient on male assailants of women, and that women victims were unfairly treated.[33]

The newspaper reports she read compelled her to overlook "standards of propriety" in detailing torture, maiming, and brutality against women.[34] Beneath the headline of "crimes against women" readers of the *Woman's Journal* found stories of wife murder, rape, incest, and wife beating; a mutual suicide agreed upon in a love pact; physical assaults by boys against girls; and even felonies committed by women, such as infanticide or crimes of passion in which women had used violence in response to seduction, rape, or violence by men. In all these instances male lust had contributed to the victimization of women. The examples provided of wife beating or wife murder were extreme because Stone wanted to shock her middle-class readership and awaken them to action. By demonstrating how great masculine brutality was, she hoped to refute the belief that women provoked violence; nothing could justify a husband who murdered his wife with an ax or gouged out her eyes.

Stone and Blackwell opposed laws to essentially legalize prostitution, and campaigned on behalf of many social purity reforms, including the arrest of male pimps and procurers as well as of prostitutes. They also sought to raise the age of consent in Massachusetts from ten to sixteen.[35] In their analysis of crimes against women, the abuse of wives was a form of "domestic tyranny" that grew out of a husband's ownership of his wife as a form of personal property, as well as from the "hydra-headed monster" of intemperance and male licentiousness. Crimes against women were committed regardless of whether the victims were "living in or out of the marriage relation."[36] Although they believed that wife beating occurred in every class and ethnic group, they held that "a large majority of such crimes" occurred among immigrants, because women were held in low regard in the countries from which the immigrants came.[37]

In 1879 Stone lent her support to a bill in the Massachusetts legislature to protect a wife whose husband had been convicted of criminally assaulting her. The proposed law gave an assaulted wife the right to apply at a neighborhood police court for a legal separation, an order requiring her husband to pay support for her and her children, and the award of child custody. Three times Stone introduced this legislation—in 1879, 1883, and 1891—and three times it failed.[38]

The idea for this bill came from the prominent English suffragist Frances Power Cobbe, who had sent Stone a copy of the protection bill she helped pass in Parliament. Cobbe's article, "Wife Torture in England," published in the *Contemporary Review* in 1879, had shocked the English public with tales of wives who were "trampled on" by their husbands. Cobbe was as famous for her antivivisectionist activism as for her concern about battered women. Born into an aristocratic Anglo-Irish family, Cobbe gained firsthand knowledge of the suffering of poor women from doing charity work in Bristol. Cobbe's understanding of wife beating was more sophisticated than that of most American reformers. The assaulted wife, she acknowledged, was not always innocent or defenseless, but sometimes fought back or even initiated violence. Wife beating, she argued, was caused by several factors: male belief that women were their property, the squalor of working-class living conditions, drunkenness, overcrowded housing, jealousy, and "heteropathy," the impulse to hurt partly aroused by the helplessness of the victim. She began to think about the necessity of some kind of legislation when members of Parliament failed to pass a law requiring the flogging of convicted wife beaters. Cobbe opposed whipping wife beaters because she believed that a husband who had been so cruelly treated would retaliate against his wife. She also feared that the punishment of flogging would deter wives from testifying against their abusive husbands. She favored a protection bill instead, especially for working-class women, among whom assaults "were tenfold as numerous and twenty times more cruel" than among women in "the upper ranks of society."[39] Divorce was an alternative many women could not afford because of the problem of how to feed, clothe, and house themselves and their children. Most wives, she realized, needed economic support from their ex-husbands to survive.

When Cobbe's bill was introduced into Parliament, it was quickly attacked as a threat to the institution of marriage. Parliament was at the time considering a rather noncontroversial bill to amend divorce legislation. Lord Penzance, perhaps influenced by Cobbe's article, attached an amendment to the divorce bill, which contained the substance of Cobbe's reform. Penzance, a former head of Parliament's divorce court, was well-respected by fellow members of Parliament. His amendment, however, made clear that any wife proven to have committed adultery was to be denied child custody and maintenance paid by her husband. This clause helped to neutralize the fear that Parliament was encouraging sexual license. Perhaps because of Penzance's amendment this legislation passed. Among the manuevers of Lord Penzance in his sponsorship of the bill, was the good use he made of public fears of brutish working-class men.[40]

When Lucy Stone received a copy of Cobbe's article and the protection bill, she immediately published both in the *Woman's Journal*. Wife beating, Stone noted, occurred in every country and was increasing in the United States. Boston police statistics indicated that there were five hundred arrests for wife beating every year. The protection bill Stone favored would grant the assaulted wife child custody and order the husband to pay child support. A wife could apply for a separation at a neighborhood police court. Stone argued that although the remedy of divorce on grounds of cruelty was available in Massachusetts, many women could not afford to hire a lawyer. In addition, wives often found it difficult to attend a court hearing downtown. Stone believed that Catholic women, who were opposed to divorce, would benefit from being able to secure legal separations. Massachusetts legislators raised several objections to Stone's bill. Support orders, they claimed, were unenforceable because abusive husbands would flee the state. Assaulted wives would not make use of the law, and if they did, legal separations would become too easy to obtain. No one seemed to notice the inconsistency in claiming that not many women and too many of them would use the law. Massachusetts legislators simply did not want to make legal separation easy to obtain. Stone, who had been so careful to distance herself from support for divorce, had been accused—as all feminists were—of encouraging the breakup of the family. Both Stone and Cobbe were attacked for the same reasons, but Stone lacked a powerful legislative advocate, such as Lord Penzance, who could make her legislation more palatable.

Had Stone's bill become law, it would have protected only legally married women, but not those who cohabited with men. Even the law Cobbe helped pass proved extremely difficult to enforce. Under English law, a wife who had committed adultery could be denied separate maintenance or custody of her child. The protection the English magistrate's courts (the equivalent of American police courts) offered was extended only to women whose husbands had been convicted of aggravated assault and those who could demonstrate that their future safety was in peril. Thus, most battered women did not qualify for a protection order. The major advantages of Cobbe's reform were twofold: battered wives were granted custody of their children (under ten years of age) and a magistrate could issue an order requiring a separated husband to pay a weekly sum for support of his wife and children. However, many husbands separated from their wives refused to pay these maintenance orders, left town, or angrily attacked their wives or children who demanded the money. Indeed, making the wife the collector of her husband's payment was a situation bound to engender further abuse, as even some British magistrates admitted.

Even if support was paid, it was usually insufficient for a woman to live on. The unwillingness of police court judges to enforce support orders discouraged many women from taking a case to court and led many others to drop their complaints. Church of England missionaries stationed in the magistrate's courts often counseled battered women applying for a separation to forgive their mates. The Matrimonial Act of 1895 ordered that the husband make his payment to the court rather than to his wife, but commentators reported that this change in procedure was "universally disregarded." Nonetheless, the act also expanded the grounds for separation, making it easier for women to obtain separation and support. Between 1897 and 1906, English magistrate's courts granted over 87,000 separation and maintenance orders.[41]

The failure of Stone and Blackwell to achieve passage of any legislation against wife beating strengthened their belief that women would never be protected from male brutality until their legal rights were guaranteed. Changes in social attitudes, they concluded, required overturning the legal structure favoring male domination. Because women were unable to vote, Stone and Blackwell argued, penalties for wife beating were mild. If women were enfranchised, then fear of the women's vote would compel judges to sentence wife beaters to long prison sentences. Lucy Stone insisted that battered wives could never "be adequately protected . . . until women would help make the laws."[42] Enacting statutes to ensure equality between the sexes would help remove prejudice against women. Even the former wife beater would no longer regard his wife as his property, since he would realize the general esteem in which women were held.[43]

Stone and Blackwell contended that when women possessed the vote, assaulted wives would recognize that they were protected under the law and would become willing to complain to the police and press their cases in the courts. Judges who had to reckon with the wrath of the female electorate would sentence wife beaters to long prison terms and governors would refuse to pardon wife murderers. Enfranchised women would demand the removal from office of judges who ordered lenient sentences against male sex criminals.

Although women's suffrage was claimed to be the cure for every social ill from child labor to world war, Stone and Blackwell were the only suffragists to assert that enfranchising women would reduce wife beating. After their deaths the suffrage movement went on to achieve great victories, but the issue of wife beating disappeared. Of course, the enfranchisement of women did not reduce wife beating. (It is equally implausible to think that the passage of the Equal Rights Amendment would have that effect, as some well-intentioned proponents of the amendment in the 1970s insisted.) Wife beating seems to be one of those social issues that inspires naive optimism about the possibility for reform. Some legislation, whether a temperance bill or a constitutional amendment for woman's suffrage, always appears to offer the solution, but while necessary, never turns out to be the panacea that is promised. Although wife beating is surely connected with the general status of women, no single change or set of changes can be expected to permanently alter women's role in marriage and their options outside of marriage. The existence of a powerful women's movement offers no guarantee for concern about abused women, either. Women won the right to vote in 1920, but the suffrage movement from the 1890s through the end of World War I had shown no interest in the issue of crimes against women.

As believers in the Victorian sexual moral code, social purity reformers tried to control male brutishness and protect the purity of the home. Reformers were able to press strategies that were perceived as empowering women within the family. Some urged the passage of new laws, and others concentrated on appeals for moral reform. A diverse but nonetheless haphazard and uncoordinated quality characterized these efforts. The Protective Agency for Women and Girls, the single most important organization of the time, had to confront the charge that it was encouraging the breakup of the family. Among reformers concerned about family violence, the conservative defenders of the family gained the most respectful hearing. The efforts that could be accommodated were those that were perceived as helping to strengthen the family. As long as male dominance was confronted indirectly, women temperance reformers could succeed. But their remedies, while useful, failed to recognize that for many abused women, the best hope was separation or divorce and child custody. Feminism should have been involved in raising the status of families headed by single mothers so that women could have had an alternative to an abusive marriage. Any efforts that came close to making separation, divorce, child custody for women, and court-ordered support more available went down to defeat. The public was unwilling to subsidize the creation of a new family form. It believed instead that women had to reshape the traditional family and make men more responsible.

In the reform of the private sphere, social purity enjoyed greater success, even if purchased at the price of denying women sexual freedom. Social purity reformers deserve credit for advocating and helping to diffuse new (and lasting) norms about woman's rights in marriage. Wives were encouraged to demand from their husbands better treatment, greater dignity, and autonomy—a marriage free of violence and brutality and a union committed to the principles of caring and mutual respect.

6

Bringing Back
the Whipping Post

AFTER HER PROTECTION BILL FAILED for the second time, Lucy Stone began to favor punishment of wife beaters rather than just the protection of their victims. A Republican state legislator and friend of Stone's sponsored a bill in the Massachusetts state legislature in 1885 to punish wife beating with the whipping post. Stone wrote favorably about the proposed legislation in the *Woman's Journal* and organized a group of women to lobby for its passage. She had been quietly championing the whipping post for wife beaters in the *Woman's Journal* for almost a decade. In this sense she was perhaps less of a humanitarian than Francis Cobbe, who never capitulated to the demand for flogging wife beaters. The law for the use of the whipping post, Stone wrote, "should exist in every state."[1] The abusive husband did not fear a month in jail or a fine, she believed, but dreaded the pain and disgrace of a whipping. Stone seemed unworried about the safety of a woman whose husband, just having been flogged, returned home. In fact, she considered whipping the best form of protection for the assaulted wife because a fine or imprisonment would merely deprive the wife beater's family of economic support. In 1885 the whipping-post bill Stone supported passed the Massachusetts House by a vote of 96 to 24, but lost by a wide margin in the state Senate.[2]

Occasionally American opponents of the whipping post suggested that the wife beater should be allowed to earn wages while in prison and thus provide support for his family. But the only serious effort to propose alternatives to corporal punishment was Stone's protection bill. When Stone supported flogging, she may have sensed that it appealed more to the public than aiding assaulted wives.

In the United States, antebellum feminists regarded wife beating as a crime, but they were primarily interested in providing abused women with divorce on grounds of drunkenness or cruelty. (They failed to pass divorce reform legislation in a single state.) Elizabeth Cady Stanton's reasons for favoring divorce for the drunkard's wife touched on the nature of marriage and a woman's right to independence. However, in the late nineteenth century, wife beating became a law-and-order issue, buried in an avalanche of arguments about the best means to deter violent crime.

Of all the reform campaigns against family violence in the late nineteenth century, this one most clearly expressed the desire to control the lower classes. Between 1876 and 1906, eminently respectable, mostly Republican, male lawyers, judges, district attorneys, and other law enforcement officials led a movement to punish wife beaters with lashings. (Republicans favored government efforts to legislate morality, such as prohibition of the sale of alcoholic beverages and blue laws restricting Sabbath activities.) Elbridge Gerry and Henry Bergh of the NYSPCC also backed the cause. Gerry even sponsored a bill in the New York state legislature to flog child molesters and fathers guilty of incest. The head of the Illinois Humane Society supported a similar bill in the Illinois state legislature to physically punish wife beaters, armed robbers, child molesters, and habitual criminals. Editorials in major newspapers such as the *Chicago Herald* and the *Washington Post* favored whipping-post legislation.[3]

Nonetheless, the whipping-post campaign led to the passage of laws in only three states—Maryland in 1882, Delaware in 1901, and Oregon in 1905.[4] This campaign, by comparison with the child protection movement of roughly the same period, was an abysmal failure. During the nineteenth century the English had four times considered and four times defeated bills to punish wife beating with the whipping post. By these standards, the American whipping-post crusade enjoyed modest success.

This campaign emerged in the 1870s, the same decade as the founding of the anticruelty societies. Both movements fed on the same fears of violent crime and "brutish impulses," and made similar demands for the state to punish violations of morality. Both campaigns emerged at the end of a liberal period of reform, as a conservative tide set in.[5]

One goal of the whipping-post campaign was to stifle even more vociferous demands for cruel punishment of lawbreakers. The men who championed state-sponsored flogging worried about the vigilante mobs in the South and Midwest taking the law into their own hands. Beginning in the 1870s, the Ku Klux Klan in the South and the White Caps in the Midwest singled out for whippings child abusers and drunken men, adulterers, prostitutes, and mothers of illegitimate children. On their Saturday night patrol, the White Caps of

Indiana, their faces and necks hidden by white hoods, delivered threatening notes on the doorsteps of known offenders. Among the eighty targets of White Caps in Harrison County, Indiana, in the 1880s, nine were assaultive husbands or fathers. Although the Ku Klux Klan, which rose from the ashes of the Confederacy's defeat, mostly targeted independent-minded ex-slaves, they also threatened to whip abusive husbands, both white and black. A few husbands in Southern or Western states who had brutally beaten or murdered their wives were lynched.[6] Upstanding judges believed that if the nation's legal institutions did not take a stronger stand against crime, vigilantes would get the upper hand.

The child rescue, temperance, and social purity causes of the late nineteenth century shared with the whipping-post campaign a belief in strong and effective criminal punishments. Flogging had earned a secure place as a time-honored and acceptable punishment in America and England. The temperance and social purity movements of the late nineteenth century, however, focused more on the issue of woman's rights. With the exception of Lucy Stone, campaigners on behalf of the whipping post for wife beaters steered clear of feminist rhetoric. There was no claim that women had the capacity to protect other women, no insistence that women must monitor agencies of criminal law to insure justice for women victims, no effort to free women from the bonds of an assaultive marriage and secure for them child custody and economic support. Supporters of the whipping post also differed from advocates of temperance, social purity, and woman's rights in emphasizing the criminal nature of wife beating, rather than civil remedies for its victims. The penalties of fines and imprisonment, advocates of legalized flogging argued, had not controlled or reformed the brutish husband. Because of this, different—and harsher—punishments were needed.

The first bill in the United States to punish wife beating with the whipping post was introduced in California in 1876. It was defeated. The same year, North Carolina rejected a statute to reintroduce the whipping post as a punishment for rogues and thieves. In 1876 the Indiana legislature also failed to pass a bill to punish unspecified offenses with flogging. The Nevada legislature in 1877 passed a law to tie for two to ten hours, to a permanent post erected in the county seat, any man convicted for the first time of beating his wife or another woman. The offender at the post was to wear a sign that read, "Woman or wife beater." The act did not state whether the offender was also to be flogged. The law apparently was never enforced. In 1879 the Missouri legislature debated a bill to punish wife beating, as well as petty larceny and cruelty to children, with flogging. One legislative sponsor of the whipping post hoped to save the state the cost of imprisoning wife beaters. His colleague and adversary insisted that the whipping post would destroy the manhood of the criminal who was whipped. This representative's supporters carried the day and helped defeat the bill handily. The same year Kentucky considered but rejected a bill to punish unnamed offenses with the whipping post.[7]

In 1882 Maryland became the first state to pass a law punishing brutal wife beating with the whipping post. The sponsor of the bill was W. T. Handy, a prominent lawyer, member of the American Bar Association, and chair of the judiciary committee in the Maryland House of Delegates. He gained his committee's support and led the fight for his bill in the House of Delegates. Handy made an impassioned plea on behalf of wives who suffered brutal beatings on Saturday nights from drunken husbands; whipping was an appropriate punishment for such cruelty because it "did not make the poor woman suffer as well."[8] The image that appealed to these legislators was that of the state as a moral father, punishing a brutish son-in-law. In fact, Handy justified governmental intervention by arguing that "the man who beats his wife and is cowhided for it by her father or brother is thought by all to have received his just reward; and why then cavil at a similar punishment inflicted in an orderly way, after a full hearing of his defence, by an officer of the law?"[9] Although opponents believed whipping to be a cruel and barbarous punishment, they were in the minority, and the bill passed by a margin of two to one.[10]

Maryland became the first state to pass a law punishing brutal wife beating with the whipping post. The post was already used in the neighboring state of Delaware, although not to punish wife beaters. Maryland legislators were convinced that flogging in Delaware effectively deterred crime. The Maryland statute limited flogging to extreme cases of wife beating. Only "brutal" assault of a wife was punished, and a judge was given discretion in ordering a flogging, a year in prison, or both.

Because of the legislative success in Maryland, similar whipping-post bills were introduced in Massachusetts, Pennsylvania, and New Hampshire in 1884 and 1885. Legislators in both political parties and religious groups—especially Quakers—led the opposition to the whipping post. A prominent liberal Republican, Robert Adams, advocated the merits of flogging wife beaters before the National Social Science Association in 1885. The same year Adams had unsuccessfully led the fight to punish wife beating with the whipping post in the Pennsylvania legislature. Daniel Chamberlain, a New York lawyer, prominent Republican, and former governor of South Carolina during Reconstruction, presented a resolution before the American Bar Association in 1885 calling for a study of the desirability of whipping as a punishment. Three eminent lawyers, one of whom was Simeon Baldwin, were appointed to prepare a report for the annual meeting of the association the following year, with Baldwin as the leader.

Born in New Haven, Connecticut, in 1840, Baldwin hailed from a distinguished Connecticut family descended from colonial settlers and patriots, including an ancestor who was a signer of the Declaration of Independence. His father had been a U.S. senator and governor of the state. Baldwin trained for the bar in his father's law office, at Yale, where he was a classmate of Chamberlain, and at Harvard. An eminent legal authority, Baldwin was respected for having streamlined Connecticut's legal procedure. He was a faculty member of Yale Law School, served as justice of the Connecticut Superior Court, and was one of the founders of the American Bar Association, eventually becoming its president. Between 1900 and 1914, Baldwin, known as "the first citizen of Connecticut," served two terms as governor of the state.

Simeon Baldwin, who considered himself a tough crime fighter, believed imprisonment had not deterred crime. He favored short prison terms for repeat offenders, with subsequent police supervision for life, or at least for a term of years.[11] Baldwin's committee was asked to investigate the punishment of whipping not just for wife beating but also for "assaults committed with slung-shots, sand-bags, brass-knuckles or similar weapons."[12] His committee's report, published in 1886, argued that the whipping post would deter wife beating and other types of crime. The ranks of the criminal class continued to grow, the report stated, while the weapons at the disposal of society were reduced in number and efficiency. To lawyers like Baldwin, sentimental and confused reformers had demonstrated more concern about the condition of the criminal than about the suffering of his victim. Too often it was impossible to secure a conviction for notorious offenders. Nonetheless, so many criminals preyed on the public that the number of men behind bars soared. For the hardened criminal, the report stated, fear of imprisonment had not deterred crime. Prisons actually helped to perpetuate crime by confining men to a foul and contaminating atmosphere.

At a time of national economic depression, the rising militance of American workers, the desperation of the great army of the unemployed, and the specter of a permanent criminal class haunted the committee. Tramps who roamed the countryside taking any odd job and begging for a few crumbs of bread seemed to present a potential criminal menace. Lacking any moral sense, these vagabonds were seen as capable of rape, arson, or murder. Any police court judge knew that as the cold weather set in, "men commit a certain class of petty offenses so as to secure comfortable quarters for the winter."[13]

The membership of the American Bar Association in 1886 considered

Baldwin's report. The arguments of each side foreshadowed those that would appear in subsequent legislative debates. Baldwin's supporters believed that the whipping post would prevent crime. Deterrence was the most important consideration, not whether a punishment was "civilized or uncivilized."[14] When one wife beater was flogged, other husbands would fear brutalizing their wives. A punishment had to fit the crime, conveying to the potential criminal the gravity with which violation of the law was regarded. A fine was not a serious or severe enough penalty for wife beating, and it imposed financial suffering on the wife. Baldwin believed that before committing an offense, criminals did not much ponder the length of their prison sentence; if they were apprehended, the average offender was incapable of distinguishing between a term of a few months and one of many "for the simple reason that the criminal classes are devoid of imagination."[15]

The Bar Association members in favor of the whipping post believed that the one thing the brutish wife beater dreaded was pain. Once he had been scourged, he would be so afraid of the cat-o'-nine-tails that he would cease to beat his wife. Pain was also a highly appropriate punishment because it inflicted physical suffering on the person who caused it, meeting force with force, blow with blow. Although legal proponents of the whipping post claimed they sought only deterrence, not retribution, their statements suggested otherwise. One lawyer from New York remarked that "some few years ago in the city of New York a shoemaker drove his awl into the eyes of his young wife, an eighteen-year-old girl, because she had looked admiringly upon some men. As to that man, I would regard it as no offense to have him stripped once a week during his life and thirty lashes applied to his back."[16]

The passage of the Maryland law figured prominently in the debate. Handy of Maryland, a member of the American Bar Association (ABA), claimed that since the law went into effect, Maryland had virtually eliminated wife beating. Baldwin's committee, which had been asked to investigate the results of the whipping-post law in Maryland, agreed. In the first year after Maryland's law was passed, no wife beater was charged under the statute, although 156 husbands were brought before a judge on the lesser offense of "assault upon wives." The next year a black husband was convicted under the act and sentenced to be punished with seven lashes. No men were indicted the following year. The year after, a white husband and a notorious thief was convicted under the statute. He was sentenced to a whipping of twenty lashes and a year in jail. After his well-publicized flogging, police in Baltimore claimed that the number of wife beating cases was cut in half, and those they saw were of a much less serious character. Everyone agreed there had been fewer reported cases of wife beating in Maryland after the whipping post was introduced.

By insisting on the efficacy of harsh punishment, Baldwin's supporters managed to avoid the controversy about interference in the privacy of the family that had plagued reform efforts against wife beating up to this time. When charged with threatening the stability of the family, proponents of the whipping post argued that they were helping to preserve the home by quickly restoring the family breadwinner—after having been whipped—to his home. They rarely, if ever, were asked to defend themselves against the charge that the state was wrongfully interfering in the family.

The whipping-post campaign seemed a novel solution to the problem of a battered woman's economic dependency. The imprisonment of wife beaters depended on a woman's willingness to prosecute. The assaulted wife might be willing to bring a complaint to the police, but she and her children could not welcome the prospect of having to subsist while the male provider served a term in jail. A whipping appeared to offer a solution to the special financial vulnerability of battered women. Very rarely, however, did the advocates of the whipping post put the argument in these terms.

In the debate about the merits of the whipping post at the annual meeting of the ABA, a lawyer from Louisiana voiced the most frequent objection to the whipping post. He argued that the state was needlessly and with malice causing a man pain. God's law was violated when the criminal was degraded instead of being treated with dignity and respect. The wife beater, suffering disgrace, would become a pariah in his own community. His wife—an innocent victim—would be met with scorn and his children would be ashamed. Society was permitted to select a punishment that protected itself from the repetition of crime, but was not permitted to indulge in vengeance and retaliation. Civilization would revert to barbarism if the whipping post was reintroduced. Even the man who administered flogging was degraded. Knowledge that criminals were whipped also inflamed the passions of the public and encouraged others, especially impressionable children, in cruelty to helpless animals.[17]

The practical objection to the whipping post was that it had not deterred crime. Cruel punishment and torture, relied on for thousands of years, had not eliminated criminal wrongdoing. Its apparent success in Delaware was due to the fact that Delaware was a small agricultural state that would be relatively free from crime regardless of what criminal measures it invoked. Those who opposed the whipping post for practical, rather than moral, reasons viewed the wife beater as a drunkard who beat his wife in a moment of passion, with little thought to the consequences. They believed that such men were incapable of being rehabilitated, and that the cause of crime was the low level of civilization. Thus wife beating never could be prevented or even reduced, and no effective means lay at hand for deterring it.

Some opponents of the whipping post feared that the flogged husband would take out his rage and humiliation on his wife and children. Others predicted that such a man would desert his family rather than seeing the disgrace he suffered reflected in their eyes, thus reducing them to permanent economic desperation. Employers would refuse to hire a man who had been so shamefully punished.

While most of the ABA debate about the whipping post was serious, one lawyer, seeking some amusement, rose to ask how the wife who beat her husband would be punished. His colleague from Maryland, who favored the whipping post, responded that "I would take a woman who beats her husband and send her to a private apartment with three good wives, the first of whom would lecture her severely, the second of whom should whip her moderately, and the third of whom should instruct her in the art of managing her husband without beating him."[18] A lawyer from Louisiana who opposed the whipping post wanted to amend the resolution by adding "that any one convicted of the crime of rape should be burned at the stake." After the laughter died down, the original resolution in favor of the whipping post was tabled by a vote of 63 to 28.[19]

As the ABA debate about the merits of whipping the wife beater was repeated in legislative chambers across the nation, the arguments offered by each side were much the same. Even the same kind of jocular resolutions reappeared. Some legislative opponents of the whipping post considered wife beating a trivial matter—a situation in which the wife often provoked her husband to violence. A few lawyers favored divorce for brutalized wives, and others believed that temperance would eradicate wife beating. Because the women's movement had not placed wife beating high among its legislative priorities, opponents of whipping were not forced to devise and sponsor alternative legislation to aid assaulted wives.

In 1898 Simeon Baldwin began to champion the whipping-post legislation again, in spite of recent defeats of such bills in New York, New Jersey, and Virginia. He drew encouragement from the fact that influential citizens were more receptive to corporal punishment of criminals. A Boston judge called for the whipping post; a New Jersey grand jury was sympathetic. Before a friendly audience of Connecticut municipal court judges, Baldwin delivered a paper summarizing his ideas. Baldwin continued his advocacy of the whipping post in an article in the *Yale Law Journal* in 1899, in which he also favored castration as a punishment for rape. Two years later he renewed his plea for whipping wife beaters and juvenile delinquents, although he dropped his demand for the castration of rapists.[20]

Some white Southern lawyers, judges, and police thought the whipping post was especially suited for black criminals, who they believed possessed innate criminal tendencies and whose inferior culture exhibited no respect for law and order. Black criminals actually enjoyed imprisonment, it was argued, because they could lie idle, eat free meals, and associate on a basis of equality with whites. Imprisonment did not disgrace the black offender, they held, and he suffered no loss of esteem in the eyes of his comrades upon his release. But blacks feared the sting of the lash because they considered it a badge of slavery. Advocates of the whipping post often remarked that in Delaware no white man ever went to the post twice, implying that the whipping of blacks would have to be repeated.

One of the reasons interest in the whipping post reemerged in the 1890s was because of increased fears of black criminals. The nature of racism in the United States had changed since the Civil War. The American slave had often been regarded as childlike rather than animal in nature. During Reconstruction, the white imagination replaced the trustworthy and gentle slave with the hostile and dangerous freedman. The racist thought of the 1890s held that emancipation revealed the innate brutishness of an inferior race. In the 1890s white Southerners for the first time described openly their fears of blacks raping white women. Joel Williamson has attributed this sudden appearance of the image of black men as rapists to several factors. First, whites were frightened by the assertion of Southern black political power, especially in the Populist movement. Second, periodic agricultural depressions endangered the white standard of living and increased resentment of black economic competition. Third, white men who were unable to provide for their families found an opportunity to prove their manhood by defending to the death the purity of white womanhood. Thus white political fears and economic anxieties created the image of the black rapist of insatiable sexual appetite who preyed on helpless white women. White men believed that in order to protect white society from the "drunken, ravening beast," they had to resort to lynching.[21] In the 1890s angry white mobs murdered hundreds of blacks during the high point of racially motivated lynching fever.

If Southern whites were so fearful of blacks, why was the whipping-post crusade not more successful in the South? The U.S. Congress rejected flogging legislation in 1906, but most of the votes in favor of it came from Southern congressmen. Still, the leaders of the whipping-post campaign were Northern Republican lawyers who found supporters in their own region. Perhaps the reason that the South did not pass whipping laws was that lynching blacks offered a more direct release of their racial fears than legalized flogging. The whipping post appealed more to law enforcement officials than to a vengeful public. Baldwin also recognized later in life that Southern legislators may not have reinstituted the whipping post because they feared being criticized for "reinstituting the methods of slavery."[22]

In the 1890s flogging as a punishment was gaining advocates in England as well as America. As early as 1863 Parliament passed an act sentencing garroters (muggers who strangled their victims) to flogging. Then in the 1890s Parliament passed laws punishing male procurers and mutinous prisoners with lashings. A parliamentary report in 1895 in Scotland favored whipping rather than imprisonment as a punishment for juvenile delinquents. (It was already common in the United States for the police to whip juveniles caught stealing rather than arresting them.) Baldwin was also encouraged by Virginia's enactment in 1898 of a law authorizing whipping for juvenile criminals.

Baldwin finally found an ally who believed in the whipping post as much as he did. Clark Bell was a distinguished lawyer and president of the Medico-Legal Society. The son of a blacksmith, Bell made his fortune as the lawyer for the Union Pacific Railroad in charge of purchasing the acquisition rights for the railroad's right-of-way. In his middle and later years, Bell gave less attention to his law practice and devoted more time to his hobbies of grape cultivation, wine making, and breeding trotting horses. He also spent more time with the Medico-Legal Society, an organization composed of doctors and lawyers who were interested in the professional reform of the law. The society favored the appointment of trained, nonpartisan physicians as coroners, expert medical testimony in legal suits, and advocated the insanity defense in criminal proceedings. It also championed the cause of women physicians and included several prominent women among its members. Bell, one of the society's founders, had been its president intermittently for many years and had served as an editor of its journal.[23]

Bell and Baldwin believed they could achieve legislative victory in at least one state—Delaware. In 1898 Baldwin delivered a major address before a banquet of the Medico-Legal Society, with Bell inviting speakers, mostly law enforcement officials, from across the country to react to the idea.[24] Among those Bell welcomed at the banquet were three of Delaware's supreme court justices, the state's fire commissioners, and the chief of the Wilmington police. The banquet received enthusiastic coverage from the *Washington Post*. The entire event was restaged before a meeting of the American Association of Physicians and Surgeons the next week. During the following year, newspapers in Chicago, Philadelphia, and New York City carried stories favorable to the use of the whipping post. A Boston magistrate, in sentencing a wife beater, hoped "to live to see the day when I can order the lash to be applied to the naked back of the man who assaults his wife." Theodore Roosevelt, governor of New York, went on record in favor of flogging husbands who assaulted their wives. At Baldwin's suggestion, the Connecticut Congregational Association, an organization that included both lay and clerical members, adopted a resolution in favor of the whipping post as a punishment for petty crimes and offenses committed by youths. However, the whipping of wife beaters was not mentioned.[25]

Delaware's whipping post served an important function in a state that had not erected a state prison, but instead relied on county jails to incarcerate inmates. Most Delaware prisoners were sentenced to a short jail term, along with a fine and a whipping. Periodic efforts to abolish the whipping post had been handily defeated. The only restriction to succeed was a prohibition on whipping females. Delaware officials liked to point to the simplicity and lack of expense of the cat-of-nine-tails. They also worried about the daily stream of thirty to forty tramps, riding the rails, who entered the state. These "vicious classes" were unafraid of a term in jail; in fact, they welcomed the warm place to stay and the steady meals prison provided. But any tramp who had been flogged in Delaware would not soon return. The officials liked to refer to a kind of testimonial from well-known out-of-state robbers who, having been flogged in the state, swore never to return. (Presumably these men were undeterred from committing crimes elsewhere.)

Bell's friend and a longtime vice president of the Medico-Legal Society, Chief Justice Charles Lore of the Delaware Supreme Court, led the campaign in his state to extend the punishment of whipping to wife beaters. In the confusing world of Delaware politics, Lore was considered a liberal reformer. He favored building a state prison and led the movement to abolish the pillory. Lore had also been the state's attorney general and served two terms in congress. A former minister, he remained active in the Methodist Episcopal church. Lore felt strongly that the wife beater should be punished by a whipping. He was fond of saying, "I'd have the wife whip him if I could get her to do so, I would like to stand beside her at the time."[26] A bill introduced in the state legislature in 1901 classified wife beating as a misdemeanor to be punished at the discretion of the court by a fine, imprisonment, and a whipping of not less than five nor more than fifty lashes. Serious opposition was limited to the Society of Friends, which had long campaigned against the pillory and the post. In the Delaware legislature, the effort to abolish the post was led by a representative from New Castle, a county with a large Quaker and Scandinavian population. Hoping to defeat the bill by ridicule, he introduced a countermeasure to provide a whipping for a wife convicted of beating her husband. His amended legislation was soundly defeated, and the original bill passed easily.

President Theodore Roosevelt, in his fourth annual message to Congress in

1904, gave the campaign an unexpected boost. He inserted a paragraph decrying "brutality and cruelty toward the weak." He wrote, "The wifebeater, for example, is inadequately punished by imprisonment; for imprisonment may often mean nothing to him, while it may cause hunger and want to the wife and children who have been the victim of his brutality. Probably some form of corporal punishment would be the most adequate way of meeting this crime."[27] No president before had ever mentioned the issue of wife beating in his annual message to Congress. (Ronald Reagan was the first president since Roosevelt to do so.) Roosevelt, a longtime advocate of social purity and a champion of the whipping post, was also a personal friend of Clark Bell and Simeon Baldwin. His presidential address appears to have influenced legislators in Oregon, who passed a whipping-post bill in 1905.[28] No information is available about the sponsors of this legislation. Victory in Oregon was unusual, since the only two other states to punish wife beating with whipping were in the upper South. The passage of Oregon's law was the final legislative success for the whipping-post campaign.

In 1906 a vigorous supporter of this legislation, Robert Adams, a congressman from Pennsylvania, introduced a bill in Congress to punish wife beaters in the District of Columbia with the whipping post. (Congress acted as the law-making body for the District of Columbia.) President Roosevelt seems to have withdrawn from the fray by the time this legislation was introduced. Most congressmen saw the floor debate on the whipping-post bill as an opportunity for amusement before the lunch-hour recess. They introduced a series of amendments to put on the rack a husband who failed to support his wife, burn at the stake a man who refused to marry, and appropriate $10,000 so that the commissioners of the District of Columbia could purchase a whipping post, a pillory, and a stake. An amendment was offered to exempt from whipping the president, his cabinet officers, congressmen, and senators, and another, to punish any wife who became a common scold with a ducking in the Potomac River.[29] All of these amendments were greeted with loud guffaws.

Having had their fun, members of the House voted to table Adams's resolution by 153 to 60. The opposition to tabling the motion, which presumably consisted of supporters of the whipping post, was bipartisan and comprised largely of Southerners and representatives from Pennsylvania, colleagues of Robert Adams.[30]

Even after this defeat, Maryland and Delaware continued to find merit in and enforce their whipping-post laws. In the 1920s, Maryland judges still sentenced a few wife beaters to floggings. There is no information as to the enforcement of the whipping-post law in Oregon. In Delaware between 1901 and 1942, six whites and fifteen blacks were flogged for wife beating. The largest number of whippings for wife beating in Delaware was administered in the early years of the twentieth century.[31]

Even in Delaware, use of the whipping post was being challenged. Reformers there scored a partial victory when the state legislature abolished the pillory in 1905, although the whipping post was retained. A Montana congressman in 1913 introduced legislation in the U.S. House of Representatives to abolish Delaware's whipping post on the grounds that it was a cruel and unusual punishment prohibited by the federal Constitution. He requested that the U.S. attorney general prevent Delaware officials from administering floggings. But the Justice Department ruled that the federal courts did not have the power to issue an injunction. Their decision silenced congressional debate about Delaware's whipping post.[32]

In Progressive era America, the whipping post was an anachronism. In 1911 the public was outraged by the sentence of a notorious burglar and horse thief (who was white) to seventy lashes at Delaware's whipping post. Baldwin and Bell rose to the defense of "Red Hannah," as Delaware's post had come to be called by some of the black prisoners who had been manacled to it. Baldwin, now governor of Connecticut, lectured the state's Conference of Charities and Corrections on the merits of the whipping post.[33] Meanwhile Clark Bell was still denouncing "the mock humanitarians of our age. . . Give me a Delaware whipping post in New York City," he requested of the readers of the *Medico-Legal Journal*, "and I will eliminate wife-beating in that city or any other American city."[34] One magistrate began to advocate the whipping post for husbands who deserted their wives.[35]

Between 1911 and 1917 the movement to end capital punishment was revived. Newspapers that once called for a return to the whipping post now denounced it as uncivilized. A warden of the Delaware state prison in 1925 explained, "We haven't had a wifebeater for years." Whenever a whipping was administered, he said, he received a flood of protest letters from all parts of the country.[36] The whipping post was finally abolished in Maryland in 1948 and Delaware in 1952.

The whipping-post campaign dissolved at the same time that Victorian rhetoric about male brutishness and female purity began to recede. Social reformers were less interested in denouncing and punishing brutish men than in eradicating the social conditions believed to cause crime. Never again would there be such maudlin sympathy for the protection of female sexual virtue. The brutish drunkard became the pitiable alcoholic who suffered from a curable medical disease or, in more severe cases, from genetic abnormality.

No permanent gains on behalf of battered women resulted from the whipping-post campaign. Had there been more legislative success, Baldwin and Bell were prepared to champion the castration of rapists and the flogging of juvenile delinquents. If punitive measures made sense as a penalty for some kinds of crime, why not employ them to deter others? And given the class and racial biases of many of the people who administer justice, it is likely that the poor, immigrants, and ethnic minorities would have been the most frequent recipients of physical punishment.

Perhaps the greatest significance of Baldwin's crusade lay in its failure. The antebellum feminist crusade proved that an attack on marriage killed any chances of legislative success. The men who favored the whipping post hardly ever discussed marriage, divorce, or woman's rights. Yet they lost, too, because state legislators were unwilling to reimpose a barbaric form of punishment.

Nonetheless, the public often supports physical punishment for some types of crimes. In the late 1940s, one-third of those questioned in a social survey agreed with the statement, "prison is too good for sex criminals. They should be publicly whipped or worse."[37] This high rate of approval for corporal punishment disturbed social researchers who held that such attitudes demonstrated authoritarianism. An Anderson, South Carolina, circuit court judge in 1983 sentenced three rapists to a choice between castration and thirty years in prison. About the same time, bills were introduced in the Maine and Massachusetts legislatures to punish rape with castration. Some members of the contemporary women's movement have been known to wear buttons and carry signs that read "Castrate Rapists."[38] One feminist journalist in her book on "conjugal crime" came across a library reference to Adams's whipping-post bill in the Pennsylvania legislature. She wrote, "Justice at last! The proposed bill, however, did not pass."[39] Phyllis Schlafly, well-known as an ERA opponent, objected to shelters for battered wives, but appeared to favor instead—perhaps tongue-in-cheek—the whipping post. "The public whipping was a rare occurrence," she arged, "because the threat of it had made Delaware one of the most crime-free states in the country."[40] Extreme violence in the family, rape, and sexual molestation, even in the modern era, arouse vindictive impulses in the public. In responding to public outcry, the values of those who dispensed justice were scarcely more advanced than those of the lynch mob and vigilantes. The powers of the state must be limited to ensure that, when punishing criminals, the bounds of humanity are not overstepped.

The stocks and whipping post in colonial Boston, 1657.
(*Courtesy of the Bostonian Society*)

MEMOIRS

OF

Mrs. Abigail Bailey,

WHO HAD BEEN THE WIFE

OF

MAJOR ASA BAILEY,

FORMERLY OF LANDAFF, (N. H.)

WRITTEN BY HERSELF.

SHE DIED IN BATH, N. H. FEBRUARY, 11, 1815.

TO WHICH ARE ADDED SUNDRY ORIGINAL

BIOGRAPHICAL SKETCHES.

EDITED BY ETHAN SMITH, A. M.
MINISTER OF THE GOSPEL IN HOPKINTON, N. H.

"Behold, and see, if there be any sorrow like unto my sorrow." JEREMIAH.
"Many are the afflictions of the righteous; but the Lord delivereth him out of them all." DAVID.

BOSTON:
PUBLISHED BY SAMUEL T. ARMSTRONG,
Theological Printer and Bookseller, No. 50, Cornhill

1815.

The year 1815: the first autobiographical account of family violence,
by the mother of an incest victim.

The first American depiction of family violence, from a temperance almanac, 1835.

A New York City police court, 1853.

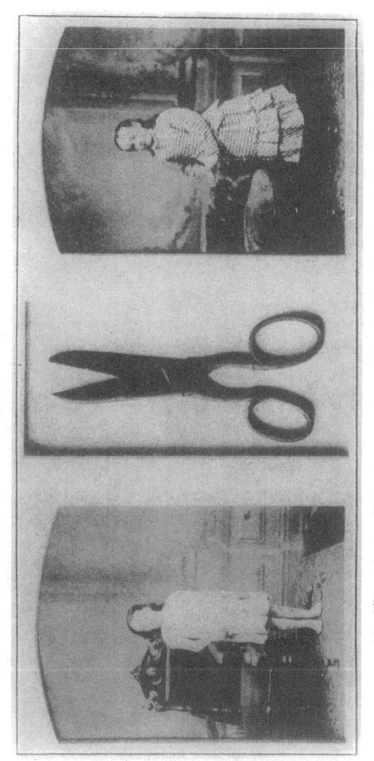

Mary Ellen: at the time of her rescue, one year later, and the scissors Mrs. Connolly used on her, 1875.

The Delaware whipping post and pillory in use, 1897.

A father uses the shingle on his son, c. 1897.
(Courtesy of the American Antiquarian Society)

A mother does the same, c. 1897.
(*Courtesy of the American Antiquarian Society*)

A mother demonstrates "spanking," c. 1897.
(Courtesy of the American Antiquarian Society)

A boy in the judge's chambers of the New York City juvenile court, 1920.

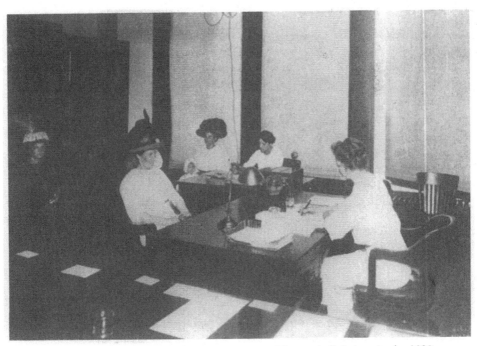

The complaint department at Chicago's Court of Domestic Relations in the 1920s.

A child guidance clinic in the 1950s.

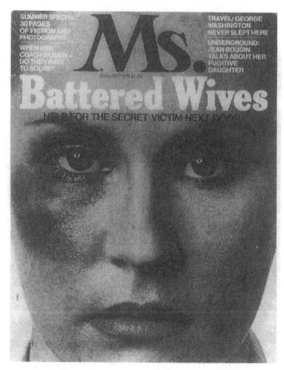

A women's movement magazine discovers wife beating: 1976.
(Courtesy of Ms. Magazine)

III

Reform,
the Psyche,
and the State

7

The Socialized
Courts

A NEW YORK CITY FAMILY COURT JUDGE in the 1920s tried the case of a husband, married for twenty years, who squandered his wages and, when drunk, beat his wife. The husband explained that his marriage was placid until the previous year when his wife began nagging him. He insisted that if is his wife only "showed him some affection, everything would be all right." The psychiatrist who headed the court's neurological institute examined the husband and wife. He reported to the judge that the wife was undergoing menopause, which made her upset and undemonstrative toward her husband. Apparently satisfied with this explanation, the judge agreed with the psychiatrist "as to the need for tender care and attention on the part of the husband, particularly during this trying change of life." The wife, accompanied by her husband, "left the court with a paper marked 'Complaint Withdrawn.'"[1]

This case, despite the absurd conclusions of the court's psychiatrist, still shows elements of a new approach toward family violence. Wife beating was being dealt with in a new type of court, where a judge was free to inquire into the couple's sexual life and personal misunderstandings, relatively unencumbered by the legal rules of evidence. Psychiatrists and social workers had become the handmaidens of judicial decision-making. Wife beating was attributed to the sexual and biological problems of women. It was seen as a form of domestic dispute best left to the counseling services of the family court. Family violence was regarded as a domestic difficulty rather than a violation of the criminal law. Criminal prosecution of incest was looked upon as wasted effort; child cruelty was dealt with in a noncriminal manner.

The distinguishing feature of the modern approach toward family violence was that criminal cases of child cruelty or spouse abuse were being heard in separate tribunals—juvenile and family (or domestic relations) courts. These new courts were designed to handle certain categories of people who committed crimes—children or other family members—rather than punish criminal offenses. The basic goal of these courts was to preserve the family, act in the best interests of the child, and offer a curative rather than punitive approach to family problems. Proponents of the juvenile courts argued, for instance, that mixing juvenile offenders with adult criminals simply afforded youths a better education in crime. Because childhood was believed to be a separate, more innocent stage of life, reformers wanted the court to provide a form of justice that prevented the juvenile from growing up to become a public menace. Similarly, judges who favored the establishment of family courts argued that relatives who committed crimes against each other ought not to be punished as common criminals, since they were merely ignorant, mentally deficient, or perhaps lazy and shiftless.

The juvenile and family courts were one of many reforms developed in the Progressive era, the two decades following the turn of the century. This period of American history was as important for the cause of protecting women and children as the New Deal was in aiding organized labor. Progressives passed hundreds of state and federal laws to limit the hours and improve the working conditions of women and children. At the same time, discussion of family violence as such ceased; few if any new state laws were passed concerning child cruelty, wife beating, or incest. As already noted, the heads of SPCCs at the turn of the century believed child cruelty was no longer an important issue. Interest in wife beating ended with the demise of the whipping-post campaign. Family violence, stigmatized by its association with old-fashioned moralism, was believed to be a problem of the past. Reformers found other social problems more interesting and pressing. Concern about family violence had little, if anything, to do with the formation of the juvenile and family courts, but the procedures these courts established directly affected how instances of family violence would be understood and handled.

The Illinois legislature created the first juvenile court—in Chicago—in 1899. Twenty years later all but three states had established such courts. Progressives hailed the creation of a tribunal designed to meet the unique needs of children.

Why was the juvenile court established? The immediate circumstances that led to its founding was indignation at the inhumane treatment of children in criminal courts and the barbarity of conditions under which child criminals were confined. Yet these conditions had been present for almost a century and had not given rise to new forms of children's justice. Some scholars interpret the juvenile courts as a new form of social response to the problems of the urban-industrial society. But an embarrassingly long stretch of time separates the emergence of modern social problems—poverty, illiteracy, unemployment, and the dislocations produced by immigration—from the appearance of the juvenile courts. Others hold that the impetus for their creation was humanitarianism.[2] These generalizations provide part of the reason, but still do not make clear why the juvenile courts did not appear earlier. At first, the reasons behind the establishment of juvenile courts resemble those that led to the formation of the SPCC. The women's club leaders and male judges who founded the juvenile court appear remarkably similar in social background and philosophy to late nineteenth-century social purity reformers and whipping-post campaigners. Yet juvenile justice reform added some new themes to the Victorian concern with the protection of children. First, the revival of interest in rehabilitation and treatment that had spelled the end of the whipping-post crusade also gave rise to the juvenile court. Poverty and poor housing, rather than faulty moral character, were cited as the most frequent causes of crime. Second, Progressive era reformers sought to create a judicial administrative apparatus, a bureaucratic system capable of handling a large caseload. The courts allied with "the helping professions" of psychiatry and social work in providing continuing supervision of families. Finally, settlement-house reformers and other Progressives believed the immigrant family, especially the immigrant mother, capable of raising respectable children who would be valuable future citizens. Where the previous generation had rebuked depraved parents, the Progressive reformers tried to see behind domestic rage to the "natural affection" between mothers and their children.

Thus, founders of the juvenile court, as true exemplars of an optimistic age, hoped to offer children a special kind of justice uniquely suited to their needs. Judges in these courts were not restricted to the rules of evidence, but could inquire freely into the particular circumstances of each child. Legal reformers in the 1960s, however, criticized the juvenile court for failing to provide the youthful offender with the protection of due process. They noted specifically that juvenile courts did not offer children legal representation and had no procedure for appeal of judicial decisions. The court may have been designed to meet children's needs, but later reformers felt it violated their constitutional rights.

Others accuse the juvenile courts of violating *parents'* rights, especially their right to privacy. Jacques Donzelot, a French sociologist, has indicted French juvenile courts and the helping professions for their extensive surveillance of the working-class family. He traces the failings of these courts to

Progressive era reform (or its French equivalent). Christopher Lasch has similarly rebuked American social service professions for destroying family autonomy. Both Donzelot and Lasch have argued that the courts intruded upon the family life of the poor, usurping functions that had been traditionally performed by the family, and taking power away from the working-class father.[3]

From her study of the case records of the Massachusetts SPCC and other Boston social welfare agencies between 1880 and 1930, Linda Gordon has offered a number of criticisms of the ideas of Lasch and Donzelot. She believes that although elements of social control can be found in the actions of these organizations, they have also provided genuine help. Agency intervention was often initiated at the request of the families themselves. Gordon argues that the concept of family autonomy is a myth: families have always been regulated by relatives and neighbors. Indeed, informal intervention was often more unjust—in that it was likely to side with the more powerful members of the family—than initiatives taken by courts, clinics, and SPCCs. She points out that Lasch and Donzelot assume that the family is an independent entity of shared interest, rather than one consisting of different generations and genders; MSPCC intervention in the family often violated male authority but came to the aid of women and children. Gordon argues further that modern social control theory appears to view family violence and child neglect as an invention of social workers, rather than a real and troubling social ill. From her study of the case records of the MSPCC, she concluded that its clients wanted assistance and often benefited from the help that was offered.[4]

Gordon's criticisms apply with equal force to the work of the juvenile courts. Juvenile and family courts allied with the father against the mother and child, with the child against his or her parents, or with mothers against their children. Lasch and Donzelot emphasized only one type of action, that of the court interceding against the parent, usually the father, when, in fact, it was involved in diverse proceedings, acting on behalf of mothers and fathers, as in petitions to have an incorrigible child removed from home and sent to an industrial or reform school. The court also prosecuted mothers and fathers (but especially mothers) for contributing to the dependency, neglect, or delinquency of their child, and removed children from a "destitute" or "unfit" home. The court also tried children for truancy or for specific offenses, such as theft.

The juvenile courts had been founded to "preserve" the family. Reformers during the Progressive period hoped to shore up the male-headed nuclear family, so that children would not have to be removed from abusive or neglectful parents and marriages would not be broken up. They believed that a family dependent on charity would be undermined, so they felt the government, through the judiciary and its special agencies, should try to make the family self-sustaining. Thus, the ideal of family privacy, which had served as a barrier to government intervention for decades, now provided the justification for state intervention. The Progressives sought a family in which the father was the primary (if not sole) breadwinner, children went to school full-time, and mothers remained at home, devoting themselves to housekeeping and care of their children.

Judge Bernhard Rabbino, an immigrant from Eastern Europe and a former rabbi who became the first judge to preside over New York City's Court of Domestic Relations, offered one of the most complete rationales for the work of the new courts in his autobiography, *Back to the Home*. The title is expressive of the author's viewpoint. Rabbino feared that the employment of mothers would lead to child neglect, and that single women, the future childbearers of the nation, were ruining their health by working in factories. If mothers remained at home caring for their children and being supported by their husbands, they would be able to raise healthier children and prepare their children to become responsible citizens. The family was giving way under the impact of industrialization, he argued, and it was ceding power over children to the schools. Rabbino favored eliminating women workers from stores and offices, replacing them with men. Although some Progressive era reformers felt that the immigrants, as genetic inferiors, would never be able to raise productive children, Rabbino held out the hope of helping America's newcomers and their children escape from poverty. [5]

In every reform effort against family violence up to this time, the emphasis on preserving the family (namely, a male-headed household) appeared in one form or another; in the Progressive era it meant extensive efforts by professionals and court personnel to alter the values and behavior of the poor, without having to break up the family. Children were not to be taken from their parents on account of poverty alone; it was unclear what should be done on behalf of abused and neglected children, where parental malfeasance, rather than low income, was the reason for considering removal.

Cases of abuse appeared before the juvenile court in many guises. A truant boy might have been absent from school because he had been beaten and neglected and did not want to admit it to his teacher or classmates. An "incorrigible" girl could have been rebelling against her parents who had whipped her for disobedience or against a father who raped her. In short, the stubborn, truant, or homeless juvenile may often have been an abused or neglected child.

The juvenile courts replaced "child cruelty" with the term "child neglect," subsuming under the label a variety of other conditions affecting the child, such as destitution, homelessness, abandonment, dependence upon public support, growing up without proper parental care, begging, living in a brothel or with a disreputable person, living in an unfit home because of parental neglect, peddling, playing a musical instrument in public, singing in a public place, or living in surroundings dangerous to morals.[6] Incest and sexual abuse were fitted into the category of "sexual delinquency" or moral neglect of the child. The courts handled many more cases of neglect than of physical abuse. The U.S. Children's Bureau, compiling yearly figures on the work of some sixty to eighty juvenile courts across the nation between 1929 and 1935, determined that only 2 percent of cases of dependency and neglect involved charges of child cruelty.[7] Had the total caseload of the courts been considered, the percentage of abuse cases before the juvenile courts would have been even lower.

Juvenile court proceedings for handling cases of neglect might involve two separate actions: a criminal charge against the parents for contributing to the neglect of a child, and a civil proceeding to remove the child from parental custody. Jurisdiction over cases of child cruelty and neglect was handled by the family courts in some cities, by juvenile courts, or by both juvenile and criminal courts in others.[8] A case of child abuse or neglect came before the juvenile court as a result of a complaint, usually from a social agency, an anticruelty society, a relative, or a schoolteacher. The probation officer or some other court employee interviewed the complaining party. Two out of every five cases appearing before Cook County Juvenile Court in 1918 were "adjusted" without being referred to the formal proceedings of the court. For Toronto's juvenile court, the figure was more than four out of five in 1912.[9] Of all the cases brought before the juvenile court, those concerning neglect and abuse were probably the least likely to result in dismissal. Even so, most abuse and neglect cases seem to have been "adjusted" without any charges being brought.

The anticruelty societies had encouraged fear of their agents; the juvenile courts hoped that probation officers would be liked and respected.[10] The difference had to do with changing public attitudes toward outside intervention in the family. The anticruelty societies recognized intervention as unpopular, but were ill-equipped to back up their threats with actions; the juvenile courts believed their actions were beneficial to families and probation officers were capable of exercising greater supervision over cases than agents of the anticruelty societies in the late nineteenth century. The Progressives viewed the probation officer as a friend of the child, a visitor to the home who would study the family's circumstances and offer helpful suggestions. He or she was supposed to be "tactful, skillful, firm and patient," a benevolent stranger "endowed with the strength of Samson and the delicacy of an

Ariel."[11] Hastings Hart, one of the leading child welfare experts of his day, noted that "it is interesting to see how the probation officer, distrusted and disliked at first, comes to be recognized as the best friend of the family . . . It is interesting to see, also, the surprising improvement which takes place in many families under the influence of the probation officer, strengthened by the fear of having the child taken away from his home by the court."[12] But many immigrant parents recognized that probation officers were usurping traditional parental prerogatives and objected to state interference with their authority. A Russian father, appearing before the juvenile court in Los Angeles, grieved that he was unable to keep his eight-year-old son at home and out of trouble. He angrily told the judge, "Oh, Fred! . . . He is wicked. I beat him to death,—then they say—it is against the law."[13]

Yet these parents perceived courts as more powerful than they were. As late as the 1920s, only one juvenile court out of five could afford to hire a probation officer. The one city with a significant number of probation officers was Chicago, with sixty-five. In Manhattan there were only three, St. Louis had eleven, and Cleveland and Cincinnati had six each. In Cleveland the chief probation officer directed the work of women volunteers as well as several dozen members of the fire department.[14]

In spite of all their efforts to preserve the family, the courts and their personnel often had to remove children from the home. While juvenile delinquents were frequently placed on probation and rarely committed to institutions, the reverse was true of neglected children. At the Boston Juvenile Court between 1906 and 1916, 16 percent of the cases of juvenile delinquents, but 65 percent of the child neglect cases, led to committing a child to an institution. (However, because juvenile crime was far more frequent, the majority of children institutionalized were nonetheless delinquents.) The courts in modern times have been more reluctant to take children from their parents. In 1979, about 20 percent of maltreated (abused and neglected) children were removed from their homes and placed in foster care, according to summary statistics from all juvenile courts in the United States.[15]

The number of children under sixteen in children's institutions rose from 60,981 in 1890 to a high of 204,888 in 1923, and then fell by a third in the next decade.[16] Since most of the residents in these institutions were delinquents or orphans, rather than neglected children, these figures suggest only that institutionalization of all types of children was increasing. Additional evidence indicates the growth in committing to institutions abused and neglected children. The U.S. Census Bureau in 1910 conducted a survey of the practices of anticruelty societies across the country, which was expanded in 1923 to include a larger number of societies. In Table 1, only the data from societies that reported information for 1910 and 1923 was included, so as to

Table 1. Disposition of Neglected Children by 49 Child Protective
Societies, 1910 and 1923[a]

	In Families (%)	In Institutions (%)	N
1910, overall	24	76	10,160
MSPCC	n.a.	n.a.	n.a.
NYSPCC	1	99	2,823
PSPCC	n.a.	n.a.	n.a.
1923, overall	14	86	2,907
MSPCC	100	0	120
NYSPCC	0	100	201
PSPCC	36	64	88

[a]Information from the same anticruelty societies in 1910 and 1923; data for 1910
applies to dependent and neglected children disposed of during the year; information
for 1923 pertains only to neglected children handled by protective societies in a four-
month period.

Sources: U.S. Bureau of the Census, *Benevolent Institutions, 1910* (Washington,
D.C.: U.S. Government Printing Office, 1913), Table II, 158–173; U.S. Bureau of
the Census, *Children Under Institutional Care, 1923* (Washington, D.C.: U.S.
Government Printing Office, 1927), Table 30, 202–209.

compare the work of the same organizations at two periods of time. The
percentage of neglected children committed to institutions rose from 76 percent in 1910 to 86 percent in 1923. As more children's institutions were built,
larger numbers of abused and neglected children were placed in them. The
wealthier and more reform-minded the state, the greater the likelihood that it
had recently built an agricultural, industrial, or manual training school.
However the budgets of these states made no provision to pay for foster care
for needy children.

Progressive era reformers never entirely succeeded in eliminating the drab
living arrangements in children's institutions. Even in the 1920s, the atmosphere of such places seemed to resemble the military more than the family.
Because the superintendents of many of these institutions were devoted to
regular drills, children were lined up in rows and marched about during the
day in close-order formations. Most of the staff consisted of grammar school
graduates who had formerly been employed in menial positions at other state
institutions. The average children's asylum offered little training or education
and expected its inmates to perform domestic chores, farm labor, or repairs.
Visitors to one of these schools observed that "the whole institution is kept
spotlessly clean—the girls are constantly on their hands and knees scrubbing
and polishing floors."[17] Ironically, abused and neglected children at these

institutions often found themselves the victims of assault. This was not a new story but the Progressives did not want to believe that their dreams of familylike institutions had so quickly turned into a nightmare of administrative incompetence and malfeasance.

An unusual verbatim transcript of a neglect hearing by a California juvenile court judge, published in 1922 and reprinted in *The Journal of Delinquency,* described a "representative" juvenile court hearing. The children were treated kindly, as one might have expected, but the mother of these neglected boys was subjected to unfriendly inquiries. The transcript provides the human story behind the placement of neglected children in state industrial schools. The hearing involved two brothers, aged twelve and ten, who admitted to the judge that they had stolen $90. The boys were the oldest children in a family of six. Their parents (identified in the transcript under the fictional names of Mr. and Mrs. Smith) had been married for fourteen years. Mr. Smith, who was illiterate, was employed steadily as a carpenter, and Mrs. Smith, who had a grammar school education, had been working sporadically, probably as a domestic, during the last four years. Since the previous summer, the Smith's babysitter had been in the hospital, and the children, all of whom were of school age, were left unattended from the time school ended until their parents came home from work. The judge questioned the assistant probation officer, who reported that the boys' home was "dirty. Everything was on the floor, this is in front of the house; I don't know about the back part. The children were all dirty." Then the judge interrogated Mrs. Smith about who was caring for the children while she was working. He told Mrs. Smith that he would not remove her sons if she quit her job. She refused.

THE COURT: The other day I asked you, when the boys got into trouble, to stay home and take care of your family, and you refused?

A. Yes.

THE COURT: You still refuse?

A. I certainly do.

THE COURT: Do you know, Mrs. Smith, that when you left, you simply turned around and walked off, didn't speak to the boys, or say goodbye to them.

A. Yes, I did. I didn't wish to hurt their feelings. I didn't want to put them up aginst [*sic*] any harder proposition than was necessary, or make things harder for them.

THE COURT: The boys' feelings have been pretty badly hurt already.

A. No doubt about it.

THE COURT: You turned around and walked off without even saying goodbye. Your husband came over and shed tears because he thought he was going to lose his children; but you showed no emotion, no care at all. Are you aware of that?

A. I know it; yes sir.

THE COURT: As far [as] you are concerned, you are perfectly willing that the children should be taken away and cared for by other people?

A. I am, yes sir; because home conditions are not what could be wished for and will not be.

THE COURT: Not so long as you are running it, they will not improve.

A. I should say so.

THE COURT. How much are you earning?

A. Three and a half a day.

THE COURT: Well, for the sake of these children, we are going to take care of them from now on. I do not want you to think Mrs. Smith, that you can bring children into the world and then turn them loose on the state, for the state to take care of.

A. I understand that, thoroughly.

The judge declared the boys to be wards of the court and committed them to the Whittier State School until they reached the age of twenty-one. He ordered the Smiths to pay $40 a month toward the support of their sons, which was about one-seventh of the family's monthly income. He turned to Mrs. Smith.

THE COURT: I am afraid if you continue to do as you are now doing, I will have to take all the rest of your family away from you.

A. Regardless of what may happen to me or my family, I will not live with my husband.[18]

The father of the boys was called on to testify, and he was told, matter-of-factly, how much he was required to pay in support. The judge was not finished with Mrs. Smith, however.

THE COURT: [To Mrs. Smith] How many more children have you?

A. I have four more.

THE COURT: You still refuse to stay home and take care of these children?

A. I certainly do. I stand pat. I have my own way to make in the world.

THE COURT: Do you know that we could file a charge against you for contributing to the delinquency of these children? Do you know that they have become delinquent children, dependent on the state; and that you have directly caused the situation by not remaining at home? That you could be arrested on that charge and sent to jail for contributing to the delinquency of these children?

A. Send me to jail; put me behind the jail doors; but I will never change my mind. He has abused me and mistreated me; I don't care what becomes of me. Place me behind the jail doors if you want to, but I will say there is no justice. I will prove to you that I am in the right.

THE COURT: Then, why don't you produce the evidence? I will give you a chance to prove it. We will have to have a hearing in regard to these other children. You have a daughter fourteen years old, growing into womanhood. Certainly she ought to have a woman to take care of her, someone to keep her from falling into bad company. You know that. You know you ought to do it. If you do not, it will be a case of the court having to take care of her. We will probably file a petition. We will not do it today. I think within the next few days we will proceed along that line with the rest of the children. We want your children to grow up right. We want to put them in a position in life where you can say, "Those are my children, I am proud of them," not to have them brought into a juvenile court by a policeman for trouble they have got into because you did not do your part.

A. Only one thing you fellows can put against me, you can only arrest me for working hard at an honest day's work. That doesn't hurt me a bit.

THE COURT: Honest day's work is right, Mrs. Smith. You probably are rendering faithful service to your employer for what you receive. But you are not doing right to leave these little children to get into mischief, while you are doing other work. These little boys have been before the court before. They are two good bright boys. They would be good boys and grow up as useful citizens, if you did your part. You neglect them, leave them alone and they get into trouble.

I will say to these boys, as I did the other day; I am not going to punish you for stealing this money, because you have never been given a chance; you have been allowed to run the streets, no one looking after you. I am going to put you in a good home where you will be taken care of.

I am sorry you take the position you do, Mrs. Smith . . . I am here to give these boys a chance in life. I don't believe you take sufficient interest in your children to care about them, but your husband will be proud of these boys when they grow up. Boys, we will take care of you from now on. Each of you [addressing parents] will receive from Whittier State School a copy of the rules and regulations. You can go down there at certain reasonable times to see the boys. They will be glad to see you, and you will be glad to see them. They will be much better off there under present conditions."[19]

The father was not held accountable for inadequate care of his children or the filthiness of his home. Nor were the boys censured for stealing. But the mother was blamed for having a dirty home, no child-care arrangements, and refusing to quit her job. Mrs. Smith claimed she was a battered woman, but the judge of the juvenile court would only discuss the charge of neglect against her. Although it was clear that Mrs. Smith had to work, she was seen as neglecting her children. To keep her sons out of trouble, the judge urged Mrs. Smith to quit her job and remain at home. If she refused, then he threatened to remove her sons and place them in an institution. The judge advised Mrs. Smith to obtain a divorce and child custody. He also added that he did not believe she had been abused and mistreated because "employers of Mr. Smith all speak well of him. All say he is a faithful employee, and they like him. True, he cannot read and write. That probably isn't his fault, his parents did not give him the chance they should."[20] Any man pleasant at work, this judge appeared to believe, could not be assaultive at home.

Mr. Smith cried when he learned his sons were to be removed from his custody, but Mrs. Smith simply walked away. She may have done so because she felt depressed or helpless, rather than because she was unconcerned about her children. The commentary following this transcript suggests that if after-school child care had been provided, the boys would not have been taken from their parents. Nonetheless, no effort was made to help the Smiths secure adequate child care or pay for an after-school babysitter. The Progressives favored a policy of preserving the family, but they were unwilling to commit the resources necessary to achieve this. Juvenile court judges hoped to keep children with their natural parents, and even improve conditions for young-sters, but they had not yet developed adequate social services to meet the needs of a family like the Smiths. Mothers were called upon to change the conditions producing neglect, yet they were often unable to do so. As a result, placement of neglected children in an institution became the easiest solution. Juvenile court judges hoped for cooperation, but when confronted with a hostile and depressed defendant like Mrs. Smith, they resorted to insults and threats.

The court of domestic relations, with legal authority over "family crimes" such as domestic assault and non-payment of child support, emerged as the adult extension of the juvenile court.[21] The first court of domestic relations was established in Buffalo, New York, in 1910, and was given jurisdiction over all criminal matters related to the family. In the next decade, ten major cities followed Buffalo's lead. Most large cities set up similar courts by the 1920s. Studies conducted in that decade showed considerable overlap in the handling of cases between juvenile and family courts. In some cities, the two courts were merged into one, whereas in others, they remained separate. The purpose of Cincinnati's domestic relations court, according to the judge who presided over it, was to provide "for the consideration of all matters relating to the family in one court of exclusive jurisdiction, in which the same methods of procedure shall prevail as in the juvenile court and in which it will be possible to consider social evidence as distinguished from legal evidence."[22] A judge of the New York City court of domestic relations believed that cases of husbands and wives needed to be heard separately from those of "drunkards, pickpockets, and highwaymen." The court, according to this judge, provided "very delicate treatment in an atmosphere that is purer and more wholesome than that of the Police Courts."[23] It was less a legal tribunal than a "great social agency," not "limited to the trial of bare issues of fact."[24]

Family court judges believed they were helping to decriminalize family violence. Judge Bernhard Rabbino held that "domestic trouble cases are not criminal in a legal sense" and insisted that the men and women who were brought to family court were not hardened lawbreakers.[25] The judge of Philadelphia's Court of Domestic Relations preferred to avoid issuing warrants for arrest because "warrants involve usually a bond and a bond involves the husband or the wife lying in jail in a filthy cell over night for an offense which is not really a crime; it is a matter of laziness or shiftlessness or indifference or incapacity or negligence or mental or physical deficiency on the part of the husband."[26]

A sociological survey described the average couple that came before the reconciliation department of the Dayton, Ohio, court of domestic relations in the 1920s. They were white, Protestant, and working class, and had not graduated from high school. The wife was usually a homemaker, the typical husband was a factory worker; the couple had been married on the average eleven years and had several children. In more than a third of the cases, one member of the couple—usually the wife—brought charges of assault; in fact, physical abuse was probably the single most common reason for complaining to the courts.[27]

The official policy of courts of domestic relations was to urge reconciliation ("home mending") whenever possible. Judges did so "for the sake of the children, to make the home what it should be—a haven of rest, peace, comfort and happiness."[28] Wife abuse was often believed to be "due to the extravagance of the wife and the arrogance and lack of understanding on the part of the husband who is abusive in manner."[29] Each spouse was regarded as equally at fault in creating a troublesome but trivial misunderstanding. Philadelphia's court of domestic relations in the 1920s claimed to have reunited 90 to 95 percent of the couples that appeared before it.[30] During the same decade, only one out of ten couples that met with the reconciliation bureau of Dayton's court of domestic relations went on to secure a divorce.[31] Social workers frankly admitted that one reason for bringing the couple together was a mother's inability to support herself and her children. But marital reunion was not only preferable for the family but for society. An interpreter employed in the Philadelphia courts anticipated the domestic happiness that would arise when a husband and wife buried their differences.

> The relations of the members of the family to one another become different . . . The head of the house shows more consideration for the women

and children, the wife begins to dress and act like American women, the family larder is kept in good condition, the father begins to patronize the savings bank and is well toward being a good American citizen.[32]

The procedures of the court of domestic relations were designed to discourage separation and divorce whenever possible. At Chicago's domestic relations court, an abused wife who wanted to file charges against her husband came to the office of the court. She was questioned by a woman interviewer, while other mothers, accompanied by their children, waited patiently to be interviewed. Since most women who brought complaints to the court were immigrants (at Chicago's court of domestic relations in 1911, the largest single group was German, followed by the Irish, Russians, and Poles), the court's interpreter was frequently called upon.[33] A mother could leave her children to be supervised by a nurse in a medium-sized room, largely filled with cots covered with army blankets. The police court, usually located in a corner of the neighborhood police station, offered none of the feminine atmosphere or children's services of the court of domestic relations. It reeked of stale cigar smoke and human sweat and was crowded with male bondsmen, messengers, and lawyers soliciting clients. No women interviewers were available there.

Before a woman complainant left the office of the court of domestic relations, she and her husband were given an appointment for a conference five days later. If the woman was not in severe distress, she was sent home and visited within a few days. The court's social service department sent a letter to the husband inviting him to the department for a "friendly talk" with a caseworker or the judge of the court. If he failed to appear, the interviewer notified the judge of the court, who could issue a summons for the man's appearance. A caseworker could arrange for a clinical examination if any of the family members was believed to be suffering from mental illness. To prepare her report, the caseworker spoke with the husband's employer and found out how much the man earned. In some cities caseworkers conducted perfunctory investigations, whereas in others, they made extensive inquiries into the family's history, economic condition, present difficulties, and child-care arrangements.

The caseworker would go to the woman's home to learn what kind of housekeeper she was and observe the neighborhood where the family lived. The investigation of a woman's housekeeping reflected the belief that one of the central elements of the housewife's role was to maintain a high standard of cleanliness and neatness. One of the founders of modern social work, Mary Richmond, claimed in *Social Diagnosis* that "the household speaks for the wife, answering unasked questions about her as it does not about the husband."[34] The caseworker would caution the wife to keep her home and children clean if she wished to command the respect of her husband. She also told the wife to have her husband's meals ready on time when he returned from a hard day's work.

The kind of advice the social worker gave abused wives was not always welcome, as in the case of Mrs. K, who appeared before Chicago's court of domestic relations in the 1920s. Mrs. K had complained because her husband, who had served time in prison, had been released and was beating her. Mrs. K was told to stop taunting her husband by telling him he was not supporting the family, and that he was living off her earnings. The caseworker advised Mrs. K to "educate her husband up to the position of the head of household and allow him to assume the responsibilities which are rightfully his." The husband, she counseled, should handle all the finances and apply for relief, if the family needed it. Mrs. K became furious. The caseworker, she said, was the only woman she had spoken to who had not sympathized with her. Mrs. K adamantly refused to turn her earnings over to her husband. Mrs. K's treatment was insensitive even by the standards of the 1920s. Caseworkers, who were mainly women, often felt compassion for the suffering of other women. But those who failed to enforce agency policy were regarded as hopelessly naive.[35] Judges of the courts of domestic relations warned caseworkers against encouraging a wife to separate "because if she thought she would be upheld in such a step she would be much less likely to put up with [her husband]."[36]

Although most of the complaints to the court of domestic relations came from married women, a large number were brought by husbands who charged their wives with failure to care for sick children, keep the house clean, or prepare their meals. A few husbands accused their wives of beating or threatening them or abusing the children. Many of these charges were made by husbands who believed their wives were about to institute civil or criminal proceedings against them. Some husbands wanted to force their wives to return to them. Others sought sole custody over their children (or claimed they wanted it as a means of getting revenge against their wives). Still other men hoped to be able to commit a sick or mentally ill wife to a state institution.[37]

By the time of the conference, a wife may have decided to drop her complaint. But if both parties did appear, the interviewer talked with the husband first to get his side of the story and reassure him of her impartiality, before including the wife. The goal of this meeting was for "both parties to return home and forget the past and make a fresh start."[38] Interviewers were credited with having achieved marital peace through patience, wisdom, and impartiality. Their job was to "put the proper perspective on the heart-burning incident recalled" and soften the harsh words husbands and wives had uttered. They knew their work was a success when "a little smile breaks into the sullen face of the man, a dimple appears in the tearful face of the wife. And presently they both smile—not to [the caseworker] but to each other."[39]

Many wives who came before the family court dropped their complaints when they realized the economic burden that would befall them and their children. Caseworkers deliberately sought to sabotage the efforts of a divorce attorney, who they believed lacked "social insight."[40] While the procedures of the family court appeared designed to aid a woman filing charges, they in effect encouraged her to return home, where she might be beaten precisely because she came forward. The court offered no physical protection for the woman who made a complaint. The wife who sought a warrant for her husband's arrest was instead persuaded to send her husband a letter summoning him to a conference with a social worker.

If the couple was willing to reconcile, their case was turned over to a private social welfare agency which sent a social worker to visit them. But continuing supervision was the exception, not the rule. In most cases, the wife was simply told to contact the court if her husband beat her again or failed to provide. Some persistent wives sought to press their complaints at a family court hearing. Even then, however, the judge usually tried to persuade the wife to withdraw her complaint and extract from each spouse a promise that they "will do all they can to forget" that they had ever been in court.[41]

Sometime in the 1920s, the judge of New York's court of domestic relations tried John Polsan, a "tenement dweller" and father of five, for beating his wife regularly. According to the judge, the quarrels that led to Mr. Polsan's beatings resulted from "the sameness of the menu, the wife serving only hash and stews." Probing further, the judge learned that Mrs. Polsan was nearly toothless and prepared food that she could eat. Mrs. Polsan complained that her husband did not take her to entertainments in the evening. Her husband responded, "Look at her. I wouldn't take her to a dog fight." The judge concluded that "no purely judicial decision could straighten out this situation." Instead, he referred the Polsans to the Big Sister Organization. They helped Mrs. Polsan obtain a pair of dentures and accompanied her to a beautician for a haircut and a permanent wave. They also took her shopping for fashionable clothes, instructed her in applying cosmetics, and gave her a few lessons in "acting coy." Soon after the Big Sisters had wrought their transformation, Mr. Polsan proudly took his wife out for an evening on the town. Mrs. Polsan reported to the judge that "everything was better than ever." The judge's conclusion: "Case withdrawn. Law? No! Common sense."[42]

This judge apparently believed that serving soft food and neglecting one's appearance were sufficient reasons for a husband to beat his wife. Who would not pummel regularly a woman who was pale, almost toothless, and wore her hair in an unattractive knot? The judge viewed this case not as a criminal complaint of assault, but as a family problem. He enlisted the aid of a social service organization in teaching an immigrant wife how to make herself more attractive. Mr. Polsan was not expected to make himself more pleasing to his wife. It is true that the Big Sisters helped Mrs. Polsan secure a pair of badly needed dentures, and she probably did feel less depressed when her hair and face were made up. But teaching a woman who had been badly beaten to act seductively was a cruel joke. There is a patronizing quality to the counsel the Polsans received. One will never know whether the Polsans were as passive and accepting of this advice as the court believed them to be. Certainly the judge in this case viewed them as grateful but simple-minded recipients of agency intervention.

Despite their policy of family reconciliation, a few courts of domestic relations did grant divorces. Those who could not afford a lawyer—the majority of complainants—were sent to a legal aid society. New York City Legal Aid in the 1920s handled divorce cases for women with children, but not for men. Their policy was to assist women who were "worthy" and "too poor to afford the services of a private attorney."[43] But most legal aid societies turned away indigent applicants for divorce. The Detroit bureau referred women seeking divorces to lawyers who charged fees, because "divorce is a luxury and should be paid for." In Chicago, the legal aid society would not handle a divorce case unless "social treatment had failed." The Boston legal aid society frankly admitted that it did not do divorce work because their contributors did not approve.

With access to divorce so limited, the only other alternative an abused wife had was a legal separation and a judicial order requiring her husband to pay a weekly sum for support. The husband who was ordered to contribute to his family signed a bond agreeing to pay the court order, and immediately handed over his first week's sum to the accounts department of the court. A probation officer was assigned to the case to insure that the man met his obligations. Unemployed, ill, disabled, or alcoholic men were unable to pay; others were negligent or deliberately spiteful. The wife whose husband defaulted in his payments had to bring yet another complaint before the court. A husband was given more leeway if he was sick or out of work. A man able but unwilling to provide for his family could be sentenced to jail, usually for thirty days. Judges often took into account the wife's morality in deciding whether to order support. The judge of Philadelphia's court of domestic relations admitted that if "the woman has not been living the right kind of life, I will not make an order on the man to support her." He often ruled against wives, he added, "for, if you make it easy for a woman to live apart from her husband she may not feel that necessity for seeking him, and reuniting the home."[44]

Failure to provide support was a misdemeanor, punishable by a fine (in the range of $500 to $1,000), imprisonment, or a fine and imprisonment. The judge who granted a legal separation also issued an order of protection that compelled a husband to stay away from his wife and punished him if he disobeyed. The procedure for insuring payment of support was swifter and cheaper than civil proceedings. The burden of enforcement was placed on the court's probation officer rather than on the woman and her lawyer. A woman victim was also somewhat more protected from further abuse, since the husband paid the support payment directly to the court, rather than to the woman. (These had been the procedures that Lucy Stone had urged some forty years earlier.) Child support orders were not always enforced, and the amount that a woman received then—as today—was barely adequate to live on. Nonetheless, in attempting to enforce child support and protective orders, the court of domestic relations was compelled to acknowledge that a mother residing with her children constituted a viable family unit.

In many ways, the new approach toward family violence in the social courts resembled the justice meted out in the police court. Still, most abusive husbands and parents probably preferred some meetings with a caseworker to a fine and spending a few nights in jail. It was relatively easy to bring a complaint in either type of court. Most charges of physical assault brought before the police court, juvenile, or family courts were dropped, either at the insistence of the victim or at the urging of the judge or district attorney. The procedures in both types of courts left the victim relatively unprotected. Lawyers were generally absent from the family court as well as the police courts. Even when they were present in the police courts, the quality of their representation was poor. Nonetheless, there was a difference between the police courts' dismissal of the seriousness of family violence, and the domestic relations courts' denial that physical and sexual assault constituted criminal behavior. In addition, judges of courts of domestic relations, in cooperation with caseworkers, had discretionary powers in deciding whether victims of violence were entitled to their feelings of injustice and rage.

In their classic study of Polish immigration to the United States, *The Polish Peasant in Europe and America*, Florian Znaniecki and William I. Thomas contended that American laws on marriage, support, and American courts helped "dissolve the Polish family in this country, chiefly by giving the wife an exaggerated conception of her rights."[45] Yet the new courts were less concerned about enforcing woman's or children's rights than in assigning personal accountability for family problems. Men were irresponsible when they failed to be good providers and drank to excess; women caused most other family problems. Since the juvenile court held the parent responsible for the child's behavior, it was mothers, more than fathers, who were to blame.

At the same time, the court of domestic relations made child support easier to obtain. By insisting that the husband live separately from his wife, the family court held out to many victims a remedy that had been unavailable before. It permitted a woman the freedom to live separately from her husband and offered the promise of a steady income sufficient to support one's children, without having to commit them to an institution or parcel them out among relatives. In order to secure court-ordered support, however, a woman had to endure a period when she was offered no physical protection, prove herself worthy to the court's investigators, and undergo the court's attempts at marital reconciliation.

The juvenile or family courts expanded the discretionary authority of judges and other court personnel. The courts now had the power to increase their inquiries into the character, habits, and even genetic background of the offender. No domain of personal life was left unexamined. Reginald Heber Smith, an astute early critic of the new courts, was forced to admit that a "weak, or incapable, or narrow-minded judge can do more harm in courts of wide discretion, such as small claims, a juvenile or a domestic relations court, than anywhere else."[46] And, indeed, many did. There were few, if any, legal restraints on the discretionary powers of the judges. The zeal to intervene was held in check only by the underfunding of the judicial system and the absence of sufficient staff. No matter how limited the efforts were, the coordination of social service work with judicial decision-making represented a departure from the work of the police court. In some cases, this combination was patronizing and misogynist, in others helpful, and sometimes both. The results of court intervention fell far short of the impartial but compassionate assistance Progressive reformers had hoped to offer. Nonetheless, complainants to these courts often came away satisfied that their needs had been met.

How successful were Progressive reformers in meeting their objectives? The goal of the juvenile and family courts was to make it possible for a nuclear family, headed by a wage-earning father, to survive intact without economic aid from the state. The juvenile court was designed to protect society from future criminals without having to remove children from their parents. Progressive reformers were interested in reshaping the immigrant and lower-class family along middle-class lines. At the same time, they also sought to restore a husband's authority in the home by urging wives to become more subservient, compliant, and dependent economically. But the intervention of the social courts was often unable to achieve these results. Neglected children were placed in children's asylums, battered wives were granted legal separations and support and protection orders, and parents or spouses were often able to commit their relatives to state institutions. Progressive reformers failed in their reform of the family for several reasons. It was extremely expensive to offer the social services that were needed. Mothers benefited from being able to live separately from their husbands and still raise their children. State asylums and children's institutions often relieved families of burdens they were unable to carry. Thus, the actual practices of the juvenile and family courts often led not to preserving the home but to breaking it up. Given the pressures on the family in modern society, bureaucratic mechanisms for committing relatives and enforcing child support were inevitably used.

8

Psychiatry
Takes Control

BEFORE THE LATE 1920S PSYCHOANALYTIC THEORIES had little impact on the practice of psychiatry in the United States. Psychiatrists in mental hospitals and the psychopathic laboratories attached to the courts of domestic relations relied on the diagnostic categories of pre-Freudian, "constitutional" (i.e., inheritance-based) psychiatry, founded in Europe by pioneers such as Emil Kraepelin and Eugen Bleuler. The standard diagnosis of the wife beater, for example, was feeble-mindedness combined with dementia praecox, in other words, mental retardation combined with schizophrenia. Feeble-mindedness and dementia praecox were believed to be hereditary and particularly common among immigrants, vagrants, and prostitutes. Abused wives and battered adolescent children were often similarly diagnosed. Pre-Freudian psychiatry did not deny abuse existed, but it tended to condemn both the victim and the perpetrator as social, even genetic, inferiors.[1] Psychiatric units in courts and mental hospitals as late as the 1920s often employed a eugenics researcher to draw up a family tree tracing the prevalence of alcoholism, syphilis, and criminal tendencies to the grandparent's generation. Psychiatrists hoped that patients could learn to control their impulses, without having to be sent to prison or an asylum. Psychoanalytic theory, however, rejected genetic determinism and held out hope for the triumph of the human spirit through self-understanding.

The main contribution of psychoanalytic ideas was to introduce a "sexual" way of understanding family violence. Freud exhibited a brief interest in the sexual molestation of children before turning to other matters. The ideas of his disciple, Helene Deutsch, regarding female masochism had a profound effect on the way wife beating was understood. By the 1930s, their ideas began to affect psychiatrists and social workers in the United States. Although actual work with patients represented a blending of Freudian and non-Freudian approaches, psychoanalytic theories affected the way that victims and perpetrators of family violence were treated.

Psychoanalytic ideas helped to liberate the modern world from the moralistic categories of the Victorians. Reformers in the nineteenth century viewed the child as sexually innocent but capable of being ruined by the immoral advances of a depraved man. The idea of male brutishness in the nineteenth century never directly led to the passage of laws or public policy against family violence, but it did serve to release anger at male perpetrators of violence against women. With the advent of Freudian thought, rhetoric about the brutish criminal and his helpless victim all but disappeared. New explanations of behavior undermined the notions of child or female innocence and purity. Unfortunately, psychoanalysis resurrected the much older, more misogynist images of the seductive daughter, the nagging wife, and the lying hysteric. It furnished new ideas that undercut the moral outrage that family violence reform needs to flourish. If family violence loses its emotional salience, its appeal as a social issue also begins to fade.

In the 1920s, American social workers and psychiatrists still gave advice and offered concrete, if limited, assistance. But a decade later, the therapeutic ideal became one of greater neutrality and distance between the clinician and the patient, with more sustained inquiry into the victim's complicity in having caused abuse. Victims were encouraged to minimize the external fact of abuse and instead examine their own psychic need to be abused. If many previous reforms put the goal of family preservation ahead of that of physical protection of victims, this approach removed itself entirely from concern with their safety. The helping professions still affirmed the importance of outside intervention in the family; indeed, psychiatric professionals had become expert advisers on childrearing and marriage. But they favored family intervention by professional psychiatrists rather than intercession by the police and the courts. The dispute was not about whether outside intrusion in the family was required, but who was to be in charge of it.

Those in the helping professions believed they should be in charge. Their efforts cannot be so easily categorized as attempts to preserve the family; most did aim to achieve that goal, although some psychiatric social workers also hoped to strengthen the individual's capacity to make choices, no matter what effect on the family those decisions had.

We have already observed the tendency of each generation of reformers to condemn the practices of the previous one. Progressive era reformers embraced social casework as an advance over the police work practices of late nineteenth-century anticruelty societies. In the 1920s, psychiatric case-workers criticized the coercive methods of their predecessors, the social case-workers, who, it was now believed, had naively sought to rescue lost souls, many of whom could not be saved. They had mistakenly posed the question, "what shall I do?" at the expense of asking "why did this happen?"[2]

By allying with the medical profession, psychiatric social workers hoped to elevate their professional status and place their work on a scientific plane. Graduate schools of social work, established in the 1920s, instructed their students in a somewhat diluted form of psychoanalytic thought. By the end of the decade, psychiatric social work had become the most prestigious branch of social work. Psychiatry provided a new vocabulary and a more elaborate therapeutic technique. The psychiatric clinic promoted cooperation between social workers and physicians in a medical setting, and offered more training and freedom for independent action than other types of social work. Under the supervision of a psychiatrist, the psychiatric social worker attached to the clinic learned the techniques of psychotherapy. The interest in personality rather than social problems arose during this decade of general disillusionment with politics and an intensive quest for personal fulfillment.[3]

One of the first settings in which psychiatric social work flourished was the child guidance clinic. In 1921, the Commonwealth Fund, established by the heirs of a partner of John D. Rockefeller in Standard Oil, launched a five-year program for the prevention of juvenile delinquency, and to further this aim funded the first child guidance clinic in St. Louis in 1922. Eleven years later there were forty-two such clinics across the country. By 1946, 285 child guidance clinics were serving children exclusively and another 350 were counseling adults as well as children. The unique feature of these clinics was that therapy was provided by a multidisciplinary team consisting of a child psychiatrist, child psychologist, and psychiatric social worker.

Most of the early patients at these clinics were "problem" children referred there by the juvenile courts, which sought a psychiatric evaluation of the child. The staff of the clinics grew dissatisfied with the rigid demands of the courts. They wanted to cure mental illness rather than just "readjust and rehabilitate in order to reduce social nuisance." By severing their close ties with the courts, the schools, and social agencies, the clinics hoped to be "free to explore and assist without exciting suspicion or arousing prejudice of being a subtle tool of these agencies."[4] Still, most of their clients came from working-class families.

Parents brought children to these clinics for complaints such as bedwetting, masturbation, truancy, and stubbornness; while investigating such problems, a caseworker might occasionally discover child abuse. When they did, they tended to regard it as a form of parental "domineering, repressive behavior," which they attributed to "deep-lying causes," such as the parent's abuse in childhood.[5] Clinicians believed that parents who had been beaten as children unconsciously repeated this abusive pattern with their own children.

Although the child was the ostensible patient at the clinic, a psychiatric social worker, usually a woman, also counseled the mother, as it was believed that treating the illness of the child required making changes in the parent. Although the literature of child guidance was careful to refer to the gender-neutral "parent," rather than to mothers, in reality, very few fathers were seen at these clinics, both because the clinics believed that most of the child's problems were caused by the mother, and because fathers were reluctant or unable to visit the clinic. Thus, paternal involvement was not encouraged, but maternal interest was expected and sought out. The social workers probed the mother's attitude toward childrearing and often counseled her on how to discipline without hitting. The blaming of mothers, however, was nowhere as condemnatory or as severe as in the juvenile courts.

In analyzing the case records of Philadelphia's child guidance clinic in the 1920s and 1930s, Margo Horn has noted the decline of the therapist's moralistic attitude toward the patient and the rise of what she terms "the therapeutic stance," a position of neutrality and objectivity toward the client. Psychiatric social caseworkers stopped issuing orders and instead encouraged clients to arrive at their own decisions. They were also less likely to tell mothers not to work outside the home. The psychiatric caseworker was more likely to be an educated guide than a friendly instructor.[6] (Horn implies that the phrase, "Well, what do you think?" was invented by psychiatric social workers in the 1930s.)

The therapeutic stance also affected the new academic discipline of family sociology. In the 1920s family sociologists cooperated with child guidance clinics and courts of domestic relations to introduce new techniques in the counseling of families. The leaders of this movement were Ernest R. Mowrer, a sociologist at Northwestern University, and his wife Harriet R. Mowrer, a psychiatric social worker employed by the Social Service Bureau of Chicago. The Mowrers influenced the training of a generation of psychiatric social workers. Separately and together, they published a number of articles and books on "family disorganization" and "domestic discord."[7] Physical abuse interested them only as a manifestation of "domestic discord." They held that differences in the attitudes and circumstances of each spouse created discord, which surfaced whenever the couple faced a difficult decision.

The Mowrers portrayed social casework in a highly unfavorable light. They believed it assumed that individuals had inherited destructive personality traits, emphasizing eugenic and biological causes of family problems at the expense of psychological ones. Social workers, they contended, were overly moralistic and condemnatory. Rather than undertaking a deeper inquiry into the couple's emotional problems, the social workers jumped in to solve the immediate problems of the family—finding them housing or material aid—while rarely taking into account the couple's sexual problems or cultural background. At the same time, the Mowrers believed that therapy with a husband and wife was preferable to individual counseling.

As adherents of "the therapeutic stance" in counseling, the Mowrers believed that the counselor should remain neutral as to whether the couple should remain together. They instructed therapists to tell the couple, "It is a situation where neither of you is to blame. I cannot tell you whether you should or should not live with your husband. That is for you to decide."[8] Influenced by Freudian ideas about repression, the Mowrers believed that if a husband were simply ordered to stop beating his wife, he might do so, but only for a short time. His aggression would reemerge or find expression in some other form. A jail term or even the threat of it would only strengthen the "resistance" of the husband to more fundamental change. In fact, the psychiatric caseworker was cautioned to deliberately avoid the subject of physical abuse in the husband's initial interview, especially when the wife had brought a complaint to court. "In dissolving [the husband's] antagonism," the Mowrers believed, they hoped to create "in him a receptive mood." The Mowrers failed to realize that the typical abuser often insists that he has done nothing wrong, since he believes his wife provoked him to hit her. By not inquiring into the specific incidents of abuse, the caseworker was inadvertently helping to maintain the abuser's facade of denial.

Although the Mowrers never established their own domestic discord clinics, they influenced the practice of "family case work for marital difficulties." Marriage counseling clinics began to appear in major U.S. cities beginning in the late 1920s. Although therapists at these clinics hoped to counsel both husband and wife, they soon found that husbands were reluctant to enter therapy. The wife was often seen alone, and counselors sought to strengthen her ability to adjust to her marriage, even when her husband resisted making any changes. Caseworkers often assumed that if a wife was encouraged to make "an attractive home and [be] an adequate wife and mother," many of the marital difficulties of the couple would disappear.[9] Although marriage counselors saw themselves as different than social caseworkers of the Progressive era, much of their advice was remarkably similar.

There were both positive and negative aspects of the new attitudes of social workers. On the one hand, the more neutral stance of therapists conveyed respect for the rights of the patient, refusal on the part of the therapist to become an agent of social control, and sympathy and support for the patient. Therapists allowed patients to make choices for themselves, including the wrong ones. It is obviously a difficult task to counsel someone who deliberately chooses to return to an environment fraught with physical danger. Thus in some cases, the counselors chose to maintain professional neutrality rather than intervene on behalf of the victim. In those situations where there was potential for further violence the therapists should have been more like the Progressive era caseworkers they looked down on, making victims aware of remedies available to them, such as emergency housing, charity, medical care, and legal aid. A blending of the two styles of social work would have vastly benefited victims of domestic violence, but, as is so often the case, supporters of the new approach were too intent on rejecting the old to appreciate its merits.

Beginning in the 1930s, the ideas of Sigmund Freud, the great explorer of psychic processes buried in the human mind, influenced a new way of defining and understanding family violence in the United States and Western Europe. Before there can be any comprehension of how completely Freud influenced the nature of social work, it is necessary to reexamine some of his famous cases of paranoia and hysteria.

To begin with, Freud was more interested in the internal psychic reality of the individual—the dreams and fantasies of his patients—than in their actual social experience. He often failed to examine abuse as a cause of mental illness. A case in point was Freud's analysis of an eminent German lawyer and judge, Daniel Paul Schreber, who suffered from periodic nervous breakdowns and was committed to an insane asylum. Freud never met Schreber and knew almost nothing about him, except what he read in Schreber's memoirs. On the basis of this evidence, Freud concluded that Schreber's frequent hallucinations of being persecuted resulted from paranoia, caused by unresolved homosexual conflict.[10] Freud knew that Schreber's father was famous for having written dozens of popular books on childrearing, which went through numerous editions and were translated into many languages. But Freud did not consult these books in arriving at his analysis. Recently, psychoanalysts have returned to the writings of Schreber's father and noted an uncanny similarity between the bizarre techniques the elder Schreber used in rearing his children and his son's paranoid delusions. Schreber's father was a talented amateur inventor who devised an array of straps, belts, chin braces, and iron bars for straightening a child's posture and curbing youthful masturbation. The elder Schreber's childrearing books were richly illustrated with drawings of the contraptions that Schreber recommended and used on his own children. The head-compressing machine, for example, consisted of a strap clamped at one end to the hair and at the other to a child's underwear. A boy's hair was pulled if he turned in the night while tethered to it. It is not surprising that a boy who was strapped to a harness called "the straightener" would suffer as an adult from delusions of chest compression, in which he felt his whole chest wall caving in. Schreber's "writing down" miracles in which he was racked by bodily pain bore a striking resemblance to his father's punishment board, which listed after each child's name the fault that had been committed.

How much Freud can be faulted for misdiagnosing a patient he never met is open to question. It might be thought that Freud did not have much to say about abuse because he rarely heard about it from his patients. In the 1890s, however, Freud was seeing a number of patients, mostly women, who had been sexually molested or raped as children.[11] They described assault by adult strangers in their dreams, and relatively mild sexual molestation (tickling of the genitals) by nurses and governesses or older siblings. In "The Aetiology of Hysteria" (1896), Freud devised his "seduction" theory, arguing that hysterical symptoms, such as double vision, seizures, paralysis, sudden blindness, or throbbing abdominal pains, were caused by the child's early experiences of sexual trauma. By 1897, Freud had decided that his patient's dreams represented not childhood memories, but fantasies, unconscious wishes that had not been fulfilled. Years later he wrote, "Almost all my women patients told me that they had been seduced by their fathers. I was driven to recognize in the end that these reports were untrue and so came to understand that the hysterical symptoms are derived from phantasies and not from real occurrences."[12]

Freud's renunciation of his seduction theory is usually seen as the turning point in the history of psychoanalysis, because in its place, Freud constructed the theory of the Oedipus complex, the fantasied sexual desire of the child for the parent of the opposite sex. Most analysts believe that Freud's renunciation of his seduction theory was not only correct but essential for the growth of psychoanalysis. This is now a major subject of major dispute. Freud's stature as one of the great thinkers of the twentieth century is not in question here, but it is important to appreciate how, in helping to overthrow Victorian attitudes about sexuality, his ideas also contributed to the decline of interest in family violence.

Jeffrey Masson, in *The Assault Upon Truth: Freud's Suppression of the Seduction Theory* (1983), charged that Freud made a serious error that forever doomed the subsequent course of the psychoanalytic movement. Masson argued that Freud's new "interpretation—that the sexual violence that so affected the lives of his women patients was nothing but fantasy—posed no threat to the existing social order. Therapists could thus remain on the side of the successful and the powerful, rather than of the miserable victims of family violence."[13] Even after he renounced the seduction theory, Freud still recognized that sexual abuse of children occurred. His statements nonetheless tended to minimize the extent of abuse. In his *Introductory Lectures* of 1916, for instance, Freud wrote, "Do not suppose, however, that sexual misuse of children by the nearest male relatives is entirely derived from the world of phantasy; most analysts will have treated cases in which such occurrences actually took place and could be established beyond doubt; only even they belonged to later years of childhood and had been transposed to an earlier time."[14] Even in this statement, he refused to acknowledge that patients experienced and could recall abuse they suffered in their early years.

Freud seemed reluctant to believe that fathers "seduced" their young daughters even before he rejected his seduction theory. He deliberately chose the milder term "seduction," rather than abuse or cruelty; he altered two of his case histories to indict the uncles of his patients rather than their fathers, and in his private correspondence he referred to "father etiology" as the cause of hysteria while failing to use the term in his publications. This challenges Masson's view that Freud had once been a courageous champion of sexual assault victims.

A letter Freud wrote to his friend and confidant, Berlin physician Wilhelm Fliess, in December 1897, provides more telling information about Freud's attitudes. (It was written after Freud "abandoned" his seduction theory in public, revealing that he had not yet done so in private.) Freud describes a woman patient who told him of being raped by her father when she was two. From the rape she contracted gonorrhea and nearly died from loss of blood and vaginitis. Freud was shocked. The rest of his letter concerns the "infantile trauma" his patient suffered from having witnessed when she was three anal intercourse between her parents, which was very painful to her mother. Freud confided to Fliess, "A new motto: What have they done to you, poor child?"— the line from a poem by Goethe.[15] Freud clearly meant to implicate both parents. His seduction theory held that repression of the memory of infantile trauma, not abuse, caused hysterical symptoms. Dream analysis could uncover the trauma, and Freud could then help his patient recall these painful incidents and work through her emotions about it. He overlooked the actual abuse this woman suffered as a child and concentrated on what he viewed as the single traumatic event of her childhood—the father's brutal forcing of his wife in anal intercourse.

Freud's seduction theory dealt not with the consequences of physical and sexual abuse of children, but with the causes of hysteria. Ever since the Greeks, hysteria was believed to be a woman's disease, the illness of the wandering womb. Most psychiatrists today regard symptoms of hysteria as a response to extreme stress. The reason hysteria is found primarily among women is now believed to be because the "sick role" among women is more acceptable. Being ill permits a woman to escape from responsibility for her life and remain dependent on her relatives.[16] Some deep psychological disturbance appears to cause hysteria, but it is doubtful, as Freud originally claimed, that repressed sexual abuse was the single or even major contributor. Freud finally had to face up to the fact that his original explanation was incorrect.

There are many reasons for Freud rejecting his original theory of hysteria and seduction. For one, he believed that for a theory to be correct, it had to provide a cure in every case. His lack of complete success stymied him. Through self-analysis, he recognized that many of his dreams resembled those of his patients, although he knew that he had not been molested as a child.[17] To Freud, this suggested the possibility that the unconscious could fantasize events that never occurred. Finally, Freud did not believe—he did not want to believe—that molestation and rape were as common as he knew hysteria to be. This last point is the only one that demonstrates Freud's lack of interest in the pervasiveness of abuse. But the other reasons for his change of mind appear reasonable. Thus, it seems unfair to charge, as Jeffrey Masson does, that Freud abandoned his seduction theory because of cowardice, a desire to protect an incompetent medical colleague, and unwillingness to risk his reputation among the Viennese medical establishment. If Freud had been so fearful of tangling with public opinion and his fellow doctors, how can one explain that he replaced his seduction theory with an even more unpopular view, that children (and adults) have deep but unconscious sexual urges?

The considerable confusion over Freud's renunciation of his seduction theory has to do with the fact that two separate issues were involved. The first was whether hysteria was always caused by a patient's repression of childhood sexual molestation. The answer to that question was no. The second was whether Freud's patients in dream analysis were able to recall their early childhood sexual abuse. The answer to that question is probably yes, based on Bernard Glueck's observations in the 1960s of patients in a psychiatric hospital. Many of Freud's cases, Glueck believed, were schizophrenics. Glueck's schizophrenics often suffered from complete amnesia, later seeming to act out early childhood experiences. Gradually, they were able to recover their memories, including an early childhood experience of molestation or rape. He became increasingly aware of his patients' history of incest or molestation from their intense emotional reactions when discussing a certain period of their childhood and from their manner of sexual acting out with fatherlike members of the hospital staff.

Glueck questioned the parents of his patients, who confirmed that abuse had occurred in the patient's childhood, although they tended to deny that they were at fault. Whether Freud could have confronted the parents of his patients is not clear, but that he should have done so before deciding that his patients were lying is obvious. Recently, Swiss psychoanalyst Alice Miller also confirmed Freud's original findings of parents sexually abusing their children. Her patients were able to recall extremely early incidents of sexual molestation, otherwise forgotten, during their dream analysis.[18] These early memories would have remained buried in the unconscious, had she not made a special effort to elicit them.

The reasons that Masson offers to explain Freud's renunciation of his theory are unconvincing. Masson is on much firmer ground when he argues that abandonment of the seduction theory had profound and damaging effects on the victims of abuse. The seduction theory gave the impression that sexual molestation and abuse of children was as common as hysteria, which in Freud's day was quite prevalent. Freud's theory also suggested that people bore lasting psychological scars from childhood abuse. Thus, renouncing the theory suggested that (1) sexual molestation and abuse were infrequent, (2) children are not deeply scarred by abuse in later life, and most importantly, (3) children often lie about abuse.

After Freud changed his mind, as Masson points out, he refused to listen to analysts who disagreed. One of Freud's disciples, Sandor Ferenczi, had been working with many patients who were able to recall sexual trauma through dream analysis. In "The Confusion of Tongues Between Adults and Children" (1932), Ferenczi observed that out of fear, children surrendered to abuse and molestation and even came to identify with its perpetrator. The victimized child felt confused, guilty, and ashamed, while the abuser often acted as if nothing had happened. Ferenczi noted that many of his patients, when they were children, were unable to express rage at what had happened to them; instead, they became either mechanically obedient or extremely defiant. Ferenczi also argued that sexual trauma in childhood could lead to the development of a split personality as an adult. As Jeffrey Masson points out, Ferenczi's short paper represented a great lost opportunity to develop treatments appropriate to sexual abuse. Instead, Freud ridiculed Ferenczi's ideas and tried to pressure him to recant his position.[19]

Freudian ideas were often grafted onto other ideas and methods of treatment. Yet even these hybrid forms represented a new method of handling cases of family violence. Psychoanalysis appeared to offer a more complex understanding of human nature that took into account the sexual side of human beings. As a new system of thought, it made many cultural attitudes appear outmoded, unscientific, and naive. Psychoanalytic ideas seemed to be most painfully at odds with the legal approach to family violence. The law held individuals accountable for their actions; psychiatry assumed that human beings were governed by urges and drives of which they were barely aware.

One clear message from Freud's rejection of his seduction theory was that children or women who bring charges of rape or sexual molestation cannot be believed. In their clinical training, therapists were cautioned not to inquire about a patient's past history of abuse, and when they learned of it, to doubt its veracity. Bernard Glueck, Jr., learned these lessons soon after graduating from Harvard Medical School and embarking on his psychiatric residency around 1940. He later recalled, "I was taught in my residency and during my early years in psychiatry, as most of us were, to look very skeptically upon the incestuous sexual material described by my patients. . . Any inclination on my part, or that of my colleagues in the training situation, to look upon these productions of the patient as having some reality basis was scoffed at and was seen as evidence of our naiveté and inexperience in appraising and understanding the mysterious world of the unconscious."[20]

Trained in social work in the mid-1950s, Florence Rush was instructed as a matter of agency policy to avoid the subject of incest in her therapy with children. Acting against instructions, she decided to draw out twelve-year-old Annie, who had been involved in an incestuous relationship with her father for two years before being admitted to a home for delinquent girls. Rush, who had access to Annie's case record, made a point of telling Annie that she knew of her incestuous relationship. "Do you want to talk about what happened to you?" Rush asked Annie. Annie hung her head and changed the subject. The psychiatrist supervising Rush was appalled when she told him about this conversation. He insisted that Annie felt guilty and ashamed because of her deep, unconscious wish to have sex with her father and that Annie should not have been encouraged to discuss her past. Rush recollected that if a child did not appear to have been psychologically damaged by incest, "it was assumed that the experience had been harmless, but if she had problems, was difficult, angry, failed in school, attracted boys or became pregnant, she was diagnosed as acting out her incestuous wish for her father or other sexual fantasies."[21] Frequently, the diagnosis entered in the case records was "adjustment reaction of adolescence with tendency to act out hostility and repressed sexual fantasies."[22] Incestuous girls were often labeled as seductive yet frigid, while the men who raped or molested them were sympathetically portrayed as sexually deprived. Of course, there was nothing new in disbelieving women and children who bring charges of molestation and rape. Victorian doctors often thought that mothers induced children to cry rape as a means of getting revenge, and that women who seduced men often claimed to have been raped.[23] But as a modern and objective science claiming to offer genuine sympathy and compassion for its patients, psychiatry should be held to a higher standard of ethical conduct than Victorian medicine.

Psychiatrists assisted judges in deciding whether victims were telling the truth and determining whether offenders were mentally competent to stand trial.[24] In a move that would have made Simeon Baldwin cringe, the American Bar Association in 1936 appointed a committee, headed by the noted legal scholar, John Henry Wigmore, to revise the rules of criminal court testimony for female victims of incest, rape, and sexual molestation. The ABA report advised judges to order a psychiatric examination of victims in any case that went to a jury because of the well-known psychiatric finding that women and children often lie about rape. Psychiatric examination was particularly important because in most cases of sexual assault, it was a matter of the woman's word against the defendant's. The report noted, "the erotic imagination of an abnormal child of attractive appearance may send a man to the penitentiary for life. The warnings of the psychiatric profession, supported as they are by thousands of observed cases, should be heeded by our profession."[25]

In his legal textbook, which was standard in the field, Wigmore repeated the recommendation of the ABA report. Too often, he believed, the real victim was the "innocent man." He quoted extensively from the leading psychiatric authorities of the day. He also published their responses to his inquiries. All women have fantasies of rape, wrote Dr. Karl Menninger of the Menninger Clinic, but some neurotic women could not distinguish between fantasy and reality. Another, less well-known, psychiatrist explained that "a woman or girl may falsely accuse a person of a sex crime as a result of a mental condition that transforms into fantasy a wishful biological urge." A German psychiatrist warned of the young girls whose intense "hussy-type" eroticism could "be detected in the wanton facial expression, the sensuous motions, and the manner of speech."[26]

Psychiatrists and criminal lawyers did encounter instances where they knew that sexual abuse had indeed taken place. Frequently in these situations, they would refer to Freud's disciple, Karl Abraham, who argued that children unconsciously desire sex with an adult. Two American psychiatrists in the 1930s, Lauretta Bender and Abram Blau, of New York's Bellevue Hospital, relied on Abraham's clinical work to argue that sexual assault was not traumatic for most young children. The children they observed did not feel guilt or shame, except when confronted by moralistic adults. Nonetheless, they were considered sufficiently disturbed to be admitted to a children's ward of a psychiatric hospital; many of them were found to be suffering from venereal disease. Bender and Blau believed that the whole subject of incest and molestation had been cloaked in outmoded beliefs about the innocence of children, when in fact, "the child may have been the actual seducer rather than the one innocently seduced." Many of their patients, who ranged between the ages of five and twelve, were unusually charming and attractive personalities. "Even in cases in which physical force may have been applied by the adult," Bender and Blau argued, "this did not wholly account for the frequent repetition of the practice."[27]

Bender and Blau failed to acknowledge what Ferenczi had realized, that in relations between adults and children, adults hold the upper hand and bear the responsibility for self-control. Psychoanalytic arguments cast the issue in black-and-white terms; the child was either innocent or guilty, the seducer or the seduced. If the child was guilty, then there was no moral or legal problem. In fact, incestuous relations can last over a period of several years; the child has to be willing to keep the family secret. The child may understand incest as a form of love, or feel ambivalent about what has occurred. Children often seek attention, hugging, and cuddling from adults, and some older children may seek intercourse, too. As with all stereotypes, there was a grain of truth in the myth of the seductive child. Adult molesters, having been absolved of responsibility for the nature of the sexual encounter, greatly benefited from this myth.

This questioning of the innocence of the child was reflected in the general culture. Novelists rediscovered the seductive nymphet, a young girl who initiates sexual contact with an otherwise respectable adult man. Vladimir Nabokov's *Lolita* (1954), an entertaining combination of murder mystery and black comedy, described a middle-aged pedophile and the twelve-year-old stepdaughter he beds down in motel rooms across the Southwest. But Nabokov always insisted that he did not believe in Freudian "nonsense," basing his heroine on prototypes in Victorian pornography. The stereotype of the seductive young girl extends as far back as the Bible, when two of Lot's daughters got their father drunk and "preserved his seed" by "lying down" with him.

Freud blasted through the bedrock of Victorian belief to uncover the intense sexual feelings of women and children. As with many significant and worthwhile ideas, this one was placed in the service of oppressive rather than uplifting aims. The popularization of Freud simply added scientific weight to those who believed that childhood sexual innocence disguised the child's true seductive nature.

Freud's view of masochism was as important in presenting a new view of the adult woman as his theories of infantile sexuality and the Oedipal complex were in portraying the child as a sexual being. When I first encountered the title of one of Freud's papers, "A Child is Being Beaten," I thought I had uncovered material showing that Freud was actually more interested in child abuse than I had previously thought. But "A Child is Being Beaten" consists of the case histories of three women patients who dream that an authority, perhaps a parent, is beating a child (who clearly is not themselves).[28] Freud found that none of these girls had been whipped or hit as children. (This was one of those rare instances when Freud did try to learn whether his patients had suffered abuse in childhood.) Freud's paper argued that fantasies of being beaten revealed the unconscious wish for it, a perverted sexual desire known as masochism. Five years later Freud published another essay on the subject, in which he claimed that masochism was instinctual in women, although he did not have a great deal to say about it. Indeed, the examples of female masochism he discussed were those of men whose fantasies represented an expression of their desire to play the feminine role. Although Freud recognized that sadism was as common to men as masochism was to women, he did not offer the parallel argument that male aggression was an outcome of instinctual sadism.

Freud never mentioned wife beating as an instance of female masochism. Similarly, most male analysts did not make the connection, either; they described neurotic women patients whose masochism manifested itself in poor school performance, fear of traveling, and the like. Women patients furnished Freud's women disciples, especially Helene Deutsch, with the material from which to develop a comprehensive theory of female masochism.[29]

Helene Deutsch and Karen Horney were the first analysts to apply the concept of masochism to women who had been beaten or raped. Deutsch, a physician of Polish-Jewish birth, was psychoanalyzed by Freud. She helped found the Vienna Training Institute and served as its director. At age forty-three she was living in Vienna and working closely with Freud when she lectured about masochism. In 1930 she published one of her lectures, entitled "The Significance of Masochism in the Mental Life of Women." Deutsch believed that masochism was more common in women than in men, indeed, a central element in the psychology of normal women. She argued that female masochism begins when the little girl notices she lacks a penis. The girl mistakenly concludes that her clitoris is what is left after someone has cut off her penis. Who was the culprit? At first she angrily accuses her father. But then her rage disappears, and she realizes instead that she wants her father to rape and impregnate her.[30] The young daughter's sadistic fantasies, generated by her penislike clitoris, are now turned inward to produce pain and also bring her sexual pleasure. Without this combination of violence, pain, and desire, the little girl would be unwilling to undergo the normal pain of childbirth when she became a woman.

Deutsch's theory became the dominant psychiatric explanation for the victimization of women. The concept of masochism seemed to explain why abused women remained with their assailants—they secretly enjoyed the pain that was inflicted on them.[31] In fact, some women were so masochistic that they continually sought out men who would mistreat them. The idea of female masochism changed the debate about why women remained in violent relationships. Pre-Freudian psychiatrists tended to believe that abused women remained with abusive men because they were stupid or feeble-minded. It now appeared that they derived psychic and sexual gratification from being beaten and humiliated. Deutsch urged therapists to help women patients admit to and accept their masochistic impulses, so that they could reconcile with the deepest part of their feminine selves.[32] Although Deutsch held that masochism was common to all women, she believed it was stronger in some than in others. In 1944 and 1945, she published *Psychology of Women*, summarizing the ideas she had been working on over the previous fifteen years. Deutsch now cleverly divided women into different types, depending on the relative strength of narcissism, passivity, and masochism in their personalities. Masochism was the strongest element in the personality of "the erotic woman."[33]

The 1920s and early 1930s were a period of great controversy among psychoanalysts about the nature of feminine psychology. Even the psychoanalytic movement was forced to reckon with the enfranchisement of women and their new mood of cultural and sexual freedom. Three years after the publication of Deutsch's essay on the significance of masochism, Deutsch's colleague, Karen Horney, offered a rebuttal of it. Karen Horney was born in Germany, the daughter of an aging Norwegian sea captain and a vibrant young Dutch woman. Over her father's opposition, she attended and graduated from medical school in Berlin. Originally trained as a neurologist, she began a psychiatric practice in Berlin just after the end of the World War I. At that time Berlin rivaled Vienna as a center of Freudian thought. Horney presented her paper on masochism one year after she moved to the United States from Germany. She explained that the chief reason for her initial break with Freudianism was its faulty view of womanhood. At the time she delivered this paper, she had already publicly criticized many Freudian concepts, especially for ignoring the impact of culture on personality.

Her essay exhibited an unswerving belief that psychoanalysis required logic and evidence other than that adduced from neurotic women patients. Because Horney rejected Freud's theory of penis envy in women, she considered any idea, such as female masochism, based on it as fallacious. Horney insisted that masochism was abnormal in women and should not be encouraged, defining it as a set of adult attitudes and behaviors, rather than an inclination developing out of infancy. It was manifested by the inhibition of self-assertion and aggression, a weak, helpless, or inferior self-image, self-sacrifice, submission, feelings of being exploited, and using weakness and helplessness as a means of enticing men. Horney believed that masochism was rooted in misogyny, women's economic dependence on men, and the exclusion of women from public life. She branded the belief in female masochism a "fixed ideology about womanhood" that served to reconcile women to their subordination, and plant in them the belief that masochism "represents a fulfillment they crave, or an ideal for which it is commendable and desirable to strive." She agreed that the example of a Russian peasant woman who does not feel she is loved by her husband unless he beats her was an instance of female masochism. But she indicted psychoanalysis for ignoring cultural or social factors that influenced the development of masochism in women. Like many of her generation, her model of liberated womanhood was "the self-assertive Soviet woman," who, Horney contended, "would doubtless be astonished if beatings were administered as a token of affection."[34] (Horney no doubt would have been dismayed to learn of the prevalence of wife beating in contemporary Soviet society.[35])

Deutsch won this debate, largely by default. Horney's essay on female masochism was the last paper she published on the subject of feminine psychology. Instead she established herself as a theorist of neurosis. Horney may have feared that her professional confrontations within the analytic community had given her a reputation as a critic rather than an original thinker. Her ability to obtain referrals of patients from other analysts may also have been in danger. Dee Garrison, who has studied Horney's career, has added that without a vigorous women's movement, the intellectual debate about the nature of womanhood was silenced, and there was no audience for an alternative female psychology.[36] Even had Horney continued to defend her position, it seems unlikely that hers would have become the dominant point of view. Deutsch's theory was more palatable for the decade of the Great Depression; in a period in which the male ability to provide had been threatened, the theory offered the comfort of male dominance and control.

American popular culture had since the 1920s begun to express similar views. Hollywood films, with their interest in human motivation and the standard plot of boy-meets-girl, were eager to try out new ideas. The lesson of many American films in the 1940s was that violence occurred naturally in male-female relations. Sexuality involved domination, and domination is what women secretly desire. Male heroes in these films long to beat women as proof of their love, The films of screen heroines such as Katharine Hepburn, Joan Crawford, and Rosalind Russell are usually seen as cinematic representations of the new woman. But beneath the surface zest for life, self-assertion, and independence of the female protagonist lay a yearning for submission.

Hollywood censors often eliminated much on-screen violence, leaving only the suggestion of it in verbal repartee or exaggerated gestures. In *State of the Union* (1948), Katharine Hepburn is married to Spencer Tracy, who plays a businessman intent on gaining the presidential nomination of the Republican Party. He has been unfaithful to his wife, and they have grown apart, although his wife still loves him. Hepburn mentions to a friend that her husband used to hit her on the buttocks when she swore. Since he began having an affair the last several years, he no longer did so, or demonstrated any other form of affection toward her. Hepburn longs for a return of her husband's love. She confesses to a friend, "I'd give anything for one good smack on the south end." (In the same film, she offhandedly remarks that a woman could never run for president because she would have to confess that she was over thirty-five.)

In *Frontier Gal*, another film from the 1940s, Rod Cameron spanks his daughter, who thanks him for treating her "like other girls." When he does the same thing to a saloon singer, played by Yvonne De Carlo, the daughter is able to tell her future stepmother, "if he beats you, it's because he loves you." The classic modern romantic situation was that of the brutish and crude man of the working class who masters the over-educated and slightly prudish heroine. *Adventure,* filmed in 1948, starred Clark Gable as a sailor on shore leave and Greer Garson as a sexually repressed librarian. Gable and Garson meet and immediately dislike each other. He disturbs the other patrons in the reading room of the library by talking too loud. On their first date, Gable gets entangled in a barroom brawl, and to avoid arrest he and Garson run off to her apartment. She continues to verbally challenge him. In exasperation, he tells her, "a good crack in the jaw would do you good. She responds, "If it would, I'd love it." They trade insults; he moves to the balcony of her apartment and describes to her the awesome power of the sea. She follows him there, and they embrace passionately. The scene fades; in the next frame, they are seen driving off to Nevada to get married.

Since the theme of controlling the uncontrollable woman could be traced back at least to Shakespeare's *The Taming of the Shrew*, Hollywood screenwriters were probably not directly influenced by the ideas of Helene Deutsch. American movies simply added current ideas to age-old elements of romantic fantasy. The "emancipated" screen heroine in the talking pictures appeared on the surface to be the verbal equal of the hero. Underneath this facade, however, she was seeking to resolve a deep personality conflict, her suppressed need for love. These films offered an explanation for a troubling feature of human behavior that seemed to fit with the current interest in unconscious sexual motivations.

Deutsch's ideas had a large, direct impact on psychiatric practice. The adjective "masochistic" was rarely used before she popularized it in the *Psychology of Women*. Her book appears to have led to the extensive use of the concept in the 1940s and 1950s. The first psychoanalytic articles on the psychology of the rape victim began to appear in the 1940s.[37] Predictably, these articles noted the victim's unconscious desire to be raped. The psychiatric view of the alcoholic's wife held that a woman unconsciously encouraged her husband's drinking through her "irrational" and inconsistent behavior. The "doormat wife," as one psychiatrist termed the battered woman, was unable to examine her own complicity in her marital problems. She permitted her husband to beat her as a way of enabling "her, however passively to hold on to him." The overt reason for complaining to a family service agency—a husband's drinking or abuse—was not the real reason for doing so; instead, the wife of an alcoholic was unaware of her own unconscious anxiety and fears, which needed to surface before she could be helped.[38]

The goal of the Family Service Association of Cleveland, Ohio, in the 1950s, for example, was to counsel the wife so that she and her husband "may have more satisfaction in their life together." During the initial interview, caseworkers do not appear to have asked many questions about the extent of sexual or physical abuse. Instead, they were advised to learn more about the nature of the woman's childhood relationship with her mother. They often found it had been unsatisfactory, and that the woman came from a "disturbed background." A deprived childhood, they theorized, had created "deep seated dependency problems" and sexual anxieties, which produced tension. Marriage was seen as an escape from an unhappy childhood, but women often grew dissatisfied in marriage. Some of the women's feelings of deprivation, left over from childhood, were manifest in "unsatisfied oral needs." Women overate and became obese, it was presumed, because they were literally hungry for love.[39]

A disturbed childhood had also left many women with "guilt over masturbation and deep sexual anxiety, specifically of a sado-masochistic nature." The caseworkers believed it was too easy "to blame the difficulties on the man's lack of appeal or on his technique when drunk." A typical example of the emotionally dependent and sexually anxious woman was Mrs. K, a heavy-set, twenty-seven-year-old mother of two young girls, who had been married six years. Her husband was an alcoholic and had been one when she married him. She came to the Family Service Association because she hoped they could persuade her husband to reduce his drinking. Most recently, her husband had confessed to her that he had had intercourse with a woman he met one night at a bar during one of his drinking binges. Mrs. K had been repeatedly physically and sexually abused by her husband. Her husband worked the night shift and wanted her to get up in the middle of the night when he came home to serve him dinner and have sex with him. The agency felt that Mrs. K's obesity was a manifestation of her psychological problem, rooted in her deprived childhood.

> Her father was a miner who was often out on strike and who drank and beat the children. Her mother was a rigid, unhappy woman, who tried to stretch the limited food budget by filling the children with starches. The diet never satisfied Mrs. K and certainly did not help her figure.[40]

When they learned about her husband's demands for sex, to which Mrs. K refused to respond, the agency sought to work with Mrs. K to "bring out some of her anxiety about sex activities."[41]

What nineteenth-century social purity activists would have regarded as evidence of male brutishness was now seen as proof of female frigidity. The caseworker appeared too squeamish to inquire into the details of the violent rape and beatings Mrs. K mentioned. The treatment Mrs. K received reinforced her feelings of guilt for her marital problems and placed on her the major burden to change. The counseling agency made no attempt to assess the danger Mrs. K faced or provide her with information about how to contact the police or a hospital emergency room if she was attacked again.

The Mowrers had been somewhat more evenhanded. They had stressed that each partner was equally to blame, and they did not urge reconciliation. The message of marital adjustment was stronger in the 1950s, and the concepts used to explain the couple's problem were psychoanalytic.

Thus, psychiatric methods represented a promise of humane treatment for victims of family violence that went unfulfilled. Instead, repression or denial of abuse was encouraged. In the name of professional neutrality, psychiatrists and analysts either refused to take sides or denied the credibility of the victim. How and why this occurred does not rest on one single turning point in Freud's thought; a whole series of intellectual and cultural influences shaped the development of psychoanalysis. In overthrowing Victorian attitudes toward sexuality, Freudian ideas also discarded a system of morality in which perpetrators of family violence were held responsible for having committed illegal and immoral acts. In retrospect, Freud may have overreacted to Victorian sexual repression. At the time he formulated his ideas, repudiation of the past was probably necessary to create a revolutionary way of thinking. Treatment methods were designed to offer a more professional and objective form of counseling. Instead they tended to make matters worse for victims, adding psychic abuse to their physical and sexual violation. In exploring other areas they believed were more important in causing psychological problems, psychiatric professionals chose to ignore or minimize the seriousness of family violence.

9

The Pediatric
Awakening

As IN PREVIOUS ERAS, the fear of violent crime in the 1950s stimulated the rediscovery of family violence. Various social commissions in that decade reported that muggings, assaults, and murders committed by youths were getting out of hand. The caseload of juvenile courts quadrupled in the two decades after 1940. Whether an epidemic of juvenile delinquency had occurred is difficult to know. Certainly the public had grown apprehensive. On their way to the subway the ordinary New Yorker dreaded encountering such youth gangs as the Egyptian Kings, the Henry Street Dragons, or the Conservative Gents, composed primarily of black and Puerto Rican male adolescents. [1]

In the mid-1950s the specter of violent teenagers menacing the public compelled social caseworkers to abandon their professional offices and reach out to troubled youth. In New York City, social workers, scrapping traditional casework methods, visited their adolescent clients at home, in school, at youth clubs, or at community institutions to offer concrete services as well as psychological counseling. [2] Aiding the neglected child was justified as a means of combating juvenile delinquency. "Aggressive casework," as the new approach was called, recognized that the agency could intervene, and had the right to do so, even if uninvited. [3] As had been true in the 1640s and the 1870s, public fears of crime and a spirit of governmental responsibility and innovation, especially in safeguarding the rights of minorities, set the stage for the rediscovery of family violence. But a small group of reformers—lawyers, social workers, physicians, and government officials—took the lead in making child abuse a social issue.

164

Vincent DeFrancis, former director of the NYSPCC, helped to introduce aggressive casework into child protective services. A lawyer who singlehandedly invigorated the child protection movement with the force of his ideas, he was the modern incarnation of Elbridge Gerry. In 1954 DeFrancis became the head of the Children's Division of the American Humane Association. The AHA, founded in 1886, still maintained its dual focus on animals and children, although animal protection remained the main priority. DeFrancis hoped to transform the AHA Children's Division into a major national organization providing scholarly and training materials for social workers and lobbying for the passage of state and federal legislation. In 1954 DeFrancis conducted the first national survey of the extent of child neglect, abuse, and exploitation. The results, published the next year, were distributed to child welfare professionals, the public, and the U.S. Children's Bureau. DeFrancis demonstrated the problems caused by the lack of specialized agencies within child welfare departments capable of handling cases of abuse and neglect. He mobilized support for increased federal funding to establish adequate protective services throughout the United States, having noted the lack of anticruelty societies and other child welfare services outside the Northeast and Midwest. He favored social casework for neglectful parents, which he believed a better alternative than resorting to the courts and/or placing a child in foster care or an institution.

He was not one to favor the coddling of abusive parents, however. If a parent beat a child in front of the caseworker, he insisted that the caseworker call the police. Many lawyers and psychiatrists would have regarded some of his proposals as violations of a parent's civil liberties. DeFrancis urged accurate recording by the caseworker to distinguish the "good neighborhood" from the "slum area," and to separate the "orderly well-kept" apartment from the "unsanitary" one. Caseworkers needed to pay attention to "moral and spiritual neglect" by the parent, which was manifest in "disrespect for authority, disregard for the property rights of others, immorality, licentiousness, obscenity, profanity, and possibly sexual deviations." DeFrancis believed moral and spiritual neglect to be "highly contagious and communicable parental patterns which too readily and too often contaminate children exposed to them at home." He could not stress enough "the deleterious effect of a home climate polluted by a smog of crime, immorality, or irreligion."[4]

DeFrancis called a conference of child welfare professionals in 1955 to discuss his report about the inadequacy of child protective services. Some traditionalists contended that social caseworkers should not intervene in families unless the child's parents wanted them to do so. Others appeared to believe that "aggressive casework" was required. DeFrancis invited to the meeting a social worker on the staff of the U.S. Children's Bureau who conveyed to the agency the interest of the AHA in child's protective services and the greater vitality of the organization under DeFrancis's leadership.

In 1957 the Bureau, whose budget for research had recently grown, issued its own report suggesting that the child welfare department in each state investigate the neglect, abuse, and abandonment of children, offer social services, or call these cases to the attention of the police.[5] This report represented the first major recognition by the federal government of child abuse as an issue of national public policy.[6] Four years later the Bureau compiled an inventory of the child protective services available in each city and county in the United States. The Children's Bureau still recommended the use of traditional casework methods. The focus of treatment was on the parent, not the child. A social worker was expected to visit the home, and perhaps in an unusual situation, offer some social service, such as day care or a live-in homemaker. Temporary removal of abused or neglected children was considered unnecessary. The Bureau appeared to maintain the traditional social work assumption that there was no such thing as a parent who could not be helped.

While the AHA rediscovered the old problem of child cruelty, their efforts alone would not have been sufficient to generate sympathy among the general public. DeFrancis defined the problem not as child abuse but as neglect and was mainly interested in providing improved social services. To capture the public interest, child cruelty required a new approach and a new label to get the attention of the print media and television. This was provided by the medical profession, particularly radiologists and pediatricians, who reversed the previous lack of attention shown by doctors to the existence of abuse. The medical discovery of child abuse was initiated by pediatric radiologists studying the X-rays of children who had suffered fractures, or blows to the skull. The first separate X-ray department in a children's hospital was established in the mid-1930s. About fifteen years later, radiologist John Caffey, a professor of pediatrics at Columbia University, noted how frequently one found in children subdural hematomas resulting from head injuries or associated with fractures of a child's long bones. Caffey was not willing to speculate on what caused the child's injuries.[7] His peers, slightly less circumspect, blamed childhood accidents on "parental carelessness" and suggested that a child's injuries arose from playing crack-the-whip with other children, a parent tugging roughly on the child's arm, or playful tossing of a child back and forth to a family friend.

Why were X-rays so important in establishing that children were abused? Many injuries to children were obvious without any X-rays. Further, close questioning of the child—other than infants or very young children—or of suspected parents might have produced proof of deliberate injury. X-rays were important because they could reveal bone fractures in various stages of healing and in locations that had already healed, suggesting injuries that had occurred more than once. Thus radiological evidence could cast doubt on the claim of a parent or guardian that a child had not been previously injured.

However, clinicians often ignored cases of child abuse and failed to report it when they saw it. Some doctors, who hoped to avoid getting involved, did not want to take time from their practice to appear in court. Others feared a libel suit brought by the parent. Then there were the physicians who convinced themselves that the child's injury was not so serious or severe, and that any parent under the right circumstances might injure a child. Medical residents sometimes joked that they would never bring their own bruised child to a hospital because someone might suspect them of abuse and call the police.[8]

The more removed the physician was from personal contact with the child's parents, the more likely the diagnosis of abuse. Private doctors, often acquainted with the family, rarely if ever wanted to report child battering. Radiologists turned out to be much better observers than pediatricians precisely because they did not personally know the child or the child's parents. They may also have had professional motives for becoming involved in child abuse. Radiology was at that time a less prestigious medical specialty, as it did not have the drama of surgery or of rescuing patients from the edge of death. Cases of child abuse brought radiologists closer to saving lives. Rarely before had articles by radiologists appeared in the *Journal of the American Medical Association* and received so much favorable attention from their colleagues in other specialties.[9]

In 1962 the U.S. Children's Bureau held a small conference composed of twenty-five lawyers, psychiatrists, pediatricians, and representatives of social service agencies to consider how to reduce the incidence of child abuse and neglect. At the meeting Dr. C. Henry Kempe, a pediatrician on the staff of the University of Colorado Medical School, presented the findings of a survey he and his colleagues had conducted to determine the prevalence of child abuse. They learned that hospital emergency rooms and district attorneys across the country had reported several hundred cases of child battering in the last few years. Many babies and infants had been severely injured, some had been maimed, and a few had died. The state of California was commended for the recent passage of a law that required hospitals and doctors on their staff to report cases of child abuse to the police. A committee, appointed at the conference, met subsequently to draft a model statute similar to the one enacted in California.

In July 1962, Kempe's report appeared in the prestigious and influential

Journal of the American Medical Association. An accompanying editorial pointed out that child abuse was a frequent cause of death in children. A few weeks later *Time* magazine's "Medicine" section devoted a column-and-a-half to Kempe's findings.[10] From episodes of "Ben Casey, M.D." and "Dragnet," television viewers learned that children were treated brutally. Over the next few years, the *New York Times* featured dozens of stories about battered children; many more articles appeared in professional, legal, medical, and educational journals.[11] By 1965, 90 percent of adults in a national survey had heard of the problem of child abuse.[12]

The growth of public and professional concern about battered children occurred in the early 1960s, a time of social turbulence and national reform. Jobs were plentiful in the 1960s, inflation was low, and average family income was rising: it was a decade of national economic prosperity. The gross national product of the nation doubled in the two decades after 1950; it grew 60 percent between 1961 and 1967. In a spirit of social justice and optimism about the government's capacity to solve social problems, Congress appropriated large sums for social welfare programs.

Although the 1960s was an idealistic age, it was not an epoch that countenanced legislated morality; indeed, the motto of the decade was "do your own thing." The vigorous protests orchestrated by the civil rights movement to eliminate racial discrimination created a national crisis of conscience that forced the federal government to respond. The dominant moral concern of the decade was the protection of minority legal rights. A children's liberation movement, much smaller in scope than campaigns on behalf of minority groups and women, attracted support, especially from lawyers, writers, and social critics. Children, the liberationists argued, should enjoy the same constitutional rights as adults (with the exception of the right to vote). Supporters of children's rights wanted to guarantee children their legal rights in order to protect them against the arbitrary authority of juvenile court judges, government agencies, and abusive parents.[13] At the same time, civil liberties lawyers found themselves defending the individual against the intrusions of the state. The suspicion of government interference in what was regarded as a private matter had always in the past dampened reform against domestic violence. But the apparently disinterested professionalism of physicians helped minimize fears of government intervention in family autonomy.

Radiologists joined forces with pediatricians and psychiatrists, particularly under the leadership of the dynamic and dedicated C. Henry Kempe. Kempe, who was born in Germany, fled the Nazis before World War II. He received his undergraduate and medical education at the University of California at Berkeley. Trained as an immunologist, he studied the response of patients suffering from complications of smallpox vaccinations. He and his wife, also a pediatrician, were the authors of a well-regarded textbook in pediatrics. By 1956, Kempe was supervising pediatric interns at the University of Colorado Medical Center. Although he came across many cases of child abuse at the hospital, the house staff refused to believe it and diagnosed the child's injury as "obscure bruising, osteogenesis imperfecta tarda, or spontaneous subdural hematoma."[14]

In 1962, Kempe's landmark article, "The Battered-Child Syndrome," which appeared when he was forty years old, was the result of his collaboration with a psychiatrist, an obstetrician, and two radiologists.[15] The presence of psychiatrists in this medical reform coalition is puzzling since their field had helped contribute to the denial of abuse and neglect in the first place. Just as "aggressive casework" revised traditional social work practices, so, too, the reformer-psychiatrists rejected the earlier psychiatric denial of abuse. Kempe and his collaborators were on the staff of a major metropolitan hospital; none of them practiced privately or even in a group clinic. Hospital-based medical practice, which had grown enormously since the end of World War II, was a form of healing highly dependent on technology and the federal government for much of its funding. Hospital practioners were more likely than private physicians to be concerned about their ethical responsibilities and less suspicious of cooperation with the state.

Kempe received funding for some of his studies from the U.S. Children's Bureau, and his research and that of others furnished the Bureau the evidence it needed. When asked the reason for convening the national conference in 1962, Dr. Katherine Bain, a deputy chief at the Bureau, explained that "while child abuse is no new problem to the Children's Bureau, our deep concern today is motivated by its apparent increase and by its particularly violent nature."[16] She added that since 1959, the Bureau had been receiving an increasing number of reports from pediatricians and hospitals regarding physical abuse, and the cases they were learning about were particularly violent ones.

Kempe and his colleagues contributed what became a key term, "the battered-child syndrome," quite by accident. As chair of the program committee of the American Academy of Pediatrics, he organized a plenary session on child abuse. Two years before he had delivered a paper before this group entitled, "parental criminal neglect and severe physical abuse of children." A fellow pediatrician suggested that he should choose another, more attention-getting title. A decade later Kempe admitted that the term he did popularize was unclear, although he had intended it to refer to nonaccidental physical injury to a child.[17]

Two sociologists, Malcolm Spector and John I. Kitsuse, argue that "when terminologies change, when new terms are invented, or existing terms are given new meanings, these actions signal that something important has happened to the career or history of a social problem."[18] The "battered-child syndrome" was at once both a more objective, yet more emotional and vivid phrase than the radiologists' "unsuspected trauma" in infancy, or the legal definition of abuse as parental assault. The battered-child syndrome focused attention on the victim, an innocent child, often assumed to be an infant, and helped gain public sympathy. Louise Armstrong notes ruefully that Kempe did not choose the term "the battering parent syndrome," because he preferred to focus on the child, not the parent.[19] Moreover, the definition of child abuse as a syndrome may have served to reassure the public that corporal punishment of children, especially for acts of disobedience, was not considered child abuse.

In his now famous publication, "The Battered-Child Syndrome," Kempe and his co-authors assumed that the abused child would be temporarily separated from its parents, because of the likelihood of further harm or even death. The child would be placed for a time with relatives or in a foster home and would return home after the parents completed therapy or the home was determined safe for the child. If there was a choice between the child's safety and the parent's right to custody of the child, Kempe and his associates believed that the "bias should be in favor of the child's safety."[20] They appeared to favor termination of parental rights if abuse continued. It is true that "The Battered-Child Syndrome" did not argue that the child had "a right" to protection. It remained for later reformers to argue that the child had an inherent right to life that superseded the parent's right to custody.

The publication of "The Battered-Child Syndrome" in 1962 was accompanied by an editorial in the *Journal of the American Medical Association* that established the significance of abuse by asserting how frequent it was. According to the AMA's editorial, "It is likely that [the battered-child syndrome] will be found to be a more frequent cause of death than such well recognized and thoroughly studied diseases as leukemia, cystic fibrosis and muscular distrophy and may well rank with automobile accidents."[21] There was no evidence at the time for making these comparisons, although the fact that a statement about the prevalence of abuse appeared in such a prestigious medical journal led to subsequent citation of this statement as if it were fact.

Because everyone agreed that reports of abuse to social agencies represented only a fraction of the dimensions of the problem, sociologists set out to learn, independent of social agencies, the prevalence of physical violence in the entire population. David Gil designed a national survey, conducted in 1965, that asked respondents whether they personally knew of families involved in physical injury to a child during the last twelve months. (He may have feared a libel suit if he asked adults directly if they had abused a child.) Three percent of his respondents knew such a family; extrapolating from this percentage to the national population, he came up with a figure of 2.53 to 4.07 million adults who *knew* an abusive family. Richard Light, who reexamined Gil's figures, calculated that there were about half a million cases of physical abuse in 1965.[22] Subsequent newspaper reports and magazine articles inflated the numbers; indeed, those who tried to determine the extent of abuse were embarrassed by the exaggerated claims. Richard Gelles, a sociologist who conducted one of the most frequently cited studies of the extent of family violence, used the phrase the "Whoozle Effect," to describe the successive increases in estimates of abuse, which could often be traced back to the survey he conducted.[23]

Why did physicians not call attention to other forms of family violence as they did to battered babies? Hospital emergency rooms nightly treated older children and adult victims of all kinds of family violence. The abused patients of pediatricians and radiologists, however, were mainly infants. The suffering of the innocent and helpless young child—who, unlike the older child or adult woman, could not be accused of provocation—made a powerful claim on the medical conscience.

The medical definition of abuse rested on the belief that child abuse was a "syndrome," that is, a set of symptoms associated with a disease, namely, inadequate parenting. According to this point of view, the parent was unwilling at first to confess to injuring the child and might even have been unaware that he or she was suffering from an illness. Nonetheless, despite repeated denials, the parent's condition justified the intervention of doctors, trained in correctly diagnosing and treating disease. Physicians criticized social workers for the prompt return of an injured child to the parents; social workers, it was maintained, were insufficiently worried about the physical safety of the child, believing they could treat the abusive parent without removing the victim. Physicians also favored much greater involvement of the courts in child abuse cases than was generally done at the time.

Battering of children, the experts claimed, occurred equally among all social classes. The case for the "classlessness" of child abuse went as follows. Official agencies were mainly concerned with the poor. The middle class, by contrast, were not policed by social welfare agencies. Therefore, its domestic violence was hidden from view. The poor, it was assumed, were unable to conceal their family life from outside scrutiny, so that the reported incidence of abuse was more or less an accurate estimate. It was reasonable to expect, however, that family violence among the most deprived social groups was even more common than reports suggested. The argument came down to a question of who concealed how much and how often.

Although middle-class parents were more able and perhaps more eager to hide family violence, two kinds of evidence suggest that abuse is in fact related to social class. First, domestic murder is the most serious form of family violence and the least likely to be concealed. The poor and racial minorities commit most family homicides. Second, the national survey conducted by Murray Straus, Richard Gelles, and Suzanne Steinmetz in 1976 asked a representative sample of parents how often they kicked, bit, punched, beat, threatened, or used a knife or gun on their children. Straus and his colleagues designed their questionnaire in such a way as to minimize the stigma of admitting to abuse. Parents earning less than $6,000 a year were twice as likely to report such activities as parents making $20,000 a year or more. Similarly, the rate of abuse was almost twice as high in families with an unemployed or only partially employed father as in families in which the father held a full-time job. Nonetheless, as Leroy Pelton notes, the "myth of classlessness" persisted, and those who argued that violence against children was concentrated among low-income groups were often accused of class prejudice. [24]

Why was the idea of classlessness so necessary to modern reform? For one thing, child battering is shameful; pointing out its higher frequency among the poor appears to be a slur on their family life. For another, the myth of classlessness fits with the medical definition of social problems. Child abuse was alleged to be an epidemic that could strike anyone. If it were associated with poverty, then federal effort would have to be directed toward people at the bottom of the social scale. But by the early 1970s, the public was in a less generous mood toward federal spending for poverty programs. Middle-class taxpayers were more sympathetic toward a social problem believed to affect people like themselves.

The medical definition of child abuse, including the key element of class-lessness, provided more humane treatment for the parent than the view of child abuse as a sin or a crime. It implied that the assailant was not a criminal, but someone unable to control his or her behavior. The family of the abuser, even society, could hope for a cure, even if that expectation was unrealistic. Classifying child battery as a syndrome also increased public compassion; people were more sympathetic toward someone who couldn't help it than toward the mother or father who was deliberately cruel. Peter Conrad, a sociologist, identifies the several benefits to be gained from the medical definition of a social problem: the creation of humanitarian and nonpunitive sanctions; the extension of the "sick role" to abusive parents; a reduction of individual responsibility, blame, and possible stigma; an optimistic therapeutic ideology; care and treatment rendered by the medical profession; and the availability of a flexible and often more efficient means of social control. [25]

Most social workers, doctors, and even many lawyers and judges agreed that imprisoning abusive parents—other than those who had murdered their children—was counterproductive. Police and judges were not qualified to handle family problems. Even the dean of the University of Virginia Law School reasoned that "all in all, criminal sanctions can do little to help a child. The major problems concern his care and custody."[26] A legal definition of abuse, the dean argued, demanded punishment, rendering the parent's rehabilitation difficult or impossible. If the parent could not be rehabilitated, then the domestic unit had to be broken up. The law, it was believed, imposed adversarial methods on troubled parents and children in need of counseling.

Reformers were reluctant to invoke cruelty statutes already on the books because they believed that criminal sanctions against parents only exacerbated domestic difficulties. New, nonpunitive laws were required instead. Between 1963 and 1967, every state passed a child abuse reporting bill, usually after lobbying by pediatricians. Indeed, no other piece of modern social legislation had been so quickly adopted by all the states. Most reporting laws were passed without much opposition. The problem addressed by these statutes was not child abuse, but the unwillingness of professionals to notify the police about it. The first reporting laws were specifically designed to protect physicians from lawsuits and to overcome their reluctance to violate the confidentiality of the doctor-patient relationship. Although nurses and social workers as well as doctors know about instances of abuse, they were not included. The laws usually did not call for any funding of programs to respond to the cases that were reported.

To encourage the public to report abuse, many states also established twenty-four-hour telephone hotlines and commissioned television and radio advertising. Once a complaint was received, it was assumed that someone would investigate it and provide therapy for the parents. In fact, social services for abusers were inadequately funded. Callers to the hotlines often got a busy signal. Deluged by reports that they did not have the resources to investigate, caseworkers succumbed to fatigue and burnout.

Physicians sought to understand why parents committed abuse and formulate the best kinds of therapy for treating them and their children. Kempe's collaborator at the University of Colorado, psychiatrist Brandt Steele, argued that assaultive fathers and mothers lacked the "ability to mother, a role reversal in which parents act like a needy child and expect their child to take over the role of a satisfying parent."[27] Abusive parents had not learned how to cope with the everyday stress of raising children. They expected their children to deal with the parent's needs and problems. Another of Kempe's colleagues developed a questionnaire to identify parents who had the capacity to abuse. The data indicated that such mothers and fathers felt isolated, held unusually high expectations for their children, and were estranged from their mothers.

The child batterer was not identified by gender. Most of the psychiatric literature never made clear which parent was more likely to commit abuse or whether the victim was more often a girl or a boy.[28] Instead, the psychiatrists argued that the sex of the child who was attacked was related to the parent's personality dynamics. These experts advised agencies not to spend much time figuring out which parent had beaten the child. Two major studies yielded contradictory results as to the parent more likely to be an abuser. David Gil, analyzing reports to child protective agencies in 1965, found that 45 percent of physical abuse complaints concerned mothers or mother substitutes and 39 percent fathers. A much more comprehensive inquiry, conducted by the American Humane Association in 1978, determined that 55 percent of the physical abusers were male.[29]

Nonetheless, Kempe and his collaborators believed that mothers, although not necessarily the only abusers, bore special responsibility for the care of children. Kempe recognized the difficulties mothers faced. Because abused children are often the result of an unwanted pregnancy, Kempe called for making birth-control information and abortion accessible. He also blamed society for encouraging women to have children as a means of self-fulfillment. He urged the establishment of crisis nurseries where a parent could leave a child for a few hours and commended Mothers Anonymous, a self-help group for abusing mothers.

In the late nineteenth century, SPCCs were more interested in condemning abuse than in understanding its causes. In the 1960s, a decade of dramatic social change, social movements strove to analyze the source of the problem they were addressing. Although several explanations were offered, the most frequent, and the one in Kempe's "Battered-Child Syndrome," was that child abuse or neglect resulted from "a cycle of violence" in which parents (presumably fathers as well as mothers) who had been mistreated now abused their own children.[30] In a section of the paper labeled "psychiatric aspects," Kempe and his co-authors argued that the parent had been injured before even being able to speak and might have repressed this early abuse. By treating the child the way he or she had been treated, the parent identified with his or her aggressive mother or father. Moreover, the child's needs triggered memories of early fear and rejection. Thus, abusive parents repeated the cruelties they had suffered. This "cycle of violence" theory provided the rationale for therapeutic intervention, even if the parent at first objected. The more abusive the childhood, the greater the unwillingness of the parent to seek help. Without therapeutic intervention, the child was in danger of growing up to become a batterer or a violent criminal.[31]

Psychiatrically influenced child guidance workers first proposed the cycle of violence theory in the 1920s. But they did not suggest that some underlying psychological process was involved. Some childrearing experts a decade before had argued that abused children became doting rather than assaultive because they wanted to compensate for how they had been treated.[32] In attempting to validate the cycle of violence theory, researchers found themselves unable to establish strong correlations between an abusive childhood and adults who became abusers. Most studies purporting to prove the link had no comparison group and were based on small samples. Many abused children grew up in deprived, multiproblem families, where other factors may have contributed to early learning of aggression.

Interrupting the cycle of violence and teaching the abusive parent how to "mother" was the therapeutic objective for a model program Kempe established at the University of Colorado Medical Center in Denver. His treatment team consisted of a pediatrician, a psychiatrist, a nurse, a social worker, and a lay therapist. One of them was available twenty-four hours a day. Kempe claimed that in five hundred cases of child battering, four out of five parents were reunited with their children without any subsequent recurrence of abuse. If a maltreated child was admitted to the hospital, a child protection agency was notified within twenty-four hours. Six days later a caseworker evaluated the parent's home to determine if the child could be safely returned upon release from the hospital. If not, then the child was temporarily placed in foster care. Parent's aides, mostly women, visited the abusive or neglectful mothers once or twice a week over an interval of six to nine months. An aide or a substitute was available for the mother to telephone at any time. The medical team preferred aides from the same class, racial, and economic background as the abusive or neglectful parent. The aide also tried to arrange for day care for the children or some additional homemaker services to relieve stress in the home.

The parent was also encouraged to enter individual or group therapy. Later on, Kempe experimented with residential treatment for the whole family, lasting three to six months. Parents and their children lived at the center, and each family member met separately with a counselor and participated in group sessions. In some cases, only the child lived at the center, while the parents visited daily and received therapy.

After the passage of the reporting laws, it was unclear what needed to be done next. The first congressional representative to show interest in child abuse was Mario Biaggi of Brooklyn, who knew about it from his service on the New York City police force and from contacts with specialized hospital teams treating abused children. Biaggi could not move the child abuse legislation he sponsored out of the powerful House Ways and Means Committee, which had a reputation for blocking social legislation. It took a much more powerful advocate to bypass the logjam created by this committee. The chair of a newly created Senate subcommittee on children was Walter Mondale, a Democratic senator from Minnesota, who used his subcommittee to hold hearings on child abuse. As a child, Mondale had often been whipped by his father as punishment for disobedience, boasting, or lying. Mondale believed his father's methods were stern, but correct, and had helped him.[33] He was not one of those reformers who opposed corporal punishment of children.

Mondale established the subcommittee as a means of advancing proposals made by the 1970 White House Conference on Children. One of the conference's recommendations was federal funding for programs to prevent child abuse and neglect. Since other Senate committees were already concerned with other aspects of child welfare, Mondale's subcommittee, with a large socially committed staff, searched for an issue to establish its reputation. A longtime advocate of social welfare legislation, Mondale had been unable to enact a comprehensive children's social services act during the Nixon administration, which wanted to reduce federal support for social programs. But child abuse was a single, emotionally strong issue, where legislation might be easier to pass. Mondale once quipped, "Not even Richard Nixon is in favor of child abuse."[34]

In 1973 Mondale introduced the Child Abuse Prevention and Treatment Act. Describing his subcommittee's hearings, he later wrote that in his nine years in the Senate, he had seen nothing "as disturbing or horrifying, or as compelling, as the stories and photos of children, many of them infants, who had been whipped and beaten with razor straps; burned and mutilated by cigarettes and lighters; scalded by boiling water; bruised and battered by physical assaults; and starved and neglected and malnourished."[35] Most members of Congress, including Mondale, wanted priority for funding to go to programs for children who were victims of physical abuse. The medical definition of child abuse dominated the subcommittee hearings. Only one lawyer and one family court judge testified; most of the other witnesses were members of hospital treatment teams. The committee met in Denver to take testimony from Dr. Kempe and the members of his team. Kempe's program at the University of Colorado Medical Center was seen as a model worth replicating throughout the nation. The *Denver Observer* succinctly summarized Kempe's testimony as: "The Child-Beaters: Sick but Curable; 'Mothering,' not Prison, is the Best Hope for Helping These Parents, Experts Say."[36] No abused child testified, but the committee heard from Jolly K., an ex-abuser who had founded a self-help organization for mothers. She had tried to murder her daughter and had sought help from many different agencies before starting her own support group. Her testimony helped convince the subcommittee that child abusers could be rehabilitated.

Expert witnesses went on to allege that the incidence of child battering had reached epidemic proportions. Ninety percent of the parents most likely to injure their children were not mentally ill, it was argued, but had been mistreated as children. Parents harmed their sons and daughters out of frustration or unrealistic expectations. Some witnesses emphasized that most violent parents were mothers, while others were vague as to which parent was at fault. The witnesses contradicted each other as to whether child abuse—which was not carefully distinguished from child neglect—was found primarily among welfare mothers, drug addicts, or alcoholics, or was equally common among every social group. Virtually all the witnesses, however, agreed that intervention was required not only to protect the child but also to interrupt "the cycle of violence" so that the victimized child would not become a juvenile delinquent, a murderer, assassin, or a child batterer.

The Child Abuse Prevention and Treatment Act passed easily in both houses of Congress in 1973. Authorizing $85 million to be spent over four years, it provided funding for demonstration programs to handle cases of child abuse and established a National Center on Child Abuse and Neglect, located within the Children's Bureau. Only a few conservatives objected that the program constituted unnecessary intrusion by the federal government into the family.

Congressional representatives insisted on adding a definition of abuse to the legislation. National social work organizations lobbied to include funding for child neglect. Kempe, who had been treating many victims of rape and molestation, wanted to incorporate sexual abuse as well. As a result, the 1973 law considered "child abuse and neglect" to be "physical or mental injury, sexual abuse, negligent treatment, or maltreatment of a child under the age of eighteen by a person who is responsible for the child's welfare under circumstances which indicate that the child's health or welfare is harmed or threatened thereby."[37] When the act was renewed in 1978, the meaning of child abuse was expanded further to encompass sexual abuse, abduction, impairing the morals of a child, sodomy, incest, and taking indecent liberties.

The 1973 act and subsequent renewals required a state to amend its laws by adding protective custody provisions sufficient to meet federal standards. These provisions gave a state child welfare agency the power to remove a child for three days if it believed the child was in danger. During that time, the caseworker was required to file a petition in the juvenile court for custody of the child, even though parental rights had not been terminated. Barbara Nelson believes that these provisions generated the first round of contention for a hitherto noncontroversial issue. She argues that the inclusion of protective custody provisions "firmly connected strong, easily administered reporting systems to lumbering, conflict-ridden legal and welfare systems. Reporting legislation was no longer a blend of public health do-goodism and malpractice insurance for physicians concerned about mistakenly labeling an injury as abuse. Instead reporting legislation became child welfare legislation subject to all the tensions over family autonomy, individual rights, and the role of the state that welfare legislation engenders."[38]

The protective custody provisions instituted no standardized pattern of action. Investigation of a report might consist of sending a letter, making a phone call, or visiting the family. The typical case was, as in the late nineteenth century, the "unfounded" one: the alleged perpetrator, as well as friends, relatives, and others who knew the family denied abuse. Rarely were the police involved. Very few parents were prosecuted on criminal charges of child abuse or neglect, and fewer still were found guilty.

In the late nineteenth century, the anticruelty societies simply dismissed unfounded complaints. In the 1970s about half of such cases were referred to agencies that provided social services to the parents or the child. When there was evidence of neglect or abuse, the child usually remained with the parent, and the family was placed under "home supervision," in which the caseworker monitored the care that the child was receiving, and the parent underwent therapy. Supervision generally consisted of about five home visits during a period of six months, after which the case was ignored, dismissed, or the parent was referred to a mental health clinic or family service agency. Some psychological counseling was provided, but only on a limited basis. The abusive or neglectful parent was not the kind of client these agencies were easily able to help. Critics of the medical model of abuse, who feared that the abuser would be subjected to an unending therapeutic regimen, were unaware of how little treatment was actually available.

The child protective agencies of the 1960s and 1970s were less likely to take children from their parents than the late nineteenth-century SPCCs. Most modern agencies justified removal of a child only if social services alone could not prevent future harm. About one in five children was placed in foster care, according to figures collected in 1978 by the National Center for Child Abuse and Neglect. Nonetheless, this percentage was substantially higher than in the 1950s, when Vincent DeFrancis estimated that less than 10 percent of substantiated cases of abuse and neglect had this outcome.

While there had been few respected critics of the federal legislation when it first passed, by the 1970s some highly influential lawyers and psychiatrists worried that too many children were being removed from their homes. Foster care was supposed to be temporary, but in fact over half of all children in it in the mid-1970s remained there for more than two years, and three out of ten lingered in foster homes for six years or more.[39] The critics, repeating arguments that had been heard in the 1950s, charged that judges and social workers were indulging in "rescue fantasies" in failing to appreciate the child's love for even neglectful parents. Children were being taken from their homes simply because of lack of appropriate services.

Michael Wald, a professor at Stanford University Law School, was one of the main proponents of the anti-interventionist point of view. He argued that state intrusion separated mainly poor and minority children from their families. Most foster homes, he argued, were as bad as the original home from which the child was removed. He opposed criminal prosecution in cases of incest and insisted that sexual abuse was not always harmful.[40] Wald, along with many other lawyers, was concerned about class prejudice and tended to side with the rights of neglectful parents against courts and social agencies.

Other opponents of state intervention included Anna Freud, a noted child psychiatrist and the daughter of Sigmund Freud, Joseph Goldstein, a lawyer, and Albert Solnit, a professor of pediatrics and psychiatry at Yale University. Their landmark book, *Beyond the Best Interests of the Child* (1979), argued that the child needed a stable family life—a continuing relationship with the mother or a substitute throughout the early years. Foster care, they believed, should be limited to a short time. They called for psychiatric treatment for the abusive parent, "not for the battered child for whom this comes too late, but for those children they might have and care for in the future."[41]

Freud and her colleagues were anti-interventionist in cases of incest and neglect. They supported removal of the incest victim only if the parent had been convicted of criminal assault; otherwise, they recommended psychiatric help for both parents and the continued presence of the incestuous father in the home. Emotional neglect, they argued, was too vague a category to warrant any action. Mandatory reporting laws, these critics argued, had not protected children, but had simply increased the number of investigations of the family, thus constituting "an unwarranted intrusion into family privacy, weakening the integrity of the families involved."[42] They opposed corporal punishment at home or at school, but believed the state should take children from parents only if there was "serious bodily injury." Ironically, in these kinds of situations, Freud and her collaborators were far more in favor of permanent revocation of parental rights than Kempe. In cases of serious bodily injury, they advocated immediate removal of the child, swift termination of parental rights, and permanent adoption of the child. They did not believe in giving seriously abusive parents "a second chance," particularly if the child had been in foster care for several years. In such a situation, they felt the foster parents had become the child's psychological parents. They even

wanted to deny visitation rights to an abusive parent who had at one time tried
to murder his or her children.

Freud, Goldstein, and Solnit believed that neglectful parents would benefit
most from the provision of voluntary services—services that they were not
required to use. They referred here to a grab-bag of social programs, including
homemaker aides, crisis nurseries, day care, economic aid to the family, and
free health care. They and other social welfare advocates argued that only by
attacking poverty, unemployment, inadequate housing and health care, and
the lack of day care would one solve the problem of child abuse and neglect.
The Western European countries provided more comprehensive child welfare planning than did the United States and as a result, it was claimed, had
done more to eliminate child abuse and neglect.[43] This view was reminiscent
of the arguments of the Progressives, who favored social reforms from mothers' pensions to building children's playgrounds as a means of preventing the
mistreatment of children. It was undeniable that the American welfare state
was a sorry shambles of problem-specific, uncoordinated social programs. But
advocates of the social welfare approach cited no evidence that the Western
European nations had indeed reduced child abuse and neglect.

The problem of violence in the family came to the public, state legislatures, and the Congress in an extremely oversimplified form. In this respect,
the modern effort was no different from previous ones. Indeed, if the issue
had been presented as child neglect, as Vincent DeFrancis had originally
proposed, there would have been no major federal legislation, no national
agency, and far fewer demonstration programs. The pediatricians and social
workers established clear control over the issue and helped obtain federal
funding on an unprecedented scale for programs to aid abused children.
Barbara Nelson concludes that national legislation was "good for its sponsors,
good for the professionals who supported it, and—though more difficult to
prove—probably good for the children whose lives it touched."[44]

The presentation of the issue as the battered-child syndrome was a well-
intentioned cover-up in the service of a worthy cause, which unraveled as
professionals began to realize that the issue was more complex than they had
originally thought. Battering was not confined to infants; abuse was not as
clearly deviant as commonly believed, since corporal punishment was widely
accepted and used. National surveys showed that many forms of domestic
violence occurred too frequently to be considered aberrant. Gradually, other
victims of violence in the family were discovered—the sexually abused child,
the battered wife, the abused elder, even the battered husband. Soon there

were as many varieties of domestic assault as there were relationships in the family.

Greater state intervention had increased the services and protection available to abused and neglected children and their parents. But federal programs had raised expectations too high. More public attention had led to more reporting, and thus more investigations of abuse that subsequently turned out to be unfounded. Even the substantiated cases overwhelmed the protective agencies, which were unable to provide the kind of services they believed were required. Ironically, the more that was done, the more unsatisfied the reformers became. By the standards of the past, the respect for the rights of the child and the parent had never been so great. But the heightened concern for individual rights contributed to a greater fear of the state. Reformers were forced to realize that state intervention produced negative as well as positive results, and sometimes a little bit of both.

Once again, reformers against family violence rejected the policies of their immediate predecessors, an attitude which time and again has proven short-sighted. Because physicians were so prominent in this latest movement, they naively assumed that *their* actions were good for everyone involved. Disillusion soon followed. Government intervention created its own abuses, for which legal safeguards were required. The national effort had not failed; instead, it had reached a new stage of maturity. Inevitably, the social problem of child abuse confronted genuine dilemmas that could no longer be avoided or brushed aside. Devising policies toward family violence forced reformers to face up to zero-sum situations—one group gained at the expense of another. Choices had to be made between treatment or punishment, too much intervention or not enough, and between ensuring parental liberties or protecting children.

10

Assault at Home

THERE WAS VIRTUALLY NO PUBLIC DISCUSSION of wife beating from the turn of the century until the mid-1970s. Wife beating was called "domestic disturbance" by the police, "family maladjustment" by marriage counselors and social caseworkers. Psychiatry, under the influence of Helene Deutsch, regarded the battered woman as a masochist who provoked her husband into beating her. In the *Journal of Marriage and the Family*, the major scholarly journal in family sociology, no article on family violence appeared from its founding in 1939 until 1969.[1]

Very few modern novels contained scenes of marital violence. In spite of the rediscovery of child abuse in the 1960s, newspapers did not begin to report on abuse of wives until 1974. The next year, however, women activists organized conferences in several cities to establish shelters for battered women, demand arrest of wife beaters by the police, and draft new legislation. In 1977 the *New York Times* carried forty-four articles on wife beating, ranging from stories about hotlines and shelters to the trials of women who had murdered their assaultive husbands.

The course of political reawakening retraced the path of late nineteenth-century campaigns. Wife beating began as a women's rights issue and picked up support as a law-and-order (and social work) issue. As in the nineteenth century, conservative feminists (and nonfeminist reformers) were more likely than radicals to succeed in achieving reform. Still, modern-day feminists did not have to assert a woman's right to leave her husband. Instead, they found themselves countering others who wondered why battered women remained in abusive marriages.

The rebirth of feminism was necessary for the rediscovery of wife beating. The women's movement put pressure on the police, social agencies, and the state and federal government to respond adequately to the problem. It forced policymakers to consider remedies that had been unthinkable only a few years before. As in the nineteenth century, feminism questioned the nature of the family and espoused greater options for women. Nonetheless, for reform on behalf of abused women to succeed, feminism—a controversial ideology—had to be tamed. The battered women's movement, having been born out of grass-roots feminism, enjoyed only brief periods free from controversy. In the modern era, as in the nineteenth century, feminism was perceived as an attack on the family. Women reformers deliberately tried to avoid rancorous debate in order to pass legislation. Their strategy eventually succeeded. The innovative social reforms of the 1970s increased the possibilities for women to escape in safety from violent husbands.

Although many women campaigned against child abuse, it was defined as a public health problem, not a feminist issue. Child protection reformers had always overlooked gender, even in the nineteenth century. The anticruelty crusade had been separate from the women's cause. In the 1970s, the only common ground shared by feminists and advocates of children was concern about victims of incest and sexual molestation.

Although the National Organization for Women was founded in 1966, wife abuse was not recognized as a "woman's issue" until the International Women's Year Convention in Houston some eleven years later. Instead, the National Organization for Women (NOW) in the late 1960s devoted its attention to such concerns as public funding for child-care facilities, banning employment discrimination against women, legal access to abortion, and passage of the equal rights amendment; rape and wife beating were not mentioned.

Some might suggest that wife beating went unnoticed in the early years of the women's movement because it did not affect the middle-class, highly educated women attracted to the movement. In fact, several leaders and members of NOW, as well as younger activists in more radical groups, described in print beatings or rapes inflicted upon them by their husbands or lovers. Even Betty Friedan, the founder of NOW, had once heaved a mirror at her husband, hitting him in the knuckle; her husband had on another occasion thrown a bowl of sugar at her face. One of the women who established Cell 16, a women's liberationist group in Boston, was Betsy Warrior—she adopted this last name to symbolize her feminist militancy. Warrior, married at seventeen, was so brutally beaten by her husband when she was pregnant that her child was stillborn. Andrea Dworkin, a radical feminist writer, had been badly bruised by her husband. A number of women's auto-biographies published in the late 1960s—Sally Kempton's recollection of her marriage in "Cutting Loose," and Sara Davidson's *Loose Change*, about three young female graduates of the University of California at Berkeley—chron-icled violence in women's personal relationships with men. In the autobiogra-phy, *I Know Why the Caged Bird Sings*, Maya Angelou described a sexual assault by her uncle when she was quite young. Traumatized by this rape, Angelou for many years lost her ability to speak. Most critics and readers interpreted these accounts as sagas of women's "coming of age" rather than as memoirs of female victims. [2]

Radical feminism, most critical of the traditional family, was responsible for the subsequent rediscovery of wife beating. Younger women, dissatisfied with the male prejudice they had encountered in the civil rights, antiwar, and the New Left movements, withdrew to establish small local women's groups. Some of these groups experimented with "consciousness-raising," in which women exchanged personal experiences revolving around sexuality, mar-riage, attitudes toward one's mother, and housework. Women, in sharing the intimate details of their lives, sought to generalize from their own personal history to a larger understanding of women's condition. [3]

In the late 1960s, abortion was the first major issue for radical feminism. It was illegal in many states, and those women who secured one were often too frightened to admit they had done so. Feminists believed that women had a right to control their bodies. The abortion issue joined other feminist demands and was linked with equal pay for equal work and the call for sexual liberation. Since abortion touched on female vulnerability concerning preg-nancy and a woman's right to chose motherhood, younger, college-educated women believed that an unplanned pregnancy could disrupt their lives and careers. Thus, access to abortion was seen as necessary for women's equality; otherwise, her biology left her disadvantaged in the workplace. [4]

In 1969 the New York radical women's liberation group, the Redstockings, organized a "speakout" for women to share their experiences about abortion. Two years later, they held another one on rape. At these events, the dominant theme was that males created and perpetuated a definition of women as sexual objects and pressured them into heterosexual intercourse. It was ironic that rape appeared as a women's issue before wife beating, because complaints of wife abuse to the police far exceeded reports of sexual assault. Nonetheless, the issue of rape was focused on first because it fitted more closely the radical feminist emphasis on the deliberate channeling of female sexuality into the service of male domination.

The issue of rape emerged out of and contributed to the growth of radical feminism. Susan Brownmiller of the New York Radical Feminists described the transformation of her own attitudes toward rape. In the fall of 1970, she had insisted to her women friends that "rape was a sex crime, a product of a diseased deranged mind . . . it wasn't a feminist issue."[5] Brownmiller was stunned by the size of the crowd at the speakout on rape she helped organize and shocked by the revelations she heard. As a result, she arrived at "a way of looking at male-female relations, at sex, at strength, and at power."[6] The same year, another feminist writer, Susan Griffin, published her article, "Rape—an All-American Crime." Rape was not an act of sexuality, she argued, but an act of domination, a form of "mass terrorism" against randomly chosen women victims.[7] All women lived in dread of sexual assault, she held; in fact, the function of rape was to keep women fearful and dependent on men.

The first rape crisis hotline, established in Berkeley, California, in 1972, took phone calls twenty-four-hours-a-day from victims. The service offered counseling to women who had been raped and encouraged them to press criminal charges against their assailants. The next year, the New York Radical Feminists, among others, called for judicial review of courtroom procedures in rape cases, stronger punishment for rapists, and increased criminal penalties for sex crimes. They also sought to broaden the definition of rape to include sexual assault by a husband or a boyfriend.

The antirape movement provided the ideology, methods, and public acceptance necessary for the emergence of the battered women's cause. Misogyny, psychoanalytic belief, public apathy, and police practices were the common enemies of both campaigns. Rape and wife beating were often compared; each was a taboo subject, rarely discussed in public, except as a joking matter. Victims of rape and wife beating were made to feel guilty for having provoked their attack and often failed to report assaults or press charges with the police. Some victims of rape or wife beating took the law into their own hands in murdering their assailants.[8]

A standard women's liberation pamphlet against rape described a series of "myths" about rape accompanied by a list of "facts" designed to refute them. The myths derived from the Bible (women acted seductively, lied about rape to punish men who spurned them, and provoked men to violence) and from popularized psychoanalytic theory (women actively sought rape and secretly enjoyed it). This myth versus fact presentation was appropriated by the battered women's movement. The antirape movement also provided a model of social services and victim advocacy in the battered women's movement.[9] The campaign against wife beating attracted antirape activists, who organized conferences about wife beating and demanded increased police protection for women victims. Feminist lawyers criticized the failure of the police to enforce criminal laws against male assailants.

The federal government had funded community legal aid services in the 1960s in poor urban neighborhoods. Poor women used them to obtain divorces. Women lawyers at these agencies, often influenced by feminism, became de facto divorce lawyers. At the South Brooklyn Legal Services Corporation, the attorney who handled divorces was Marjory Fields, a native New Yorker and recent law school graduate. The police, she learned, refused to come when her clients called them. In 1974 Fields, who was unable to secure an appointment with the New York City police chief, told her story to a *New York Times* reporter. His article was syndicated in newspapers across the country.[10] Fields called for the inclusion of women police officers in special police units to handle complaints of wife beating.

About the same time, two women law students at the University of Michigan documented the lack of responsiveness of Washtenaw County, Michigan, police and judges to complaints from battered women.[11] They learned that the police told battered women complaining of assault that "if you are married, there is nothing we can do." The police often relied on a "stitch rule"— arresting an abusing husband only if his wife had been injured badly enough to require a specific number of surgical sutures.

Police practices were the first to be criticized, because they could be so clearly documented. Later, social workers and hospital emergency room personnel came in for scrutiny.[12] Police reports of "domestic disturbance calls" provided the first evidence about the extent of wife beating. Law enforcement publications favored arrest only as a last resort. The modern approach was to mediate domestic disputes or refer victims to family court or social agencies for counseling.[13] Since officers who intervened in violent families were often injured or even killed, a policy aimed at reconciliation, it was believed, would lower the rate of injuries among the police.

Feminist lawyers directed their efforts at changing such policies. Laurie Woods, a twenty-nine-year-old attorney with a federal legal services organization in New York City, explained that "it was upsetting for me to tell these women with bruises, black eyes and sometimes broken bones about their rights to legal protection and have them come back to me with stories about the runarounds they got." She started by calling up specific police officers or court personnel but she soon discovered, "I could spend a whole morning trying to get action on behalf of one woman." She realized that it was more efficient to attack "the whole problem with a suit."[14] In 1976 women lawyers in Oakland, California, and Fields, Woods, and other legal advocates in New York City brought class-action suits against the police in their respective cities, hoping to force major procedural changes. They charged that the police refused to arrest assaultive husbands. The legal brief by the New York lawyers also accused court personnel of denying women access to judges who could issue orders of protection. Feminist lawyers also began to defend battered women who had murdered their husbands. Not all battered wives could claim they killed in self-defense, although most were able to show they had endured beatings and terror over a number of years. The function of dramatic courtroom trials, one feminist lawyer explained, was to "raise the level of public awareness about the pervasiveness of the physical abuse of women."[15]

Other early efforts evolved from local chapters of NOW, where women could establish a task force on a subject of their choice. By 1973, some chose the topic of "displaced homemakers," widows and divorcees who were unprepared to reenter the job market after having spent their adult years as full-time housewives. The members of these task forces were generally divorced women, some of whom had been beaten by their husbands. NOW members organized a separate task force on battered women. In 1973 Nancy Kirk-Gormley, a divorced mother of two who fled her marriage after enduring ten years of beatings, established the first task force. A year after joining NOW, she realized that the organization had addressed almost every women's problem except abuse. She formed a self-help group for battered women that eventually led to the founding of the Pennsylvania Task Force on Household Violence. It stressed divorce as the long-term solution for battered women, along with self-defense and prosecution of the abuser, and sought reform of police practices and legal aid for victims. Much like Protective Agency members in nineteenth-century Chicago, women from NOW task forces accompanied battered women to courts and assisted in pressing criminal charges against their husbands.

An abused woman should have been able to call upon police to evict her assaultive husband from the home. In practice, the law, the courts, and the police were unwilling to provide this kind of protection. Thus battered women required emergency housing as well as legal assistance. Marjory Fields, for example, objected to the idea of a wife going into hiding while her assailant was free, but she "received too many calls from women huddled in phone booths with their children, asking where they should go" to question the urgent need for shelters.[16] A shelter could provide an abused woman and her children a place to stay while she decided whether to return to her husband or get a divorce. Most U.S. cities at this time furnished emergency housing only for derelicts. Children could be accommodated on a temporary basis at these refuges, but the mother was generally not permitted to accompany her children.

Americans had first learned about emergency housing for women victims in England. Erin Pizzey, a modern-day counterpart of Francis Power Cobbe, devised the idea of temporary residences for battered women. Born in China of English parents, Pizzey had been imprisoned by the Japanese during World War II. She recalled that her father, although not a wife-beater, had bullied and tormented her mother. At the age of forty-two, Pizzey was married and living in a London suburb. She joined with a group of women to establish a neighborhood center, Chiswick, that offered a child-care center and a refuge for homeless women. Many of those attracted to the center had been abused by their husbands.[17] Pizzey soon learned that police, social workers, and physicians did not want to help these women, and that local social services had refused to house them.

Chiswick admitted any woman who arrived at its doorstep. It attracted women from all parts of England and Scotland. Local groups of women began to establish shelters across the country. Pizzey used her personal connections—her husband was a journalist for the BBC—in publicizing her work. She supplied newspapers and television stations with a steady stream of horrible accounts about violent treatment of women and demonstrated the need for battered women's refuges by showing the large numbers of women who flocked to Chiswick. A self-identified feminist, but uninterested in radical ideology, Pizzey allied herself with psychiatrists and other "experts" who approached wife abuse as a problem of "a cycle of violence." The abusive childhood of the wife beater, she argued, contributed to his assaultive behavior as an adult. She was fond of saying that "a man who batters is a child who was battered that nobody helped."[18] The Chiswick model inspired other women's groups, most of whom were more hostile to community authorities and established professionals than Pizzey.

Dozens of Americans visited the English shelters in the first years after they were founded. Others learned of the experiments from articles in *Newsweek*, *Ms.* magazine, and television programs.[19] Between 1975 and 1977, a brief media flurry about wife beating spurred the growth of the movement in the United States. From the media's point of view, wife beating was new, controversial, and somewhat titillating in that it involved the staple of modern American culture—sex and violence. The issue of wife beating provided a vehicle for a popular discussion of family life and feminism and supplied the human element and dramatic urgency the media require. Magazine and newspaper articles were emblazoned with close-up photographs of women's bruised faces and blackened eyes, and generally portrayed the battered woman as a helpless victim overpowered by a savage brute. Television soap operas and police dramas featured sympathetic portrayals of abused women that diminished public apathy.[20]

In the United States safe houses for wives of alcoholics were the only available model of shelters for abused women. The founding of Women's Advocates in St. Paul, Minnesota, in 1974, although not the earliest refuge for battered women in the United States, was still the first to reflect the impact of the modern feminist movement. It was founded by a consciousness-raising group, Women's Advocates, that had previously produced a divorce rights handbook and organized a legal information phone service for women. Most of its members were single, in their twenties, and none had ever been beaten themselves. One leader, Sharon Vaughan, recalled, "Personally, I didn't call myself a feminist when we started. It sort of snuck up and embraced me as I lived it."[21]

Abused women who required emergency housing called the group's telephone hotline. Because there was often no emergency housing available, some of the staff began to house these callers in their own apartments. The service moved its office to a one-bedroom apartment, so that it could provide housing for a few women and their children; responses from a mailing provided the funding. Because of the steady stream of women and children arriving and leaving the premises, Women's Advocates was evicted from this apartment, and temporarily moved into the dining room of a private home and secured pledges for a loan to purchase a three-story, five-bedroom older house not far from St. Paul's downtown. A twenty-four-hour crisis telephone line was operated from an office in the house. Twelve women and their children could be accommodated at one time.

Women's Advocates had a paid staff, at least one of whom was always available, augmented with volunteers. They explained the criminal procedure in assault cases to each woman who arrived at the shelter. When the woman was ready, she was taken to a lawyer, a doctor, or the welfare department. A social worker from a local family counseling agency led a support group for current and former residents of the shelter, babysat, and arranged for temporary enrollment of the children in school or a day-care center. The Advocates operated as a collective and divided administrative responsibilities; they opposed hiring staff based on professional credentials. A founder of the shelter said, "A shelter is not a treatment center; residents are not described as clients, battering is not described as a syndrome. Women are not thought of as victims except as victims of a crime requiring redress."[22]

The average length of stay for a resident was about ten days. Women were required to attend nightly house meetings to decide on how to divide the next day's tasks; they also prepared and cooked their own meals. The rules of the house prohibited violence, but staff members were often forced to intervene to keep tempers in check. If a mother appeared about to strike her child, they tried to stop her or divert her attention by playing with the child. [23]

Many residents of the shelter subsequently returned to their husbands. Women were encouraged to make their own decision about whether to remain apart. Even if a woman did go back, Advocates sought to "support her choice and urge her to keep in contact with the shelter and return to the weekly support group." [24] Sharon Vaughan learned the lesson that "each woman must be free to choose her own consequences . . . Our final communication is that the door is . . . open." [25]

Most subsequent shelters copied the model of Women's Advocates in St. Paul. They provided battered women with counseling about jobs, schooling, and legal remedies. Many residents were assisted in obtaining food stamps or welfare. Some activists were concerned that welfare and food stamps substituted economic dependency on the state for financial subservience to a husband. Given that most women who fled to refuges were poor and ill-educated, welfare was the only realistic temporary (and for some, more permanent) alternative. One survey estimated that about 47,000 women were housed at shelters throughout the United States in 1977. Most residences received some federal money, especially from a national job-training program, which employed some of the staff at about half of all shelters. [26] In 1978 the Florida legislature imposed a $5 tax on marriage licenses, providing $600,000 a year for shelters in the state. About sixteen other states imitated this scheme. The single largest source of funds for shelters came from the Social Security Administration's program for the temporary housing of neglected and abused children.

Shelters legitimized the issue of wife beating. If there was a place for battered women to go and if large numbers of women went there, then a social problem clearly existed. Women's refuges also created jobs (albeit at a subsistence wage) that supported activists helping battered women. The staff and residents of shelters also served as an organized pressure group, demanding better treatment for victims from police and hospital emergency services and lobbying for legislation.

Women's refuges multiplied rapidly, especially in California, New York, and other states where the women's movement was strongest. In August 1976, a *Ms.* catalog of services available for battered women listed only twenty shelters in the United States; by 1982, there were about three hundred, as well as coalitions to provide services to battered women in forty-eight states. Although feminists who had been heavily involved in the antirape movement began the first shelters, their influence soon began to wane. A survey of 127 shelters in 1981 found that fewer than half developed out of a women's group or included a board of directors or staff members who defined themselves as feminists.[27] The more "radical" shelters, which often included lesbian feminists on their staff, frequently did not survive. The more long-lasting ones commonly drew their support from churches, community groups, and established social service agencies, which preferred to employ social welfare professionals rather than feminist activists.

By the late 1970s, many of the surviving refuges had been transformed from "self-help" organizations into social agencies. The evolution of a shelter in Arizona illustrated this process. It received funding from the state's mental health bureau, which mostly handled programs for drug abusers, alcoholics, and the mentally ill. The state agency required the shelter to maintain case files and devise treatment plans with concrete goals for each woman. (Similarly, federal regulations mandated reporting welfare and parole violations, and drug addiction.[28])

Some of the original feminist founders left because of their distaste for bureaucratic and casework procedures. The new board hired a male professional social worker to supervise the counselors, many of whom were former battered women. Staff meetings, once largely rambling discussions, now consisted primarily of structured, formal presentations of cases. Clinical language was used in meetings, reports, and training sessions. The staff "began to view each woman as a case requiring psychotherapeutic intervention and were rewarded for using that approach in their case files and presentations." They saw the refuge as a "therapeutic milieu" where women freed themselves from dependence on batterers and on counselors. Eventually the shelter hired psychologists and social workers, who were less likely to become emotionally drained or exhausted by their work, but were also less dedicated and committed. One of the disappointed founders regretted that the shelter "no longer provided a 'homelike' atmosphere, but was more of an 'agency,' where clients befriended one another, but not the staff."[29]

No matter what their style of operation, refuges were still crucial for women victims. The demand for services of every kind far outstripped the supply. In 1979, a survey of abused women in Kentucky—none of whom were current residents of shelters—found that about half would have like to have received counseling, but only 7 percent had. Many had needed legal aid and child care. Quite a few had required medical care for their injuries, although they had been reluctant or ashamed to see a doctor or go to a hospital. About a third said they would have fled to a shelter if one had been available. Most had not turned to anyone, not even friends or relatives, when they had been beaten.[30]

The next step in the evolution of programs was services for batterers, first established in 1975. Either a social service agency or a woman's shelter began most of these efforts. This kind of service was quite new; its only precedent was the counseling for male alcoholics provided by psychopathic hospitals in the 1920s. Unlike previous approaches, the new programs saw violence as "the man's problem," and their goal was to teach abusers to become non-violent.[31] Although preservation of the marriage was no longer the major objective, these programs held out the possibility of a nonviolent, egalitarian family. Counselors, some of whom were ex-batterers, were often more optimistic about the couple's chances for reconciliation than the staff who worked at shelters.

By 1976, the first new state laws concerning wife abuse were passed. They provided funding for shelters, improved reporting procedures, repealed intra-spousal immunity from torts, and established more effective criminal court procedures. By 1980, all but six states had enacted such laws. By the late 1970s, women's coalitions also lobbied to eliminate the marital exemption from rape statutes.[32] The first states to do so were those where the battered women's movement was strongest.

Much like child abuse reporting laws, domestic violence legislation was quickly adopted because it was inexpensive. There was a fairly predictable pattern in these legislative efforts. An interested "insider" working for a state representative helped mobilize women's groups and the state's commission on the status of women. Liberal Democratic men or women legislators from both political parties were sponsors. Viewed as nonpartisan, and noncontroversial, these domestic violence laws were passed without lengthy hearings or legislative debate.[33]

Most activists had never clearly formulated an explanation for the causes of wife abuse. An American couple teaching sociology in Scotland and active in the movement there to establish shelters provided the major feminist analysis of wife beating. In *Violence Against Wives* (1979), R. Emerson Dobash and Russell Dobash argued that marriage was an institution based on the subordination of women, and that wife beating was an extension of male domination and control. The patriarchal family, they believed, permitted male violence against wives and children as long as it did not exceed certain limits. Communities and social institutions silently tolerated violence; the police and the courts refused to enforce criminal laws. They insisted that wife beating was normal, not pathological; the abusive husband was merely living up to cultural expectations to beat a provocative wife. The quality of the marriage deteriorated, the Dobashes found, as battered women experienced loss of affection, fear, depression, withdrawal, and participated in violence themselves.[34] Far more influential as a practical guide to grass-roots organizing was

Del Martin's *Battered Wives*, published in 1976. Martin, a founder of NOW and an important advocate of lesbian rights, attributed wife beating to a husband's belief that his wife was his property.[35]

Various groups involved with the issue of battered women posed the query, "Why do they stay?" Their assumption was that battered women ought to get a divorce; something was wrong with women who did not do so. In the nineteenth century, it was thought that a woman *should* remain married out of religious duty and responsibility to her children. Feminists fought for a woman's right to leave a violent marriage and opposed the stigma surrounding divorce. The question "why do they stay?" was first posed in the 1920s, perhaps coinciding with the rise of modern psychology. The answer given then was that battered women were of low intelligence or mentally retarded; two decades later, it was assumed these women did not leave because they were masochistic. By the 1970s, an abused woman stayed married, the experts claimed, because she was isolated from friends and neighbors, had few economic or educational resources, and had been terrorized into a state of "learned helplessness" by repeated beatings.[36] The modern answer was not necessarily wrong—it was certainly less insulting—but it was far less revealing than the persistent need to pose the question.

Although modern psychology has since debunked stereotypes about masochistic women, it did not have a clearly defined explanation of why men batter. Some attributed it to childhood abuse, or alcohol and drugs. Others argued that husbands were threatened because their wives demanded too much power in the family. Aggressive and domineering behavior toward women, it was claimed, compensated for insecure masculine identity. No one tried to integrate these different suggestions into a single theory, nor was any one of them dominant.[37]

The lesson of child abuse reform was that in order to receive federal funding and attention, a social problem had to be widespread and cut across class lines. Federal funding—more than one million dollars in government grants—went into the research of sociologists Murray Straus, Richard Gelles, and Suzanne Steinmetz to determine the prevalence of different types of domestic abuse. In 1976 they surveyed several thousand people, considered representative of the U.S. population. Their statistics were then used to prove the common occurrence of diverse forms of violence in the family. Mary Jane Cronin was a member of a group in the federal government that met regularly to coordinate federal efforts regarding domestic violence. In retrospect she claimed that "there was a federal response because the problem cuts across class and race. If domestic violence affected only poor women, it would have been dismissed."[38] Women in the government, along with anti-wife beating activists, worked at orchestrating both media coverage and pressure from women's groups. Their efforts led to government action on behalf of battered women and helped shape national legislation.

Wife beating entered the federal bureaucracy as a law-and-order issue. The Law Enforcement Assistance Administration (LEAA), the major funding source of local rape crisis programs across the country, also provided money for battered women's shelters and other programs on behalf of women victims. Congress established the LEAA in 1968 to help the criminal justice system. Most of the agency's money was distributed to the states, which in turn channeled it to local organizations. In its discretionary budget for 1977, LEAA devoted about $700,000 to domestic violence projects; spending quadrupled by 1980. LEAA tended to prefer shelters established by the Salvation Army or the United Fund to those identified with feminism. Critics charged that the agency was more concerned with "criminal justice improvement" than with aiding victims.[39] Although the official federal policy was to encourage victims to bring complaints, some local programs hoped to "save resources" by discouraging victims from doing so. LEAA programs often diverted batterers from the courts to court-ordered counseling programs. Offenders who could afford to pay for therapy were permitted to enter private programs or choose their own therapist; others were sent to jail or enrolled in government-funded programs.[40]

As the problem of wife beating gained more national attention, it was officially called "domestic violence" in both state and federal legislation, and in the office established within the Department of Health and Human Services in 1979. Until the 1970s, the phrase "domestic violence" was understood as referring to the riots in ghetto areas during the 1960s; some congressional representatives thought the term meant urban terrorism.[41] The NOW chapter of Ann Arbor, Michigan, may have first applied it to the family in their Domestic Violence/Spouse Assault Task force in 1975. University of Michigan women law students were analyzing local police records to document the incidence of wife assault. Domestic violence may have been a close but more vivid equivalent for the "domestic disturbance calls" the police received. "Domestic" replaced "family" because police records showed that complaints came from the wives, girlfriends, and divorcees. Domestic violence was defined to include abuse of the elderly and incest, and efforts to combat them were developed. Battered husbands were theoretically served by "spouse abuse" programs.[42] Only abused and neglected children were excluded, on the grounds that they were already covered by child abuse prevention programs.

In all, this new label deemphasized the woman as the victim. The problem was in domestic life generally. The term appealed to social workers, who believed their field had special expertise in treating family problems.[43]

Still, there was no C. Henry Kempe of wife beating, no single national leader who could command the respect of politicians. Erin Pizzey was the closest equivalent, but she was not an American. In 1977 several members of Congress attended a luncheon with Pizzey, who was on a fund-raising tour in the United States. One of the staff members of a congressional representative who met her reported, "It was the first time that many members of Congress had really heard a heavy discussion about the plight of battered women and their families. Ever since then, things have been snowballing."[44]

The Senate, the House, and the U.S. Civil Rights Commission held hearings on battered women in 1978. To those who listened to the testimony at Mondale's subcommittee hearing five years before, the arguments were familiar. Witnesses claimed that the incidence of wife abuse had reached epidemic proportions. Intervention was required not only to protect the battered wife but also to interrupt the cycle of violence so that children would not sustain permanent psychological damage. While these statements in some ways paralleled those made about child abuse, there were differences as well. In the hearings about child abuse, witnesses tried to explain why parents abused their children; in the hearings about wife abuse, experts gave reasons why battered women were willing to be beaten. The motivations of abusers went unanalyzed. Moreover, the calls for treatment and rehabilitation, voiced frequently in Mondale's hearings, were noticeably absent. Except for a few feminist psychiatrists, physicians were rare among the group of reformers who testified. Some abused wives appeared before the committee, but no abuser testified (the exact opposite of the deliberations on child abuse). Although several feminists were witnesses, their analysis was reduced to the assertion that sex-role stereotypes and conditioning contributed to domestic violence. The preferred explanation, given by psychologists and sociologists, was that domestic violence arose from stress and frustration, compounded by alcoholism and drugs.

Several witnesses at the U.S. Civil Rights Commission's hearings cautioned against equating wife with child abuse. They argued that the battered wife was an adult who did not need the same degree and type of protection as the abused child. The victim of wife abuse, they claimed, could obtain assistance on her own, whereas the abused child could not. (This statement was an exaggeration, since many battered children did seek help.) Quite a few

experts hoped that shelters for battered women would not become demonstration programs and hospital treatment units like those for abused children. The
solution to wife beating was to enforce the criminal law.

President Jimmy Carter established the Office of Domestic Violence in
1979. It served as a national clearinghouse and center for dissemination of
information. Women in federal agencies and on the White House staff who
had successfully lobbied for the creation of this office overcame the fear of
male officials that it would be too controversial and excessively feminist. In
1980, the Office had a budget of $900,000 for demonstration grants, research,
and dissemination of materials. This level of funding was minuscule in comparison with federal expenditures against child abuse. Nonetheless, the
employees of the Office drummed up support for the passage of federal
domestic violence legislation and coordinated programs between agencies.[45]

The next step was a bill providing much larger sums for social services. The
first such act was co-sponsored by a Republican, Newton Steers of Maryland,
and a Democrat, Lindy Boggs of Louisiana. Steers represented Montgomery
County, Maryland, the site of one of the early task forces on battered wives,
which had received much favorable publicity and enjoyed wide support.
Boggs was on the board of a Washington, D.C., shelter for battered wives.
The sponsor of the other House bill was Barbara Mikulski, a feisty con-
gresswoman from Baltimore, a former social worker, and a feminist. Mikulski
wanted to give more funds to social programs and less to research. Each bill
called for $125 million in federal funds to be spent over five years. Steers,
Boggs, and Mikulski reached a legislative compromise, which favored
Milkulski's emphasis on social service programs. Introduced in 1977–1978,
the bill passed in the Senate but lost in the House.

During the next congressional session, similar legislation was passed by the
House but lost in the Senate. Its opponents were Republicans and Southern
Democrats. Domestic violence legislation was reintroduced a third time in
1980. Two conservative Republican senators, Orrin Hatch of Utah and S. I.
Hayakawa of California, led the opposition. They circulated a letter to their
colleagues which stated that such "legislation represents one giant step by the
federal social service bureaucracy into family matters which are properly,
more effectively and democratically represented by the states and local
communities."[46]

By 1980, conservative groups across the country targeted this legislation for
defeat.[47] The Old Right crusade against anticommunism receded in favor of
the "New Right," which blossomed in the early 1970s, partly in opposition to
the U.S. Supreme Court ruling in *Roe* v. *Wade* (1973), which legalized
abortion. The New Right was a coalition of conservative, fundamentalist
Protestant ministers, born-again Christians, anti-abortion Catholics, Mor-

mons, and Orthodox Jews. Many were disturbed by what they saw as the "breakdown of the American family"—the prevalence of abortion, the increase in teenage pregnancy, and the steady parade of mothers leaving their homes each morning to go to work.

The banner of the New Right was "strengthening the American Family," quite along the lines Progressive reformers advocated; it favored a household whose fathers supported the family and exercised authority, whose mothers kept house and looked after the children—a home whose privacy was protected from unnecessary interference by the state and liberal experts. In the 1970s many fundamentalist religious groups advocated more corporal punishment. Some carried their desire to whip Satan out of children to the extreme; students at fundamentalist schools and children of parents who belonged to extreme Christian religious sects were beaten for hours at a time, handcuffed, or shoved into padlocked cells for punishment.[48]

The New Right identified domestic violence legislation with feminism, which in turn they associated with an attack on "motherhood, the family, and Christian values." They hoped to restore the family as an institution separate from the public world. At the same time, they wanted to win the state over to their own view of morality. This New Right favored federal legislation to outlaw abortion, prohibit teenagers from receiving birth control information, and to reinstate prayer in public schools.

A Moral Majority lobbyist who opposed domestic violence legislation feared that radical feminists will be "coming to the federal trough for a $65 million feed if the domestic violence bill becomes law."[49] He organized a campaign in fifty states to inundate senators with phone calls and telegrams opposing domestic violence legislation. As part of this effort, ministers in Tennessee told their parishioners that the pending legislation would prohibit parents from spanking their children.[50] Senators began to receive letters asserting that "battered women's shelters make women promise to divorce their husbands in order to enter the shelters."[51]

Gordon Humphrey, a conservative Republican senator from New Hampshire, worried that the federal government would be subsidizing opponents of the nuclear family "Sixty-four percent of the funding under the proposal would go to sustain so called 'homes' for battered women," he said. He wondered "what kinds of values and ideas . . . these homes [would] advance? The federal government should not fund missionaries who would war on the traditional family or on local values."[52] As Congress drew to a close before the presidential election of 1980, supporters of the legislation, threatened with a filibuster, decided not to bring the bill up for a final vote.

The resurgence of conservatism targeted not only domestic violence legislation but also child abuse laws. One conservative Republican senator, Paul

Laxalt of Nevada, introduced a Family Protection Act in 1979 that had been written by Karl Moor, the executive director of the Moral Majority. Among other provisions, it eliminated federal expenditures specially designated for child abuse prevention, and reallocated funding to the states, where such programs would compete with other social service programs. It further proposed to amend the definition of child abuse to exclude corporal punishment of a child by a parent or a parental designate. And it stipulated that no federal law, grant, program, or directive could broaden or supercede existing state laws relating to spousal abuse. The Family Protection Act, which never had much chance of being passed, was intended mainly to remind liberal legislators and their sympathizers of the potential wrath of conservative voters.

The combination of budget cuts and diminishing sympathy for battered women led to the closing of the federal Office of Domestic Violence in 1981, soon after Ronald Reagan became president. The Office was dismantled and the few staff who remained were reassigned to the National Center on Child Abuse and Neglect. Eventually, however, the New Right discovered that child abuse reform could serve its purposes. Advances in medical technology made it possible to keep alive extremely premature and ever more handicapped infants; doctors sometimes simply permitted these babies to die. Anti-abortionists broadened their agenda by attacking this practice. They seized upon the denial of medical care to a "Baby Doe," a catastrophically deformed and mentally retarded infant in Bloomington, Indiana, whose parents had refused surgery to prolong their daughter's life. While measures to pass a constitutional amendment criminalizing abortion bogged down, legislators sympathetic to the Right to Life movement decided to tack on to the renewal of the Child Abuse and Prevention Treatment Act of 1983 a provision to protect handicapped infants.[53]

Meanwhile, domestic violence legislation, calling for federal funding for shelters along the lines that Mikulski had originally proposed, was also attached to this bill. The Reagan administration, although opposed to funding shelters, favored the infant protection amendment and thus was willing to compromise. In 1984, President Reagan signed the bill, and $6 million was appropriated—a sum less than a quarter of the original request, but in an era of unabashed budget cutting, a significant victory. Seven years had passed from the introduction of the first domestic violence bill to the passage of this legislation.

The battered women's movement, although worried about financial cutbacks and the threat of the New Right, could take pride in its accomplishments. Within a decade, hundreds of women's shelters were established across the country, state and federal funding was secured for them and other advocacy programs for victims, and new state and federal laws were passed. A network of activists in almost every state acted as a pressure group on behalf of women victims. Although progress was slow, many police and judicial practices had changed. Wife beating was once again taken seriously. Feminist novels from Marge Piercy's *Small Changes* to Alice Walker's *The Color Purple* portrayed strong women who freed themselves from sexual and physical abuse. Although rock videos, pornographic magazines, even fashion photography glamourized the brutalization of women, the wife-beating joke had virtually disappeared from American popular humor and the movies. Many stereotypic attitudes fostered by psychoanalysis were in retreat. If child abuse reform was good for everyone concerned, reform on behalf of women victims was just as beneficial.

The rediscovery of crimes against women aided modern feminism, strengthened the radical wing of the women's movement, and deepened thinking about the nature of male-female relations, marriage, and the family. The myth of the happy family was shattered. The establishment of shelters helped to broaden the constituency of the women's movement. It was often thought that the major beneficiaries of modern feminism were well-educated, middle-class women with access to lucrative careers in business or the professions. The existence of shelters proved that the women's movement also served the needs of desperate, mainly poor, women and their children.

In an era when every other marriage ended in divorce, who could have expected that the sanctity of traditional marriage could have become the basis for a backlash movement? Yet conservatives were frightened precisely because modern marriage and family relations were undergoing dramatic change. Feminists once again had to defend themselves against the charge that they were encouraging the breakup of the family. Some insisted that their aim was only to protect victims from further violence. Others claimed that "by reducing and discouraging violence, the family is *strengthened*."[54] Activism on behalf of women victims had always been more controversial than child abuse reform. The issue of wife beating was tethered to criticism of the traditional family. In addition, wife beating emerged as a social issue just at a time of increasing national conservatism, with accompanying drastic reductions in federal spending.

No social movement survives the process of community acceptance with all of its radical ideas intact. The battered women's cause had been considerably tamed by the coalitions and compromises it made in order to receive state and federal funding. Wife beating and rape became law-and-order issues. To be sure, there were some Victorian echoes in the periodic calls for the harsh punishment of perpetrators, although these cries for vengeance were considerably muted. Law enforcement agencies were concerned—as before—with strengthening their control over violent criminals. But the needs of women victims received a higher priority now than in the nineteenth century. Broadening the movement diluted its feminism and altered the character of battered women's shelters. The issue of wife beating has always had a protean character, appealing to divergent groups for different reasons. And yet the modern coalition of social casework, feminism, and law and order proved to be more successful than any preceding effort.

11

Epilogue

FROM THE VANTAGE POINT of more than three hundred years of American history, the family has become a less hierarchical institution. It is no longer viewed as a little kingdom but as an intimate grouping of individuals bound by affection and companionship. Children are seen as having rights to minimum standards of care and to physical and emotional safety. They are no longer expected to submit to parental commands with unquestioning obedience. Women have acquired a separate legal identity not subsumed by their husbands. A wife, no longer expected to be submissive, is thought to possess even the right to refuse intercourse with her husband. Many women now approach the altar expecting a violence-free relationship, one that if not fully egalitarian, at least permits a high degree of autonomy and self-assertion.

These changes, however, have not reduced family violence. Indeed, it may flourish as much in the context of disappointed hopes for warmth, support, and love as in a climate of authoritarianism. There is thus no simple relationship between family norms and the frequency or character of contemporary family violence.

As late as two centuries ago, the best a battered woman could hope for was to run away and live alone. She could obtain a divorce only with difficulty and could not expect to secure legal custody of her children. Today divorce is commonplace—about one in two American marriages ends in divorce—and socially acceptable. In many states, couples are not required to supply any grounds for dissolving a marriage. It is also a realistic option for many women because programs provide a minimal level of support to divorced mothers and their children. However, such women still have great difficulty raising children on their own; even with state support or their own earnings, they often live in poverty.

Many social programs have been established to respond to spouse abuse and other types of domestic violence. In almost every major city there are self-help groups for victims or former abusers. They have helped families undergoing immediate crises and supported former victims trying to free themselves from their family histories. The field of social work has returned to the more active role it took during the Progressive era. Hospitals now sponsor special treatment teams concerned with abused and neglected children. Indeed, all of the helping professions have repudiated the Freudian denial of abuse and emphasis on the victim's complicity. Shelters and social caseworkers often act as victim advocates, bringing pressure on the family courts, lawyers, or welfare departments. Historically a recent innovation, shelters for battered women, are now believed to be an absolutely necessary community institution.

The history of social policy against family violence has been one of persistent, even inherent, conflict between protecting the victim and preserving the family, and the gradual development of alternatives within and outside the family for victims of abuse. Programs since the 1960s have been more concerned about ensuring the physical safety of victims than ones earlier in this century, but nonetheless still cling to the belief that the family, after undergoing some sort of treatment, can and should be restored. Modern policies often favor "temporary" removal from the home, either of the victim or the abuser, combined with therapy for both. This is accomplished in a number of different ways. The battered child remains in protective custody while the parent enters a treatment program; the incestuous father must live away from home while he and other family members receive therapy; the abused woman lives in a shelter or apart from her husband while he attends a therapy group for batterers.

Temporary removal has the advantage of appearing to reconcile preservation of the home with protection of the victim. In both the past and present, great faith has often been placed in therapeutic efforts to restore family harmony. In milder cases of abuse, this faith may be reasonable. However, the success of therapy should not be judged by whether the family unit is "preserved." The expectation that treatment should and will maintain the family often comes at the expense of victims who will be reinjured. It also diverts attention and resources from other approaches.

Some have argued, for example, in favor of considering family violence as a criminal matter, arresting abusers and sending them to jail. This strategy may or may not be effective in reducing violence. It has the advantage of offering victims what they want—a way of threatening the abuser and being taken seriously. However, the family usually is economically dependent on the perpetrator of abuse. Thus, criminalizing family violence can go only so far before the family must be provided with other economic resources.

Although therapy may help in milder cases and criminalization in more serious ones, what is really needed is a variety of programs that increase or strengthen the alternatives to maintaining the family. Concern about abused children can be measured by the amount and quality of foster care available and the likelihood that a child can be placed permanently with adoptive parents. Efforts to help abused women or incest victims are only as good as the living conditions for single mothers and their children. By these measures, we have a long way to go in creating an effective policy against family violence.

To strengthen the alternatives to the traditional family involves vastly expanding and improving foster care and adoption programs for children; providing legal aid for women seeking separation, protection orders, divorce, and child custody; offering job training, child care, decent housing, and welfare; and enforcing child support. In sum, it demands social services on a scale far larger than the public appears willing to support. A Swedish-style welfare state, though perhaps needed, is impractical, at least for the present conservative moment. Even such piecemeal remedies as restoring legal aid for the poor, expanding child care, reforming the foster care system, and so forth, may be difficult to implement. Nonetheless, these remedies are far more important than 24-hour hot lines and public awareness campaigns. Many more resources should go into strengthening alternatives to the family and many fewer into "prevention" programs of dubious utility.

Thus, a policy against family violence is only as far-reaching as the alternatives to the traditional family it makes available. The barrier to achieving this goal, however, is not only its monetary cost but also the challenge it represents to the Family Ideal. Most Americans support such abstractions as parent's rights, family autonomy, and domestic privacy, especially when these values are presented in opposition to the power of the state. In an era when almost every politician holds aloft the banner of "family values," an attack on the Family Ideal is unlikely to be popular. Yet it is precisely the family values that contemporary politicians so much affirm that permit, encourage, and serve to maintain domestic violence. The solution to family violence is not to appropriate this vacuous rhetoric—no matter how effective such a strategy has proven in the past—but to affirm the individual liberty of women and children within the nuclear family and legitimize and expand the alternatives to it.

Appendix A:
Patterns of Childhood
Punishment

THE RECOLLECTIONS INCLUDED DIARIES (twenty-nine), autobiographies (forty-two), biographies (twenty-nine), a published defense by a stepfather accused of child cruelty (one), a father's magazine article describing his punishment of his son (one), letters (six), and oral interviews (two). A single source might also provide evidence about the punishment of a niece and nephew, or two daughters. Sources had to indicate whether physical punishment in childhood had occurred, and state directly or by inference its frequency. All documents described actual behavior, not merely attitudes toward whipping. Travelers' accounts and observations by third parties (other than a child's tutor) were excluded. Childhood physical discipline had to take place in the United States or the American colonies, not in a foreign country, some time between 1650 and 1900. Table I arranges the recollections according to the birth date of the child.

Several stages of research were involved in assembling the recollections. All published diaries listed in William Matthews, *American Diaries* (Berkeley: University of California Press, 1945) and every sixth entry from Louis Kaplan, *A Biography of American Autobiographies* (Madison: University of Wisconsin Press, 1962) were examined. If the book listed in Kaplan could not be obtained, I located the entry just prior to it. Original sources quoted in scholarly monographs and biographies and autobiographies published subsequent to Kaplan's listing were added. The final list of sources was checked against those in Linda Pollock's *Forgotten Children: Parent-child Relations from 1500 to 1900* (Cambridge, Engl.: Cambridge University Press, 1983), 143–188 and 296–321 to insure that every source she examined had been included.

Table 2. Physical Punishment of American Children from Firsthand Sources

Child's Name	Source	Social Characteristics	Punishment
1650–1699			
1. Samuel Sewall's son	Father's diary	Boston Puritan merchant[h]	Father whips only once[a]
2. William Byrd's nephew	Uncle's diary	Va. plantation owner, Church of England	Uncle whips[c]
3. William Byrd's niece	Uncle's diary	Va. plantation owner, Church of England	Uncle whips[c]
4. Increase Mather	Father's diary	Boston Puritan minister[h]	Father gives blow occasionally[a]
1700–1749			
5. Sarah Homes	Son's memoir	N.J./N.E., Presbyterian	Father boxes ears[a]
6. Joseph Bean	Diary	Boston Puritan	Parents do not spare the rod
1750–1799			
7. Isaac Hooper	Biography	Rural N.J. farmers	Both parents whip
8. Davy Crockett	Autobiography	Rural Tenn. farmers	Father whips often with hickory stick[a]
9. Henry Clarke Wright	Autobiography	Rural Ct., N.Y. Calvinist farmers	Father often whips[a]
10. Arthur Tappan	Biography	Small town Mass. Congregationalist store owner & goldsmith[h]	Both parents whip
11. Daniel Stafford	Wife's memoir	Rural Mass. Calvinist farmers	Father uses correction often[a]
12. Aaron Burr	Biography	Small town N.J. Presbyterian minister	Uncle "licked me like a sack" once[e]
13. Sally Burr	Mother's diary	Small town N.J. Presbyterian minister	Mother whips, probably rarely[b]
14. Landon Carter, Jr.	Grandfather's diary	Va. plantation owner, Church of England[h]	Grandfather whips, causing bruises, once
15. Bob Carter	Tutor's diary	Va. plantation owner, Church of England[h]	Father and tutor whip[a]
16. William Buffum	Daughter's diary	Rural R.I. Quaker farmers	Mother horsewhips often[b]
17. Horace Lane	Mother's diary	Rural N.Y. farmer and rafting pilot	Father occasionally whips[a]
18. Abigail Bailey's daughter	Mother's diary	Rural N.H. wealthy Protestant farmers	Father rapes, beats with horsewhip[a]
1800–1849			
19. Sile Doty	Autobiography	Rural Vt., N.Y. farmer/landowner[h]	Father and mother often whip
20. Richard Malcolm Johnston	Autobiography	Rural Ga. Baptist minister, plantation owner[h]	Both parents use switches

continued

Table 2. *Continued*

Child's Name	Source	Social Characteristics	Punishment
21. John D. Rockefeller	Biography	Rural N.Y. peddlar, farmers, Baptist/Dutch Reformed	Mother often uses rod[b]
22. Almon Pray	Stepfather's defense	Small town N.H. minister[h]	Father whips with rod, horsewhip once, causing bruises and marks
23. Heman Wayland	Father's magazine article	Providence, R.I. Baptist minister[h]	No mention of corporal punishment
24. G. Stanley Hall	Autobiography	Rural Mass. Protestant farmers	Father slaps, boxes ears[a]
25. Robert E. Lee	Biography	Rural Va. Episcopalian planter	Aunt whips often[c]
26. Ernest Chaplin	Diary	Rural S.C. planter	Father whips[a]
27. Thomas Edison	Biography	Small town Ohio lumber dealer[h]	Father whips publicly, once
28. J. S. Clinkscales	Autobiography	S.C. planters	Mother beats every week[b]
29. Henry Lyman	Autobiography	Honolulu Presbyterian missionaries	Both parents use whips and rod frequently
30. Anna Lowell	Mother's diary	Boston Congregationalist minister[h]	No corporal punishment
31. Georgina Lowell	Mother's diary	Boston Congregationalist minister[h]	No corporal punishment
32. Tennessee Claflin	Biography	Small town Ohio, Methodists, Father = postmaster, mother = tavernkeeper	Father whips frequently[a]
33. Victoria Claflin	Biography	Small town Ohio, Methodists, father = postmaster, mother = tavernkeeper	Father whips frequently[a]
34. John Muir	Autobiography	Rural Wisc. Presbyterian farmers	Father whips frequently
35. Mary Van Lennep	Diary	Protestant missionaries	Father hits on hand[a]
36. Ann Branson	Journal	Rural Ohio Quaker farmers	Both parents seldom use rod
37. Nellie Kinzie	Biography	Small town wealthy Protestant[h]	Father whips only once[a]
38. Amanda Smith	Autobiography	Slaves in Maryland	Aunt whips severely[c]
39. Caroline Lovell	Mother's diary	Small town Mass. Quaker[h]	Father and mother rarely use rod
40. Anna Alcott	Father's diary	Phila./Boston schoolteacher, Transcendentalist[h]	Both parents spank but rarely
41. Louisa Alcott	Father's diary	Phila./Boston schoolteacher, Transcendentalist[h]	Both parents spank but rarely

continued

Table 2. *Continued*

Child's Name	Source	Social Characteristics	Punishment
42. Lucy Stone	Biography	Rural Mass. Congregationalist, wealthy farmer and tanner[h]	Father whips often[a]
43. Elizabeth Sedgwick	Mother's journal	N.Y.C. Protestant lawyers[h]	Both parents whip but rarely
44. Abigail Walker	Mother's diary	Rural Ore. Methodist/ Congregationalist farmers	Mother beats with rod[b]
45. Cyrus Walker	Mother's diary	Rural Ore. Methodist/ Congregationalist farmers	Mother beats with rod[b]
46. Charles Pancoast	Diary	Rural N.Y. Quaker farmers	Father uses switches frequently[a]
47. Cassius Clay	Autobiography	Calvinist Ky. plantation owner[h]	Father uses rod only once[d]
48. Benson Bidwell	Autobiography	Small town Mich. Protestant shoemaker[h]	Father whips with strap, mother doesn't whip
49. Millard Fillmore Kennedy	Grandson's autobiography	Rural Ind. farmers, father also a schoolteacher, Universalist/ Congregationalist	Mother spanks, uses shingle and switch[b]
50. Alexander Stephens	Biography	Rural Ga. teacher & store clerk, Presbyterian	Father whips[a]
51. Theodore Cuyler	Autobiography	N.Y. Presbyterian lawyer[h]	Mother whips[b]
52. Nathaniel Harris	Autobiography	Small town Miss.	Both parents do not "spare the rod"
53. Adolphus Greely	Biography	Rural Mass. farmers	"Moral suasion" the rule
54. E. C. Dudley	Autobiography	Rural Mass. farmers	Mother hits with slipper, father whips
55. Abraham Lincoln	Biography	Rural Ky., Ind. poor farmers	Father whips, hits with fist[a]
56. Buck Barry	Biography	Rural Texas farmers	Mother whips[b]
57. Charles Minor	Diary	Va. planter	Father whips daily[a]
58. Lucy Tappan	Father's diary	N.Y.C. Free Church merchant[h]	Father whips only once[a]
59. Sally Lacy's son	Mother's letter	Southern planter[h]	Mother whips often, father doesn't
60. John Douglas' daughter	Mother's letter	Southern planter[h]	Father whips
61. Henry Ward Beecher	Autobiography	Small town Ct. Calvinist minister	Father occasionally hits with switch[a]
62. Alice Banning	Biography	Rural Del. farmers	Mother boxes ears
63. Eliza Wood Farnham	Autobiography	Western N.Y. atheists	Foster father frequently beats, foster mother doesn't

continued

Table 2. *Continued*

Child's Name	Source	Social Characteristics	Punishment
1850–1899			
64. Turner Pender	Parent's correspondence	Rural N.C. general, plantation owner	Mother whips[b]
65. Theodore Roosevelt	Biography	N.Y.C. Episcopalian[h]	Father hits only once[a]
66. Walter J. Stevens	Autobiography	Boston laborer, African Methodist Episcopal[h]	Father whips often, mother doesn't
67. Ed Rickenbacker	Biography	Columbus, Ohio, Swiss Lutherans subcontractor[h]	Father whips with switch often[a]
68. Logan Pearsall Smith	Mother's journal	Phila. Quakers, manufacturer[h]	Mother whips black and blue once[b]
69. Lincoln Steffens	Autobiography	Sacramento merchant[h]	Mother spanks hard[b]
70. Owen Kildare	Autobiography	N.Y.C. Irish Catholic poor	Foster father beats often[a]
71. William Randolph Hearst	Biography	S.F. mineowner, Presbyterian, Episcopalian	Neither parent uses switch
72. Pierrepont Noyes	Biography	Rural N.Y. farmer, utopian community leader, Perfectionist	Mother spanks, puts in dark closet, uncle whips
73. A. A. Anderson	Autobiography	N.Y. Presbyterian engineer	Father uses strap often, mother whips
74. Thomas Watson	Biography	Rural Ga. Baptist plantation owner	Governed with "fitful harshness"
75. John R. Commons	Autobiography	Small town Ind., Christian Scientist/Calvinist	Mother whips[a]
76. Evan Barnard	Autobiography	Ill. Presbyterian minister	Father uses switch[b]
77. Jules Sandoz	Autobiography	Rural Nebraska atheists, farmers	Father whips often[a]
78. Bay Clemens	Biography	Urban Ct., author[h]	Mother spanks[b]
79. Suzy Clemens	Biography	Urban Ct., author[h]	Neither parent uses corporal punishment
80. Clara Clemens	Biography	Urban Ct., author[h]	Neither parent uses corporal punishment
81. Nell Kimball	Autobiography	Ill. Catholic poor farmers	Father uses harness whip, razor strop
82. Alice Foote McDougall	Autobiography	N.Y.C. businessman, Unitarians[h]	Mother boxes ear, no other hitting[b]
83. John Franklin Carter	Biography	Small town Mass. Protestant minister	Father and mother hit with ruler and horsewhip
84. Anna Thomas	Sister's autobiography	Baltimore Quaker manufacturer[h]	Mother hits with slipper or rod[b]
85. John Thomas	Sister's autobiography	Baltimore Quaker manufacturer[h]	Mother hits with slipper or rod[b]

continued

Table 2. *Continued*

Child's Name	Source	Social Characteristics	Punishment
86. Hannah Milhous	Oral interview	Rural Ind. Quaker farmers	Father never hits, mother hits ankles with whip
87. Alfred G. Field	Autobiography	Small town Ohio[h]	Mother spanks, father uses switches
88. David Starr Jordan	Autobiography	Rural N.Y. Universalists, farmers	Neither parent uses corporal punishment
89. Rufus Jones	Autobiography	Small town Maine Quakers	Father seldom corrects, mother disciplines
90. Ennen Reeves	Autobiography	Small town Oklahoma, minister[h]	Father and mother hit with switch often
91. Mary Austin	Autobiography	Ill. English Protestant farmers	Mother spanks often[b]
92. Annie Glover	Oral interview	Rural S.C. black Protestant sharecroppers	Father and mother use horsewhip often
93. Charlotte Perkins Gilman	Biography	N.Y.C. librarian[h]	Father uses small whip once[a]
94. Anges Smedley	Autobiography	Rural Mo. Colorado, farmer/laborer[h]	Mother and father use whip often
95. May Pinzer	Letters	Philadelphia Jewish	Uncle molests, mother whips often
96. Marietta Minnegrode Andrews	Autobiography	Va. Protestant minister	Grandmother uses switch often[c]
97. Irving Greenberg	Autobiography	Brooklyn rabbi[h]	Father uses cat-o-nine tails often[a]
98. Consuelo Vanderbilt	Biography	N.Y.C. Epscopalian financier[h]	Parents whip on legs with riding crop, infrequently
99. Louise Waters	Autobiograhy	.Small town Pa. poor	Mother beats[b]
100. Lorena Hickok	Biography	Midwest traveling salesman	Father rapes daughter, whips, causes black and blue marks
101. Evelyn Walsh	Autobiography	Washington, D.C. businessman[h]	Mother uses buggy whip once[b]
102. Annie Ellis	Biography	Rural Ark. farmer	Older brother whips with plough lines[c]
103. Gertrude Atherton	Autobiography	Calif. ranch merchant[h]	Grandmother spanks often, locked in closet[c]
104. Thomas Barbour	Autobiography	N.Y. Calvinist, wealthy	Mother uses giant hairbrush often[b]
105. William Guggenheim	Son's biography	Phila. Jewish merchant[h]	Father uses rod, stick, strap, mother "gentler"
106. Elias Bond	Autobiography	Small town Ct. Presbyterian missionaries	Father uses rod often, mother uses rod as last resort
107. Samuel Chotzinoff	Autobiography	Passaic N.J. cheder teacher[h]	Father often uses belt, mother whips but less frequently

continued

Table 2. *Continued*

Child's Name	Source	Social Characteristics	Punishment
108. Ada Stoughton	Son's biography	N.Y.C. wealthy Protestant	Mother beats with whip or locks in closet[b]
109. Mary Waterman Rice's son	Mother's letters	Ill., Calif, doctor[h]	Mother hits with hairbrush[b]
110. Balfour Anderson	Mother's letters	Calif. student, teacher	Mother whips[b]

[a]Mother dead.

[b]No information regarding father.

[c]Both parents dead or absent.

[d]Father dead.

[e]However his uncle referred to Aaron as one "whom I brought, or rather suffered to grow up without the rod," as quoted in Holmes Alexander, *Aaron Burr: The Proud Pretender* (New York: Harper and Brothers, 1973), 9.

[h]Mother's occupation is primarily that of housewife; when the couple are actively involved in farm work, both parents' occupations are classified as farmers.

SOURCES FOR TABLE 2

1. Samuel Sewall, *Diary*, v. 5 (Boston: Massachusetts Historical Society, 1878–1882), 225.

2, 3. Louis Wright and Marion Tinling, eds., *William Byrd, the Secret Diary of William Byrd of Westover, 1709–1712* (Richmond: The Dietz Press, 1941), 204, 285.

4. Worthington Chauncey Ford, ed., *Diary of Cotton Mather, 1681–1724*, v. 7 (Boston: Massachusetts Historical Society, 1911–1912), 534–537.

5. Lewis Tappan, *Memoir of Mrs. Sarah Tappan* (New York, 1834), 87 and Lewis Tappan, "My Forefathers," in Lewis Tappan Mss., Library of Congress, as quoted in Bertram Wyatt-Brown, "Three Generations of Yankee Parenthood: The Tappan Family, A Case Study of Antebellum Nurture," *Illinois Quarterly*, v. 38, No. 1 (Fall 1975), 12–29.

6. Joseph Bean, "The Spiritual Diary of Joseph Bean, February 1741–January 1744," Byrn Mawr College Library, as quoted in Philip Greven, *The Protestant Temperament: Patterns of Child-Rearing, Religious Experience, and the Self in Early America* (New York: Knopf, 1977), 58.

7. L. Maria Child, *Isaac T. Hooper: A True Life* (New York and Boston: J. P. Jewett, 1853), 5, 12, 16–17.

8. David Crockett, *A Narrative of the Life of David Crockett of the State of Tennessee* (Philadelphia: E. L. Carey, 1834; revised edition, Knoxville: University of Tennessee Press, 1973), 23.

9. Louis C. Jones, ed., *Growing Up in the Cooper Country* (Syracuse, N.Y.: Syracuse University Press, 1965), 128–130.

10. Lewis Tappan, *The Life of Arthur Tappan* (New York: Hurd and Houghton,

1870), 21, as quoted in Bertram Wyatt-Brown, "Three Generations of Yankee Parenthood," 12–28.

11. Mrs. Anna Eliza Turner Safford, *A Memoir of Daniel Safford, by his Wife* (Boston: American Tract Society, 1861), 13.

12. Holmes Alexander, *Aaron Burr: The Proud Pretender* (New York: Harper and Brothers, 1937), 9.

13. Esther Burr Diary, February 1755, p. 67, Beinecke Rare Book Library, Yale University, as quoted in Nancy F. Cott, "Notes Toward an Interpretation of Antebellum Childrearing," *The Psychohistory Review*, v. 11 (Spring 1978), 19.

14. Jack P. Greene, ed., *The Diary of Colonel Landon Carter of Sabine Hall, 1752–1778* (Charlottesville, Va.: Virginia History Society, 1965), v. 1, No. 310; v. 11, Nos. 646, 647, 702.

15. Hunter Dickinson Farady, ed., *Journal and Letters of Philip Vickers Fithian 1773–1774: A Plantation Tutor of the Old Dominion* (Williamsburg: Colonial Williamsburg, 1957), 49–50, 116.

16. Elizabeth Buffum Chace and Lucy Buffum Lovell, *Two Quaker Sisters: From the Original Diaries of Elizabeth Buffum Chace and Lucy Buffum Lovell* (New York: Liveright, 1937), 2–3.

17. Horace Lane, *The Wandering Boy, Careless Sailor, and Result of Inconsideration: A True Narrative* (Skaneateles, N.Y.: Luther A. Pratt, 1839), 7–10, as quoted in Myra C. Glenn, *Campaigns Against Corporal Punishment: Prisoners, Sailors, Women, and Children in Antebellum America* (Albany: State University of New York Press, 1984), 7.

18. Abigail Bailey, *Memoirs of Mrs. Abigail Bailey* (Boston: Samuel T. Armstrong, 1815), 40–41.

19. Sile Doty, *The Life of Sile Doty, 1800–1876* (Detroit: Alved, 1948), 2.

20. Richard Malcolm Johnston, *Autobiography of Col. Richard Malcolm Johnston* (Washington, D.C.: The Neale Co., 1900), 9, 14.

21. Allan D. Nevins, *John D. Rockefeller: The Heroic Age of American Enterprise* (New York: Charles Scribner's Sons, 1940), 41.

22. Philandros, *An Astonishing Affair: The Rev. Samuel Arnold Cast and Tried for His Cruelty, Though His Cause was Advocated in Masterly Manner, by the Right Hon. Joseph Almon Clark Pray* (Concord: Luther Roby, 1830).

23. Rev. Francis Wayland, "A Case of Conviction," *American Baptist Magazine* (October 1831), 35–38, as quoted in William G. McLoughlin, "Evangelical Childrearing in the Age of Jackson: Francis Wayland's Views on When and How to Subdue the Willfulness of Children," *Journal of Social History*, v. 9, No. 1 (Fall 1975), 21–34.

24. G. Stanley Hall, *Life and Confessions of a Psychologist* New York: D. Appleton, 1923), 74–75.

25. Information provided in Mary Cable, *The Little Darlings: A History of Child Rearing in America* (New York: Charles Scribner's Sons, 1972), 86.

26. Diary of Thomas Chaplin, as quoted in Bertram Wyatt-Brown, *Southern*

Honor: Ethics and Behavior in the Old South (New York: Oxford University Press, 1982), 152.

27. Matthew Josephson, *Thomas Edison* (New York: McGraw-Hill, 1959), 13–14.

28. J. G. Clinkscales, *The One Old Plantation: Reminiscences of His Childhood* (New York: Negro Universities Press, 1969), 84–85, as quoted in Bertram Wyatt-Brown, *Southern Honor*, 152.

29. Henry M. Lyman, *Hawaiian Yesterdays: Chapters from a Boy's Life in the Islands in the Early Days* (Chicago: A. C. McClurg, 1906), 26–27.

30., 31. Diary of Anna C. Lowell, Papers of John Lowell, Jr., Lowell Family Papers, Massachusetts Historical Society.

32., 33. Emanie Sachs, *"The Terrible Siren": Victoria Woodhull* (New York: Harper and Brothers, 1928), 3–4.

34. John Muir, *The Story of My Boyhood and Youth* (Boston: Houghton and Mifflin, 1913), 34–35.

35. Louisa Hawes, *Memoir of Mrs. Mary E. Van Lennep* (Hartford, Conn.: Belknap and Hamersley, 1851), 182, 184.

36. *Journal of Ann Branson: A Minister of the Gospel in the Society of Friends* (Philadelphia: W. H. Pile's Sons, 1892), 10, 18, 19.

37. G. D. Schultz and D. G. Lawrence, *Lady from Savannah* (Philadelphia: Lippincott, 1958), 47.

38. Amanda Smith, *An Autobiography: The Story of the Lord's Dealings with Mrs. Amanda Smith* (Chicago: Meyer and Brothers, 1893), 50.

39. Elizabeth Buffum Chace and Lucy Buffum Lovell, *Two Quaker Sisters*, 84–88.

40., 41. Diary of Amos Bronson Alcott, as quoted in Charles Strickland, "A Transcendentalist Father: The Child-Rearing Practices of Bronson Alcott," *History of Childhood Quarterly*, v. 1, No. 1 (Summer 1973), 4–51.

42. Elinor Rice Hays, *Morning Star: A Biography of Lucy Stone, 1818–1893* (New York: Harcourt Brace and World, 1961), 15.

43. Elizabeth Ellery Sedgwick, "Journal-book of the first years of her child's life, 1824–1829," 1, 25, Houghton Library, Harvard University, as quoted in Nancy F. Cott, "Notes Toward an Interpretation of Antebellum Childrearing," 13.

44., 45. Clifford Merrill Drury, ed., *First White Women Over the Rockies: Diaries, Letters and Biographical Sketches of the Six Women of the Oregon Mission Who Made the Overland Journey in 1836 and 1838*, v. 2 (Glendale, Calif.: The Arthur Clark Co., 1963), 151, 176–177, 197, 273, 294–295, 299.

46. Anna Paschall Hannum, ed., *A Quaker Forty-Niner: The Adventures of Charles Edward Pancoast* (Philadelphia: University of Pennsylvania Press, 1930), 4, 6, 11–13.

47. Cassius Marcellus Clay, *The Life of Cassius Marcellus Clay*, v. 1 (Cincinnati, Oh.: J. Fletcher Brennan and Co., 1886), 20–21.

48. Benson Bidwell, *The Life of Benson Bidwell* (Chicago: Henneberry Press, 1977), 86.

49. Millard Fillmore Kennedy, *Schoolmaster of Yesterday: A Three Generation Story, 1820–1919* (New York: Whittlesey, 1940), 17.

50. Richard M. Johnston and William H. Browne, *Life of Alexander H. Stephens* (Philadelphia: Lippincott, 1884), 30–36.

51. Theodore Ledyard Cuyler, *Recollections of a Long Life: An Autobiography* (New York: The Baker and Taylor, 1902), 3, 6, 7.

52. Nathaniel E. Harris, *Autobiography, The Story of an Old Man's Life with Reminiscences of Seventy-five Years* (Macon, Ga.: The J. W. Burke, 1925), 16, 18–19.

53. Adolphus Washington Greely, *Reminiscences* (New York: Charles Scribner's Sons, 1927).

54. E. C. Dudley, *The Medicine Man* (New York: J. H. Sears, 1927), 7–8.

55. Albert J. Beveridge, *Abraham Lincoln, 1809–1858* (Boston and New York: Houghton Mifflin, 1928), 66.

56. James Buckner Barry, ed., *A Texas Ranger and Frontiersman* (Dallas: The Southwest Press, 1932), 6–7.

57. Charles Minor, autobiography, Virginia Historical Society, as cited in Dickson D. Bruce, Jr., *Violence and Culture in the Antebellum South* (Austin: University of Texas Press, 1979), 61.

58. Diary of Lewis Tappan, October 21, 1836, as quoted in Bertram Wyatt-Brown, "Three Generations," 12–28.

59. Sally Lacy to William Graham, February 7, 1819, Graham Collection, Duke University, as quoted in Catherine Clinton, *Plantation Mistress: Woman's World in the Old South* (New York: Pantheon, 1982), 47–48.

60. John Douglas to Eleanor Douglas, January 2, 1823, Eleanor Douglas Collection, Duke University, as quoted in Catherine Clinton, *Plantation Mistress*, 48.

61. Henry Ward Beecher, *Star Papers* (New York, 1855), 189–193, as quoted in Milton Rugoff, *The Beechers: An American Family in the Nineteenth Century* (New York: Harper & Row, 1981), 115.

62. Papers of the Hartsuff Family, Michigan Historical Society.

63. Eliza Wood Farnham, *My Early Days* (New York: Thatcher and Hutchinson, 1859), 13–29.

64. William H. Hassler, ed., *The General to His Lady: The Civil War Letters of William Dorsey Pender to Fanny Pender* (Chapel Hill: University of North Carolina Press, 1962), 183, 222.

65. Theodore Roosevelt, *Theodore Roosevelt: An Autobiography* (New York: Macmillan, 1913), 8.

66. Walter J. Stevens, *Chip on My Shoulder* (Boston: Little, Brown, 1946), 32.

67. Edward V. Rickenbacker, *Rickenbacker* (Englewood Cliffs, N.J.: Prentice-Hall, 1967), 7.

68. Logan Pearsall Smith, *The Unforgotten Years* (London: Constable, 1938), 36.

69. Lincoln Steffens, *The Autobiography of Lincoln Steffens*, v. 1 (New York: Harcourt Brace, 1931), 10.

70. Owen Kildare, *My Mamie Rose: The Story of My Regeneration* (New York: The Baker and Taylor Co., 1903), 30.

71. W. A. Swanberg, *Citizen Hearst: A Biography of William Randolph Hearst* (New York: Charles Scribner's Sons, 1961), 12.

72. Pierrepont Noyes, *My Father's House: An Oneida Boyhood* (New York: Farrar and Rinehart, 1932), 61–63, 66–67, 100, 110, 155, 219–221.

73. Colonel A. A. Anderson, *Experiences and Impressions: The Autobiography of Colonel A. A. Anderson* (Freeport, N.Y.: Books for Libraries Press, 1933), 12.

74. C. Vann Woodward, *Tom Watson: Agrarian Rebel* (New York: Oxford University Press, 1963), 17–18.

75. John R. Commons, *Myself* (New York: Macmillan, 1934), 15–16.

76. Evan G. Barnard, *A Rider of the Cherokee Strip* (Boston: Houghton Mifflin, 1936), 10.

77. Mari Sandoz, *Old Jules* (Boston: Little, Brown, 1935), 266, 284.

78., 79., 80. Caroline Thomas Harnsberger, *Mark Twain: Family Man* (New York: Citadel Press, 1960), 41–43, 62–63.

81. Stephen Longstreet, ed., *Nell Kimball: Her Life as an American Madam* (New York: Macmillan, 1970), 14, 31.

82. Alice Foote MacDougall, *The Autobiography of a Business Woman* (Boston: Little, Brown, 1928), 28–29.

83. John Franklin Carter, *The Rectory Family* (New York: Coward McCann, 1937), 72–73.

84., 85. Helen Thomas Flexner, *A Quaker Childhood* (New Haven: Yale University Press, 1940), 26.

86. Doris Faber, *The President's Mothers* (New York: St. Martin's Press, 1976), 21.

87. Al G. Field, *Watch Yourself Go By* (Columbus, Oh.: Spoke and Glenn, 1912), 4, 13, 24, 38.

88. David Starr Jordan, *The Days of a Man, Being Memories of a Naturalist, Teacher and Minor Prophet of Democracy,* v. 1 (Yonkers, N.Y.: World Book Company, 1922), 16.

89. Rufus M. Jones, *A Small Town Boy* (New York: Macmillan, 1941), 32–33.

90. Ennen Reeves Hall, *One Saint and Seven Sinners* (New York: Thomas Y. Crowell, 1959), 2–3, 14–15, 38–39.

91. Mary Austin, *Earth Horizon: Autobiography* (New York: Literary Guild, 1932), 34–35.

92. Clyde Vernon Kiser, *Sea Island to City: A Study of St. Helena Islanders in Harlem and Other Urban Centers* (New York: Columbia University Press, 1932), 236–237.

93. Charlotte Perkins Gilman, *The Living of Charlotte Perkins Gilman* (New York: D. Appleton Century, 1935), 16.

94. Agnes Smedley, *Daughters of Earth* (New York: Feminist Press, 1973), 7, 8, 16, 71, 75, 105–107, 133.

95. Ruth Rosen, ed., *The Maimie Papers* (Old Westbury, N.Y.: The Feminist Press, 1977), 192–193, 270.

96. Marietta Minnigerode Andrews, *Memoirs of a Poor Relation* (New York: E. P. Dutton, 1927), 71, 74–75, 115, 131, 135–136, 138, 339–340.

97. Stanley F. Chyet, *Lives and Voices: A Collection of American Jewish Memories* (Philadelphia: Jewish Publication Society of America, 1972), 315.

98. Information provided in Mary Cable, *The Little Darlings*, 136.

99. Ethel Waters, *His Eye is on the Sparrow: An Autobiography* (New York: Doubleday, 1951), 4.

100. Doris Faber, *The Life of Lorena Hickok: Eleanor Roosevelt's Friend* (New York: William Morrow, 1980), 14, 16, 21–22.

101. Evelyn Walsh McCleon, *Father Struck It Rich* (Boston: Little, Brown, 1936), 11–12.

102. Anne Ellis, *The Life of an Ordinary Woman* (Boston and New York: Houghton Mifflin, 1929), 2.

103. Gertrude Atherton, *Adventures of a Novelist* (New York: Liveright, 1932), 10, 14.

104. Thomas Barbour, *Naturalist at Large* (Boston: Little, Brown, 1943), 10.

105. Gatenby Williams, *William Guggenheim* (New York: The Lone Voice, 1934), 18.

106. Ethel M. Damon, ed., *Father Bond of Kohola: A Chronicle of Pioneer Life in Hawaii* (Honolulu: The Friend, 1927), 74.

107. Samuel Chotzinoff, *A Lost Paradise* (New York: Knopf, 1955), 68–79.

108. Lynn Z. Bloom, *Doctor Spock: Biography of a Conservative Radical* (Indianapolis: Bobbs-Merrill, 1972), 6.

109. Mary Waterman Rice to Robert Waterman, September 25, 1885, Robert Waterman Papers, Bancroft Library, University of California at Berkeley, as quoted in Carl N. Degler, *At Odds: Women and the Family from the Revolution to the Present* (New York: Oxford University Press, 1982), 90.

110. Charlena Anderson to Melville Anderson, July 20, 1881, Anderson Papers, Stanford University, as quoted in Carl N. Degler, *At Odds*, 88.

Appendix B:
Changes in the Incidence
of Family Murder

No question about family violence is asked more often than whether it is increasing or decreasing. Those who argue that it has fallen point to the growth of humane sentiments, respect for the rights of women and children, and egalitarianism in domestic life. Their opponents feel the reasons for an alleged increase in family violence can be found in the sexually violent imagery of films, rock video, and television, the crisis of the contemporary family, the assassinations and urban riots of the 1960s, and the high level of assault and murder since then. There is thus a clear division of opinion. Is the modern family more violent than in the past? Or has the reporting of family violence increased, while the actual level of it has remained the same?

Family murder is the one form of family violence about which relatively reliable historical statistics exist. Of all the types of family violence, it is always recognized as a serious crime. If thought of as "successful assault," the rate of domestic murder provides a rough indicator of the overall level of severe family violence. It is usually expressed in terms of the number of family murder victims per year per 100,000 population. But determining the number of such victims and the population in the past can be exceedingly difficult. Population estimates before national censuses are not necessarily reliable. Modern homicide data often comes from official police statistics, and those before the end of the nineteenth century from indictments for murder or manslaughter. The investigative methods of long ago were primitive by today's standards; many killers were never brought to trial. Even so, watchful relatives and neighbors in past centuries probably reported most murders to the authorities.

One possible confusion in homicide statistics is that murder can involve multiple killers and multiple victims. Whenever possible, data was selected about the number of homicide victims. Otherwise, information about murderous offenses or family murderers was substituted. But the homicide rate derived from the number of victims

217

is roughly similar to that computed from the number of murders for the years in which both were available.[1]

Most studies of historical trends in family murder note that it now comprises a greater proportion of all murders. These studies do not demonstrate that family murders are becoming more frequent in absolute terms.

Table 3 is a compilation of family homicide rates in England and America going as far back as the fourteenth century. During the medieval period, the rate of family murder varied greatly from one locale to another. Since the populations of all the medieval English towns except London were small, these estimates of their family murder rates are less stable than the later figures in the table. Medieval rates for family murder, as indices of overall family violence, are probably inflated, relative to later periods, by the high level of mortality among wounded assault victims. Still, the family murder rate in thirteenth- and fourteenth-century England was much higher than the early modern period. It fell by the middle of the sixteenth century and remained quite low both in sixteenth-century England and the New England colonies. It then began to rise gradually in the nineteenth century and more rapidly in the twentieth. The rate of family murder in the United States between 1962 and 1984 was 1.4 per 100,000. The highest rates of family homicide in Western European and American history have been recorded in twentieth-century American cities: Detroit between 1926 and 1929, Houston and Detroit in the 1960s, Philadelphia in 1972. The national family homicide rate in the 1980s is slightly below the records set in these cities.

Evidence from Philadelphia, Detroit, or Houston may not be representative of national trends. Nationwide statistics on the incidence of family homicide, however, were not compiled until the 1960s. Before then, the only data available were limited to specific American cities. The best information comes from Philadelphia, where evidence about family homicide can be obtained as far back as 1839. In that city, the rate of family homicide tripled between 1839 and 1972: from 1.0 per 100,000 in 1839–1873 to 3.6 per 100,000 in 1972.

The trends in Table 3 shed light on a number of speculations about changes in family murder. One suggestion is that divorce has become its modern substitute. Modern marriages, so the argument goes, break apart before one spouse kills the other. Since the largest component of family homicide is murder between spouses, the overall trend in domestic murder would undoubtedly reflect changes in spousal murder. The steady increase in the family homicide rate during the twentieth century suggests that access to divorce has not diminished marital murder. Indeed, a wife's threat to leave her husband sometimes escalates into homicide. In this way, the increasing access to separation and divorce may even have *raised* the level of marital homicide.

Another theory holds that modern males have responded to contemporary feminism with increased violence against women. Men, it is said, are threatened by the economically independent, sexually liberated woman. It is true that wife-killing, the single most common form of family murder, increased during the first phase of women's liberation in the 1960s. But the overall homicide rate was also increasing. It

Table 3. Reported Family Homicide Rate per 100,000 Population Per Year

Date(s)	Locale	Rate	Sources
1227–1255	Kent	2.0	Court records[a]
1221–1247	Warwick	2.1	Court records[a]
1241–1261	Oxford	1.6	Court records[a]
1202–1276	Bedford	1.2	Court records[a]
1244,1276	London	0.4	Court records[a]
1250,1269	Norfolk	0.6	Court records[a]
1221–1248	Bristol	0	Court records[a]
1342–1348	Oxford	0	Court records[a]
1559–1625	Essex, Sussex and Hertfordshire	0.8	County court assize indictments[b]
1560–1609	Essex	0.4	Coroner's inquests and indictments[b]
1610–1659	Essex	0.6	Coroner's inquests and indictments[b]
1660–1709	Essex	0.4	Coroner's inquests and indictments[b]
1630–1692	Mass. Bay Colony	0.3	Indictments[c]
1630–1692	Plymouth Colony	0.4	Indictments[c]
1839–1873	Philadelphia	1.0	Indictments[c]
1874–1901	Philadelphia	1.3	Indictments[c]
1926–1927	Chicago	1.0	Death registration
1926–1929	Detroit	3.2	Police records[c]
1930–1939	Detroit	1.2	Police records[c]
1940–1949	Detroit	1.6	Police records[c]
1948–1952	Philadelphia	1.4	Police records[c]
1950–1959	Detroit	2.2	Police records[c]
1960–1968	Detroit	3.4	Police records[c]
1961	U.S.	0.4	Police records[b]
1962	U.S.	1.3	Police records[b]
1963	U.S.	1.3	Police records[b]
1963	U.S.	1.4	Police records[c]
1964	U.S.	1.5	Police records[c]
1965	U.S.	1.5	Police records[b]
1966	U.S.	1.0	Police records[b]
1967	U.S.	1.8	Police records[b]
1968	U.S.	1.8	Police records[b]
1969	Houston	3.7	Police records[c]
1969	U.S.	1.8	Police records[b]
1970	U.S.	1.8	Police records[b]
1971	U.S.	2.1	Police records[b]
1972	Philadelphia	3.6	Police records[c]
1972	U.S.	2.2	Police records[b]
1973	U.S.	2.2	Police records[b]
1974	U.S.	2.2	Police records[c]
1975	U.S.	2.2	Police records[c]
1976	U.S.	2.1	Police records[c]
1977	U.S.	1.6	Police records[c]

continued

Table 3. *Continued*

Date(s)	Locale	Rate	Sources
1978	U.S.	1.2	Police records[c]
1979	U.S.	1.6	Police records[c]
1980	U.S.	1.1	Police records[c]
1981	U.S.	1.5	Police records[c]
1982	U.S.	1.4	Police records[c]
1983	U.S.	1.3	Police records[c]
1984	U.S.	1.2	Police records[c]

[a]Number of murderers who were related to their victims.

[b]Number of murderous offenses between family members.

[c]Number of murder victims who were related to their assailant.

Note: Infanticide and murder of servants and apprentices have been excluded. Murders between homosexual couples were also omitted.

Sources: James Buchanan Given, *Society and Homicide in Thirteenth-Century England* (Stanford, Calif.: Stanford University Press, 1977), 57; Carl J. Hammer, Jr., "Patterns of Homicide in Fourteenth-Century Oxford," *Past and Present*, No. 78 (February 1978), 3–23; J. S. Cockburn, "The Nature and Incidence of Crime in England, 1559–1625: A Preliminary Survey," in J. S. Cockburn, ed., *Crime in England, 1550–1660* (Princeton, N.J.: Princeton University Press, 1977), 155–186; 10–12; J. A. Sharpe, "Domestic Homicide in Early Modern England," *Historical Journal*, v. 24, No. 1 (1981), 29–48; Essex population was estimated at 80,000 for 1560–1659 and at 90,000 for 1660–1709; John Noble, ed., *Records of the Court of Assistants of the Colony of the Massachusetts Bay, 1639–1692*, v. 1 (Boston: Suffolk County, 1801), 14, David Thomas Konig, ed., *Plymouth Court Records, 1686–1856*, vols. 1–4 (Wilmington, Del.: Michael Glazier, 1978); estimates of population in Massachusetts Bay and Plymouth colonies can be found in Evarts B. Greene and Virginia D. Harrington, *American Population before the Federal Census of 1790* (New York: Columbia University Press, 1932), 10–18; unpublished data of criminal indictments in Philadelphia collected by Professor Roger Lane; H. C. Brearly, *Homicide in the U.S.* (Chapel Hill: University of North Carolina Press, 1932), 58; the data does not include common-law marriages; James Boudouris, "Trends in Homicide: Detroit, 1926–1968," unpublished Ph.D. dissertation, Wayne State University, 1970, 90; Marvin Wolfgang, *Patterns in Criminal Homicide* (Philadelphia: University of Pennsylvania Press, 1958), Table 20, 378; Henry P. Lundsgaarde, *Murder in Space City: A Cultural Analysis of Houston Homicide Patterns* (New York: Oxford University Press, 1977), 230–231; unpublished materials of Frank Hartleroad, supplied to me by Professor Roger Lane, data consists of one-half of all homicides known to the Philadelphia police, June 1, 1972 to December 30, 1974; U.S. Department of Justice, Federal Bureau of Investigation, *Uniform Crime Reports for the United States* (Washington, D.C.: U.S. Government Printing Office, 1961–1985).

seems more likely that the surge in family murder was associated with the rising rate of violence overall rather than with the emergence of the women's liberation movement.

The historical trend in the family homicide rate best resembles the bottom half of a dish, a gradual decline matched by an equally gradual increase. Several factors account for this pattern. First, this trend is similar to that for homicide overall. In the United States, homicide rates plummeted until the early twentieth century, then rose until around 1930, tumbled for several decades, and spurted upward again in the 1960s. There were other peaks and troughs along the way—the peaks were generally reached in wartime—but the overall curve is one of long-term decline and recent increase. [2]

The homicide rate in Western Europe fell long before the growth of modern police forces or the advent of major medical advances in treating serious wounds or gangrene. Lawrence Stone and Ted Robert Gurr, who examined the long-term course of change in Western European and American homicide, each argue that the decline in the homicide rate from the post-medieval period to the twentieth century reflects the onset of modern civilization, the emphasis on civility, politeness, propriety, and the value of self-control. [3]

There are many reasons for the high rate of homicide in the Middle Ages. Medieval men appear to have been quick to anger and anxious to fight; there was no greater glory than hand-to-hand combat. Medieval society was also a youthful one, with a high proportion of young men, the group most prone to murder. Moreover, physical aggression was acceptable in the Middle Ages; assault and battery short of murder was rarely prosecuted. A new code of nonviolent conduct, Stone and Gurr believe, first appeared among the urban upper classes and gradually spread through the rest of society. The death of the feudal order also struck a blow at the values of honor, courage, and personal violence. Stone points to "the taming of upper-class violence by the code of the duel after the late sixteenth century . . . followed by the transformation of manners in the late seventeenth century, and then by the humanitarian ideology of the Enlightenment."[4] Roger Lane attributes the falling homicide rate of the nineteenth-century American city to the imposition of time and work discipline in schools and factories. Lane also finds that Victorian society was concerned about inflicting physical pain. Increasingly, by the end of the nineteenth century, manslaughter cases were prosecuted rather than being casually dismissed. [5]

The U.S. homicide rate first began to rise from 1900 to 1930, and moved upward a second time beginning in the 1960s. [6] There are several overlapping explanations for this increase. The first is the growth in the most violence-prone segment of the population, males aged 15–29. Since children of the Baby Boom came of age in the 1960s, they increased the size of the criminal class, and thus contributed to the violent crime wave.

A second reason for the rising homicide rate is the increased use of handguns. In the medieval period, there were no guns—murderers killed with knives, clubs, and axes. In 1982, about half of all homicides in the United States were committed with firearms. Since the fatality rate from handguns is anywhere from two to six times greater than from knife wounds, an increase in the use of handguns in itself would lead to a higher homicide rate. [7]

Finally, more than half of all homicides in the United States in 1984 were committed by blacks and Hispanics. These two groups comprise about 22 percent of the U.S. population. Throughout American history a disproportionate number of family murders have occurred among racial or ethnic minorities. There are quite a few explanations for this. Minority groups have a higher birthrate than the rest of the population, and thus, a larger proportion of young males. Moreover, groups at the bottom of society learn that physical aggression is a necessary tool for survival. In addition, Lawrence Levine believes that violence appears frequently in black music and folk tales because it expresses "the profound anger festering and smoldering among the oppressed," a rage that is not romanticized, embellished or even tamed, but simply accepted as a part of life. [8] Violence has been high among many other American racial and ethnic minorities, and disadvantaged groups in other cultures. In New Zealand, for example, a disproportionate amount of violent crime is committed by Maoris. Violent crime across the globe appears more often among impoverished racial minorities than among the middle class.

Most people use resources at their command—influence, status, money, education—to achieve their goals. Minority men have fewer resources than other men, and they are thus more likely to use the one resource they do have—their physical prowess. Thus, the increasing minority share of the population helps account for the growth in the homicide rate.

The arguments advanced to explain the trend in homicide apply as well to the long-term decline and recent rise in family homicide. Clearly, the same forces that affect society in general affect the individual family. But there are others unique to families. Throughout the history of Western civilization, most murders were committed by men against other men. Family murder, by contrast, usually involves male aggression against women and girls. The most frequent type of family murder is a husband killing his wife; a wife killing her husband comes in second. It seems likely that significant changes in the nature of marriage also contribute to the rising rate of family murder.

Table 4 presents information about family killings in Western European and American history. In Elizabethan England about half of all family murders consisted of parents slaying their children; the proportion of homicides between spouses was far below what it had been in the medieval period. Table 3 showed that the overall rate of family homicide was declining during the same period. Table 4 suggests that the major reason for this falling rate was a reduction in murder between spouses.

Victorian marriage appears to have been fraught with stress and jealousy. Alcohol consumption was also quite high. The ideal of romantic love arose, leading to hopes of intimacy, sharing, and companionship which could not always be satisfied. Dashed expectations for marital bliss may have caused some murders. Whatever the reason, spousal murder accounted for an ever-growing share of family murder in the nineteenth century. The medieval pattern of family homicide returned in the twentieth century; about half of family murders consisted of murder between spouses, a smaller number were parents killing children, or vice versa, and the rest were relatives murdering each other. Lawrence Stone argues that from the sixteenth century to the modern period family homicide due to "casual brutality" fell, whereas violence growing out of sexual passion increased. [9]

Wives who slay their mates have often been beaten by their husbands over a period of years before they finally reach a breaking point. Some wives are simply defending themselves from attack, others intentionally plan murder. Husbands who murder their wives, on the other hand, are usually following their previous patterns, only escalating

Table 4. Relationship of the Victim and Offender in Family Homicides

	Victim									
	Husband	Wife	Spouse	Father	Mother	Parent	Son	Daughter	Child	Other
Selected English counties, 1202–1276 (N = 177)	18	36	54	6	3	9	4	5	9	28
Selected English counties, 1300–1348 (N = 95)			53		n.a.	10	22		n.a.	n.a.
Essex, 1560–1709 (N = 74)	11	22	32		n.a.				50	n.a.
Philadelphia, 1839–1901 (N = 176)	10	60	70		3				5	22
Philadelphia, 1948–1952 (N = 136)	35	39	74	1	2	3	7	6	13	10
U.S., 1982 (N = 2974)	22	31	53	5	4	9	1	7	8	30

Sources: James Buchanan Given, *Society and Homicide in Thirteenth Century England* (Stanford, Calif.: Stanford University Press, 1977), 57; Barbara H. Westman, "The Peasant Family and Crime in Fourteenth-Century England," *Journal of British Studies*, v. 13 (1974), 17; J. A. Sharpe, "Domestic Homicide in Early Modern England," *Historical Journal*, v. 24, No. 1 (1981), 29–48; unpublished data on Philadelphia criminal indictments, collected by Professor Roger Lane; Marvin Wolfgang, *Patterns of Criminal Homicide* (Philadelphia: University of Pennsylvania Press, 1958), 378; Federal Bureau of Investigation, *Uniform Crime Reports of the United States, 1982* (Washington, D.C.: U.S. Government Printing Office, 1982).

its level. In one contemporary study, nine out of ten women who killed their husbands or lovers claimed to have been abused.[10] Table 5 indicates that the majority of murders between spouses consist of husbands killing their wives, but the proportion of spousal killings committed by wives has gradually increased. In medieval Europe, about two-thirds of spousal murders consisted of wife killings. (In colonial New England the figure was lower, 55 percent, but the base is extremely small.) The FBI began tabulating marital murder in 1963. Since then, the rate has varied from 52 to 62 percent. The percentage of husband-wife murders committed by U.S. husbands in 1984 stood at the high point of this range. While the FBI figures from 1963 to the present show an increasing proportion of marital murders committed by husbands, wives are somewhat more likely to kill their husbands today than they were in the nineteenth century. Perhaps, as some have suggested, the handgun is the great equalizer.[11]

The evidence considered in this appendix suggest two major conclusions. First, the overall trend in family homicide from thirteenth-century England to the present is

Table 5. Percentage of Husband-Wife Murders Committed by Husbands

	Percentage	Number
Selected English counties, 1202–1276	66	96
Essex, Hertfordshire, and Sussex assizes, 1559–1625	c. 74	n.a.
Essex assizes	72	n.a.
Selected New England colonies	55	9
Philadelphia, 1839–1901	86	122
Cook County, Illinois, 1926–1927	76	55
Philadelphia, 1948–1952	53	100
Houston, 1969	41	44
U.S., 1963	55	n.a.
U.S., 1966	56	1780
U.S., 1967	55	1934
U.S., 1968	54	1870
U.S., 1969	54	1911
U.S., 1970	54	1913
U.S., 1971	52	2257
U.S., 1972	52	2315
U.S., 1973	52	2400
U.S., 1974	52	2493
U.S., 1975	52	2359
U.S., 1977	55	2944
U.S., 1978	57	1936
U.S., 1979	54	1853
U.S., 1980	56	1814
U.S., 1981	59	1725
U.S., 1982	59	1598
U.S., 1983	59	1755
U.S., 1984	62	2391

Sources: James Buchanan Given, *Society and Homicide in Thirteenth-Century England* (Stanford, Calif.: Stanford University Press, 1977), 57; John F. Cronin, ed., *Records of the Courts of Assistants of the Colony of Massachusetts Bay, 1630–1692* (Boston: Suffolk County, 1928), v. 1, 295–296, v. 2, 308; records of the colonies of Connecticut, New Haven, and Plymouth, as quoted in Lyle Koehler, *A Search for Power: The "Weaker Sex" in Seventeenth-Century New England* (Urbana: University of Illinois Press, 1980), 139, 155–156; J. S. Cockburn, "The Nature and Incidence of Crime in England, 1559–1625: A Preliminary Survey," in J. S. Cockburn, ed., *Crime in England 1550–1800* (Princeton, N.J.: Princeton University Press, 1977), 57; J. A. Sharpe, *Crime in Seventeenth-Century England: A County Study* (Cambridge: Cambridge University Press, 1983), 127; J. A. Sharpe, "Domestic Homicide in Early Modern England," *The Historical Journal*, v. 24, No. 1 (1981), 37; unpublished data from Philadelphia criminal indictments supplied to me by Professor Roger Lane; Illinois Association for Criminal Justice, *The Illinois Crime Survey* (Chicago: Illinois Association for Criminal Justice, 1929), 610; Marvin Wolfgang, *Patterns in Criminal Homicide* (Philadelphia: University of Pennsylvania Press, 1958), 378; Henry P. Lundsgaarde, *Murder in Space City: A Cultural Analysis of Houston Homicide Patterns* (New York: Oxford University Press, 1977), 230–231; Federal Bureau of Investigation, *Uniform Crime Reports for the United States* (Washington, D.C.: U.S. Government Printing Office, 1963, 1966–1975, 1977–1985).

U-shaped: relatively high in the medieval period, lower in the early era, gradually rising from the nineteenth century to the present. Second, the composition of family homicide has gradually changed from the Victorian era to the present: husband-wife murder has increased relative to the slaying of children, and has become more equal between spouses.

The rising rate of family homicide reveals growing tension, especially in the homes of the poor and of racial minorities. It is a sorry record of discontent and rage. One contemporary study determined that the police had generally been called to intervene in families where a homicide eventually took place; often the police have been summoned as many as five times before a murder occurs. [12] It cannot be proven that swifter arrest of family assailants would reduce the level of family murder. But these figures demonstrate an urgent cry for help and the drastic need to punish assault before someone gets killed.

Notes

INTRODUCTION

1. A fuller consideration of these statistics is provided in Appendix B.

2. The psychiatric literature on this subject is extensive. Some of the most recent work has compared the psychological symptoms of the abused with those of a control group, thus leading to conclusions about the specific consequences of abuse. For a study of this kind among abused and neglected children, see Arthur H. Green, "Self-destructive behavior in battered children," *American Journal of Psychiatry*, v. 135, No. 5 (May 1978), 579–582. The psychological damage incest victims suffer is assessed by Judith L. Herman, *Father-Daughter Incest* (Cambridge, Mass.: Harvard University Press, 1981), 22–49. Elaine Hilberman examined the psychological consequences of wife beating in "Overview: the "wife-beater's wife" reconsidered," *American Journal of Psychiatry*, v. 137, No. 2 (November 1980), 1336–1347. Victims of domestic violence admitted to psychiatric hospitals suffer from different psychological symptoms than non-abused psychiatric inpatients. Elaine Hilberman Carmen, Patricia Perri Rieker, and Trudy Mills, "Victims of Violence and Psychiatric Illness," in Patricia Perri Rieker and Elaine Hilberman Carmen, eds., *The Gender Gap in Psychotherapy: Social Realities and Psychological Processes* (New York and London: Plenum Press, 1984), 199–211.

3. C. Henry Kempe, Frederic N. Silverman, Brandt F. Steele, William Droegemuller, and Henry K. Silver, "The Battered-Child Syndrome," *Journal of the American Medical Association*, v. 181 (1962), 17–24.

4. Although abuse of the elderly and sibling violence occurred throughout American history, they were rarely noticed until the 1970s.

5. The state refers to the variety of public and private, voluntary and government-financed or government-chartered institutions that have been charged with responsibility for intervening in the family.

6. The similarities in these reform movements are emphasized in Peter Conrad and

Joseph W. Schneider, *Deviance and Medicalization: From Badness to Sickness* (St. Louis: The C. V. Mosby Company, 1980).

7. The Family Ideal does not fit the reality of family life or the diverse history of American families, Mary Ryan argues in "The Explosion of Family History," *Reviews in American History*, v. 10, No. 4 (December 1982), 181–195.

8. The family became a more private institution by the seventeenth century in England and the eighteenth in France. Four influential works in family history that have reached this conclusion are Philippe Aries, *Centuries of Childhood*, trans. Robert Baldick (New York: Knopf, 1965); Lawrence Stone, *The Family, Sex and Marriage in England, 1500–1800* (London: Weidenfeld and Nicholson, 1977); Edward Shorter, *The Making of the Modern Family* (New York: Basic Books, 1975); and Jean Louis Flandrin, *Families in Past Time* (Cambridge, England: Cambridge University Press, 1979).

9. John Demos, *A Little Commonwealth: Family Life in Plymouth Colony* (New York: Oxford University Press, 1970).

10. Jean Bethke Elshtain, *Public Man, Private Woman: Women in Social and Political Thought* (Princeton: Princeton University Press, 1981), 298–353.

11. Sarah B. Pomeroy, *Goddesses, Whores, Wives, and Slaves: Women in Classical Antiquity* (New York: Schocken Books, 1975), 150–155.

12. French customary rights are described in Jean Louis Flandrin, *Families In Past Time* (Cambridge, England: Cambridge University Press, 1979), 122–145. Nineteenth-century U.S. judicial opinion on the right of moderate chastisement is surveyed in Elizabeth H. Pleck, "Wife Beating in Nineteenth-Century America," *Victimology: An International Journal*, v. 4, No. 1 (1979), 60–71.

13. Rodney Stark and James McEvoy III, "Middle Class Violence," *Psychology Today*, v. 4 (November 1970), 52–65.

14. Elizabeth H. Pleck, "Challenges to Traditional Authority in Immigrant Families," in Michael Gordon, ed., *The American Family in Social-Historical Perspective*, third edition (New York: St. Martin's Press, 1983), 504–517; Linda Gordon, "Child Abuse, Gender, and the Myth of Family Independence: A Historical Critique," *Child Welfare*, v. LXIV, No. 3 (May–June 1985), 224; and Linda Gordon, "Single Mothers and Child Neglect, 1880–1920," *American Quarterly*, v. 37, No. 2 (Summer 1985), 173–192. For additional refutation of the "social control" perspective on American reform, see Gerald N. Grob, "Reflections on the History of Social Policy in America," *Reviews in American History*, v. 7, No. 3 (September 1979), 293–306.

15. Jacques Donzelot, *The Policing of Families* (New York: Pantheon, 1979); Carnegie Council on Children, *All Our Children: The American Family Under Pressure* (New York: Harcourt Brace Jovanovich, 1978); Christopher Lasch, *Haven in a Heartless World: The Family Besieged* (New York: Basic Books, 1977); Eileen Boris and Peter Bardaglio, "The Transformation of Patriarchy: The Historic Role of the State," in Irene Diamond, eds., *Families, Politics, and Public Policy: A Feminist Dialogue on Women and the State* (New York and London: Longman, 1983), 70–93; Ellen Ryerson, *The Best-Laid Plans: America's Juvenile Court Experiment* (New York: Hill and Wang, 1978); Anthony M. Platt, *The Child Savers: The Invention of Delinquency* (Chicago: University of Chicago Press, 1977); and Nigel Parton, *The Politics of Child Abuse* (New York: St. Martin's, 1985). On the "state take-over" of the battered women's movement, see Patricia Morgan, "From Battered Wife to Program Client: The State's Shaping of Social Problems," *Kapitalistate*, v. 9 (1981), 17–40. Paul Boyer

criticized nineteenth-century urban reformers for their desire to impose social control in *Urban Masses and Moral Order in America, 1820–1920* (Cambridge: Harvard University Press, 1978). For one of the first pointed critiques of the view that the state has usurped family functions, see Ann Vandepol, "Dependent Children, Child Custody, and the Mothers' Pensions: The Transformation of State-Family Relations in the early 20th Century," *Social Problems*, v. 29, No. 3 (February, 1982), 221–235.

16. Judith Areen, "Intervention between Parent and Child: A Reappraisal of the State's Role in Child Neglect and Abuse Cases," *Georgetown Law Journal*, v. 63 (March 1975), 887–937; Michael S. Wald, "State Intervention on Behalf of 'Neglected Children': A Search for Realistic Standards," *Stanford Law Review*, v. 27 (April 1975), 985–1040; and Michael S. Wald, "State Intervention on Behalf of 'Neglected' Children: Standards for Removal of Children from their Homes, Monitoring the Status of Children in Foster Care, and Termination of Parental Rights," *Stanford Law Review*, v. 28 (April 1976), 673–706.

17. Heidi Hartmann offers critical observations on these assumptions in "The Family as the locus of gender, class and political struggle: the example of housework," *Signs: Journal of Women and Culture*, v. 6 (Spring 1981), 366–394. The idea, however, has had considerable appeal in historical writing on the family, as Rayna Rapp, Ellen Ross, and Renate Bridenthal note in "Examining family history," *Feminist Studies*, v. 5 (Spring 1979), 174–200. For continuing American belief in the Family Ideal, see David M. Schneider, *American Kinship: A Cultural Account*, second edition (Chicago: University of Chicago Press, 1980).

18. In "the Bad Old Days," according to Edward Shorter, wives were frequently beaten and children maltreated. See his *The Making of the Modern Family* (New York: Basic Books, 1975), 255–268. Other works that emphasize the horror of past childrearing practices include Lloyd de Mause, "The evolution of childhood," in Lloyd de Mause, ed., *The History of Childhood* (New York: Psychohistory Press, 1975), 1–74; Lloyd de Mause, "Our forebearers made childhood a nightmare," *Psychology Today*, v. 8 (April 1975), 85–87; Samuel Radbill, "A history of child abuse and infanticide," in Ray Helfer and C. Henry Kempe, eds., *The Battered Child* (Chicago: University of Chicago Press, 1980), 3–29. Linda Pollock's *Forgotten Children: Parent-child relations from 1500 to 1900* (Cambridge: Cambridge University Press, 1983), is a necessary antidote to this point of view.

CHAPTER 1. WICKED CARRIAGE

1. I use the word "Puritan" to refer to the inhabitants of seventeenth- and early eighteenth-century New England, including the population of Plymouth Colony (the Pilgrims). To differentiate these two groups of Protestant religious dissidents, I occasionally reserve the term Puritan for the residents of Massachusetts Bay Colony and refer to the inhabitants of Plymouth Colony as Pilgrims.

2. Quoted in Lyle Koehler, *A Search for Power: The "Weaker" Sex in Seventeenth Century New England* (Urbana: University of Illinois Press, 1980), 49.

3. Benjamin Wadsworth, *The Well-Ordered Family* (Boston: B. Green, 1712), 25, 36.

4. Lyle Koehler, *A Search for Power*, 139; John Putnam Demos, *Entertaining*

Satan: Witchcraft and the Culture of Early New England (New York: Oxford University Press, 1982), 74–75.

5. John Noble, ed., *Records of the Court of Assistants of the Colony of the Massachusetts Bay, 1630–1692,* v. 1 (Boston: Suffolk County, 1901); and David Thomas Konig, ed., *Plymouth Court Records, 1686–1856,* v. 1–4 (reprinted Wilmington, Del.: Michael Glazier, 1978). Estimates of colonial population can be found in Evarts B. Greene and Virginia D. Harrington, *American Population before the Federal Census of 1790* (New York: Columbia University Press, 1932), 10–19.

6. Emil Oberholzer, Jr, *Delinquent Saints: Disciplinary Action in the Early Congregational Churches in Massachusetts* (New York: Columbia University Press, 1956), 120–121. E. William Monter described how the church court of Calvinist Geneva punished the wife beaters in "The Consistory of Geneva, 1559–1569," *Bibliothèque d'humanisme et Renaissance,* v. 38 (1976), 467–484.

7. These opinions ran counter to prevailing judicial opinion of the time. See Elizabeth H. Pleck, "Wife Beating in Nineteenth-Century America," *Victimology: An International Journal,* v. 4, No. 1 (1979), 60–74.

8. Massachusetts Colony Law Statutes, *The Body of Liberties of 1641* (reprinted Boston: Rockwell and Churchill, 1890), 51.

9. George Lee Haskins, *Law and Authority in Early Massachusetts: A Study in Tradition and Design* (New York: Macmillan, 1960), 123–140.

10. Lyle Koehler, *A Search for Power,* 49; Lawrence Stone, *The Family, Sex and Marriage in England, 1500–1800* (New York: Harper & Row, 1977), 197.

11. Nathaniel B. Shurtleff, M.D., ed., *Records of the Colony of New Plymouth in New England,* v. III (Boston: William White, 1855), 106–107, 121, 126.

12. Although church courts hoped to reconcile husband and wife, the Puritans nevertheless permitted divorce on a number of grounds, particularly in comparison with English law. Marriage, the Puritans believed, was not a sacrament but a civil contract based on the mutual consent of both parties. When the contract was broken, full divorce, including the right to remarry, was permitted. In England only the ecclesiastical courts granted partial divorce (actually, legal separation), referred to as "separation from bed and board." Divorce allowing each partner the right to remarry was not permitted there unless the marriage was nullified on grounds of consanguinity, bigamy, or sexual incapacity. Until the passage of divorce reform legislation in the nineteenth century, ecclesiastical church courts in England granted a separation on grounds of cruelty, with cruelty usually defined as life-threatening acts of violence. Even a legal separation was extremely difficult to obtain, and the woman applicant had to appear blameless, prove that she had been unwilling to live with her husband after he had threatened her, and have two witnesses ready to testify that they had seen her husband commit acts of violence. Naturally, there were few English wives who could meet all these stringent criteria. Lawrence Stone, *Family, Sex and Marriage,* 37–41. Lyle Koehler provides a list of petitions for divorce in seventeenth-century New England in his book, *A Search for Power,* 452–458. See also D. Kelly Weisberg, "Under Greet Temptations Heer: Women and Divorce in Puritan Massachusetts," *Feminist Studies,* v. 2 (1975), 183–194.

13. Nancy F. Cott, "Divorce and the Changing Status of Women in Eighteenth-Century Massachusetts," *William and Mary Quarterly,* v. 33, 3rd series (October 1976), 597. Nancy Cott generously permitted me to examine her notes on the divorce cases she consulted.

14. Nathaniel B. Shurtleff, M.D., ed., *Records of the Colony of New Plymouth in England*, v. V, 13–14.

15. Edwin Powers, *Crime and Punishment*, 305; Emil Oberholzer, Jr., *Delinquent Saints*, 124.

16. Nathaniel B. Shurtleff, M.D. ed., *Records of the Colony of New Plymouth in England*, v. V, 75; Edwin Powers, *Crime and Punishment*, 178.

17. John D. Cushing, *The Earliest Laws of New Haven and Connecticut Colonies, 1639–1663* (reprinted Wilmington, Del.: Michael Glazier, 1977), 14, 20; John D. Cushing, *The Earliest Acts and Laws of the Colony of Rhode Island and Providence Plantations, 1646–1719* (Wilmington, Del.: Michael Glazier, 1977), 140. The law in Rhode Island provided a whipping of not more than ten lashes for a child who struck a parent or a servant who abused a master. John Demos explains the symbolic importance of these laws in *A Little Commonwealth: Family Life in Plymouth Colony* (New York: Oxford University Press, 1970), 100–101.

18. The colonies of New Plymouth, New Haven, and Delaware enacted similar laws. John D. Cushing, *The Laws of the Pilgrims* (reprinted Wilmington, Del.: Michael Glazier, 1977), 4–5; John D. Cushing, *The Earliest Laws of New Haven*, 20.

19. Edwin Powers, *Crime and Punishment in Early Massachusetts, 1620–1692: A Documentary History* (Boston: Beacon Press, 1966), 283.

20. Nathaniel B. Shurtleff, ed., *Records of the Governor and Company of the Massachusetts Bay in New England*, v. 4, Pt. II (Boston: William White, 1853–1854), 196, 216.

21. Harriet Miller Skillern, "Stubborn Women: A Socio-Historical Analysis of the Massachusetts Stubborn Child Law," unpublished paper presented at the annual meeting of the Social Science History Association, November 1982, and Harriet Miller Skillern, "A Socio-Legal Analysis of the Massachusetts Stubborn Child Law," unpublished Ph.D. thesis, Brandeis University, 1977.

22. George Francis Dow, ed., *Records and Files of the Quarterly Courts of Essex County, Massachusetts* (Salem, Mass.: Essex County Historical Society, 1911–1921), v. VI, 139, 141.

23. John Demos, "Child Abuse in Context: An Historian's Perspective," in John P. Demos, ed., *Past, Present, and Personal: The Family and the Life Course in American History* (New York: Oxford University Press, 1986), 68–91.

24. Quoted in Edmund S. Morgan, *The Puritan Family: Religion and Domestic Relations in Seventeenth-Century New England* (New York: Harper & Row, 1944), 78; Alice Morse Earle, *Child Life in Colonial Days* (New York: Macmillan, 1899), 197; James Axtell, *The School Upon a Hill: Education and Society in Colonial New England* (New Haven: Yale University Press, 1974), 123.

25. Dr. Nathaniel B. Shurtleff, ed., *Records of the Colony of New Plymouth in New England, 1633–1691*, v. 1–6 (Boston: William White, 1861); and David Thomas Konig, ed., *Plymouth Court Records, 1686–1856*, v. 1–4 (reprinted Wilmington, Del.: Michael Glazier, 1978). Dallett Hemphill argues that battered women's appeals in the courts of Essex County, Massachusetts, increased by the 1670s and that appearances in court for husband abuse began to fall off by the 1640s. There were few cases, however, and thus her generalizations are based on insufficient evidence. C. Dallett Hemphill, "Women in Court: Sex-Role Differentiation in Salem, Massachusetts, 1636 to 1683," *William and Mary Quarterly*, v. XXXIX, No. 1 (January 1982), 164–176.

26. Quoted in David Thomas Konig, *Law and Society*, 131.

27. David H. Flaherty, *Privacy in Colonial New England* (Charlottesville: University of Virginia Press, 1971), chapt. VII.

28. George Francis Dow, ed., *Records and Files of the Quarterly Courts of Essex County, Massachusetts*, v. VIII, 272–274. From his examination of court records and minister's statements, David Konig argues that neighbors and Puritan communities became more reluctant to intervene in the family around the 1680s. Since information is scarce for the entire colonial period, especially the first fifty years of settlement, it is by no means clear that neighbors were not similarly reticent to become involved in family conflict before then. David Thomas Konig, *Law and Society*, 127–128.

29. The amount of change these figures suggest may be somewhat exaggerated because the overall number of prosecutions was quite small and one time period for which the data was assembled was much longer than the other. Barbara S. Lindemann, ""To Ravish and Carnally Know": Rape in Eighteenth-Century Massachusetts," *Signs*, v. 10, No. 1 (Autumn 1984), 63–82. See also Catherine S. Baker, "Rape in Seventeenth-Century Massachusetts," unpublished paper delivered at the Berkshire Conference on Women's History, June 1976.

30. Francis G. Wallett, "The Diary of Ebenezer Parkman, 1747" *Proceedings of the American Antiquarian Society*, v. 73 (1963), 82, 84, 86.

31. James Axtell, *The School Upon a Hill: Education and Society in Colonial New England* (New Haven: Yale University Press, 1974), 336.

32. Rates of accusation and conviction for child murder in colonial New England can be found in Peter C. Hoffer and N. E. H. Hull, *Murdering Mothers: Infanticide in England and New England, 1558–1803* (New York: New York University Press, 1984), 33–64. On the punishment of Elizabeth Emerson, a mother who murdered her infant, see Laurel Thatcher Ulrich, *Good Wives: Image and Reality in the Lives of Women in Northern New England, 1650–1750* (New York: Knopf, 1982), 195–201.

33. Peter C. Hoffer and N. E. H. Hull, *Murdering Mothers*, 75–78. For a more general statement about how the decline in state enforcement of morality contributed to the separation of the family from public life, see Mary Beth Norton, "The Evolution of White Women's Experience in Early America," *American Historical Review*, v. 80, No. 3 (June 1984), 593–619. Norton believes that the decades between 1730 and 1750 were the turning point in the treatment of women criminals, which she claims shows a decline in enforcement of morality. But the laws against family violence were not being enforced by the 1680s, showing that diminution of state responsibility for individual morality began about fifty years before Norton suggests.

34. Hendrik Hartog, "The Public Law of a County Court: Judicial Government in Eighteenth Century Massachusetts," *American Journal of Legal History*, v. 20 (October 1976), 282–329. See also Daniel Scott Smith and Michael S. Hindus, "Premarital Pregnancy in America, 1640–1671: An Overview and Interpretation," *Journal of Interdisciplinary History*, v. 5, No. 4 (1975), 537–580.

35. Benjamin Franklin, "What Are the Poor Young Women to Do? The Speech of Polly Baker," in Albert Henry Smyth, ed., *The Writings of Benjamin Franklin*, v. VII (New York: Macmillan, 1905), 436–467.

36. William E. Nelson, "The Larger Context of Litigation in Plymouth Colony, 1725–1825," in David Thomas Konig, ed., *Plymouth Court Records, 1686–1859*; William E. Nelson, *Americanization of the Common Law: The Impact of Legal Change on Massachusetts Society, 1760–1830* (Cambridge: Harvard University Press,

1975), 110–121; David H. Flaherty, "Law and the Enforcement of Morals in Early America," *Perspectives in American History*, v. V (1971), 248.

37. Elizabeth H. Pleck, "Wife Beating in Nineteenth-Century America," *Victimology*, v. 4, No. 1 (1979), 69–70; Lawrence Stone, *The Family, Sex and Marriage in England, 1500–1800* (New York: Harper & Row, 1977), 375; Natalie Zemon Davis, "Women on Top," in Natalie Zemon Davis, ed., *Society and Culture in Early Modern France* (Stanford: Stanford University Press, 1975), 315; Mary P. Ryan, *Cradle of the Middle Class: The Family in Oneida County, New York, 1790–1865* (New York: Cambridge University Press, 1981), 36. The European pattern of community regulation is described in R. Emerson Dobash and Russell Dobash, "Community Response to Violence Against Wives: Charivari, Abstract Justice, and Patriarchy," *Social Problems*, v. 28, No. 5 (June 1981), 563–581; E. P. Thompson, "Rough Music: Le Charivari Anglais," *Annales: E.S.C.*, v. 27, No. 2 (1972), 285–312; Martin Ingram, "Ridings, Rough Music and the Reform of Popular Culture in Early Modern England," *Past and Present*, No. 105 (November 1984), 79–114. In sixteenth- and seventeenth–century England, most community rituals were directed against wives who beat or nagged their husbands. By the nineteenth century, the main target of ritualized community anger was the wife beater.

CHAPTER 2. PARENTAL TYRANNY

1. Abigail Stewart surveyed four childrearing books and pamphlets for each of four centuries, beginning with the sixteenth century. She described her methods in Abigail J. Stewart, David G. Winter, and A. David Jones, "Coding Categories for the Study of Child-Rearing: Historical Sources," *Journal of Interdisciplinary History*, v. 5 (Spring 1975), 684–694. Her sources were supplemented with childrearing books and pamphlets listed in Alice Ryerson, "Medical Advice on Child Rearing, 1550–1800," unpublished dissertation, Harvard Graduate School of Education, 1960; and Geoffrey H. Steere, "Changing Values in Child Socialization: A Study of United States Child-Rearing Literature, 1865–1929," unpublished Ph.D. dissertation, University of Pennsylvania, 1964, 22–28, 39–40, 63–84. Steere examined all childrearing books printed in the United States from 1865 to 1929; Ryerson analyzed thirty-nine childrearing books written by physicians for parents from 1550 to 1800.

A few late Victorian childrearing advisors such as Kate Douglas Wiggin, the author of many children's stories, held that children had a "right" to kind treatment and that parents enjoyed no comparable right to physically correct their children. Her radical views held sway briefly. By the 1920s behaviorists believed that physical discipline was largely a question of proper "management of the child," a view held since by many childhood advisors. To be sure, in the first edition of *Baby and Child Care*, a book that almost rivaled the Bible in sales if not in popularity, pediatrician Dr. Benjamin Spock rejected altogether physical punishment of children. Eleven years later, however, in a new edition, he decided that corporal punishment "is *never* the main element in discipline—it's only a vigorous additional reminder that the parent feels strongly about what he says." Quoted in Lynn Z. Bloom, *Doctor Spock: Biography of a Conservative Radical* (Indianapolis: Bobbs-Merrill, 1972), 137–138.

2. John Locke, *Some Thoughts Concerning Education* in Howard R. Penniman, ed., *John Locke: On Politics and Education* (New York: Van Nostrand, 1947), 263–

264; originally published London, 1693. For a detailed interpretation of the significance of this treatise, see Nathan Tarcov, *Locke's Education for Liberty* (Chicago: University of Chicago Press, 1984); on the sources of Locke's thought, see John Dunn, *The Political Thought of John Locke: An Historical Account of the Argument of the Two Treatises of Government* (Cambridge, Eng.: Cambridge University Press, 1969), especially 256–261.

3. The influence of Locke's ideas in America are traced in Jacqueline S. Reiner, "Rearing the Republican Child: Attitudes and Practices in Post–Revolutionary America," *William and Mary Quarterly*, v. 39, No. 1 (January 1982), 150–163; Daniel Calhoun, *The Intelligence of a People* (Princeton, N.J.: Princeton University Press, 1973), 145–148; Ruth H. Bloch, "American Feminine Ideals in Transition: The Rise of the Moral Mother, 1785–1815," *Feminist Studies*, v. 4, No. 2 (June 1978), 108–109.

4. Jay Fliegelman, *Prodigals and Pilgrims: The American Revolution Against Patriarchal Authority, 1750–1800* (Cambridge, Eng.: Cambridge University Press, 1982). A similar argument is offered by Edwin G. Burrows and Michael Wallace in "The American Revolution: The Ideology and Psychology of National Liberation," *Perspectives in American History*, v. VI (1972), 167–306; and Philip Greven, *The Protestant Temperament: Patterns of Child-Rearing, Religious Experience, and the Self in Early America* (New York: Knopf, 1977), 335–364. Adams is quoted in Bernard Bailyn, *The Ideological Origins of the American Revolution* (Cambridge: Harvard University Press, 1976), 59, 93.

5. Abigail Adams to John Adams, March 31, 1766, as quoted in Alice S. Rossi, ed., *The Feminist Papers: From Adams to de Beauvoir* (New York: Bantam Books, 1973), 10–11. Mary Beth Norton describes the increase in women's power in marriage and childrearing in *Liberty's Daughters: The Revolutionary Experience of American Women, 1750–1800* (Boston: Little, Brown, 1980), 234–238.

6. The reasons why republican mothers were given special childrearing responsibilities is explained by Linda Kerber in *Women of the Republic: Intellect and Ideology in Revolutionary America* (Chapel Hill: University of North Carolina Press, 1980) and especially in chapt. 9, 269–288.

7. Jan Lewis finds that Virginia planters relinquished public service in favor of personal and family life soon after the Revolution. Jan Lewis, *The Pursuit of Happiness: Family and Values in Jefferson's Virginia* (New York: Cambridge University Press, 1983).

8. Robert V. Wells, "Family, Sex and Fertility Control in Eighteenth Century America: A Study in Quaker History," *Population Studies*, v. 26 (1971), 73–82; and Robert V. Wells, "Quaker Marriage Patterns in a Colonial Perspective," *William and Mary Quarterly*, v. 39 (1972), 415–442. The significant religious role of Quaker women is noted by Mary Maples Dunn in "Women of Light" in Carol Ruth Berkin and Mary Beth Norton, eds., *Women of America: A History* (Boston: Little, Brown, 1979), 114–136; and in her article, "Saints and Sisters: Congregational and Quaker Women in the Early Colonial Period," *American Quarterly*, v. 30 (Winter 1978), 582–601. On the involvement of Quaker women in economic affairs and political activity, see Joan M. Jensen, *Loosening the Bonds: Mid-Atlantic Farm Women, 1750–1850* (New Haven: Yale University Press, 1986), 129–166.

9. J. William Frost, *The Quaker Family in Colonial America: A Portrait of the Society of Friends* (New York: St. Martin's Press, 1973), 84–85. Quaker methods of

discipline, and for that matter, Locke's advice, correspond to what Philip Greven in *The Protestant Temperament* calls "moderate" childrearing, one distinct type quite different from two others he calls authoritarian and genteel. His three types suggest a range of childrearing practice in early American history. But they seem to obscure changes in childrearing advice and practice; the Quakers, for example, became less authoritarian and more moderate around the time of the Revolution; moderates became even more moderate, with the shift from Lockean to antebellum methods.

10. Bertram Wyatt-Brown contrasts Quaker insistence on inculcating conscience and guilt feelings in the child with the Southern emphasis on shame and humiliation. See *Southern Honor: Ethics and Behavior in the Old South* (New York: Oxford University Press, 1982), 117; and his article, "Child Abuse, Public Policy and Child-rearing: An Historical Approach," in Barbara L. Finkelstein, ed., *Governing the Young: Working Papers No. 2* (College Park: University of Maryland College of Education, 1981), 1–34. Barry Levy argues that even in colonial America, Quakers were more gentle parents than Puritans. See his article "Tender Plants: Quaker Farmers and Children in the Delaware Valley, 1681–1735," *Journal of Family History*, v. 3 (June 1978), 116–133.

11. Philip Greven, *The Protestant Temperament*, 58; Rufus M. Jones, *A Small Town Boy* (New York: Macmillan, 1941), 33.

12. Jean Straub, "Quaker School Life in Philadelphia Before 1800," *Pennsylvania Magazine of History*, v. LXXXIX, No. 4 (October 1965), 451.

13. J. William Frost, *The Quaker Family*, 122–123, 286–287; Elizabeth Buffum Chace and Lucy Buffum Lovell, *Two Quaker Sisters: From the Original Diaries of Elizabeth Buffum Chace and Lucy Buffum Lovell* (New York: Liveright, 1937), 2–3; Charles T. Congdon, *Reminiscences of a Journalist* (Boston: J. R. Osgood, 1880), 51; Logan Pearsall Smith, *The Unforgotten Years* (Boston: Little, Brown, 1939), 36; Logan Pearsall Smith, ed., *Philadelphia Quaker: The Letters of Hannah Whitall Smith* (New York: Harcourt Brace, 1950), 9; *Journal of Ann Branson: A Minister of the Gospel in the Society of Friends* (Philadelphia: W. H. Pile and Sons, 1892), 10; Lydia Maria Child, *Isaac Hooper: A True Life* (Boston: J. P. Jewett, 1854), 367; Helen Thomas Flexner, *A Quaker Childhood* (New Haven: Yale University Press, 1940); Doris Faber, *The President's Mothers* (New York: St. Martin's Press, 1976), 21. A contemporary study, conducted in the 1980s, found that rates of physical force in Quaker families were as high as those in the general population. Judith L. Brutz and Bron B. Ingoldsby, "Conflict Resolution in Quaker Families," *Journal of Marriage and the Family*, v. 46, No. 1 (February 1984), 21–26. Most of the Friends in the survey were religious converts who had not grown up as Quakers.

14. Carl N. Degler provides a general survey of maternal influence in childrearing in *At Odds: Women and the Family from the Revolution to the Present* (New York: Oxford University Press, 1982), 86–110; Nancy F. Cott, "Notes Toward an Interpretation of Antebellum Childrearing," *The Psychohistory Review*, v. VII (Spring 1978), 4–20; Bernard Wishy, *The Child and the Republic: The Dawn of Modern American Child Nurture* (Philadelphia: University of Pennsylvania Press, 1968), 42–49; and Robert Sunley, "Early Nineteenth-Century American Literature on Child-Rearing," in Margaret Mead and Martha Wolfenstein, eds., *Childhood in Contemporary Cultures* (Chicago: University of Chicago Press, 1955), 150–168.

15. Herman R. Lantz, Margaret Britton, Raymond L. Schmitt, and Eloise C. Snyder, "Pre-industrial Patterns in the Colonial Family in America: A Content Analy-

sis of Colonial Magazines," *American Sociological Review*, v. 33 (June 1968), 413–426; Herman R. Lantz, Raymond L. Schmitt, and Richard Herman, "The Preindustrial Family in America: A Further Examination of Early Magazines," *American Journal of Sociology*, v. 79 (November 1973), 566–588; Herman R. Lantz, Jane Keyes, and Martin Schultz, "The American Family in the Preindustrial Period: From Base Lines in History to Change," *American Sociological Review*, v. 40, No. 1 (February 1975), 21–36.

16. Mary P. Ryan, *Cradle of the Middle Class: The Family in Oneida County, New York, 1790–1865* (Cambridge, Eng.: Cambridge University Press, 1981), 157–162; Mary P. Ryan, *The Empire of the Mother: American Writing about Domesticity, 1830–1860* (New York: Institute for Research in History, 1982).

17. Mrs. Louisa Hare, *Hints for the Improvement of Early Education and Nursery Discipline* (New York: Wiley and Long, 1835), 47.

18. David Rothman argues that the insistence on obedience in antebellum childrearing literature betrayed hysteria, a fear of social crisis, and a decline in the enforcement by the community of a moral code. In fact, obedience in children has always been a major emphasis in childrearing from the Puritans up to the present. Rothman appears to have been surprised that training for obedience could persist amidst the gentle measures of childrearing the advisors recommended. The antebellum advisors remained wedded to traditional goals, however, and simply sought to employ new methods in realizing them. David Rothman, *The Discovery of the Asylum: Social Order and Disorder in the New Republic* (Boston: Little, Brown, 1971), 216–221.

19. T. S. Arthur, *The Iron Rule; or Tyranny in the Household* (Philadelphia: T. T. Peterson, 1853), 12; and T. S. Arthur, *The Mother's Rule: or The Right Way and the Wrong Way* (Rochester, N.Y.: Arthur E. Darrow, 1856), 21.

20. Lyman Cobb, *The Evil Tendencies of Corporal Punishment as a Means of Moral Discipline in Families and Schools,* (New York: Newman, 1847), 12, 59.

21. Theodore Dwight, *The Father's Book, or Suggestions for the Instruction of Young Children* (Springfield, Mass.: G. G. Merrimac, 1835), 124.

22. Mary P. Ryan, *Cradle of the Middle Class,* 161.

23. Henry C. Wright, *A Kiss for a Blow: Or, a Collection of Stories for Children* (Boston: B. B. Mussey, 1842). For a general survey of the themes in antebellum children's fiction, which often paralleled those of childrearing advisors, see Anne Scott MacLeod, "Education for Freedom: Children's Fiction in Jacksonian America," *Harvard Educational Review*, v. 46, No. 3 (August 1976), 425–435.

24. Lydia Maria Child, *The Mother's Book,* second edition (Boston: Carter and Hendler, 1831), 37.

25. Evelyn Walsh McClean, *Father Struck it Rich* (Boston: Little, Brown, 1836), 11–12; and John Franklin Carter, *The Rectory Family* (New York: Coward McCann, 1937), 72–73.

26. Elizabeth Buffum Chace and Lucy Buffum Lovell, *Two Quaker Sisters,* 84, 88.

27. The sources and methods used in conducting the survey of parental punishment are described in Appendix A. A cautionary tale about the pitfalls in interpreting childrearing advice is furnished by Jay Mechling in "Advice to Historians on Advice to Mothers," *Journal of Social History*, v. 9 (Fall 1975), 44–63. The discrepancy between the childrearing ideal and mother's frequent spanking, even of infants, is among the observations made by Barbara Maria Korsch, Jewell B. Christian, Ethel

Kontz Gozzi, and Paul V. Carlson in "Infant Care and Punishment: A Pilot Study," *American Journal of Public Health*, v. 55, No. 12 (December 1965), 1880–1888.

28. Linda Pollock, in a carefully researched study of actual childrearing practice in England and America from 1500 to 1900, believes that the absence of information reflects the absence of punishment. However, she also argues that autobiographies are much more likely to mention punishment than diaries, a fact that seems to suggest that punishment is commented upon mainly in retrospect. Those parents who noted punishment in their diaries were self-conscious and relatively mild in their methods. Cruel and abusive parents were not the kind of people who kept diaries.

Pollock further argues that child abuse in the past was relatively infrequent, and that in every period of history one could find enlightened parents who treated their children gently. However, her reading of the evidence is suspect: she interprets the absence of information about abuse as evidence of mild treatment; she weights her study in favor of diarists, who tended to be enlightened; and she fails to make extensive use of American autobiographies. Linda A. Pollock, *Forgotten Children: Parent-child relations from 1500 to 1900* (Cambridge, Eng.: Cambridge University Press, 1983).

29. Samuel Sewall, *Diary*, v. 5 (Boston: Massachusetts Historical Society, 1878–1882), 225. Louis Wright and Marion Tinling, eds., *William Byrd, The Secret Diary of William Byrd of Westover, 1709–1712* (Richmond: The Dietz Press, 1941), 204, 285; Worthington Chauncey Ford, ed., *Diary of Cotton Mather, 1681–1724*, v. 7 (Boston: Massachusetts Historical Society, 1911–1912), 534–537. The childrearing of Sarah Homes is described in Bertram Wyatt-Brown, "Three Generations of Yankee Parenthood: The Tappan Family, A Case Study of Antebellum Nurture," *Illinois Quarterly*, v. 38, No. 1 (Fall 1975), 12–29.

30. Lewis Tappan, *The Life of Arthur Tappan* (New York: Hurd and Houghton, 1878), 24; Bertram Wyatt-Brown, "Three Generations of Yankee Parenthood: The Tappan Family, A Case Study of Antebellum Nurture," *Illinois Quarterly*, v. 38, No. 1 (Fall 1975), 12–29.

31. My observations about antebellum childrearing literature are in general agreement with those of Carl N. Degler in *At Odds*, 86–98. He astutely observes changes in actual childrearing practice within the educated middle class, but then, I believe, mistakenly, assumes these were common in other groups.

32. Murray A. Straus and Richard J. Gelles, *Behind Closed Doors: Violence in the American Family* (New York: Doubleday, 1980), 61.

33. David Crockett, *A Narrative of the Life of David Crockett of the State of Tennessee* (Philadelphia: E. L. Carey, 1834; revised edition, Knoxville: University of Tennessee Press, 1973), 23; Allan D. Nevins, *John D. Rockefeller: The Heroic Age of American Enterprise* (New York: Charles Scribner's Sons, 1940), 41; Mary Cable, *The Little Darlings: A History of Child Rearing in America* (New York: Charles Scribner's Sons, 1972), 86; Albert J. Beveridge, *Abraham Lincoln, 1809–1858* (Boston: Houghton Mifflin, 1928), 66.

34. A general survey that portrays the similarity in antebellum reform movements against corporal punishment is Myra C. Glenn's *Campaigns Against Corporal Punishment: Prisoners, Sailors, Women, and Children in Antebellum America* (Albany: State University of New York Press, 1984). On the campaign against corporal punishment in the schools, see Carl F. Kaestle, "Social Change, Discipline, and the Common School in Early Nineteenth-Century America," *Journal of Interdisciplinary History*," v. IX, No. 1 (Summer 1978), 1–18; on the abolition of corporal punishment in the

navy, see Harold Langley, *Social Reform in the United States Navy, 1798–1862* (Urbana: University of Illinois Press, 1967), 131–206; on the efforts to abolish capital punishment, see David Brion Davis, "The Movement to Abolish Capital Punishment in America, 1787–1861," *American Historical Review*, v. 63 (October 1957), 23–46.

CHAPTER 3. THE DRUNKARD'S WIFE

1. Edmund H. Sears, *An Address Delivered at Lancaster Before the Washington Total Abstinence Society* (Boston: Isaac Butts, 1841), 19.

2. On the relation between alcoholism and domestic violence, see Richard J. Gelles, *Family Violence* (Beverly Hills, Calif.: Sage, 1979); and Richard A. Berk, Sarah Fenstermaker Berk, Donileen R. Loseke, and David Rauma, "Mutual Combat and Other Family Violence Myths," in David Finkelhor, Richard J. Gelles, Gerald T. Hotaling, Murray A. Straus, eds., *The Dark Side of Families: Current Family Violence Research* (Beverly Hills, Calif.: Sage, 1983), 197–210. W. J. Rorabaugh, "Estimated U.S. Alcoholic Beverage Consumption, 1790–1860," *Journal of Studies of Alcohol* 37 (March 1976), 360–361; W. J. Rorabaugh, *The Alcoholic Republic: An American Tradition* (New York: Oxford University Press, 1979), 225–233, concern incidence.

3. Robert L. Griswold, *Family and Divorce in California, 1850–1890: Victorian Illusion and Everyday Realities* (Albany: State University of New York Press, 1982), 105.

4. Jerome Nadelhaft, "Domestic Violence in the Literature of the Temperance Movement," unpublished paper, 1982, 13.

5. Myra C. Glenn takes the opposite position, that the ideology of domesticity prevented most antebellum reformers, other than advocates of temperance or feminism, from being interested in the issue of wife beating. In England, however, reformers of the 1850s paid much attention to the issue of wife beating, in spite of the prevalent national adherence to the ideology of domesticity. Myra C. Glenn, *Campaigns Against Corporal Punishment: Prisoners, Sailors, Women, and Children in Antebellum America* (Albany: State University of New York Press, 1984), chapt. 4.

6. *The Pearl* (June 6, 1846), 4, as quoted in Jed Dannenbaum, "The Origins of Temperance Activism and Militancy Among American Women," *Journal of Social History*, v. 15, No. 2 (Winter 1981), 287.

7. Ibid.

8. Samuel Chipman, *Report of the Examination of Poor-Houses, Jails, etc., in the State of New York* (Albany: Hoffman and White, 1834), 76; William Alcott, *The Young Wife; or, Duties of Women in the Marriage Relation* (New York, 1837; reprint, New York: Arno Press, 1972), 263. On the image of the brutish man in antebellum reform tracts, see Myra C. Glenn, *Campaigns Against Corporal Punishment*, 44–45, 77.

9. Ian R. Tyrrell, "Women and Temperance in Antebellum America, 1830–1860," *Civil War History*, v. 28, No. 2 (June 1962), 139; Lorenzo D. Johnson, *Martha Washingtonianism, or a History of the Ladies' Temperance Benevolent Societies* (New York: Saxton and Miles, 1834); Jed Dannenbaum, "The Origins of Temperance Activism and Militancy Among American Women," 235–252; Harry Gene Levine, "Temperance and Women in 19th-Century United States," in Oriana Josseau Kalant, ed., *Alcohol and Drug Problems in Women*, v. 5 (New York: Plenum

Press, 1980), 25–67; and Nancy A. Hewitt, *Women's Activism and Social Change: Rochester, New York, 1822–1872* (Ithaca: Cornell University Press, 1984), chapt. 4.

10. Declaration of Sentiments and Resolutions, Seneca Falls Convention, as quoted in Aileen S. Kraditor, ed., *Up from the Pedestal: Selected Writings on the History of American Feminism* (Chicago: Quadrangle Books, 1970), 187.

11. *Lily* (Jan. 15, 1852), 12.

12. The grounds for divorce, by state, are summarized by the U.S. Commission of Labor, *A Report on Marriage and Divorce in the United States, 1867 to 1886, including an Appendix Relating to Marriage and Divorce in Certain Countries in Europe* (Washington, D.C.: U.S. Government Printing Office, 1891), 444–601. The definition of "cruelty" varied from one state to another and was subject to interpretation by state appellate courts. In some state statutes a single blow, a push, or a shove was sufficient grounds to prove cruelty; in others, cruelty consisted of an act endangering life. In his influential legal commentaries, Joel Prentiss Bishop argued that "cruelty" consisted of past acts that caused a spouse to fear physical harm. The purpose of divorce, he argued, was not to punish past wrongs but to prevent future injuries. Most courts did not consider evidence of mental distress sufficient proof of cruelty. Similarly, drunkenness was not regarded as cruelty, whereas violent acts committed when inebriated were. A fear of future harm could be established, even if no physical injury occurred, as long as there were credible threats of future violence. Bishop considered mental suffering a form of cruelty as well, but with the exception of a few state appellate courts, he was ahead of his time in this idea. Joel Prentiss Bishop, *Commentaries on the Law of Marriage and Divorce*, v. 1 (Boston: Little, Brown, 1864), 628.

13. Nelson Blake, *The Road to Reno: A History of Divorce in the United States* (New York: Macmillan, 1962), 87. Blake traces the history of New York divorce reform in this book, especially pp. 48–63.

14. *Lily* (May 1852), 41.

15. Quoted in Nelson Blake, *The Road to Reno*, 77.

16. *Lily* (May 1852), 41.

17. Ibid.

18. Ibid. Linda Gordon, "Family Violence and Social Control," (New York: Pantheon, forthcoming), chapt. 10.

19. Elizabeth Cady Stanton, Susan B. Anthony, and Matilda J. Gage, *History of Woman Suffrage* (Rochester: Susan B. Anthony, 1881), v. 1, 496.

20. Theodore Stanton and Harriet Stanton Blatch, eds., *Elizabeth Cady Stanton as Revealed in Her Letters and Diary* (New York: Harper and Brothers, 1922), v. 2, 48.

21. Norma Basch, *In the Eyes of the Law: Women, Marriage, and Property in Nineteenth-Century New York* (New York: Cornell University Press, 1982), 179.

22. Quoted in Nelson Blake, *The Road to Reno*, 89.

23. Elizabeth Cady Stanton, Susan B. Anthony, and Matilda J. Gage, *History of Woman Suffrage*, v. 1, 492; Ida Husted Harper, *The Life and Work of Susan B. Anthony*, v. 1 (Indianapolis: The Hollenbeck Press, 1898), 200–205; Elizabeth Cady Stanton, *Eighty Years and More: Reminiscences 1815–1897* (New York, 1897; reprinted, New York: Schocken Books, 1983), 214; and Lois W. Banner, *Elizabeth Cady Stanton: A Radical for Woman's Rights* (Boston: Little, Brown, 1980), 14.

24. Elizabeth Cady Stanton, Susan B. Anthony, and Matilda J. Gage, *History of Woman Suffrage*, v. 1, 731.

25. A general review of Stanton's involvement in divorce reform in the 1850s is

provided by Elisabeth Griffith in *In Her Own Right: The Life of Elizabeth Cady Stanton* (New York: Oxford University Press, 1984), chapt. 6.

26. *Acts of the State of Tennessee, Laws, Statutes, etc. . . . for the Years 1849–1850* (Nashville: Kennie and Watterson, 1850), 300–302; Orville A. Park, Harry B. Skillman, and Harry S. Strozier, *Code of Georgia Annotated* (Atlanta, 1933), 198. On the limited enforcement of the Georgia law, see Bertram Wyatt-Brown, *Southern Honor* (New York: Oxford University Press, 1982), 281.

27. Stanton and Anthony were also uninterested in the ramifications of the civil law for battered women. The New York Married Women's Act of 1860, called the Civil Liability Act, gave a married woman the right to sue or be sued, that is, it did not explicitly prohibit a wife from suing her husband. One of the most controversial rights that abused wives or children lacked was the right to sue the husband or father for damages. Even today there are many states that do not permit such torts. The irony is that woman's rights advocates, in supporting the passage of the Married Women's Property Act, never realized the liability law had these implications. After it was enacted, Catherine Langendyke of upstate New York sued her husband for damages after he assaulted her. She won her case in lower court but her husband appealed. The New York State Supreme Court was unwilling to nullify the common-law tradition of unity of interest between husband and wife. It threw out her case and held that a wife did not have the right to sue her husband. The Court ruled that "the effect of giving so broad a construction to the act of 1860 might be to involve the husband and wife in perpetual controversy and litigation—to sow the seeds of perpetual domestic discord and broil—to produce the most discordant and conflicting interest of property between them, and offer a bounty or temptation to the wife to seek encroachment upon her husband's property." Stanton and Anthony never mentioned the Langendyke case, or its implications for the issue of woman's rights, even though it was such a clear example of the degradation of the marriage relationship. Langendyke v. Langendyke, 44 Barbour's 366. For a general review of nineteenth-century legal opinion on intra-spousal immunity from torts, see F. A. Ervin, "Assault and Battery. Wife vs. Husband," *The University Law Review*, v. 111, No. 3 (February 1897), 67–74.

28. George K. Behlmer, *Child Abuse and Moral Reform in England, 1870–1908* (Stanford, Calif.: Stanford University Press, 1982), 13–15. See also Janet R. Lambertz, "Male-Female Violence in Late Victorian and Edwardian England," unpublished B.A. thesis, Harvard University, December 1979; and Nancy Tomes, "A 'Torrent of Abuse': Crimes of Violence Between Working-Class Men and Women in London, 1840–1875," *Journal of Social History* v. 11, No. 3 (Spring 1978), 328–345. A somewhat similar law, providing steeper penalties for assaulting a woman, child, or elderly person, was enacted in France during the Revolution. Roderick Phillips, "Women and Family Breakdown in Eighteenth-Century France: Rouen 1780–1800," *Social History*, v. 1, No. 2 (May 1976), 202.

29. Quoted in Margaret May, "Violence in the Family: An Historical Perspective," in J. P. Martin, ed., *Violence and the Family* (New York: John Wiley, 1978), 44. Police statistics assembled in the first years after the law was passed showed that most of those charged under this law were men who assaulted women in public brawls. Arrests of such men were four times as numerous as arrests of wife beaters; very few parents were detained for assaulting their children.

30. Keith Thomas, *Man and the Natural World: A History of the Modern Sensibility* (New York: Pantheon Books, 1983), chapt. IV; and James Turner, *Reckoning*

with the Beast: Animals, Pain, and Humanity in the Victorian Mind (Baltimore: Johns Hopkins University Press, 1980), chapt. II.

31. The efforts of Stanton and Anthony on behalf of victimized women are described in Elizabeth H. Pleck, "Feminist Responses to 'Crimes Against Women,' 1868–1896," *Signs: Journal of Women and Culture*, v. 8, No. 3 (Spring 1983), 452–458.

CHAPTER 4. PROTECTING THE INNOCENTS

1. Mason P. Thomas, "Child Abuse and Neglect: Historical Overview, Legal Matrix, and Social Perspectives," *North Carolina Law Review*, v. 50 (1972), 344.

2. The details on the case of Mary Ellen can be found in *The New York Times* (April 10, 1874), 8; (April 11), 2; (June 2), 8; (December 7), 3–4; (December 27), 12; and (December 29), 2. Some of these news stories are reprinted in Robert H. Bremner, ed., *Children and Youth in America: A Documentary History*, v. 2 (Cambridge, Mass.: Harvard University Press, 1970), 185–192. Information about Mary Ellen's later life can be found in Catherine J. Ross, "Society's Children: The Care of Indigent Youngsters in New York City, 1875–1903," unpublished Ph.D. dissertation, Yale University, 1977, 23.

3. "The Beginning of Child Protection: 'The Case of Mary Ellen' as told by her rescuer, Mrs. Etta Angell Wheeler," *The National Humane Review* (August 1913), 183.

4. Wright's obituary appeared in *The New York Times* (August 22, 1879), 5.

5. Ibid.

6. Joseph M. Hawes, *Children in Urban Society: Juvenile Delinquency in Nineteenth Century America* (New York: Oxford University Press, 1971); Anthony M. Platt, *The Child Savers: The Invention of Delinquency* (Chicago: University of Chicago Press, 1969); Barbara J. Nelson, *Making an Issue of Child Abuse: Political Agenda Setting for Social Problems* (Chicago: University of Chicago Press, 1983), 7–8, 53–56; and Catherine J. Ross, "The Lessons of the Past: Defining and Controlling Child Abuse in the United States," in George Gerbner, Catherine J. Ross, and Edward Ziegler, eds., *Child Abuse: An Agenda for Action* (New York: Oxford University Press, 1980), 63–81.

7. Barbara J. Nelson, *Making an Issue of Child Abuse*. For an account of the origins of anticruelty societies in Britain, see George K. Behlmer, *Child Abuse and Moral Reform 1870–1908*, (Stanford: Stanford University Press, 1982) chapt. 3. More information about the founding of the societies can also be found in Roswell C. McCrea, *The Humane Movement* (New York: Columbia University Press, 1910); and Sydney H. Coleman, *Humane Society Leaders in America* (Albany, N.Y.: American Humane Association, 1924); and William J. Schultz, *The Humane Movement in the United States, 1910–1922* (New York: Columbia University Press, 1924).

8. R. E. Apthorp, *First Annual Report*, MSPCC (Boston: Wright and Potter, 1881), 7.

9. George K. Behlmer, *Child Abuse and Moral Reform*, 90. For a representative statement of children's rights from the 1890s, see Rev. Anna Garlin Spencer, "Social Responsibility Towards Child Life," in Anna Garlin Spencer and Charles Wesley Birtwell, eds., *The Care of Dependent, Neglected, and Wayward Children* (Baltimore:

Johns Hopkins University Press, 1894), 2–15. The growth in rhetoric about children's rights in the Progressive era is traced in N. Ray Hiner, "Children's Rights, Corporal Punishment, and Child Abuse: Changing American Attitudes, 1870–1920," *Bulletin of the Menninger Clinic*, v. 43, No. 3 (1979), 233–248.

10. David J. Rothman, *The Discovery of the Asylum: Social Order and Disorder in the New Republic* (Boston: Little, Brown, 1971), 206–210.

11. Neil Howard Cogan, "Juvenile Law, Before and After the Entrance of 'Parens Patriae,'" *South Carolina Law Review*, v. 22, No. 2 (Spring 1970), 147–181.

12. New York *Sun*, February 5, 1875, as quoted in Catherine Ross, "Society's Children: The Case of Indigent Youngsters in New York City, 1875–1903," unpublished Ph.D. dissertation, Yale University, 1977, 51.

13. *New York Times* (Dec. 28, 1874), as quoted in Robert H. Bremner, ed., *Children and Youth in America* (Cambridge, Mass.: Harvard University Press, 1970), 191–192.

14. The appellate cases that fell in this category were those in which a parent or guardian was charged with assault or battery on his or her child. Those upholding the more expansive definition of child cruelty were *State* v. *Bitman*, 13 Iowa 485; *Commonwealth* v. *Barker*, 1 Brewster 311; *State* v. *Harris*, 63 N.C. 1; *Fletcher* v. *People*, 52 Ill. 395; *Neal* v. *State*, 54 Ga. 281; *Stanfield* v. *State*, 43 Texas 167, and *Commonwealth* v. *Coffey*, 121 Mass. 66. The exception was *State* v. *Alford*, 63 N.C. 322.

15. The ruling in *State* v. *Alford* was also upheld in another case of child cruelty decided by the North Carolina State Supreme Court in 1886, *State* v. *Jones*, 95 N.C. 588. For a general review of this and other child cruelty cases, see Monrad G. Paulsen, "The Legal Framework for Child Protection," *Columbia Law Review*, LXVI (1966), 679–717.

16. *The People* v. *Turner*, 55 Ill. 280.

17. *Commonwealth* v. *Jane Barker*, 1 Brewster 311; and *Stanfield* v. *State*, 43 Texas 167.

18. James Turner, *Reckoning with the Beast: Animals, Pain, and Humanity in the Victorian Mind* (Baltimore: Johns Hopkins University Press, 1980), 131–133.

19. *New York Times* (January 27, 1872), 3.

20. Manuscript Docket Books, Court of Quarter Sessions, Philadelphia, Pennsylvania, 1839–1901, City Archives of Philadelphia, Pa. Professor Roger Lane graciously supplied me with this data, which he used in his study of murder in nineteenth-century Philadelphia. Edith Abbott called attention to the impact of the Civil War on crime in "Crime and War," *Journal of Criminal Law and Criminology*, v. 9 (1981), 32–45. Edwin Powell's criminal statistics for police arrests in Buffalo show that murder and assault rates rose dramatically at the end of the Civil War. This postbellum violent crime wave cannot be solely attributed to an increased willingness of the police to make arrests, since the arrest rate for violent crimes grew twice as fast as the total arrest rate. Edwin H. Powell, "Crime as a Function of Anomie," *Journal of Criminal Law, Criminology, and Police Science*, v. 57, No. 2 (June 1956), 161–171. Similarly, the crime rate in Boston between 1867 and 1874 grew twice as fast as the increase in the city's police force. Theodore H. Ferdinand, "The Criminal Patterns of Boston Since 1848," *American Journal of Sociology*, v. 73, No. 1 (July 1967), 84–99.

21. Michael Grossberg traces the late nineteenth-century appellate cases concerning the state's right to intervene in abusing and neglectful families. See Michael Craig

Grossberg, "The Law and the Family in Nineteenth Century America," unpublished Ph.D. dissertation, Brandeis University, 1979, 587–660. Mason Thomas reviews some of the same cases as well as those from the antebellum period in "Child Abuse and Neglect," 327–349.

22. "The Rise of Child Protection," *National Humane Review* (January–February 1962), 19.

23. Quoted in Sydney H. Coleman, *Humane Society Leaders in America*, 81. The standard view of the late nineteenth-century societies can be found in Joyce Antler and Stephen Antler, "From Child Rescue to Family Protection: The Evolution of the Child Protective Movement in the United States," *Children and Youth Services Review*, v. 1 (1979), 177–204; and Michael B. Katz, *Poverty and Policy in American History* (New York: Academic Press, 1983), 193–194. These authors have paid insufficient attention to the actual operation of the late nineteenth-century societies and have assumed that the societies were more powerful and more prosecutorial than they in fact were.

24. Quoted in William J. Schultz, *The Humane Movement in the United States, 1910–1922*, 202.

25. One child who published later his reminiscences about the intervention of the NYSPCC was the comedian Buster Keaton. As early as age three, he appeared in his father's slapstick act as "the human mop," batted about by his father. The act consisted of Buster's father hitting him harder and harder. Buster's three-year-old brother and five-year-old sister were brought into the act, and they, too, hit each other. Buster was frequently bruised and beaten during his performances. On one occasion his father threw him into scenery with a brick wall behind it and kicked him in the head, knocking him unconscious. After this incident, his father still allowed him to appear in the matinee right after he regained consciousness. On and off the stage, Buster's father gave him "a good clout on the backside," which Buster believed (as a child and an adult) was not cruel, but rather justifiable punishment. Americans found this stage portrayal of family violence hilarious; the English were not amused. Because English audiences did not laugh at the act, stage promoters in England urged Buster's father to temper his onstage rough treatment of his son. The English even assumed that Buster was adopted because a natural father would not treat his own son so cruelly.

Around 1900 the NYSPCC accused Buster's father of mistreating him on the stage. Acting on the basis of the society's complaints, two successive New York City mayors ordered Buster to their offices to see if he was bruised. The society also sought to prohibit Buster from working because of his age (he was seven). But the NYSPCC lost its case in court, and the Keatons were never prohibited from performing. Buster Keaton, *My Wonderful World of Slapstick* (Garden City, N.Y.: Doubleday, 1960), 12–71.

26. For the expectations of the MSPCC regarding good fathers and mothers, see Linda Gordon, "Child Abuse, Gender, and the Myth of Family Independence: An Historical Critique," *Child Welfare*, v. LXIV, No. 3 (May–June 1985), 213–224, especially 214–216.

27. The same pattern was found in the records of the MSPCC as in those of the PSPCC and the Illinois Humane Society. See Linda Gordon's article, "Incest as a Form of Family Violence: Evidence from Historical Case Records," *Journal of Marriage and the Family*, v. 46, No. 1 (February, 1984), 27–34.

28. Linda Gordon, "Child Abuse, Gender, and the Myth of Family Independence: An Historical Critique," *Child Welfare*, v. LXIV, No. 3 (May–June 1985), 220.

29. The Brooklyn Society for the Prevention of Cruelty to Children, *Fourth Annual Report, 1884* (Brooklyn: Union Book, 1884), 4.

30. *Massachusetts Society for the Prevention of Cruelty to Children, Tenth Annual Report for 1885* (Boston: Wright and Potter, 1886), 12.

31. Figures were compiled from the annual reports of the PSPCC, 1879–1883, 1886–1888, 1890–1898, 1900–1901, 1904–1913, and 1920–1935. By modern standards, 12 percent is quite high. Only 6 percent of the cases handled by the Massachusetts Society to Prevent Cruelty to Children in 1960 involved physical abuse of a child. Alfred Kadushin, *Child Welfare Services* (New York: Macmillan, 1967), 218.

32. Figures pertaining to the NYSPCC were compiled from their annual reports for 1887, 1890, and 1892–1913. In this respect, the British anticruelty societies were quite different. Of the children on whose behalf the National Society to Prevent Cruelty to Children intervened between 1889 and 1903, less than 1 percent were removed from parental custody. One does not know whether the denominator in this figure is the number of cases reported to the society or the number of such cases they investigated. If it was the latter figure, then the English anticruelty society intervened far less often than its American counterparts. The English considered legislation in Parliament to protect children from cruelty the year before the NYSPCC was founded. The bill never even came up for debate, apparently because the idea of state intervention in the family was too controversial. Actually, punishment of assault against women and children had become law by the 1850s. But the much touchier subject, from the British point of view, was the removal of children from their natural parents. George K. Behlmer, *Child Abuse and Moral Reform in England, 1870–1908*, 42–43, 175.

33. Linda Gordon argues that in providing battered women with some assistance in securing charity or legal aid, the MSPCC contributed more to helping battered women than it did to protecting children from cruelty. Linda Gordon, "Child Abuse, Gender, and the Myth of Family Independence: An Historical Critique," *Child Welfare*, v. LXIV, No. 3 (May–June 1985), 221.

34. Unpublished Case Record, Illinois Humane Society, Dec. 1881, Archives, University of Illinois, Chicago Circle.

35. The typical pattern of temporary removal of children is described by Priscilla Ferguson Clement in "Families and Foster Care: Philadelphia in the Late Nineteenth Century," *Social Service Review*, v. 53, No. 3 (September 1979), 406–420, and Catherine Ross, "Society's Children," 119, 174, 181.

36. Grafton D. Cushing, "Work of Societies for the Prevention of Cruelty to Children Essential in the Prevention of Crime," in The National Conference on Social Welfare, *Proceedings of the National Conference on Charities and Correction* (Philadelphia: privately published, 1906), 110.

37. Massachusetts Society to Prevent Cruelty to Children, *Annual Report, 1883* (Boston: Wright and Potter, 1883), 13.

38. Ibid., *Twenty-seventh Annual Report, 1907* (Boston: George Ellis, 1907), 17.

39. Ibid., *Forty-fifth Annual Report, 1925* (Boston: George Ellis, 1926), 26.

40. White House Conference on Child Health and Protection, *Section IV—The Handicapped: Prevention, Maintenance, Protection* (New York: Appleton-Century, 1933), 23.

CHAPTER 5. THE PURE WOMAN AND THE BRUTISH MAN

A previous version of this chapter appeared as "Feminist Responses to 'Crimes Against Women,' 1868–1896," *Signs: A Journal of Women in Culture,*" v. 8, No. 2 (Spring 1983), 451–470.

1. Books and articles concerning the social purity movement and the campaign against prostitution in Victorian England include Judith R. Walkowitz, *Prostitution and Victorian Society: Women, Class and the State* (New York: Cambridge University Press, 1980); Deborah Gorham, "The 'Maiden Tribute of Modern Babylon' Reexamined: Child Prostitution and the Idea of Childhood in Late-Victorian England," *Victorian Studies,* 21 (Spring 1978), 353–369; Paul McHugh, *Prostitution and Victorian Social Reform* (New York: St. Martin's Press, 1980); Jeffrey Weeks, *Sex, Politics and Society* (London: Longmans, 1981), chapt. 5; Edward J. Bristow, *Vice and Vigilance: Purity Movements in Britain Since 1700* (London: Gill and Macmillan, 1977); Judith R. Walkowitz, "Male Vice and Female Virtue: Feminism and the Politics of Prostitution in Nineteenth-Century Britain," in Ann Snitow, Christine Stansell, and Sharon Thompson, eds., *Powers of Desire: The Politics of Sexuality* (New York: Monthly Review Press, 1983), 419–438.

The major study of the social purity movement in the United States is David J. Pivar's, *Purity Crusade: Sexual Morality and Social Control, 1868–1900* (Westport, Conn.: Greenwood Press, 1973). In their books Linda Gordon, Carl Degler, and William Leach have each explored the ideas of social purity writers. William Leach, *True Love and Perfect Union: The Feminist Reform of Sex and Society* (New York: Basic Books, 1980); Linda Gordon, *Woman's Body, Woman's Right* (New York: Grossman Publishers, 1976), chapt. 6; Carl N. Degler, *At Odds: Women and the Family in America from the Revolution to the Present* (New York: Oxford University Press, 1980), chapts. IX and XI. Linda Gordon and Ellen DuBois present a cogent summary of the reasons why prostitution was the major concern of social purity reformers in their article, "Seeking Ecstasy on the Battlefield: Danger and Pleasure in Nineteenth-Century Feminist Sexual Thought," *Feminist Studies,* v. 9, No. 1 (Spring 1983), 7–25.

2. The work of antebellum female moral reform societies is described in Carroll Smith-Rosenberg, "Beauty, the Beast and the Militant Woman: A Case Study in Sex Roles and Social Stress in Jacksonian America," *American Quarterly,* v. 23 (October 1971), 562–584; and also in Mary P. Ryan, "The Power of Women's Networks: A Case Study of Female Moral Reform in Antebellum America," *Feminist Studies,* v. 5 (Spring 1979), 66–85.

3. David J. Pivar, *Purity Crusade: Sexual Morality and Social Control, 1868–1900* (Westport, Conn.: Greenwood Press, 1973), 51.

4. Victoria Woodhull, as quoted in Ruth Rosen, *The Lost Sisterhood: Prostitution in America, 1900–1918* (Baltimore: Johns Hopkins University Press, 1982), 56.

5. Joan Jacobs Brumberg, "Zenanas and Girlless Villages: The Ethnology of American Evangelical Women, 1870–1910," *Journal of American History,* v. 69, No. 2 (September 1982), 347–371. Two antebellum advocates of "free love," T. L. Nichols and Mary S. Gove Nichols, probably provided the first ethnography of the customs of other countries to demonstrate the victimization of women. Their book was entitled *Marriage: Its History, Character and Results, Its Sanctities, and its Profanities: Science and its Facts* (New York: privately published, 1854), 53–54, 60, 62–65.

6. Lucinda Chandler, as quoted in Linda Gordon, *Woman's Body, Woman's Right* (New York: Grossman Publishers, 1976), 105. For contemporary sociological studies of marital rape, see Diana E. H. Russell, *Rape in Marriage* (New York: Macmillan, 1982); and David Finkelhor and Kersti Yllo, *License to Rape: Sexual Abuse of Wives* (New York: Holt, Rinehart, and Winston, 1985).

7. Eliza B. Duffey, *The Relations of the Sexes* (New York: Wood and Holbrook, 1876), 195–224. Peter Gay challenges vigorously the stereotype of the Victorian as sexually repressed, but minimizes the frequency of violence and brutality in the Victorian bedroom. Peter Gay, *The Bourgeois Experience: Victoria to Freud*, v. 1 (New York: Oxford University Press, 1984), 287–294.

8. Page Smith, *Daughters of the Promised Land, Women in American History* (Boston: Little Brown, 1970), 228.

9. Instances of physical violence figures in 27 percent of women's complaints and 10 percent of men's in Los Angeles divorce applications from 1880. Elaine Tyler May, "The Pursuit of Domestic Perfection: Marriage and Divorce in Los Angeles, 1890–1920," unpublished Ph.D. dissertation, University of California, 1975, 212. For an additional case, see Robert L. Griswold, "Sexual Cruelty and the Case for Divorce in Victorian America," *Signs: Journal of Women in Culture*, v. II, No. 3 (Spring 1986), 529–541.

10. Robert L. Griswold, *Family and Divorce in California, 1850–1890: Victorian Illusion and Everyday Realities* (Albany: State University of New York Press, 1982), 116.

11. Elaine Tyler May, *Great Expectations: Marriage and Divorce in Post-Victorian America* (Chicago: University of Chicago Press, 1980), 35.

12. Ibid., 36.

13. David Pivar, *Purity Crusade*, 80–81.

14. William Leach, *True Love and Perfect Union*, 89.

15. Unpublished case record, Illinois Humane Society, December 5, 1900, University of Illinois at Chicago Circle, Archives.

16. *First Annual Report of the Protective Agency for Women and Children, 1897* (Chicago, 1887), 13. Mari Jo Buhle first told me about the existence of this organization.

17. Ibid., 11.

18. Ibid., 10.

19. *Third Annual Report of the Protective Agency for Women and Children, 1889*, 10.

20. *First Annual Report of the Protective Agency for Women and Children, 1887*, 10.

21. *Eleventh Annual Report of the Protective Agency for Women and Children, 1897*, 14; Reginald Heber Smith and John S. Bradway, *Growth of Legal-Aid Work in the United States*, Bulletin No. 67 (Washington, D.C.: U.S. Department of Labor, 1936), 201, 207. Legal Aid in Chicago appears to have been the only legal aid society that emerged from a woman's protective agency.

22. T. N. Soper, *Green Bluff: A Temperance Story* (Boston: Rand, Avery and Co., 1874); Rev. J. P. Newman, D. D., in *Temperance Sermons Delivered in Response to an Invitation of the National Temperance Society and Publication House* (New York, 1873), 81, 115; Ian Gough, *Sunlight and Shadow, or Gleanings from My Life Work* (Hartford, Conn.: A. O. Worthington, 1881), 256–258.

23. Quoted in Barbara Epstein, *The Politics of Domesticity: Women, Evangelism, and Temperance in Nineteenth-Century America* (Middletown, Conn.: Wesleyan University Press, 1981), 104.

24. "The Drunkard's Wife," Music by L. L. Pickett, lyrics by M. W. Knapp, 1894, reprinted in Donald M. Scott and Bernard Wishy, eds., *America's Families: A Documentary History* (New York: Harper & Row, 1982), 357–358.

25. Both Barbara Epstein and Ruth Bordin view temperance women as more concerned with defending the family than with securing for women the right to equal citizenship. Barbara Leslie Epstein, *The Politics of Domesticity*; and Ruth Bordin, *Women and Temperance: The Search for Power and Liberty, 1873–1900* (Philadelphia: Temple University Press, 1981). On Elizabeth Cady Stanton's view of the Women's Temperance Crusade of 1873–1874, the precursor of the WCTU, see Jack S. Blocker, Jr., "Separate Paths: Suffragists and the Women's Temperance Crusade," *Signs: Journal of Women in Culture and Society*, v. 10, No. 3 (Spring 1985), 460–476.

26. Barbara Leslie Epstein, *The Politics of Domesticity*, 134; Ruth Bordin, *Women and Temperance*, p. 14.

27. Janet Giele, "Social Change in the Feminine Role: A Comparison of Woman's Suffrage and Woman's Temperance, 1870–1920," unpublished Ph.D. dissertation, Radcliffe College, 1961, 120–125, 142–149.

28. Henry Campbell Black, *A Treatise on the Laws Regulating the Manufacture and Sale of Intoxicating Liquors* (St. Paul, Minn.: West Publishing, 1892), 277–377.

29. *Wilson v. Booth*, 57 Mich. 249; *Woman's Journal* (April 19, 1877), 41.

30. Ruth Bordin, *Women and Temperance*, 103; Richard D. Sexton, "The San Diego Woman's Home Association: A Volunteer Charity Organization," *Journal of San Diego History*, v. XXIX, No. 1 (Winter 1983), 1–53. The WCTU also engaged in the rescue of prostitutes and established homes for unwed mothers. Joan Brumberg provides a case study of their work in one community in " 'Ruined' Girls: Changing Community Responses to Illegitimacy in Upstate New York, 1890–1920," *Journal of Social History*, v. 18, No. 2 (Winter 1984), 247–272. On the Sanctificationists of Belton, Texas, who preached that God did not demand that a wife remain with a drunken husband and who founded their own community, see Eleanor James, "The Sanctificationists of Belton," *The American West*, v. 2, No. 3 (Summer 1965), 65–73. The Sisters of Mercy, established in 1843, provided Mercy Houses for women in distress who required temporary housing. They do not appear to have urged battered women to reconcile with their husbands. Hasia R. Diner, *Erin's Daughters in America: Irish Immigrant Women in the Nineteenth Century* (Baltimore: Johns Hopkins University Press, 1983), 57.

31. *Woman's Journal* (January 18, 1879).

32. *Woman's Journal* (December 3, 1870).

33. At the time Stone published her catalog, crimes against women were in fact specific violations of the criminal code. Wife beating was punishable as assault and battery and wife murder as murder or manslaughter. Under Massachusetts law the husband never enjoyed the right to moderate correction of his wife. If there was any remaining doubt that wife beating was a crime under Massachusetts law, it was decided by the Massachusetts Supreme Court in 1871 in *Commonwealth v. Hugh McAfee*. McAfee was indicted for manslaughter in striking and beating his wife, who was drunk, on the head and body. She fell on a chair and suffered a concussion that

killed her. The state supreme court ruled that "the beating of the defendant's wife was unlawful . . . There is no authority in its favor in this Commonwealth. Beating or striking a wife violently with the open hand is not one of the rights conferred on a husband by the marriage, even if the wife be drunk or insolent." *Commonwealth* v. *McAfee*, 458 Mass., 1871.

A wife who left her husband because he beat her could apply for both a protection order requiring him to vacate her premises and forbidding him from forcing her to return, and an order of support. If a wife or her child was injured by a drunken husband, the wife could sue the saloonkeeper for damages. Finally, a husband convicted of assaulting his wife was required to post a bond for up to two years. Yet there were difficulties in enforcing any of these provisions. A wife had to swear out a complaint against her husband, and, in some jurisdictions, police were instructed not to arrest a man unless they saw him commit a violent act. If a husband claimed to have reformed and demanded his wife's return, his wife was legally required to go back to him. On Massachusetts law regarding wife assault, see *Acts and Resolves Passed by the General Court of Massachusetts, 1874* (Boston: Wright and Potter, 1874), 132–133; George A. O. Ernst, *The Legal Status of Married Women in Massachusetts* (Boston: Massachusetts Woman Suffrage Association, 1895), 23, 24; *Massachusetts Laws, Statutes, Acts and Resolves Passed by the General Court of Massachusetts in the Year of 1879* (Boston: Rand, Avery and Co., 1879), 444.

34. *Woman's Journal* (January 28, 1877).

35. Judith Becker Ranlett, "Sorority and Community: Women's Answer to a Changing Massachusetts, 1865–1895," unpublished Ph.D. dissertation, Brandeis University, 1974, 141; Elinor Rice Hays, *Morning Star: A Biography of Lucy Stone, 1818–1893* (New York: Harcourt, Brace, and World, 1961), 266.

36. *Woman's Journal* (January 28, 1877).

37. Ibid. (May 15, 1875).

38. *Journal of the House of Representatives of the Commonwealth of Massachusetts, 1879* (Boston: Rand, Avery and Co., 1879), 110; *Documents of the House of Representatives of the Commonwealth of Massachusetts, 1879* (Boston: Rand, Avery and Co., 1879), 1–2; "Legal Relief for Assaulted Wives," *Woman's Journal* (January 11, 1879), 12; "Legal Redress for Assaulted Wives," *Woman's Journal* (January, 1879), 20; *Journal of the House of Representatives of the Commonwealth of Massachusetts, 1892* (Boston: Wright and Potter, 1892), 139, 453, 468.

39. Frances Power Cobbe, "Wife Torture in England," *Contemporary Review*, (April 1878), 57.

40. On the legislative history of the passage of the Matrimonial Causes Act of 1878, see Mary Lyndon Shanley, "Wifebeating and the Victorian Conscience: the Matrimonial Causes Act of 1878," unpublished paper delivered at the annual meeting of the American Political Science Association, September 1985. See also Carol Bauer and Lawrence Ritt, " 'A Husband is a Beating Animal': Frances Power Cobbe Confronts the Wife-Abuse Problem in Victorian England," *International Journal of Women's Studies*, v. 6, No. 2 (March/April 1983), 99–118.

Anthony Wohl provides all the reasons why the English did not take up the question of incest, and yet by American standards, they discussed incest quite often. Anthony S. Wohl, "Sex and the Single Room: Incest Among the Victorian Working Classes," in Anthony S. Wohl, ed., *The Victorian Family: Structure and Stresses* (New York: St. Martin's Press, 1978), 197–216.

41. Janet R. Lambertz, "Male-Female Violence in Late Victorian and Edwardian England," unpublished B.A. thesis, Harvard University, December 1979, 103–105, 119–120; O. R. McGregor, *Divorce in England: A Centenary Study* (Melbourne: Heineman, 1957), 23–24; Iris Minor, "Working-Class Women and Matrimonial Law Reform, 1890–1914," in David E. Martin and David Rubinstein, eds., *Ideology and the Labour Movement: Essays Presented to John Saville* (London: Croom and Helm, 1979), 103–124; and Carol Bauer and Lawrence Ritt, "Wife-Abuse, Late Victorian English Feminists, and the Legacy of Frances Power Cobbe," *International Journal of Women's Studies*, v. 6, No. 3 (May/June 1983), 195–207.

42. *Woman's Journal* (April 8, 1892).

43. Ibid. (January 11, 1879) and (January 18, 1879).

CHAPTER 6. BRINGING BACK THE WHIPPING POST

A previous version of this paper, entitled, "The Whipping Post for Wife Beaters, 1876–1906," was published in Leslie Page Moch and Gary D. Stark, eds., *Essays on the Family and Historical Change* (College Station: Texas A and M University Press, 1983), 127–149.

1. *Woman's Journal* (July 11, 1885), 220.

2. *Woman's Journal* (January 29, 1876), (June 11, 1881). When this bill was defeated, its sponsor substituted another one to punish wife beaters with a three- to ten-year prison term. The revised bill also lost. See *Documents Printed by the Order of the House of Representatives of the Commonwealth of Massachusetts, 1884* (Boston: Wright and Potter, 1884).

3. Howard M. Jenkins, "Live Wood in Our Whipping Post," *Lippincott's Magazine*, v. XXIII, No. 135 (March 1879), 368; Elbridge T. Gerry, "Must We Have the Cat-O'-Nine Tails," *North American Review*, v. 100, No. 3 (March 1895), 318–325; Thirtieth Annual Report, *Illinois Humane Society* (Chicago: privately printed, 1899), 56–58; and *Public Opinion*, v. XXVI, No. 2 (June 8, 1899), 718.

4. The twelve states that considered legislation to punish wife beating with the whipping post were California (1876), Missouri (1879), Maryland (1882), Massachusetts (1884 and 1905), Pennsylvania (1885), New Hampshire (1885), New York (1895), New Jersey (1898, 1901), Virginia (1899–1900), Illinois (1899), Delaware (1901), and Oregon (1905). The U.S. Congress, acting as the legislative body for the District of Columbia, debated a whipping-post bill in 1906.

5. American Bar Association, *Report of the Ninth Annual Meeting of the American Bar Association* (Philadelphia: T. and J. W. Johnson, 1886), 287, and Simeon E. Baldwin, "How to Deal with Habitual Criminals," *Journal of Social Science*, v. 22 (1886), 162–171.

6. Elizabeth H. Pleck, "Wife Beating in Nineteenth-Century America," *Victimology*, v. 4, No. 1 (1979), 60–74; Matilda Joslyn Gage, *Woman, Church and State* (New York: 1893; reprint, Watertown, Mass.: Persephone Press, 1981), 331; National Association for the Advancement of Colored People, *Thirty Years of Lynching in the United States, 1889–1918* (New York: National Association for the Advancement of Colored People, 1919), 63, 80, 82, 92, and Madeline M. Noble, "The White Caps of Harrison and Crawford County, Indiana: A Study in the Violent Enforcement of Morality," unpublished Ph.D. dissertation, University of Michigan, 1973, 70–71.

7. *Woman's Journal* (January 29, 1876); *Appleton's Annual Cyclopaedia and Register of Important Events, 1879,* 639; Marion S. Goldman, *Gold Diggers and Silver Miners: Prostitution and Social Life on the Comstock Lode* (Ann Arbor: University of Michigan Press, 1981), 45.

8. *Report of the Tenth Annual Meeting of the American Bar Association,* 64.

9. Simeon E. Baldwin, "Corporal Punishments for Crime," *Medico-Legal Journal,* v. 17, No. 1 (1899), 87.

10. Maryland, House of Delegates, *Journal of the Proceedings of the House of Delegates of Maryland, General Assembly, January Session, 1882* (Annapolis: State of Maryland, 1882), 62, 199, 253, 448.

11. *Report of the Tenth Annual Meeting of the American Bar Association* (Philadelphia: T. and J. W. Johnson, 1887), 293. Richard Maxwell Brown in *Strain of Violence: Historical Studies of American Violence and Vigilantism* (New York: Oxford University Press, 1975), 177, argues that Simeon Baldwin favored the whipping post and castration because of the "prevalence of lynch law and viligantism in the nineteenth century [which] had brutalized attitudes." He neglects to point out that many English favored corporal punishment for criminals, in spite of the absence of lynching there. He conveys his own attitude toward wife beating in the statement, "the White Caps were using whipping all over the country as an extralegal punishment for wife beating, immorality, shiftlessness, and petty thievery—precisely the sort of *small offense* [italics added] against which the movement to legalize whipping was mainly directed."

12. *Report of the Ninth Annual Meeting of the American Bar Association* (Philadelphia: Dando Printing and Publishing, 1886), 293.

13. American Bar Association, *Report of the Tenth Annual Meeting,* 63.

14. Ibid., 58.

15. Ibid., 57.

16. Ibid., 58.

17. Ibid., 78.

18. Ibid., 69.

19. Ibid., 78.

20. Simeon Baldwin, "The Restoration of Whipping as a Punishment for Crime," *The Green Bag,* v. XIII, No. 1 (January 1901), 66; and Simeon Baldwin, "Whipping and Castration as Punishments for Crime," *Yale Law Journal,* v. VIII, No. 9 (June 1899), 371–386.

21. Joel Williamson, *The Crucible of Race: Black-White Relations in the American South Since Emancipation* (New York: Oxford University Press, 1984), chapt. 4, especially 112–115.

22. Simeon Baldwin, *The American Judiciary* (New York: The Century Co., 1925), 246–247.

23. *New York Times* (February 23, 1918).

24. "Transactions," *Medico-Legal Journal,* v. 17, No. 1 (1899), 117–118, and Clark Bell, "Wife Beaters and their Punishment," *Medico-Legal Journal,* v. 21, No. 3 (1904), 317–322.

25. Robert Caldwell, *Red Hannah: Delaware's Whipping Post* (Philadelphia: University of Pennsylvania Press, 1947), 32; and *Public Opinion,* v. VI, No. 23 (June 8, 1899), 2718.

26. Robert Caldwell, *Red Hannah,* 33.

27. Fred L. Israel, ed., *The State of the Union: Messages of the Presidents, 1790–1966*, v. 2 (New York: Chelsea House, 1977), 2116.

28. State of Oregon, *The General Laws, 1905* (Salem, Ore.: J. R. Whitney, 1905), 335–336.

29. *Congressional Record-House* (February 12, 1906), 2451.

30. Ibid., 2452.

31. Robert Caldwell, *Red Hannah*, 131.

32. "Delaware's Whipping Post," *The Literary Digest*, v. XLVII (December 6, 1913), 1100–1101; and "The Whipping Post in Delaware," *Medico-Legal Journal*, v. 24 (1906–1907), 662–663.

33. "Whipping as a Mode of Punishment," *Journal of the American Institute of Criminal Law and Criminology*, v. III (May 1912–March 1913), 945–947.

34. Clark Bell, "The Cat as a Deterrent for Crime," *Journal of the American Institute of Criminal Law and Criminology*, v. III (May 1912–March 1913), 945–947.

35. Ibid.

36. Robert Caldwell, *Red Hannah*, 49; and *New York Times* (April 19, 1925), XX.

37. Roger Brown, *Social Psychology* (New York: Free Press, 1965), 520.

38. *Boston Globe* (November 19, 1983); *Bangor Daily News* (January 7, 1979), 34, as quoted in Douglas J. Besharov, "Child Protection: Past Progress, Present Problems and Future Direction," *Family Law Quarterly*, v. XVII, No. 2 (Summer 1983), 157–158; Vicki McNickle Rose, "Rape as a Social Problem: A Byproduct of the Feminist Movement," *Social Problems*, v. 25, No. 1 (October, 1977), 75–89.

39. Terry Davidson, *Conjugal Crime: Understanding and Changing the Wifebeating Pattern* (New York: Hawthorn Books, 1978), 103.

40. Carol Felsenthal, *The Sweetheart of the Silent Majority: The Biography of Phyllis Schlafly* (Garden City, N.Y.: Doubleday, 1981), 273.

CHAPTER 7. THE SOCIALIZED COURTS

1. Jonah J. Goldstein, *The Family in Court* (New York: Clark Boardman, 1934), 4.

2. On the rise of the juvenile court, see Robert M. Mennel, *Thorns and Thistles: Juvenile Delinquents in the United States, 1825–1940* (Hanover, N.H.: University of New Hampshire, 1973); Ellen Ryerson, *The Best-Laid Plans: America's Juvenile Court Experiment* (New York: Hill and Wang, 1978); Anthony M. Platt, *The Child Savers: The Invention of Delinquency* (Chicago: University of Chicago Press, 1969); Steven L. Schlossman, *Love and the American Delinquent: The Theory and Practice of Progressive Juvenile Justice, 1825–1920* (Chicago: University of Chicago Press, 1977); and David J. Rothman, *Conscience and Convenience: The Asylum and Its Alternatives in Progressive America* (Boston: Little, Brown, 1980).

3. Jacques Donzelot, *The Policing of Families* (New York: Random House, 1977); Christopher Lasch, *Haven in a Heartless World: The Family Besieged* (New York: Basic Books, 1977).

4. Linda Gordon, "Child Abuse, Gender, and the Myth of Family Independence: An Historical Critique," *Child Welfare*, v. LXIV, No. 3 (May–June 1985), 213–224.

5. Bernhard Rabbino, *Back to the Home* (New York: Court Press, 1933), 81.

6. Sophonisba P. Breckinridge and Helen R. Jeter, U.S. Children's Bureau Pub-

lication No. 70, *A Summary of Juvenile Court Legislation in the United States* (Washington, D.C.: U.S. Government Printing Office, 1920), 19.

7. U.S. Department of Labor, Children's Bureau Publication No. 195, *Juvenile Court Statistics* (Washington, D.C.: U. S. Government Printing Office, 1929), 31; U.S. Department of Labor, Children's Bureau Publication No. 200, *Juvenile Court Statistics, 1928* (Washington, D.C.: U.S. Government Printing Office, 1930), 26; U.S. Children's Bureau Publication No. 207, *Juvenile Court Statistics, 1929* (Washington, D.C.: U.S. Government Printing Office, 1931), 22; U.S. Children's Bureau Publication No. 212, *Juvenile Court Statistics, 1930* (Washington, D.C.: U.S. Government Printing Office, 1932), 26; U.S. Children's Bureau Publication No. 222, *Juvenile Court Statistics, 1931* (Washington, D.C.: U.S. Government Printing Office, 1933), 31; U.S. Children's Bureau Publication No. 226, *Juvenile Court Statistics and Federal Juvenile Offenders: 1932* (Washington, D.C.: U.S. Government Printing Office, 1935), 44; U.S. Children's Bureau Publication No. 232, *Juvenile Court Statistics and Federal Juvenile Offenders, 1933* (Washington, D.C.: U.S. Government Printing Office, 1936), 38; U.S. Children's Bureau, *Juvenile Court Statistics Year Ended December 31, 1934* (Washington, D.C.: U.S. Government Printing Office, 1937), 51; U.S. Children's Bureau Publication No. 245, *Juvenile Court Statistics Two-Year Period Ended December 31, 1936* (Washington, D.C.: U.S. Government Printing Office, 1939), 38.

8. In some cities, police and juvenile courts existed side-by-side with overlapping functions. It is impossible to say whether the police courts handled different kinds of children's cases than the juvenile courts.

9. Susan Tiffin, *In Whose Best Interest? Child Welfare Reform in the Progressive Era* (Westport, Conn.: Greenwood Press, 1982), 223; John Hagan and Jeffrey Leon, "Rediscovering Delinquency: Social History, Political Ideology, and the Sociology of the Law," *American Sociological Review*, v. 42, No. 4 (August 1977), Appendix 1, 596.

10. The SPCCs investigated cases for the juvenile courts. The MSPCC was the one anticruelty society to tabulate regularly data about the number of children's cases it brought to the Boston Juvenile Court. In the 1880s, the MSPCC took about a third of all children's cases to court; by the early twentieth century, the figure was closer to half. The annual report of the MSPCC between 1883 and 1935 published statistics on the number of children's cases in court for neglect, determination of guardianship, assault, and so forth.

11. Quoted in David J. Rothman, *Conscience and Convenience: The Asylum and its Alternatives in Progressive America* (Boston: Little Brown, 1980), 250.

12. Quoted in Louise de Koven Bowen, "The Early Days of the Juvenile Court," in Jane Addams, ed., *The Child, The Clinic, and the Court* (New York: New Republic, 1925), 300.

13. Miriam Van Waters, *Youth in Conflict* (New York: New Republic, 1932), 13.

14. Hastings H. Hart, *Preventive Treatment of Neglected Children* (New York: Russell Sage, 1910), 313; Susan Tiffin, *In Whose Best Interest*, 223.

15. These percentages were based on the total number of cases that appeared before a probation officer or a juvenile court judge on an official or unofficial basis. Judge Baker Guidance Center, *Harvey Humphrey Baker: Upbuilder of the Juvenile Court* (Boston: Judge Baker Foundation, 1920) 21, 49; and U.S. National Center on Child Abuse and Neglect, *National Analysis of Child Neglect and Abuse Reporting, 1978*, as cited in Douglas J. Besharov, "Child Protection: Past Progress, Present Problems, and

Future Directions," *Family Law Quarterly*, v. XVII, No. 2 (Summer 1983), 160; Robert H. Mnookin, *Child, Family and State: Problems and Materials on Children and the Law* (Boston: Little, Brown, 1978), 517. Linda Gordon explores the policy of the MSPCC toward child neglect in "Single Mothers and Child Neglect, 1880–1920," *American Quarterly*, v. 37, No. 2 (Summer 1985), 173–192.

16. U.S. Bureau of the Census, *Report of the Defective, Dependent and Delinquent Classes of the Population of the United States* (Washington, D.C.: U.S. Government Printing Office, 1888), Table CV, 443; U.S. Department of the Interior, Census Office, *Report on Crime, Pauperism, and Benevolence in the United States at the Eleventh Census: 1890*, Part II (Washington, D.C.: U.S. Government Printing Office, 1895), Table 212, 791–792; Table 213, 800–801; Table 290, 961–972; Table 291, 968–969; U.S. Bureau of the Census, *Benevolent Institutions, 1904* (Washington, D.C.: U.S. Government Printing Office, 1905), Table XII, 26; U.S. Bureau of the Census, *Paupers in Almshouses, 1910* (Washington, D.C.: U.S. Government Printing Office, 1910), Table 9, 17; U.S. Bureau of the Census, *Benevolent Institutions, 1910* (Washington, D.C.: U.S. Government Printing Office, 1913), Table 23, 31; U.S. Bureau of the Census, *Children Under Institutional Care* (Washington, D.C.: U.S. Government Printing Office, 1927); U.S. Bureau of the Census, *Children Under Institutional Care and in Foster Homes* (Washington, D.C.: U.S. Government Printing Office, 1935), Table 4, 8.

17. Quoted in David Rothman, *Conscience and Convenience*, 268–282.

18. J. Harold Williams, "A Court Hearing on Parental Neglect," *Journal of Delinquency*, v. 7, No. 3 (May 1922), 143.

19. Ibid., 144–145.

20. Ibid., 145.

21. I am using the terms "family court" and "court of domestic relations" interchangeably, although at the time, domestic relations courts referred to those courts with jurisdiction over adult cases only, whereas family courts referred to courts that handled adult and children's cases.

22. Charles W. Hoffman, "Social Aspects of the Family Court," *Journal of Criminal Law and Criminology*, (1919), 378–381.

23. Bernhard Rabbino, *Back to the Home*, 81.

24. Ibid.

25. Ibid.

26. Jacob H. Hopkins, "The Domestic Relations Court, Its Organization, Development and Possibilities," Annual Report and Proceedings, *Eighth Annual Conference of the National Probation Association* (Albany, N.Y.: National Probation Association, 1916), 64.

27. Elinor Ryan Hixenbaugh, "Reconciliation of Marital Maladjustment: An Analysis of 101 Cases," *Social Forces*, v. X, No. 1 (October 1931), 230–236.

28. Leon Stern, "Case Steps in Domestic Relations Procedure," Annual Report and Proceedings of the National Probation Association, *Social Treatment of the Delinquent* (New York: National Probation Association, 1922), 45.

29. Ibid.

30. Kate Claghorn, *The Immigrant's Day in Court* (New York: Harper and Brothers, 1923), 238.

31. Elinor Ryan Hixenbaugh, "Reconciliation of Marital Maladjustment," 230–236.

32. Leon Stern, "Case Steps in Domestic Relations Procedure," 45.

33. Sixth Annual Report, *Municipal Court of Chicago* (Chicago: no publisher, 1911), Table E, 72-F.

34. Mary Richmond, *Social Diagnosis* (New York: Russell Sage Foundation, 1917), 147.

35. Frances Perkins, who was appointed by Franklin D. Roosevelt as his Secretary of Labor, was employed after college at a social work agency. The agency's director asked her what she would do with a drunken husband who beat his wife. Perkins replied that she would have him arrested. Having come up with a response contrary to agency policy, Perkins was dispatched to "learn more of life." George Martin, *Madam Secretary: Frances Perkins* (Boston: Houghton Mifflin, 1976), 62–63.

36. Ernest R. Mowrer and Harriet R. Mowrer, *Domestic Discord: Its Analysis and Treatment* (Chicago: University of Chicago Press, 1928), 65–67; Charles L. Brown, *Address of the Municipal Court Before the Men's Club of Market Square* (Philadelphia: privately printed, 1914), 23–24.

37. Elizabeth H. Pleck, "Challenges to Traditional Authority in Immigrant Families," in Michael Gordon, ed., *The American Family in Social-Historical Perspective*, third edition (New York: St. Martin's Press, 1983), 506–509.

38. Ernest R. Mowrer and Harriet R. Mowrer, *Domestic Discord*, 65–67.

39. Ibid.

40. Ibid., 65–67.

41. Charles L. Brown, *Address of the Judge of the Municipal Court Before the Men's Club of Market Square*, 23–24.

42. Jonah J. Goldstein, *The Family in Court*, 7–8.

43. Reginald Heber Smith, *Justice and the Poor* (New York: Carnegie Foundation, 1924), 77.

44. Charles L. Brown, *Address of the Judge of the Municipal Court Before the Men's Club of Market Square*, 23–24.

45. William I. Thomas and Florian Znaniecki, *The Polish Peasant in Europe and America* (New York: 1919–1923; New York: Octagon Books, 1974), v. 2, 1143.

46. Reginald Heber Smith, as quoted in Kate Holladay Claghorn, *The Immigrant's Day in Court*, 184.

CHAPTER 8. PSYCHIATRY TAKES CONTROL

1. The work of the Psychopathic Laboratory in Chicago is described in "The Municipal Court of Chicago and Its Psychopathic Laboratory," *Medico-Legal Journal*, v. XXXIII, No. 8 (1916), 5–9. Samples of psychiatric diagnoses can be found in Elmer E. Southard and Mary Jarrett, *The Kingdom of Evils* (Boston: Little, Brown, 1922), 170–171, 260–262, 268. Battered women often tried to commit their abusive husbands to psychiatric hospitals. For some representative cases, see Elizabeth Lunbeck, "Psychiatry in the Age of Reform: Doctors, Social Workers and Patients at the Boston Psychopathic Hospital, 1900–1925," unpublished Ph.D. dissertation, Harvard University, 1984, chapt. 2.

2. Beatrice Z. Levey, "New Trends in Psychiatric Social Treatment in the Family Agency," *Mental Hygiene* (January 1929), 129–131; Dorothy Berkowitz, "Protective Casework and the Family Agency," *Journal of Social Casework*, v. XXIV, No. 7 (November 1943), 261–265; and Lois French, *Psychiatric Social Work* (New York: The Commonwealth Fund, 1940), 57, 83.

3. A brief history of the founding of the child guidance clinics is supplied by Joel D. Hunter in "The History and Development of Institutes for the Study of Children," Julia Lathrop et al., *The Child, The Clinic, and the Court* (New York: New Republic, 1927), 204–214; and the more general history of the growth of the profession of social work can be found in Lois Meredith French, *Psychiatric Social Work* and George S. Stevenson and Geddes Smith, *Child Guidance Clinics: A Quarter Century of Development* (New York: The Commonwealth Fund, 1934).

4. Porter R. Lee and Marion E. Kenworthy, *Mental Hygiene and Social Work* (New York: The Commonwealth Fund, 1928), 14, 48. Helen Witmer is critical of the links between clinics and the courts in *Psychiatric Clinics for Children* (New Haven: Yale University Press, 1940), 277–278, 293–298.

5. Mary Buell Sayles, *The Problem Child at Home: A Study in Parent-Child Relationships* (New York: The Commonwealth Fund, 1932), 98.

6. Margo Horn, "The Moral Message of Child Guidance, 1925–1945," *Journal of Social History*, v. 18, No. 1 (Fall 1984), 25–36. For an extremely positive assessment of Freud's impact on social work, see Helen Harris Perlman, "Freud's Contribution to Social Work," *Social Service Review*, v. 31, No. 2 (June 1957), 197–202.

7. Ernest R. Mowrer, *Family Disorganization: An Introduction to a Sociological Analysis* (Chicago: University of Chicago Press, 1929); Harriet R. Mowrer, "Clinical Treatment of Marital Conflicts," *American Sociological Review*, 11 (1937), 771–778; Ernest R. Mowrer and Harriet R. Mowrer, *Domestic Discord: Its Analysis and Treatment* (Chicago: University of Chicago Press, 1928).

8. Harriet R. Mowrer, *Personality Adjustment and Domestic Discord* (New York: American Book Co., 1935), 31.

9. Jeanette Hanford, "Family Case Work With Marital Difficulties," *Proceedings of the National Conference on Social Work* (Chicago: University of Chicago Press, 1938), 234.

10. Notes Upon an Autobiographical Account of a Case of Paranoia (Dementia Paranoides) (1911)," reprinted in Sigmund Freud, *Three Case Histories*, Philip Rieff, ed., (New York: Collier Books, 1963), 103–186; Morton Schatzman, *Soul Murder: Persecution in the Family* (New York: New American Library, 1973); Dr. William G. Niederland, M.D., *The Schreber Case: Psychoanalytic Profile of a Paranoid Personality* (New York: Quadrangle/New York Times Book Co., 1974); and Louise Armstrong, *The Home Front: Notes from the Family War Zone* (New York: McGraw-Hill, 1983), 17–31.

11. Around the time of the first World War, psychiatrists in the United States began to replicate Freud's work with hysterics and saw women patients who had an early childhood history of abuse. E. E. Southard and Mary Jarrett, *The Kingdom of Evils*, 336. Another early Freudian at the Boston Psychopathic Hospital, Dr. Eugene Emerson, preserved his handwritten notes on the case of masochistic young woman, a victim of sexual molestation and incest, whose father had beaten her, her brothers, and her mother. Dr. Emerson's notes and the letters to him from this young woman are reprinted in Martin Bauml Duberman, "'I Am Not Contented': Female Masochism and Lesbianism in Early Twentieth-Century New England," *Signs: A Journal of Women in Culture*," v. 5, No. 4 (Summer 1980), 825–841.

12. Sigmund Freud, *The Complete Introductory Lectures of Psychoanalysis* (New York: Norton, 1966), 584.

13. Jeffrey Moussaieff Masson, *The Assault on Truth: Freud's Suppression of the Seduction Theory* (New York: Farrar, Straus and Giroux, 1984), XXII–XXIII. Janet

Malcolm's *In the Freud Archives* (New York: Knopf, 1984) offers an insider's view of the controversy over Masson's disclosure of documents in the Freud Archives, as well as a good summary of the psychoanalytic arguments in favor of and against the seduction theory.

14. Sigmund Freud, *Introductory Lectures on Psycho-Analysis* (London: Allen and Unwin, 1922), 310.

15. Letter of Sigmund Freud to Wilhelm Fleiss, Dec. 22, 1897, reprinted in Jeffrey Masson, *The Assault on Truth*, 116–117.

16. Carroll Smith-Rosenberg has argued that hysteria was a "role option" for the Victorian woman. Carroll Smith-Rosenberg, "The Hysterical Woman: Some Reflections on Sex Roles and Role Conflict in Nineteenth-Century America," *Social Research*, v. 39, No. 1 (Winter 1972), 652–678. Edward Shorter points out that hysteria appeared commonly among working-class as well as bourgeois women in "Paralysis: The Rise and Fall of a 'Hysterical' Symptom," *Journal of Social History*, v. 19, No. 4 (Summer 1986), 549–582.

17. William J. McGrath, *Freud's Discovery of Psychoanalysis: The Politics of Hysteria* (Ithaca, N.Y.: Cornell University Press, 1986), 197–229.

18. Bernard C. Glueck, Jr., "Early Sexual Experiences in Schizophrenia," in Hugo G. Beigel, ed., *Advances in Sex Research* (New York: Harper & Row, 1963), 253–255; and Alice Miller, *Thou Shalt Not be Aware: Society's Betrayal of the Child* (New York: Farrar, Straus, and Giroux, 1984).

19. Jeffrey Masson, *The Assault on Truth*, 155–187.

20. Bernard C. Glueck, Jr., "Early Sexual Experiences," 253–255.

21. Florence Rush, *The Best Kept Secret: Sexual Abuse of Children* (New York: McGraw Hill, 1980), 100.

22. Linda Gordon, "Family Violence and Social Control," typescript, chapt. 8.

23. Jerome Walker, "Reports, with Comments, of Twenty-One Cases of Indecent Assault and Rape Upon Children," *Archives of Pediatrics*, v. 3, No. 6 (June 1886), 332–333, and Elizabeth Anne Mills, "One Hundred Years of Fear: Rape and the Medical Profession," in Nicole Hahn Rafter and Elizabeth Anne Stanko, eds., *Judge, Lawyer, Victim, Thief: Women, Gender Roles, and Criminal Justice* (Boston: Northeastern University Press, 1982), 29–62.

24. Between 1935 and 1960, twenty-nine states and the District of Columbia passed "psychopathic offender" laws, which put the incestuous father in the same criminal category with rapists, child molesters, and homosexuals who had sexual relations with a minor. Under these statutes, a father accused of incest was required to undergo a psychiatric examination. If he was diagnosed as psychopathic, he could serve his sentence in a psychiatric hospital rather than in prison. Estelle Freedman, "The Sexual Psychopath Laws," unpublished paper delivered at the annual meeting of the American Historical Association, December 1983.

25. *Annual Report of the American Bar Association*, v. 63 (Chicago: American Bar Association, 1938), 588.

26. John Henry Wigmore, *A Treatise on the Anglo-American System of Evidence*, 3rd edition, vol. 3 (Boston: Little, Brown, 1940), 744–746.

27. Lauretta Bender and Abram Blau, "The Reaction of Children to Sexual Relations with Adults," *American Journal of Orthopsychiatry*, v. 7 (October 1937), 500–518.

28. Sigmund Freud, "A Child Is Being Beaten," (1919), reprinted in Sigmund

Freud, ed., *Sexuality and the Psychology of Love* (New York: Collier Books, 1963), 107–132. Gertrud Lenzer traces the history of the discovery of masochism as a sexual perversion and Freud's transformation of it into a principal instinctual drive in "On Masochism: A Contribution to the History of a Fantasy and Its Theory," *Signs: Journal of Women in Culture and Society*, v. 1, No. 2 (Winter 1975), 277–324.

29. For other classic statements besides those of Deutsch, see Marie Bonaparte, "Passivity, Masochism, and Femininity," in Jean Strouse, ed., *Women and Analysis* (New York: Grossman Publishers, 1974), 241–249; and Sandor Rado, "Fear of Castration in Women," *Psychoanalytic Quarterly*, v. 2, Nos. 3–4 (1933), 425–475.

30. Helene Deutsch, "The Significance of Masochism in the Mental Life of Women," *International Journal of Psychoanalysis*, v. XI (1930), 48–60.

31. John Snell, Richard Rosenwald, Ames Robey, "The wifebeater's wife: A study of family interaction," *Archives of General Psychiatry*, v. 11, No. 2 (1964), 107–112. See also the comments on the belief in masochism by psychiatric social workers in the 1970s as quoted in Jennifer Baker Fleming, *Stopping Wife Abuse: A Guide to the Emotional, Psychological, and Legal Implications for the Abused Woman and Those Helping Her* (Garden City, N.Y.: Doubleday, 1979), 76.

32. Brenda S. Webster points out that Deutsch in her clinical practice considered masochism a neurotic tendency that had to be controlled. See her article, "Helene Deutsch: A New Look," *Signs: Journal of Women in Culture*, v. 10, No. 3 (Spring 1985), 553–571.

33. Helene Deutsch, *The Psychology of Women: A Psychoanalytic Interpretation* (New York: Grune and Stratton, 1944), v. 1, 239–278.

34. Karen Horney, "The Problem of Feminine Masochism," *Psychoanalytic Review*, v. 12, No. 3 (1935), 241–257, reprinted in Jean Baker Miller, ed., *Psychoanalysis and Women* (Baltimore, Md.: Penquin Books, 1973), 36. For a critique of the concept of masochism, which is often confused with female altruistic, self-denying behavior, see Paula J. Caplan, "The Myth of Women's Masochism," *American Psychologist* v. 39, No. 2 (February 1984), 130–139. For a contemporary psychiatric inquiry into female masochism, see Natalie Shainess, *Sweet Suffering: Woman as Victim* (Indianapolis: Bobbs-Merrill, 1984).

35. *Ms.* (November 1980), 83.

36. Dee Garrison, "Karen Horney and Feminism," *Signs: Journal of Women in Culture and Society*, v. 6, No. 4 (Summer 1984), 672–691.

37. Rochelle Semmel Albin, "Psychological Studies of Rape," *Signs: A Journal of Women in Culture*, v. 3, No. 2 (Winter 1977), 427–429. For the impact of psychoanalysis on social agency practice in the postwar period, see Martha H. Field, "Social Casework Practice during the Psychiatric Deluge," *Social Service Review*, v. 54, No. 4 (December 1980), 432–457. As late as 1970, a therapist in training at an eminent psychiatric hospital in Boston was advised by his psychiatric supervisors that a patient who had been violently raped two days before and complained of terrifying flashbacks of the event, would continue to do so until she could acknowledge the parts of herself that found the rape gratifying. Joseph H. Pleck, "Sex Role Issues in Clinical Training," *Psychotherapy: Theory, Research and Practice*, v. 13, No. 1 (Spring 1976), 17–19.

38. Harry F. Tashman, M. D., *The Marriage Bed: An Analyst's Casebook* (New York: University Publishers, 1959), 10; Margaret L. Lewis, "The Initial Contact with Wives of Alcoholics," *Social Casework*, v. XXXV, No. 1 (January 1954), 14. For

additional examples that battered women were regarded as "castrators" or sexually frigid in the 1950s and early 1960s, see Linda Gordon, "Family Violence and Social Control," chapt. 10.

39. Margaret L. Lewis, "The Initial Contact with Wives of Alcoholics," 12.

40. Ibid., 13.

41. Ibid.

CHAPTER 9. THE PEDIATRIC AWAKENING

1. Daniel P. Moynihan, *Maximum Feasible Misunderstanding: Community Action in the War on Poverty* (New York: The Free Press, 1969), 14–15; and James T. Patterson, *America's Struggle Against Poverty, 1900–1980* (Cambridge, Mass.: Harvard University Press, 1981), 100–102; John H. Ehrenreich, *The Altruistic Imagination: A History of Social Work and Social Policy in the United States* (Ithaca: Cornell University Press, 1985), 152–153; and James Gilbert, *A Cycle of Outrage: America's Reaction to the Juvenile Delinquent in the 1950s* (New York: Oxford University Press, 1986), chapt. 8.

2. Jane McFerran, "Parent's Groups in Protective Services," *Children*, v. 5–6 (November–December 1958), 223–228.

3. Bertram M. Beck, "Protective Casework Revitalized," *Child Welfare* (November 1955), 1–7.

4. Vincent DeFrancis, *The Fundamentals of Child Protection* (Denver: American Humane Association, 1955), 35.

5. U.S. Children's Bureau, *Child Welfare Services: How They Help Children and Their Parents* (Washington, D.C.: U.S. Department of Health, Education, and Welfare, 1957).

6. Barbara J. Nelson, "Setting the Public Agenda; The Case of Child Abuse," in Judith V. May and Aaron B. Wildavsky, eds., *The Policy Cycle* (Beverly Hills, Calif.: Sage Publications, 1978), 18.

7. John Caffey, "Multiple Fractures in the Long Bones of Infants Suffering from Chronic Subdural Hematoma," *American Journal of Roentgeneologic Radium Therapy Nuclear Medicine*, v. 56 (1946), 163–173.

8. Helen E. Boardman, "A Project to Rescue Children from Inflicted Injuries," *Social Work*, v. 7, No. 1 (January 1962), 44; and Elizabeth Elmer, "Abused Young Children Seen in Hospitals," *Social Work*, v. 5 (1960), 98–102.

9. Stephen Pfohl, "The Discovery of Child Abuse," *Social Problems*, v. 24 (1977), 310–321.

10. *Time* (July 20, 1962), 60.

11. Barbara Nelson, *Making an Issue Out of Child Abuse* (Chicago: University of Chicago Press, 1984), 23. Nelson's study is an excellent history of the modern reform movement, which traces the events described in this chapter in much greater detail.

12. David G. Gil, *Violence Against Children: Physical Abuse in the United States* (Cambridge, Mass.: Harvard University Press, 1970), 60.

13. Ruth C. Kempe and C. Henry Kempe, *Child Abuse* (Cambridge, Mass.: Harvard University Press, 1978), 120–123. Norma D. Feshbach and Seymour D. Feshbach chart the course of the children's liberation movement of the 1970s in "Toward an Historical, Social and Developmental Perspective on Children's Rights," *Journal of Social Issues*, v. 25, No. 2 (1978), 1–7. An important statement of chil-

dren's rights was Kimberly B. Cheney's, "Safeguarding Legal Rights in Providing Protective Services," *Children*, v. 13 (1966), 86–92.

14. C. Henry Kempe, "Child Abuse—The Pediatrician's Role in Child Advocacy and Preventive Pediatrics," *American Journal of Diseases of the Child*, v. 132 (March 1978), 255–260. An appreciative view of Kempe's role in reform is provided by Gertrude J. Williams, "Cruelty and Kindness to Children: Documentary of a Century, 1874–1974," in Gertrude J. Williams and John Money, eds., *Traumatic Abuse and Neglect of Children at Home* (Baltimore: Johns Hopkins University Press, 1980), 68–88. John Grady takes a more critical view of child abuse reform in "The Manufacture and Consumption of Child Abuse as a Social Issue," *Telos*, v. 56 (1983), 111–118.

15. C. Henry Kempe, Frederic N. Silverman, Brandt F. Steele, William Droegemuller, and Henry K. Silver, "The Battered Child Syndrome," *Journal of the American Medical Association*, v. 181 (1962), 17–24.

16. Charles Plato, "Parents Who Beat Children," *Saturday Evening Post* (October 6, 1962), 30–35.

17. C. Henry Kempe and Ray E. Helfer, eds., *Helping the Battered Child* (Philadelphia: J. B. Lippincott, 1972), IX.

18. Malcolm Spector and John I. Kitsuse, *Constructing Social Problems* (Menlo Park, Calif.: Benjamin Cummings Publishing, 1977), 8.

19. Louise Armstrong, *The Home Front: Notes from the Family War Zone* (New York: McGraw Hill, 1983), 3.

20. C. Henry Kempe, Frederic N. Silverman, Brandt F. Steele, William Droegemuller, and Henry K. Silver, "The Battered-Child Syndrome," 17–24.

21. *Journal of the American Medical Association*, v. 181 (1962), 17–24.

22. David G. Gil, *Violence Against Children*, 59–59; Richard Light, "Abused and Neglected Children in America: A Study of Alternative Policies," *Harvard Education Review*, v. 43 (November 1973), 556–598. The most comprehensive national survey of incidence was undertaken by the U.S. National Center on Child Abuse and Neglect, *National Study of the Incidence and Severity of Child Abuse and Neglect* (Washington, D.C.: Department of Health and Human Services, 1981).

23. Richard J. Gelles, "Violence in the Family: A Review of Research in the Seventies," *Journal of Marriage and the Family*, v. 42, No. 4 (November 1980), 880.

24. Margaret A. Zahn summarizes the literature on twentieth-century homicide in the United States in "Homicide in the Twentieth Century United States," in James A. Inciardi and Charles D. Faupel, eds., *History and Crime: Implications for Criminal Justice Policy* (Beverly Hills, Calif.: Sage, 1980), 111–131. The evidence in favor of real, rather than just observed class differences in the incidence of child abuse and neglect, is offered in Leroy H. Pelton, "Child Abuse and Neglect: The Myth of Classlessness," in Leroy H. Pelton, ed., *The Social Context of Child Abuse and Neglect* (New York: Human Sciences Press, 1981), 23–38. The national survey on the incidence of abuse was conducted by Murray Straus, Richard J. Gelles, and Suzanne K. Steinmetz. They report their results in *Behind Closed Doors: Violence in the American Family* (New York: Anchor Press/Doubleday, 1980), 31.

25. Peter Conrad and Joseph W. Schneider, *Deviance and Medicalization: From Badness to Sickness* (St. Louis: C. W. Mosby, 1982), 246–248.

26. Monrad G. Paulsen, "Legal Protections Against Child Abuse," *Children*, v. 13, No. 2 (March/April 1962), 43–48.

27. Marian G. Morris and Robert W. Gould, "Role Reversal: A Necessary Con-

cept in Dealing with the Battered Child Syndrome," *American Journal of Ortho-psychiatry*, v. 33 (March 1963), 298–229; B. F. Steele and C. B. Pollock, "A Psychiatric Study of Parents Who Abuse Infants and Small Children," in Ray Helfer and C. Henry Kempe, eds., *The Battered Child*, second edition (Chicago: University of Chicago Press, 1974), 89–134.

28. Judith Martin, "Maternal and Parental Abuse of Children: Theoretical and Research Perspectives," in David Finkelhor, Richard J. Gelles, Gerald T. Hotaling, and Murray S. Straus, eds., *The Dark Side of Families: Current Family Research* (Beverly Hills, Calif.: Sage, 1983), 293–304.

29. David Gil, *Violence Against Children*, 116; American Humane Association, *National Analysis of Official Child Neglect and Abuse Reporting* (Denver: American Humane Association, 1978), 22.

30. George C. Curtis, "Violence breeds violence—perhaps?" *American Journal of Psychiatry*, v. 120, No. 4 (1963), 388–387; and Larry B. Silver, Christina C. Dublin, and Reginald S. Lourie, "Does violence breed violence? Contributions from a study of the child abuse syndrome," *American Journal of Psychiatry*, v. 126, No. 3 (1969), 152–155.

31. For a critical review of the literature on the cycle of violence, see Mildred Daley Pagelow, *Family Violence* (New York: Praeger, 1984), 223–258.

32. Elizabeth McCracken, *The American Child* (Boston and New York: Houghton Mifflin, 1913), 9; Rudolf Dreikus, M.D., *The Challenge of Parenthood* (New York: Duell, Sloan and Pearce, 1948), 138.

33. *Wall Street Journal* (July 17, 1984), 12.

34. Quoted in Barbara Nelson, *Making an Issue out of Child Abuse*, 102.

35. Quoted in Douglas J. Besharov, "Child Protection: Past Progress, Present Problems, and Future Directions," *Family Law Quarterly*, v. XVII, No. 2 (Summer 1983), 157–158.

36. *Denver Observer* (March 23, 1973).

37. Public Law 93, 247, No. 3, January 31, 1974, 88 Stat. 5.

38. Barbara Nelson, *Making an Issue out of Child Abuse*, 125.

39. Douglas J. Besharov, "Child Protection," 160.

40. Michael S. Wald, "State Intervention on Behalf of 'Neglected' Children: A Search for Realistic Standards," *Stanford Law Review*, v. 27 (April 1975), 985–1040; and Michael S. Wald, "State intervention on behalf of 'neglected' children: Standards for removal of children from their homes, monitoring the status of children in foster care and termination of parental rights," *Stanford Law Review*, v. 28 (April 1976), 673–706. Statistics demonstrating that black and Indian children had the highest rates of "out-of-home placement" can be found in Edmund V. Meck, "Out-of-Home Placement Rates," *Social Service Review*, v. 57, No. 4 (December 1983), 659–667.

41. Joseph Goldstein, Anna Freud, and Albert J. Solnit, *Before the Best Interests of the Child* (New York: The Free Press, 1979), 143.

42. Ibid., 71. Caseworkers, following Goldstein's theories, tend to prolong temporary placement of children in foster care, so that eventually judges will permanently place the child with a foster family rather than with the child's biological parents. Goldstein's response to this and other criticisms is given in "Interview with Joseph Goldstein," *New York Review of Law and Social Change*, v. XII, No. 3 (1983–1984), 575–589.

43. Stephen Antler argues in favor of this point of view in "Child Abuse: An

Emerging Social Priority," *Social Work*, v. 23, No. 1 (January 1978), 58–61; and "Small Programs for Big Problems," *Public Welfare* (Fall 1978), 10–13.

44. Barbara Nelson, *Making an Issue out of Child Abuse*, 125.

CHAPTER 10. ASSAULT AT HOME

1. John E. O'Brien, "Violence in Divorce Prone Families," *Journal of Marriage and the Family*, v. 33 (November 1971), 691.

2. "Dossier: Betty Naomi Friedan," *Esquire* (December 1983), 518; Andrea Dworkin, "The Bruise That Doesn't Heal," *Mother Jones*, 3 (July 1978), 31–36; Sally Kempton, "Cutting Loose: A Private View of the Women's Uprisings," *Esquire* (July 1970), 53–57; Sara Davidson, *Loose Change: Three Women of the Sixties* (New York: Doubleday, 1977); Maya Angelou, *I Know Why the Caged Bird Sings* (New York: Random House, 1969).

3. Sara Evans, *Personal Politics: The Roots of Women's Liberation in the Civil Rights Movement and the New Left* (New York: Alfred A. Knopf, 1979), 212–232.

4. Kristin Luker, *Abortion and the Politics of Motherhood* (Berkeley: University of California Press, 1984), chapt. 5.

5. Susan Brownmiller, *Against Our Will: Men, Women and Rape* (New York: Simon and Schuster, 1975), 8.

6. Ibid., 9.

7. Susan Griffin, "Rape—The All-American Crime," *Ramparts* (September 1971), 26–35.

8. Barbara Deckard, *The Women's Movement: Political, Socioeconomic and Psychological Issues* (New York: Harper & Row, 1975), 405–409; Judith Hole and Ellen Levine, *Rebirth of Feminism* (New York: Quadrangle Books, 1971), 152–157; Vicki McNickle Rose, "Rape as a Social Problem: A Byproduct of the Feminist Movement," *Social Problems*, v. 25, No. 1 (October 1977), 75–89; E. O'Sullivan, "What Has Happened to Rape Crisis Centers? A Look At Their Structures, Members and Funding," *Victimology*, v. 3, Nos. 1–2 (1978), 45–62; Mary Ann Largen, "Grassroots Centers and National Task Forces: A History of the Anti-Rape Movement," *Aegis* (Autumn 1981), 46–53.

9. Kathleen Tierney, "The Battered Women Movement and the Creation of the Wife Beating Problem," *Social Problems*, v. 29, No. 3 (February 1982), 211.

10. J. C. Barden, "Wife Beaters: Few of Them Even Appear Before a Court of Law," *New York Times* (October 21, 1974).

11. Susan E. Eisenberg and Paula L. Micklow, "Assaulted Wife—'Catch 22' revisited," *Women's Rights Law Reporter*, v. 3, Nos. 3–4 (1977), 138–161.

12. Beverly B. Nichols, "The Abused Wife Problem," *Social Casework*, v. 57, No. 1 (January 1976), 27–32; Evan Stark, Anne Flitcraft, and William Frazier, "Medicine and Patriarchal Violence: The Social Construction of a 'Private' Event," *International Journal of Health Services*, v. 9, No. 3 (1979), 461–493.

13. Morton Bard and Joseph Zacker, "The Prevention of Family Violence," *Journal of Marriage and the Family*, v. 33 (February 1971), 677–682; M. Faulk, "Men Who Assault Their Wives," *Medicine, Science and the Law*, v. 14 (July 1974), 180–183; Martha H. Field and Henry F. Field, "Marital Violence and the Criminal

Process," *Social Service Review*, v. 47 (June 1973), 221–240; Raymond I. Parnas, "Judicial Response to Intra-Family Violence," *Minnesota Law Review*, v. 54 (1970), 585–644; Raymond I. Parnas, "The Police Response to the Domestic Disturbance," *Wisconsin Law Review*, v. 1967, No. 4 (Fall 1967), 914–960.

14. Laurie Woods, "Litigation on Behalf of Battered Women," *Women's Rights Law Reporter*, v. 5, No. 1 (Fall 1976), 7–33; Pauline W. Gee, "Ensuring Police Protection for Battered Women: The Scott v. Hart Suit," *Signs*, v. 8, No. 3 (1983), 564–567; Marcia Rockwood, "Courts and Cops: Enemies of Battered Wives," *Ms.*, v. 5 (April 1977), 19; *New York Times* (December 12, 1976); *New York Times* (June 12, 1977). An account of feminist protest against the lack of police protection for battered women is provided by Anne Wurr in "Community Responses to Violence Against Women: The Case of a Battered Women's Shelter," in Janet A. Flammang, ed., *Political Women: Current Roles in State and Local Government* (Beverly Hills, Calif.: Sage, 1984), 221–241.

15. *Newsweek* (January 30, 1978), 54. The biography of Francine Hughes, who killed her husband by setting fire to his bed, is recounted in Faith McNulty, *The Burning Bed* (New York: Harcourt, Brace, Jovanovich, 1980).

16. Beverly Jacobson, "Battered Women: The Fight To End Wife Beating," *Civil Rights Digest* (Summer 1977), 14.

17. Erin Pizzey, *Scream Quietly, or the Neighbors Will Hear* (Middlesex, Eng. Penguin Books, 1974); "A Refuge for Battered Women: A Conversation with Erin Pizzey," *Victimology*, v. 4 (1979), 100–112; Jo Sutton, "The Growth of the British Movement for Battered Women," *Victimology: An International Journal*, v. 2 (1978), 576–584.

18. Judith Weinraub, "The Battered Wives of England: A Place to Heal Their Wounds," *New York Times* (November 29, 1975), 17.

19. "Battered Wives: Chiswick Woman's Aid," *Newsweek* (July 9, 1973), 39.

20. Kathleen Tierney, "*The Battered Women Movement*," 213.

21. Quoted in Susan Schecter, *Women and Male Violence: The Visions and Struggles of the Battered Women's Movement* (Boston: South End Press, 1982), 65; Sharon R. Vaughan, "The Last Refuge: Shelter for Battered Women," *Victimology*, v. 2 (December 1977), 113–115.

22. Sharon R. Vaughan, "The Last Refuge," 118.

23. Sharon R. Vaughan, "Where It All Began," *Do It NOW*, v. IX, No. 5 (June 1976), 6.

24. Sharon R. Vaughan, "The Last Refuge: Shelter for Battered Women," 118.

25. Sharon R. Vaughan, "Where It All Began," 6.

26. Grace A. Franklin and Randall G. Ripley assess the success and failures of the Comprehensive Employment and Training Act in CETA: *Politics and Policy, 1973–1983* (Knoxville: University of Tennessee Press, 1984).

27. Kathleen J. Ferraro, "Processing Battered Women," *Journal of Family Issues*, v. 2, No. 4 (December 1981), 435.

28. Colleen McGrath, "The Crisis of the Domestic Order," *Socialist Revolution*, v. 9, No. 1 (January–February 1971), 27.

29. Kathleen J. Ferraro, "Processing Battered Women," *Journal of Family Issues*, 435; see also Patricia Morgan, "From Battered Wife to Program Client: The State's Shaping of Social Problems," *Kapitalistate*, v. 9 (1981), 24–25; and Lois Ahrens,

"Battered Women's Refuges: Feminist Cooperatives vs. Social Service Institutions," *Aegis* (Summer/Autumn 1980), 9–15.

30. Mark A. Shulman, *A Survey of Spousal Violence Against Women in Kentucky* (New York: Garland, 1981), 31–45.

31. David C. Adams and Andrew J. McCormick, "Men Unlearning Violence: A Group Approach Based on the Collective Model," in Maria Roy, ed., *The Abusive Partner: An Analysis of Domestic Battering* (New York: Van Nostrand Reinhold, 1982), 170–197; Albert R. Roberts, "National Survey of Services for Batterers," in Maria Roy, ed., *The Abusive Partner*, 230–243; and Carann Simpson Feazell, Raymond Sanchez Mayers, and Jeanne Deschner, "Services for Men Who Batter: Implications for Programs and Policies," *Family Relations*, v. 33, No. 2 (April 1984), 217–223; and Daniel Jay Sonkin, Del Martin, and Lenore E. Walker, *The Male Batterer: A Treatment Approach* (New York: Springer Publishing, 1985).

32. Sherry Chase, "Outlawing Marital Rape: How We Did it and Why," *Aegis*, No. 55 (Summer 1982), 21–26.

33. Jennifer Baker Fleming, *Stopping Wife Abuse* (Garden City, N.Y.: Anchor Books, 1979), 255–258.

34. R. Emerson Dobash and Russell Dobash, *Violence Against Wives* (New York: The Free Press, 1979). A highly influential feminist critique of sociological and psychological literature about family violence is Wini Breines and Linda Gordon, "The New Scholarship on Family Violence," *Signs: Journal of Women in Culture*, v. 8, No. 3 (Spring 1983), 490–531.

35. Del Martin, *Battered Wives* (San Francisco: Glide Publications, 1976).

36. Donileen R. Loseke and Spencer E. Cahill point out that among divorcing couples, the question most often asked is why did they break up; among battered women the query is why they remain married. Loseke and Cahill argued that many wives left but later returned to their husbands. Battered women's behavior was not unique. Donileen R. Loseke and Spencer E. Cahill, "The Social Construction of Deviance: Experts on Battered Women," *Social Problems*, v. 31, No. 3 (February 1984), 296–310. For a critique of social science studies of battered women, see Laurie Wardell, Dair L. Gillespie, and Ann Leffler, "Science and Violence Against Wives" in David Finkelhor, Richard J. Gelles, Gerald T. Hotaling, and Murray A. Straus, eds., *The Dark Side of Families: Current Family Violence Research* (Beverly Hills, Calif.: Sage Publications, 1983), 69–84.

37. "Insecurity" in the male sex role is often a code word for latent homosexuality. Usually, the mother is blamed for having produced male insecurity. The son's attachment to his mother, it is argued, leads him to have a "feminine" component in his sex-role identity. Male insecurity is also created by mothers rewarding femininity in their sons. Joseph H. Pleck, *The Myth of Masculinity* (Cambridge, Mass.: MIT Press, 1981), 113–115. For an example of the mélange of psychiatric and social-psychological belief, see Vee Mullin, "Wife beating—the menace we can no longer ignore," *New Directions for Women*, v. 6, No. 2 (Summer 1977), 1, 10.

38. Susan Schecter, *Women and Male Violence*, 192.

39. For a general overview of LEAA involvement, see Sandra Wexler, "Battered Women and Public Policy," in Ellen Bonepath, ed., *Women, Power and Policy* (New York: Pergamon Press, 1982), 184–204. Criticism of LEAA policy is offered by Susan Schecter in *Women and Male Violence*, 186; and Laurie Ann Wermuth in "Wife

Beating: The Crime without Punishment," unpublished Ph.D. dissertation, University of California at Berkeley, 1983.

40. Patricia Morgan, "From Battered Wife to Program Client," 30.

41. Kathleen Tierney, "The Battered Women Movement," 213.

42. Suzanne Steinmetz argued that husband beating constituted a sizeable proportion of marital violence in "The Battered Husband Syndrome," *Victimology: An International Journal*, v. 2, Nos. 3–4 (1977–1978), 499–509. For subsequent criticism of her findings, see Elizabeth Pleck, Joseph H. Pleck, Marlyn Grossman, and Pauline B. Bart, "The Battered Data Syndrome: A Comment on Steinmetz' Article," *Victimology*, v. 2, Nos. 3–4 (1977–1978), 680–683; and Richard Gelles, "The Truth about Husband Abuse," *Ms.* v. 7 (October 1979), 63–65.

43. The other definition, "violence against women," emerged in 1977 at a meeting of the National Coalition Against Domestic Violence. This term was proposed as a means of uniting the antirape and antibattering movements, and included women concerned about incest and the portrayal of women in pornography. The term "violence against women" appears reasonably similar to the phrase "Crimes Against Women" used at a 1976 International Tribunal held by feminists in Brussels, although their definition went so far as to include employment discrimination and sexual castration of African women. Joyce Gelb briefly evaluates the significance of the work of the National Coalition Against Domestic Violence in "The Politics of Wife Abuse," in Irene Diamond, ed., *Families, Politics, and Public Policy: A Feminist Dialogue on Women and the State* (New York: Longman, 1983), 250–264.

44. Quoted in Susan Schecter, *Women and Male Violence*, 200.

45. Ibid., 193.

46. June Zeitlin, "Domestic Violence: Perspectives from Washington," in Irene Tinker, ed., *Women in Washington: Advocates for Public Policy* (Beverly Hills, Calif.: Sage Publications, 1983), 263–275. See also *Congressional Quarterly*, v. 38, No. 25 (June 23, 1980), 1689–1699.

47. On the growth of the New Right, see Alan Crawford, *Thunder on the Right* (New York: Pantheon, 1980); Allen Hunter, "In the Wings: New Right Organization and Ideology," *Radical America*, v. 15, Nos. 1–2 (Spring 1981), 111–138; Rosalind Petchesky, "Anti-abortion, Antifeminism and the Rise of the New Right," *Feminist Studies*, v. 7, No. 2 (Summer 1981), 187–205; and Linda Gordon and Allen Hunter, "Sex, Family and the New Right: Anti-Feminism as a Political Force," *Radical America*, v. II, No. 6 and v. 12, No. 1 (November 1977–February 1978), 9–25.

48. *Conservative Digest* (May/June 1980), 3. Letty Cottin Pogrebin, *Family Politics: Love and Power on an Intimate Frontier* (New York: McGraw Hill, 1983), 49; and *New York Times* (September 8, 1983), III, 2; *New York Times* (May 31, 1984), II, 24; Ibid. (June 23, 1984), II, 5.

49. *Congressional Quarterly*, v. 38, No. 37 (September 13, 1980), 2719.

50. Ibid.

51. Quoted in "Domestic Violence Conference Bill to Go to Senate for Final Vote. Right Wing Targets Legislation for Defeat," *SANENEWS: A National Newsletter on Battered Women*, v. 1, No. 11 (October 1980), 1.

52. Ibid.

53. *Congressional Quarterly* (March 12, 1980), 527; Ibid. (September 28, 1984), 2410; Ibid. (September 22, 1984), 2305; Ibid. (February 4, 1984), 230.

54. Maria Roy, "The Nature of Abusive Behavior," in Maria Roy, ed., *The Abusive Partner*, 15; and Joyce Gelb, "The Politics of Wife Abuse," 258–259.

APPENDIX B

1. For a thorough review of the many problems in using criminal statistics, see Ted Robert Gurr, "Historical Trends in Violent Crime: A Critical Review of the Evidence," *Crime and Justice: An Annual Review of Research*, v. 111 (1981), 298–303; and V. A. C. Gatrell and T. B. Hadden, "Criminal Statistics and their Interpretation," in E. A. Wrigley, ed., *Nineteenth-Century Society: Essays in the Use of Quantitative Methods for the Study of Social Data* (Cambridge: Cambridge University Press, 1972).

2. The impact of war on the homicide rate is analyzed by Dane Archer and Rosemary Gartner, "Violent Acts and Violent Times: A Comparative Approach to Postwar Homicide Rates," *American Sociological Review*, v. 41 (1976), 937–963.

3. Lawrence Stone, "Interpersonal Violence in English Society, 1300–1980," *Past and Present*, No. 101 (November 1983), 122–133, and Ted Robert Gurr, "Historical Trends in Violent Crime," 295–353.

4. Lawrence Stone, "Interpersonal Violence in English Society 1300–1980," 129. J. A. Sharpe believes seventeenth-century England was an exceedingly violent place, but the evidence as to the frequency of family homicide does not support his argument. J. A. Sharpe, *Crime in Seventeenth-Century England: A County Study* (Cambridge: Cambridge University Press, 1983), 126–127.

5. Roger Lane, "Urban Homicide in the Nineteenth Century: Some Lessons for the Twentieth," in James H. Inciardi and Charles E. Faupel, eds., *History and Crime: Implications for Criminal Justice Policy* (London: Sage, 1980), 91–109; and Roger Lane, *Violent Death in the City: Suicide, Accident and Murder in Nineteenth Century Philadelphia* (Cambridge, Mass.: Harvard University Press, 1979).

6. A general survey of the homicide rate in twentieth-century America is provided by Margaret Zahn, "Homicide in the Twentieth Century United States," in James H. Inciardi and Charles E. Faupel, eds., *History and Crime*, 111–131.

7. James D. Wright, Peter H. Rossi, Kathleen Daly, *Under the Gun: Weapons, Crime, and Violence in America* (New York: Aldine, 1983), 198–199.

8. Lawrence Levine, *Black Culture and Black Consciousness: Afro-American Folk Thought from Slavery to Freedom* (New York: Oxford University Press, 1977), 408.

9. Lawrence Stone, "Interpersonal Violence in English Society 1300–1980," 27. Paul Bohannan has noted, with common sense, that murder is a "social relationship," and that some relationships, such as that between husband and wife, are more homicide-inducing than others. Paul Bohannan, "Patterns of Homicide Among Tribal Societies in Africa," in Marvin Wolfgang, ed., *Studies in Homicide* (New York: Harper & Row, 1967), 211–237.

10. Jane Totman, *The Murderess: A Psychosocial Study of Criminal Homicide* (San Francisco: R. E. Research Associates, 1978), 3, 48. For a study of the motives and social attitudes toward female murderers, see Ann Jones, *Women Who Kill* (New York: Holt, Rinehart, and Winston, 1980).

11. James Wright, Peter Rossi, and Kathleen Daly argue that people, not guns,

cause homicide. They cast doubt on the association between handguns and crime. Murderers, they argue, choose guns because they want to commit homicide, and those who opt for knives rather than guns are less intent on taking a life. It seems likely that the motives of wives who kill have remained the same over the centuries, although they more often resort to lethal weapons. James Wright, Peter Rossi, and Kathleen Daly, *Under the Gun*, 175–212.

12. M. L. Marcus, "Conjugal Violence: The Law of Force and the Force of Law," *California Law Review* (December 1981), 1657–1733.

Index

The University of Illinois Press
is a founding member of the
Association of American University Presses.

———————————————————————————

University of Illinois Press
1325 South Oak Street
Champaign, IL 61820-6903
www.press.uillinois.edu